Peppers

of the
Americas

Peppers
of the
Americas

The Remarkable Capsicums That Forever Changed Flavor

Maricel E. Presilla

Photographs by Romulo Yanes
Botanical Illustrations by Julio J. Figueroa

LORENA JONES BOOKS
An imprint of TEN SPEED PRESS
California | New York

Dedicated to my father, Ismael Espinosa, and grandfather, Santiago Parladé, two remarkable men who shaped my love for food gardening. And to my husband, Alejandro Presilla, for cheerfully surrendering our home and backyard to a pepper invasion.

Contents

A PEPPER EPIPHANY

At the end of September 2009, I was winding up a trip to Peru with a visit to Cusco, the great capital of the Inca Empire. As I walked through the Temple of the Sun, musing about the trappings of ancient royal power, my phone rang. It was someone in Washington, DC. At first I thought it might be a prank, but after some confusion, I gathered that the White House was asking me to cook for the first presidential Fiesta Latina, a salute to Latin American culture and music.

When I returned home to New Jersey and continued the conversation, I realized that I was to be responsible for the entire menu with less than two weeks' notice. The household staff was expecting me to settle innumerable details for a 400-guest event (even down to the flower arrangements). I knew this was the opportunity for peppers, the great staple food of the New World, from the Caribbean and Mesoamerica to the Andes, to tell their story. When the staff in Washington asked what kind of flowers I wanted to order, I replied, "No flowers . . . *peppers*!" And that was the sight that eventually greeted guests as they entered the Blue Room on the evening of the Fiesta Latina: tall cylindrical glass vases holding glowing rainbows of green, yellow, ivory, lavender, purple, orange, and red New World peppers in every shape.

The Fiesta Latina was a pivotal moment in my relationship with peppers—or *capsicums*, chiles, "chillis," or *ajíes*, depending on one's culinary culture. When I picked up the phone in Cusco, I was already deep into a personal pepper exploration that had begun decades earlier in Latin America and continues to this day. This book—not an encyclopedic catalog, but a highly subjective record of my own garden and kitchen encounters with these remarkable plants—is one result of that decades-long fascination.

The story of my backyard pepper laboratory begins in the summer of 2002, when an overnight thunderstorm sent a giant Norway maple tree crashing down into my backyard in Weehawken, New Jersey. I mourned the old shade tree but rejoiced that it and its shade-producing companion, a massive wisteria vine draped around its branches, would no longer block my dreams of a sunny backyard kitchen garden.

Unwisely rushing to plant all the sun-loving herbs that I'd longed for, I soon found that I'd created my own little shop of horrors, an aromatic menace with mint, lemon balm, and epazote dominating every inch of my yard and even sprouting from cracks in the brick-paved patio. Plan B was to concentrate on something less invasive. I instantly thought of hot peppers, which I had been gradually discovering during years of travels and explorations while researching *Gran Cocina Latina*, my book on the cuisines of Latin America, not from my own less fiery Cuban culinary heritage.

My upbringing in Cuba had been a great help in talking to non-Latin cooks about the full diversity and excitement of New World peppers—not because I grew up knowing all about peppers, but because I didn't. My maternal aunts, the marvelous cooks in our family, scarcely ever ventured beyond the perfumed but sweet *ají cachucha*, the gentle bell pepper, and a few other mild varieties, either fresh or canned, though my father simply adored cooking with a tiny, very hot wild pepper called *ají guaguao*. Living in Miami and New York City as a refugee, and later as a citizen, I discovered the cuisines of Mexico and India, two important countries for peppers. This is when I truly began to appreciate the magic of hot peppers in cooking, which my father had so well understood when we lived in Cuba. It took many more years for me to thoroughly explore the pepper map of the Americas.

Looking back on my first experiments with pepper cultivars, chosen for their suitability to the warm, humid summers of New Jersey, I now realize how strategic I was to focus on a few sturdy members of this fertile, ever-surprising New World botanical clan. During many years of research for *Gran Cocina Latina*, I had already traveled extensively and frequented farms, markets, and home kitchens where skilled women had taught me as much about the special qualities of Mesoamerican chiles and Caribbean or Andean ajíes as any visiting cook-historian could absorb. But that wasn't the same responsibility as nurturing even one pepper plant from infancy to harvest. The leap to handling peppers as a home gardener added new dimension to my perspective. It brought home the importance of direct engagement with these strong yet delicate living organisms.

Pepper plants in many containers soon filled every sunny patch of ground in my backyard. At first the overflow was perched on garden tables and chairs, and then it required roomier quarters on improvised trestle-and-plank arrangements. I scoured the Internet for more and more varieties and forged relationships with suppliers, such as Happy Quail Farms in Palo Alto, California, whom I would later call on to help me create the Fiesta Latina arrangements at the White House. When I went back to South America in 2003 and again in 2006, exploring the ancient foundations of northern Peruvian civilization and cuisine to research an article for *Saveur,* it was with a better understanding of how peppers fit into the panorama of native New World foods. By 2006 I presented a seminar on peppers at the Culinary Institute of America at Greystone in Napa Valley and discovered that people wanted to learn still more. So did I.

Opening my Hoboken restaurant, Cucharamama, had already yielded new opportunities to showcase my own New Jersey–grown South American peppers in South American dishes. By now, my selection of peppers included many dozens of cultivars obtained from US sources or during my Latin American travels. During the growing season, I often had a platter of assorted homegrown peppers (mild flavored, medium hot, scorching hot) on the counter at Cucharamama, changing it as I harvested new ones. One of those pepper platters was sitting on the bar one evening in 2007 when James Oseland, then editor of *Saveur*, arrived for dinner and bravely ate his way through every kind of pepper on display, inspiring him to suggest that we collaborate on an article for the magazine that would be a pictorial guide to major pepper varieties. Throughout the 2008 growing season, I planted, tended, and harvested about 100 cultivars, sending them to the New York office for Jim to photograph and winnow to roughly 50 kinds.

The year of 2009 turned out to be my wonder year for peppers. I was engaged in a new push on my big Latin American cookbook and eager to work in the results of my ongoing Caribbean and South American pepper research. Meanwhile, the second edition of my earlier book, *The New Taste of Chocolate*, was published, enriched by new ideas that I'd formed about the intertwined history of cacao and peppers in the pre-Columbian as well as post-conquest New World tropics (especially Guatemala, where I had become fascinated with the wonderful local dried chiles). The *Saveur* article, "A World of Peppers," appeared in September while I was again in Peru attending a Lima-based food festival called Mistura. There I was awestruck at the brilliant multicolored displays of Andean and Amazonian peppers, far surpassing the selection I'd been able to bring to my backyard garden. The sights, smells, and tastes of Peruvian peppers were still vividly etched in my memory when I went on to Cusco, where I received that call from the White House.

The pepper-filled vases that lit up Fiesta Latina were an implicit promise to myself that I would go on with the story begun in my article, "A World of Peppers." I recruited *Gourmet* veteran photographer Romulo Yanes, a New Jersey neighbor (and fellow Cuban), and I rolled up my sleeves to do plantings that would be more ambitious than my prior effort (which had taken over not only the backyard but the driveway too).

In the fall of 2012, *Gran Cocina Latina* was published, and I was ready to concentrate on my biggest pepper harvest yet. I'd forgotten that nature tends to follow her own, not gardeners', plans. At the end of October, Superstorm Sandy battered the entire Northeast coast. Somehow I managed to bring every plant in to the house and garage until the storm had passed. Congratulating myself on having avoided disaster, I got everything outside again—just in time for a freak snowstorm and freeze that wiped out most of my entire growing season's work.

It was back to square one in 2013, with more careful planning. This time the weather gods were on my side—but my new Shiba Inu puppy was not! He tirelessly scrabbled out a deep hole under one end of the biggest trestle table until that whole side collapsed. We found him happily playing with the pots and running around the yard with whole fruit-laden pepper plants dangling from his jaws. Luckily I'd been prudent enough to institute a backup policy much earlier in my love affair with peppers: three specimens of each cultivar, to be planted in separate pots at separate spots. So I was able to get back on course without losing much time. But we now faced a new roadblock: Romulo, the photographer, had moved to San Francisco on a long-term assignment just as the earliest peppers started ripening.

Proving that where there's a will there's a way, we worked out a system of shipping freshly gathered specimens across the continent as carefully as if we'd been handling organs for transplant. I devised a packaging protocol involving resealable plastic bags, florists' water tubes, and wads of water-saturated paper towels, with bags of dry ice taped to the inside walls of Styrofoam coolers to keep them from banging around and damaging the peppers during transit. As we grew more skilled, I was able to graduate from sending single pods to packing entire branches with leaves, flowers, and pods at various stages of ripeness.

These peppers have been part of my education as a cook and gardener firmly rooted in the New World. But the beginning of the journey is just as important. How did the *Capsicum* complex come into being, and where? How did members of the genus first reach kitchens in South America and Mesoamerica? What transformed them from tiny wild berries with a hidden sting into five domesticated species and hundreds of cultivars with a dazzling range of culinary possibilities resting on a unique flavor chemistry? How did they insinuate themselves into indigenous and, later, colonial cuisines everywhere in Latin America before setting off on world travels that forever changed flavor everywhere people cook today? The answers to these questions, and more, have emerged—and continue to unfold—through the many paths of research that I have traveled with the patience and curiosity of an explorer.

This book presents the fruits of my labors. It is a selective compendium with descriptions and photographs of about 180 peppers (roughly one-third of the cultivars that I've planted). For context, brief introductions to the botanical, historical, cultural, and culinary significance of peppers tell the story of their march to global popularity. To help you start cooking with more types of peppers in more ways, you'll find forty-one recipes that illustrate my own discoveries as a Latin American cook with a garden-to-table supply of many cultivars and a keen interest in the flavor possibilities that these remarkable plants create wherever they take root.

THE SILENT GARDENERS

Whenever I prepare a handful of peppers for the cooking pot, I feel that living history rests in my hands. I marvel at the course of events that brought these beautiful creations to my kitchen, thankful that the many mysteries of their birth, spread, and domestication in the Americas are gradually yielding to the work of dedicated researchers. Without detailing the complexities of this real-life detective story, retracing peppers' pathways to our kitchens has been more involved than I ever expected, and a window into the whole panorama of Latin American cooking from prehistoric times forward.

Like me, the "peppers" of this book are Latin American natives. I am not talking about black or white peppercorns or any unrelated spice that happens to share the "pepper" name (for example, pink peppercorns or Sichuan peppercorns). What I mean by "peppers" are the pods born by plants (mostly perennial) of the genus *Capsicum*, a member of the *Solanaceae*, or nightshade family.

"Nightshade" may be a byword for "poison," but in the New World some very ancient nightshade predecessor gave rise to several of the world's most nourishing food plants—potatoes, tomatoes, and tomatoes' closest botanical cousin, peppers. (Scientists who study plant relationships believe that the forebears of today's peppers and tomatoes split off from a common ancestor about twenty million years ago in South America.) All three would later travel around the globe. But to this day, all yield their most telling insights when *you* travel to *them*—that is, if you become acquainted with them in their original New World ecological and cultural contexts, voyaging to their homes either in person or via the printed page. This is especially true of peppers.

About twenty miles from the city of Trujillo in northwestern Peru stands a narrow wedge-shaped strip of plateau sandwiched between green sugarcane fields and the Pacific Ocean. This site, El Brujo (the shaman), has been continuously occupied almost as long as we have evidence of human beings in western South America. Temples, burial chambers, subterranean dwellings, and other remnants of successive civilizations, both before

and after the Spanish conquest, have yielded remarkable discoveries for archaeologists. Possibly the most important of all is a huge, sprawling heap close to the southern tip of the wedge. Its name, Huaca Prieta, means "dark-colored mound," and that is what it looks like. Here, in 1946 through 1947, Junius Bird led an American Museum of Natural History archaeology team. Along with dwellings and kitchens they found ancient garbage dumps and latrines laid down in stages, layer by layer, over many thousands of years.

This refuse heap was a discovery more exciting than the gold ornaments and jewelry that fill many archaeological museums. Why? The simplest answer is that the refuse is more difficult to come by. Gold can survive all kinds of climatic conditions unharmed. This is not so for food and other organic remains, which rapidly break down and disappear in all but the driest climates—and El Brujo happens to have a very dry climate. Digging through successive strata from the outer layers of the mound, Bird and his associates found recognizable evidence of what prehistoric and indeed preceramic peoples ate, in an extraordinary state of preservation. Among the still-recognizable remnants were a few whole peppers and other fragments, along with close to one hundred pepper seeds.

Peppers' First Spread

Peppers were not native to this small corner of South America. By studying patterns of species distribution throughout the continent, botanical sleuths have concluded that the first ancestral wild capsicums appeared between 15,000 BP and 20,000 BP somewhere in central Bolivia—more precisely, the piedmont region between Bolivian Amazonia and the eastern slopes of the Andes. The climate there is moist, with cloud forests covering the uplands, lowlands, and rain forests. (Today's archaeologists and archeobotanists generally use a scale for dating plant and other remains on which they count backward from 1950 AD to a fairly precise number of years "before present," or BP. As of approximately 1950, radiocarbon dating—based on the rate at which certain radioisotopes decay—has made it possible to measure the passage of time over millennia with some accuracy. Unless otherwise stated, BP dates in this book are based on sources' use of this now widely accepted system.)

Eventually prehistoric peoples carried peppers across the Bolivian and Peruvian *cordillera* (mountain ranges) as far as the arid Pacific Coast. By a fluke of climate, identifiable remains of peppers survived at Huaca Prieta, while corresponding evidence in their place of origin east of the mountains was quickly lost to cycles of decay. This same divide between dry and moist regions is one of the long-standing frustrations of all research on ancient civilizations throughout the Latin American tropics, with new technologies only now beginning to mitigate the challenges. This is the reason that scientists understand so little of how peppers—which flourished along with all the great

clockwise from top: Huaca Cao Viejo at El Brujo's archaeological complex; a Peruvian woman gathering fish and seafood at the beach by Huaca Prieta; a vivid mural at Huaca Cao depicts *life*, a staple food (fish) of the ancient inhabitants of this region.

pre-Hispanic civilizations—spread from their Bolivian birthplace to nearly every part of South America, Mesoamerica, and the Caribbean.

Some facts are beyond question. The wild Bolivian *Capsicum* ancestors, like all later peppers, were perennial, but unable to survive frost. They bore tiny fruits like scintillas of brilliant scarlet. These might have been a magnet for hungry mammals, except that every fruit contained the basic *Capsicum* defense strategy: a devilish though non-poisonous sting in the form of capsaicin, an alkaloid so painful to most animals' taste buds that they avoided the fruits like hornets' nests. (See pages 17 to 22 for more about capsaicin chemistry.) Birds, however, were unaffected. They could happily eat their fill of tiny hot peppers before excreting the seeds whole and still viable. In other words, from the start, peppers had adapted in ways that would enable the colonization of new territories through aerial dispersal while repelling animals whose more complex digestive systems were likely to break down the seeds.

How did humans first realize that the superhot ancestral mini-fruits held any potential as food? This, too, is still unknown. But over several millennia, the first parent diversified into many wild species scattered throughout the Bolivian piedmont and some neighboring regions. The sight of the widespread plants must have been familiar to prehistoric hunter-gatherers, giving them ample opportunity to experiment with specimens close to their own settlements and discover that eating the jewel-bright fruit didn't kill anyone.

It's a safe bet that, after this, peppers followed the same course as other major food plants—that is, people first encouraged the wild plants to grow in dedicated sites, and then cultivated them through simple measures like seeding and weeding. Last came true domestication, which created five species wholly dependent on human skills. Many people in different locations independently practiced cultivation, and most scholars believe that domestication took place at various centers rather than spreading out from one definitive point of origin. In any case, many wild and domesticated members of the *Capsicum* clan proved remarkably able to adapt to either lowland or moderate highland altitudes, semi-desert or rain forest conditions, and a wide range of temperatures (with frost as the limiting factor). Over millennia, variant forms with different colors or particular flavor notes appeared. Even capsaicin, the plant's default defense, sometimes was absent. These lucky genetic accidents would be skillfully exploited by both prehistoric and modern growers to produce a rainbow of possible colors and a range of hotter, milder, and sweeter flavors.

In pre-Hispanic times, the amazing, intelligent *Capsicum* plant had already spread throughout huge swaths of South America, from the eastern foothills of the Andes to the Pacific and Atlantic Oceans and throughout the Amazon and Orinoco basins, the Caribbean islands, and every part of Mesoamerica between Mexico and the Isthmus of Panama. Peppers even reached the deserts of what we know today as Arizona and New Mexico. Still more surprising, one wild species, *C. galapagoense*, grows on only two of the twenty-plus Galapagos Islands—a fact that surely would have fascinated Charles Darwin.

Huaca Prieta mound and the dwellings of the neighboring fishing village.

To this day, more wild *Capsicum* species flourish closer to their ancestral Bolivian homeland than anywhere else. And though the peppers originally domesticated in South America were slow to receive detailed English-language coverage and adoption, they are now starting to enter US kitchens thanks to immigrants from Peru, Ecuador, Colombia, Brazil, and other parts of the continent, as well as the Caribbean.

It is astonishing to realize that some of these "new" hot peppers were being eaten at Huaca Prieta by at least 6500 BP or perhaps even earlier. Nowhere else have I experienced a more powerful sense of the past and present of Latin America meshing through the magic of food. On different visits I walked through the complex of ruins at El Brujo, feeling bones crunch under my feet and glimpsing still-familiar kitchen objects like a *batán* (stone grinding slab) or *lapa* (hollowed-out half gourd shell used as a food vessel) protruding from the earth. At the Huaca Prieta mound I gazed at the traces of past excavations before strolling a few hundred feet to a neighboring cluster of shacks by the ocean to watch fully dressed women gathering fish or shellfish by hand in the breakers. Propped up to dry against walls were the graceful *caballitos* ("little horses," small floating crafts made of dried bulrushes), astride which the men of the village ventured into deeper waters in search of larger fish. It was as if no time had passed since their predecessors fished the same spots.

Freshwater canals run past this tiny hamlet. Between the nearest canal and the backs of the houses, people grow food plants identified as ancient staples by archaeologists. The canals of the region still support the highly prized *life*, a member of the South American "pencil catfish" group (*Trichomycterus spp*.), which appears on the Moche period murals of Huaca Cao Viejo, elsewhere at El Brujo. In the villagers' homes I watched families preparing simple dishes based on corn, sweet potatoes, other root vegetables, shellfish, and little else. It struck me that what elevated this cooking from subsistence rations to a true cuisine was the skilled use of peppers, the beautiful local *ajíes* that I'd seen the women crushing into sauces on the *batán*. It was a permanent enlargement of flavor that first began at Huaca Prieta more than seven thousand years ago. This wasn't the only evidence of prehistoric Latin American foodways transformed by the invention of pepper-based seasonings. Later, in other South American centers of pepper cultivation and cooking, I would have the same realization.

Huaca Prieta: Food Archaeology Game Changer

The 1946 to 1947 expedition to Huaca Prieta was a turning point in food archaeology. Junius Bird and his associates had the luck not only to find one of the longest unbroken records of food use anywhere in the Americas but also to start working with it just as a revolution in the tools of archaeological analysis was dawning. Seventy years later, the huge mass of materials that they collected and brought to New York is still yielding priceless discoveries about peppers and many other things, thanks to a deluge of new analytical methods in the last few decades.

When Bird's party pitched their tents by the Huaca Prieta mound, the field of systematic archaeology was about sixty years old and already depended on many advanced skills that are still the backbone of investigation. The primary job was usually to uncover buried remains of structures (such as walls belonging to residences, temples, tombs, or whole cities), artifacts (anything from clay tablets to gold rings), or natural objects (for example, bones). In some sites, such as caves used as dwellings or camps, artifacts and bones might be left on or close to the surface. Otherwise, it was necessary to excavate the soil stratigraphically—that is, carefully cutting down from the surface through upper and lower layers of deposits belonging to successive groups of inhabitants until the bottom (the oldest) layer of remains had been reached.

The pioneer archaeologists had only occasionally focused on food (as opposed to clues about ruling dynasties and monuments) and had few specialized tools for analyzing it. Huaca Prieta would inspire a cascade of changes. Bird himself was more interested in textiles than food. But sets of fine-mesh screens that he had designed for sifting through soil samples proved excellent at catching small food remnants, such as pepper seeds.

After the team returned to New York, Bird sent some of the expedition's findings for analysis using the new technique of carbon-14 dating, which was starting to replace guesswork about the true age of samples with objective evidence based on rates of decay in radioactive isotopes. It was soon clear that the earliest Huaca Prieta remains must be many millennia older than anything else at El Brujo. The most recent estimates, based on more refined technology, suggest that humans had colonized the site as early as the late Pleistocene epoch, and dated the first evidence of pepper use circa 7600 BP.

Bird also turned over other acquisitions to Eric O. Callen, the founding father of coprolite analysis, a new branch of research based on the study of desiccated or fossilized feces. Still regarded as on the fringe in the 1940s, this line of investigation has turned out to be one of the essential tools for any serious study of ancient diets today. (If you think about it, examining the contents of people's digestive tracts is a foolproof way to tell which specific foods were eaten—not thrown out uneaten—and how individual items were combined at meals.) Examining several Huaca Prieta coprolites as well as specimens collected from the abdomen of a mummified body at the site, Callen concluded that people were eating several kinds of peppers (though usually discarding the seeds first) together with seafood.

The Bird expedition broke new ground. It was the start of a revolution in methods of analysis that has gained momentum in the seventy years since. In fact, every year or so another technique or way of combining techniques forces plant-history sleuths to adjust previous beliefs. We are now experiencing a golden age of food-focused archaeology that yields new branches and sub-branches of investigation, like a young tree growing in speeded-up motion. One advance leads to another in the blink of an eye. For instance, the technique of flotation, using the water to isolate tiny and light materials and passing soil samples or lake-bottom sediments through a series of increasingly finer screens to obtain smaller particles of organic or nonorganic matter, are enhanced versions of Bird's sifting methods. Carbon-14 dating quickly gave way to accelerator mass spectrometry (AMS), a far more precise way of estimating the age of samples.

The Miracles of Microremains Analysis

I can only touch on some—by no means all—of the many analytical tools that today's bioarchaeologists, paleoethnobotanists, archaeological chemists, and others are bringing to pepper history and prehistory.

Some of the most advanced methods involve microremains, or bits of matter too small to see with the naked eye. Using electron microscopes, scientists can now directly examine pollen grains recovered from soil or lake-bottom samples. They can study phytoliths, microscopic silica-based structures found in the tissues of some plants.

And they can search ancient cooking pots or grinding stones for evidence of fossilized starch granules.

Microremains of these kinds have two huge advantages over macroremains, meaning those large enough to be seen without a microscope. First of all, they are unique fingerprints establishing the species identity of a plant beyond any doubt. Second, they do not decay in any climate. This means that they can provide conclusive evidence about peppers' origin and development in the steamy regions east of the Andes where experts once thought all plant remains must decompose in a few years. As a result, the long-standing imbalance between arid-climate and moist-climate pepper research is starting to be righted. And by the same token, all parts of the New World tropics are yielding a stream of discoveries about other foods that peoples of the Americas have prepared, cooked, and eaten with peppers.

With such archaeological context, we can begin to understand the solid pre-Hispanic culinary underpinnings that I have found again and again surviving in today's Latin American kitchens. Take the example of starch granules: Under the microscope, starch is not one undifferentiated substance. It occurs in granules of particular shapes and sizes that are unique to each starch-containing food—and though plants of the *Capsicum* genus don't contain much starch by comparison with potatoes or wheat berries, they do have small amounts that can't be confused with starch from any other source. Dolores Piperno, Linda Perry, and other pioneers of starch-grain analysis are conducting exciting research at sites with crucial evidence of pepper use. Repeatedly, they mention a pattern that I noticed when I was invited into indigenous peoples' kitchens to see how they worked with ingredients. Almost invariably, I found cooks grinding a staple starchy food like maize or yuca with some preferred local tool—a heavy stone rubbed like a pestle over a *batán* or other stone mortar, or a handmade wooden grater studded with quartz or metal teeth—that also was used for grating or grinding peppers. So it did not surprise me when archaeologists reported often finding pepper starch granules on the same grinding stones or graters as starch from the great root crops of the Andes and the tropical lowlands: yuca, potatoes, sweet potatoes, and other root vegetables, such as *achira* (*Canna edulis*, a classic coastal Peruvian crop that is still being grown on canal banks next to El Brujo).

Another analytic method also confirms that peppers had commonly kept the same company in ancient as in modern kitchens. The wizardry of high-performance or ultra-high-performance liquid chromatography makes it possible to identify the separate components in traces of food found in vessels—for instance, a sauce or beverage with residues including capsaicin with boiled-down, fermented yuca juice, or with theobromine (the chemical marker for cacao, from which chocolate is made). For me, all of these methods shine a direct light on the hands of cooks at work in past centuries or millennia.

Grinding was the foundation of serious food processing for major staples in all pre-Hispanic civilizations. The pairing of certain foods with certain flavorings shows cooks thinking like cooks. When I learn that microremains of squash, maize, sweet potatoes, yuca, *malanga*, or *achira* have been found somewhere in company with one of the capsicums, in my mind I see generations of women wielding their remarkably efficient crushing or grinding tools to extract maximum pepper flavor for a sauce or to bring bland staple foods to life with pepper heat.

Microscopic study can also be applied to macroremains, as in a novel technique devised by Katherine L. Chiou and Christine A. Hastorf of the UCLA anthropology department. While examining pepper seeds under a scanning electron microscope, they found that the characteristic shapes and proportions of seeds vary by *Capsicum* species. The measurement system they worked out promises to be an invaluable tool for tracking the early movements of the five domesticated species through the Americas—better evidence than the main techniques of microremains analysis, which are only sometimes able to narrow down identity beyond the *Capsicum* genus.

Fittingly enough, seeds from Huaca Prieta and Paredones, a site less than a mile north of Huaca Prieta, were among the first archaeological samples that Chiou and Hastorf examined. It appeared that at an early date (more than 8000 BP), local people were using the four species *Capsicum baccatum, C. chinense, C. frutescens,* and *C. pubescens* with some frequency, but that by 4500 BP the baccatum—a star pepper in today's Peruvian cuisine—already outshone all the rest. This is the kind of evidence that needs to be applied to every archaeological site of the New World tropics to tell us how and when different peppers took root in regional cuisines.

Eclectic Use of Techniques

Broadly speaking, all archaeological research on native New World food crops has moved from complete reliance on macroremains to a strong—not exclusive—focus on microremains. At the same time, completely different lines of investigation are opening other vistas. Genome sequencing has been performed on several wild and domesticated species as well as some individual cultivars.

A striking feature of twenty-first-century archaeologists' mentality is a multi-disciplinary approach that brings many detective tools to bear on the lives—and food culture—of ancient peoples. One example is a 2013 paper by an international team of plant scientists, anthropologists, and other researchers of prehistoric foodways and food crops; they used *C. annuum* peppers in Mexico to demonstrate the advantages of a multipronged effort to pin down the first area of domestication. Some of their evidence came from the various archaeobotanical methods described previously, as well as comparative DNA analysis of wild and domesticated pepper populations. But they also used a technique known as species distribution modeling to predict the statistically most likely parameters of ecological factors, such as local temperatures and rainfall, for early domestication efforts. An entirely different kind of evidence was sketched by Cecil H. Brown, one of the founders of the new field of paleobiolinguistics, which applies comparative linguistic analysis to the challenges of reconstructing the names of food plants and animals in the extinct ancestors of known languages.

In the researchers' opinion, the most likely site of origin for domesticated *C. annuum* is an area of east-central Mexico between southern Puebla and southern Veracruz State. They presented this conclusion as the explanation most consistent with a careful weighing of all these clues. To me, this is a perfect example of the directions in which modern pepper research is going, giving us incomplete answers to all questions about capsicums through the ages while continually evolving bits and pieces of answers that show how archaeology itself is a living, ever-changing fusion of disciplines.

C. annuum var. *glabriusculum* (Sonora chiltepín)

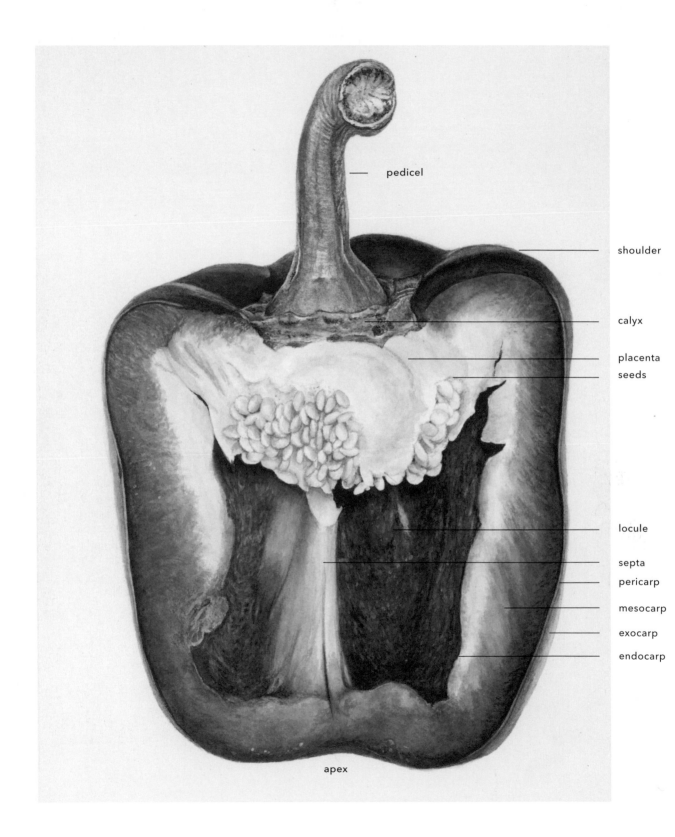

pedicel

shoulder

calyx

placenta

seeds

locule

septa

pericarp

mesocarp

exocarp

endocarp

apex

PEPPER ANATOMY
AND HEAT

Pepper plants defy quick generalizations based on appearance. The more than thirty-five wild and domesticated species grow in a fantastic range of forms. They can be spindly stalks less than 2 feet/.60 meters high, many-branched and woody like small trees, or dense bushes. The peppers that they bear can be equally confusing to the eye. Looka-likes are often only distantly related. If you have ever had trouble sorting out the kinds in a market display, you are not alone. Nevertheless, wild and domesticated peppers of all species have certain ancient structural traits in common in contrast to more recently acquired features that differentiate, say, a poblano from a habanero. Though we eat them as vegetables or condiments, all are technically fruits or, more specifically, berries, with small seeds borne inside a fleshy envelope. In everyday usage, the fruits are called pods.

Pepper Anatomy: Pod, Calyx, Flower, Seed

In all pepper plants, from tall old shrubs to tender garden specimens, the flowers and, later, the fruits are attached to the branching stems by *pedicels* (the botanical term for short individual stems) in either erect, pendant (hanging), or intermediate positions. A green *calyx* first encloses the flower bud, and remains around the base of the opened blossom and then the fruit when it develops. Both flower and calyx display particular features that differ by species. These have been of great importance to botanists who study wild or domesticated peppers in tracking the New World travels of the *Capsicum* genus's individual members.

Pepper pods can have remarkably diverse shapes, resembling string beans or diminutive bananas, cherry tomatoes, or miniature lanterns, and botanists have selected particularly illustrative pod types from known cultivars as examples. The kinds closest to the original wild prototype always look like tiny beads. But all peppers, both wild and domesticated, retain parts of the same ancestral anatomy. Their kinship is clear when you compare cross sections or lengthwise sections of different kinds.

Every pepper contains a fleshy outer structure called the *pericarp*, which you will recognize as the only part of a bell pepper (and some other large peppers) that is eaten. It consists of three layers: the *exocarp* (skin), the thicker and meatier *mesocarp*, and the thin, membranous *endocarp*. On the inner side, the pericarp has two, three, or four lengthwise ridges called ribs, or more precisely *septa* (from the Latin for "partitions"). These run down all or part of the pod and loosely divide the interior into chambers, or in botanical terms *locules* or lobes. (In very small, skinny peppers, the ribs may be colloquially called veins.) The chambers that they form are partly hollow, which makes some peppers (especially large ones) ideal for stuffing.

The crucial contents of the pod's interior are the reproductive organs of the fruit. Starting from the top end, the most conspicuous feature is a pulpy structure called the *placenta*, which supplies nourishment to the developing *seeds* just as a mammalian placenta nourishes the fetus. In some kinds, such as the familiar bell pepper, the placenta-seed complex may look like a whitish plug attached to the top; in others, as for the Peruvian *ají amarillo*, it runs the entire length of the pepper. The number of seeds carried on the placenta varies strikingly between different kinds of peppers, from about a dozen to more than two hundred per fruit.

In every wild species and almost all domesticated cultivars, tiny cells lying close under the surface of the placenta secrete a unique chemical weapon. This fiery substance, produced by capsicums and no other plants, has often been labeled capsaicin. Today it is known to be a complex of several alkaloids more correctly called capsaicinoids. (The pericarp contains another group of related compounds called capsinoids, responsible for the nonhot flavors that are most pronounced in "sweet" cultivars.) It used to be thought that the placenta was the only source of true pepper heat, partly communicating its fierceness to the flesh, veins, and seeds. However, recent research by horticulturist Paul Bosland at the Chile Pepper Institute in New Mexico, has established that in a few superhot cultivars, capsaicin secretion also occurs in the pericarp, meaning that every bit of the flesh can be as incredibly searing as the placenta itself (see more information on capsaicin on pages 17 to 19).

These physical structures are universal features of pepper fruits, though it may take a careful eye to recognize them in examples as different as a tiny *chiltepín* and a *cubanelle*. But when experts try to distinguish among different species, they generally concentrate not on the fruit but on two other sources of information: One is the blossom. The other is the calyx, the green "cap" that covers the top of the blossom and remains attached to the pod, where it joins the pedicel. There may be other clues,

C. annuum (chile huacle)

C. frutescens (Tabasco)

C. Chinense (dátil)

C. pubescens (rocoto)

such as whether the pedicel attachment is flush with the top of the fruit, or (as in bell peppers) somewhat sunken; some pedicels also are enlarged toward the attachment point. The shape of the calyx, however, usually produces better evidence of species identity than the shape of the pod.

In many members of the *C. annuum* species (which includes bell peppers and nearly all the varieties first developed in Mexico), the outer margin of the calyx is marked into five or more oblique angles like a pentagon or other polygon, with a small rib running to the pointed tip of each angle. In others, it shows a few rounded or blunt projections. In the South American *C. pubescens*, the calyx is conspicuously dentate—that is, it has long, sharp teeth extending beyond the rim. The pretty calyx of *C. baccatum* (also from South America) is also dentate, but the shape is more like the outside of a miniature parasol with delicately marked rib tips instead of toothlike projections. *C. frutescens*, a species with members widely distributed throughout the New World tropics, has a nearly circular calyx with less evidence of teeth. That of the more narrowly distributed South American and Caribbean *C. chinense* (whose most famous members are habanero and Scotch bonnet peppers, found in the United States) displays a narrow constriction where the pedicel meets the calyx.

Pepper flowers also show some clear differentiation by species. Each contains a *corolla* (Latin for "little garland") of five to seven petals arranged in a circle around the stamens and pistil in the center. *C. pubescens* is distinguished by a purple corolla, sometimes with a narrow white border around the edges of the petals. *C. baccatum* has characteristic tan spots at the base of its white petals. The *C. chinense* corolla is a slight greenish white; that of *C. frutescens* is a clearer, more definite white. Most *C. annuums* have white flowers, though some are purple. These details are better markers of identity than other aspects of pepper morphology (that is, form and structure), but there is one additional major source of clues to species identity: the seeds.

Until very recently, researchers paid scant attention to distinctions between the seeds of different species other than noting that *C. pubescens* has black (sometimes

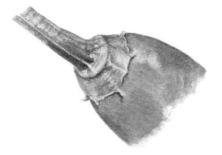

C. baccatum (ají amarillo)

dark brown) seeds with a rough, wrinkled exterior, while the seeds of other species are smooth coated and never darker than light tan, yellow, or off-white. But in the last few years, some pioneering work has been done on systematic measurement of seed shapes and proportions that has furnished new tools for identification—a very important development because seeds are often the only recognizable evidence remaining at archaeological sites when other plant matter has decayed.

In 2012, a pair of archaeobotanists at the University of California, Berkeley, developed a system of measuring features, including shape, proportions, seed coat texture, the tiny protrusion called the beak, and the scar indicating the point where a seed detached from the placenta, to identify the species to which seeds belong.

What Makes Peppers Hot

Forty years ago, fans of pepper heat got very simple answers to questions about its source. They were told that their favorite Mexican chiles were hot because of a substance called *capsaicin*, an alkaloid located in pepper seeds and ribs. At that time, we were just learning to roughly measure amounts of this substance in Scoville units, tallying degrees of zero pepper hotness along a scale (established in 1912 by pharmacist Wilbur Scoville), starting with bell peppers and rising to stratospheric heights for the then newly popular habanero. At that point, "stratospheric" probably meant less than 500,000 units.

How much has changed since then! The more I learn about capsaicin, the more I realize how much there is still to know and the more convinced I become that cooking with peppers is one of the most important ways to understand their heat. And growing them in my own garden has taught me even more. Tasting hundreds of peppers at various stages of growth and taking notes on their development through the years has

given me an increased sense of the plants' intelligent survival strategies. I am sensitive now to the ways in which weather fluctuations and even minor details, such as where a certain pepper is planted in the garden, will affect its pungency.

I believe that the best way to tackle this very intricate subject is to begin by thinking not about capsaicin chemistry but about the living plants of the *Capsicum* genus in their South American place of origin. Their capacity to secrete capsaicin is unique, shared by no other member of the plant kingdom. Though destined to become an attraction for humans, capsaicin paradoxically started out as a repellent for other creatures—a powerful irritant. The original evolutionary strategy of capsicums in the wild depended on driving away potential eaters whose teeth and digestive systems would damage the seeds and hinder the plant from reproducing. But the savage bite that fended off mammals was not at all repellent to birds, whose wings could carry them for miles and whose simpler digestive tracts excreted the seeds intact, allowing them to germinate and take root across a wide range.

But a pepper plant doesn't just pump a precise, uniform dose of capsaicin into each fruit like an injection on an assembly line. The plants respond flexibly to different environmental factors by secreting varying amounts, a fact well recognized by gardeners.

In 2008, researcher Joshua Tewksbury was able to document surprising variations in capsaicin production by the wild South American species *C. chacoense*. When attacked by insects that bore into the fruit and leave it open to invasion by the fungus *Fusarium*, it mounts a direct counterattack by ramping up capsaicin production in *Fusarium*-affected areas. But capsaicin production can deplete the plant's energy. In other settings, where drought replaces fungi as the main environmental threat, the same species is capable of shutting off capsaicin production altogether while altering the distribution of *stomata*—the pores of the leaves through which transpiration takes place—in order to conserve water. The domesticated capsicum plants can't match these drastic, purposeful switches in pungency, but within narrower limits, they can swap one quality or function for another.

It is known that factors like altitude, ambient heat, sunlight exposure, drought, excessive rain, and stress also affect capsaicin levels in domesticated peppers. For instance, the higher the altitude, the higher the capsaicin content in some Himalayan *chinense* cultivars. *Frutescens* peppers grown in the torrid climate of eastern Africa develop much more intense heat than anywhere else. The Padrón, an *annuum* cultivar, is far hotter when grown in Florida than when grown in Palo Alto, California.

The original balance of environmental influences in the wild was altered with domestication, and even more so with the change from perennial to annual growth when three of the domesticated species (*C. annuum, C. frutescens,* and *C. chinense)* were successfully transferred from the tropics to temperate zones with strongly marked seasonal growth limits. Having to grow each year from seed introduced more generation-to-generation variables. And having to flower and fruit within a certain time range imposes serious constraints. Simply put, the plants need to manage the energy that goes into making capsaicin. They can't dole out equal amounts of capsaicin to every pepper at every stage of the growing season.

I see some of the resulting variations in all my hot pepper plants. The first flowers to develop will yield hotter peppers than the later ones. In fact, something red-hot close to the stem end may be noticeably cooler a knuckle's length or two farther toward the tip. Contrary to popular belief, the true source of heat is not the seeds but the placenta. This is where the capsaicin is actually secreted, though the seeds may pick it up through contact.

More Than Capsaicin

As with everything about peppers, the properties of heat are also complex. Anyone who learns to appreciate the spectrum of flavors that the many different hot peppers bring to sauces and soups also appreciates that their heat has many nuances. So it should come as no surprise to learn that the single term "capsaicin" long ago became inadequate.

Beginning with improved analysis in 1961, it has been conclusively established that the hotness of chiles and other pungent peppers actually comes from a cluster of closely related compounds officially known as capsaicinoids. Although more than twenty have been isolated, the principal five are capsaicin, dihydrocapsaicin, nordihydrocapsaicin, homodihydrocapsaicin, and homocapsaicin. For the sake of convenience, writers still loosely use the term "capsaicin" for the total package, but at times it's necessary to refer more precisely to capsaicinoids. What's important to know is that each contributes different notes to the sensation of hotness, and that their overall balance can vary greatly in individual cultivars. Our understanding of the genetic variables behind these factors is still fairly rudimentary. Whole genome sequencing has been done on several *C. annuum* cultivars and at least one *C. chinense* landrace (the term for when a species has been developed over many years in a specific area through traditional farming practices, not agricultural science). But given the notorious talent of annuums for producing mutations to aid survival through switching the position of transposons (short segments of DNA) on a chromosome, and the huge mild-to-superhot range of chinenses, these are only baby steps in understanding the subtle intricacies of pepper heat.

Tables of average capsaicinoid content generally list the relative amounts of capsaicin and dihydrocapsaicin at respectively about 69 and 22 percent of the total, with nor-dihydrocapsaicin a distant third at 7 percent and each of the last two registering only 1 percent or less. But these are only averages that don't really tell us much.

Researchers are just starting to grapple with two important facts: first, that each of the principal five capcasinoids registers in a different way on the palate; and second, that the balance of capsaicin, dihydrocapsaicin, and nordihydrocapsaicin can be as sharply affected as total capsaicinoid content by environmental factors. And even the tiny amounts contributed by homodihydrocapsaicin and homocapsaicin are likely to be crucial to the overall sensory effect. We perceive pepper heat not just in one big blast, but as an intricate blend of sensations. Depending on the pepper in question, the heat may be either quickly dissipating or lingering, most strongly felt on the tip of the tongue or the back of the throat, delivered evenly throughout the tasting process or gradually blossoming in the mouth. These are the kind of mysteries that further capsaicinoid research promises to unlock.

The Science of Tasting

We've come a long way since fans first started using Scoville readings like baseball scores. For the record, the scale that Wilbur Scoville devised involves diluting alcohol extracts of dried peppers in progressively larger amounts of a water-based sugar solution until a panel of tasters can detect no heat. If it sounds a little unscientific, it is. Getting human tasters to quantify their sensations by exact numbers is like herding a pack of Shiba Inus. Meanwhile, we've seen the Scoville scores of the 1970s eclipsed by a generation of carefully bred superhot peppers that keep revving up the voltage. The current record-holder (but for how long?) is a cultivar called the Carolina Reaper, coming in at more than 2 million Scoville units. Examining superhot peppers, Paul Bosland found that they are an exception to the rule that the real source of capsaicin is the placenta. They carry excruciating heat in tiny vesicles distributed throughout the pericarp (see page 12), and I suspect that they are also visible under the skin as a kind of pimply eruption. All of my superhots have that strange skin-rash look. When you dare to face a Carolina Reaper, Bhut Jolokia, Trinidad Moruga Scorpion, or any of the other superhots, expect no mercy from even the tiniest bite of the flesh.

PEPPERS AND NUTRITION

Peppers are an excellent addition to any diet aimed at making the most of fresh vegetables. Very low in calories, they contain small amounts of a few minerals, including calcium, phosphorus, and zinc, but considerably more significant amounts of several vitamins. The most important are vitamin C, vitamin E, and vitamin A in the precursor form of beta-carotene and other carotenoids. Green bell or hot peppers have enough of all three to supply substantial percentages of the adult recommended daily allowances; note, however, that some of the vitamin C will be destroyed by cooking.

The picture for yellow and (especially) red peppers is similar, except that the amounts of all three vitamins are much greater. All raw red peppers are among the richest sources of vitamin C known, and a good amount remains even after cooking or processing in such forms as canned roasted red peppers. Both vitamin A activity and vitamin E content are multiplied several times and are not affected by cooking. In fact, ground dried red pepper in the forms enjoyed by many of the world's peoples from Spain and Hungary to Turkey and Korea can be a significant dietary source of vitamin A.

Scoville scores are fun to read about, but you'll notice that I very seldom mention them except when Guinness World Records are involved. Not only are these numbers much more subjective and variable than many people realize, they are a diversion from what I consider the true culinary role of capsaicin in real peppers—as a flavor enhancer. At either fairly low or fierce heat levels, Mexican chiles and South American *ajíes* matter in the kitchen because the capsaicinoid complex has the power to bring the other components of a dish together, to give them clarity and definition. This wonderful talent needs to be recognized for its own merits. For me, plain English terms like "mild," "moderately hot," "very hot," and "excruciatingly hot" are more dependable than strings of zeros. And having seen supposedly very hot cultivars in my own garden that taste as meek as a dull jalapeño one summer and blazing hot the next, I place very little reliance on numbers. I prefer to taste a pepper for myself before I stir it into a pot of soup or crush it in a mortar for a salsa.

I believe that science has much to contribute to the art of tasting peppers, mild or hot. Already we know that the most strongly and subtly individualized contributors to pepper flavor and—just as important—aroma are not the capsaicinoids but a host of unrelated substances known as volatile organic compounds (VOCs). If you sniff a Caribbean chinense and then a Peruvian *rocoto* and note the floral perfume of the first and the green bell pepper aroma of the other, their individual VOC profiles are the main source of the difference. Today, the preferred methods of measuring both VOCs and the individual capsaicinoids are high-performance liquid chromatography or combined gas chromatography–mass spectrometry. Both yield accurate readings of very tiny amounts. They are sensitive enough to have detected traces of capsaicin residues along with cacao in a fifth-century AD Mayan cooking pot.

Capsinoids: Heat-Free Anomaly

In every pepper-growing country of the world, research institutes are zeroing in on manifold refinements of pepper chemistry using new methods of analysis and a wide spectrum of other investigative tools, including genomic studies. Their advances are interesting to home gardeners like me, but of much greater concern to commercial pepper growers. Everything that affects flavor and hotness also affects the bottom line of a huge, rapidly growing international agro-industry that needs hard facts about how factors like capsaicin or VOC will be expressed in the flesh and placenta of a certain cultivar under varied conditions, at different stages of growth, or when subjected to different kinds of processing, such as drying and grinding, freezing, pickling, and fermenting. The giant seed-breeding companies are equally dependent on reliable chemical profiles of the strains they are working with and knowledge of the terroirs where the peppers will be grown.

One completely unexpected aspect of pepper chemistry was revealed in 1989 by a team of Japanese scientists investigating an unusual laboratory-bred nonhot pepper labeled CH–19 Sweet. To their surprise, they found that it contained a kind of "silent army"—a group of compounds resembling the capsaicinoids, but without their heat. They have been christened capsinoids, and include capsiate, dihydrocapsiate, and nor-dihydrocapsiate. Subsequent research has established that they are present in all peppers in smaller amounts. The discovery of capsinoids is tremendously important for medical researchers studying the health effects of peppers, and also notable for those of us who are mostly interested in flavor.

Capsaicinoids, Capsinoids, and Health

For decades, capsaicin (meaning the capsaicinoid complex) has been used for topical pain relief. Does this sound like a contradiction in terms? Contradictions and surprises have accompanied the whole pepper story since the original repellent became an attraction for prehistoric humans. Ointments and salves containing capsaicinoids are known to have an initial irritating effect followed by reduced pain; this is a suggestive parallel to the effect on people raised on hot peppers who eat dishes liberally seasoned with them. Strangers and small children flinch from the burn, but everybody else not only tolerates it but also finds a sense of rapturous pleasure in it—a kind of learned behavior unlike other acquired tastes. If, like me, you have a fairly high tolerance but sometimes reach your limits, I drink whole milk or take a spoonful of plain yogurt or sour cream. Do not try drinking water! Capsaicin is not water-soluble, and you will only prolong the ordeal. Creamy dairy products are useful because capsaicin dissolves in fat.

Neurological research has determined that the capsaicinoids trigger responses in a certain receptor along particular nerve pathways. The activation of TRPV1 (transient receptor potential vanilloid receptor 1) by exposure to dangerous heat is responsible for the pain of an actual burn. Strong concentrations of capsaicinoids cause the same sensation on skin and mucous membranes as on the mouth, though without the tissue damage of a real thermal burn. With repeated exposure, they soothe rather than exacerbate pain. Of course, the extreme concentrations in hot pepper spray are another story, capable of immobilizing a healthy person for forty-five minutes and lethally injuring people with already impaired breathing and other medical conditions.

The significance of the capsinoid discoveries is that these compounds have many of the capsaicinoid effects but produce no irritation—a great advantage when administering them. A promising future is starting to open up for new medical uses of both capsaicinoids and capsinoids. It is too early to sort out truth from fiction in the many enthusiastic health claims made for products based on either. But both complexes appear to be antioxidants and potential anti-inflammatories. In laboratory animals, they have been found to modulate blood insulin spikes after meals, suggesting possible benefits for diabetics. They produce temporary increases in body temperature, perhaps pointing to a slight metabolic speeding up capable of discouraging the proliferation of fat cells or promoting actual weight loss. The jury is out on blood pressure effects, asthma relief, and tumor suppression, but there is much to indicate exciting future uses for peppers. I do not yet recommend taking capsaicinoid or capsinoid pills as supplements, but I do cook with hot and nonhot peppers as an everyday pleasure that just may produce health benefits.

THE CAPSICUM CLAN

When Spanish voyagers first returned from the New World with an unexpected alternative to the East Indian black pepper that Columbus had hoped to find, scientists of the time thought that they were looking at a single new variety. It wasn't until two centuries later that Linnaeus decided available specimens must belong to several distinct species, leading him to conclusively establish *Capsicum* as the name of the parent genus. Since the nineteenth century, scholarly plant hunters have managed to identify five domesticated and several dozen wild species (about thirty-five at last count). Most were found close to the east-central Bolivian piedmont, an important area for the exchange of influences between the main lowland and highland regions of the South American tropics.

The relationships of pepper clan members are intricate and still not fully understood. This is partly because they present an enormous diversity of phenotypes, a word embracing the entire complex of outward qualities that greet an observer, from size, color, and shape to smell and taste. In the case of peppers, it also includes varying amounts of capsaicin, the source of pepper heat. Aspects of phenotype related to form and structure are collectively called morphology. Phenotype and morphology can, but often do not, furnish helpful evidence about a plant's genotype, or the sum total of the genetic makeup underlying its external characteristics.

Members of the *Capsicum* clan share a common basic anatomy, as well as a few other major traits. All are tropical natives that were born in or close to the original Bolivian center of dispersal. All are natural perennials that easily grow to the dimensions of woody shrubs on home territory but are cold intolerant, some to a greater degree than others. They have beautiful star-shaped flowers in various shades of white, greenish, or purple. The capsaicin responsible for their heat is a unique and defining feature of the genus, but a mutation that suppresses capsaicin production occurs in "sweet" cultivars of at least two domesticated species.

The extensive range of different reds seen in ripe peppers—from rosy to flame colored to rich crimson—reflects the fact that small amounts of certain pigments that are not unique to peppers can figure in the equation. In fact, some cultivars produce little or no capsanthin and capsorubin (pigments responsible for red colors). In these kinds, it is yellow pigments, chiefly lutein and beta-carotene, that become visible with the breakdown of chlorophyll. If there is some production of both red and yellow pigments, different shades of orange result. And when peppers contain large amounts of anthocyanins—a family of red, purple, and blue pigments unrelated to capsanthin and capsorubin—they can turn out a striking lavender, magenta, or purple.

External clues to species identification can be especially elusive. Taxonomists trade arguments about the validity of some distinctions and point out that the Latin names of most species are based on mistakes. But for purposes of discussion everyone is willing to acknowledge the following five domesticated capsicums: *C. annuum, C. baccatum, C. chinense, C. frutescens,* and *C. pubescens.* They were created when wild peppers were strategically altered by human effort at several times and places that are still under investigation, then carried to new homes far from the original point of the *Capsicum* genus's origin. The most mysterious of these prehistoric journeys took one species—*C. annuum*—to Mesoamerica, while all the others stuck closer to the South American lowland tropics.

The Call of the Wild

Peppers have been bound up with the lives of Latin American peoples for millennia. The prehistoric voyages of people and cuisines were also voyages of wild and domesticated peppers from region to region. *Capsicum* remnants in kitchen middens or on the walls of ancient cooking pots are fragments of great stories waiting to be pieced together by a new generation of specialists in Latin American paleobotany. Essential to the story line are the classic regional pairings that evolved between hot peppers and other foods before the dawn of history, and that have triumphantly survived to this day.

Traveling and cooking through many Latin countries over the last thirty years, I repeatedly found the backbone of regional cuisines to be a starchy ingredient (or complex of several) given life and soul by some form of hot peppers. This pattern seems to have begun with wild peppers. Take one example: Wherever yuca has been exploited by indigenous peoples in the moist tropical lowlands of South America, so have fierce, tiny capsicums. The staple food (in its original form or fermented into vinegar) and the classic seasoning ingredient became joined during the early transition from wild to domesticated pepper species.

But what is a wild pepper? The answer is twofold. We can apply the name to the dozens of *Capsicum* species that have never undergone any process of domestication.

All of these share a few crucial qualities, starting with a bitter taste and the fierce blaze of capsaicin. The pods are tiny, very seedy berries, usually smooth and round or like slightly elongated beads, though they can take other shapes. They grow upright on the pedicel (the stem where the flower and later the fruit are attached to a branching stalk) instead of dangling from it. As they ripen, they turn bright red and eventually fall from the pedicel, to be pecked up by birds and shunned by other wildlife.

Five of these original species were coaxed into larger, very different domesticated phenotypes through the genius of indigenous peoples in the American tropics. But peppers of "tame" species have a stubborn penchant for escaping from gardens back into the wild and reverting to something resembling their original form. They are very small, very hot, and usually ripening to a blazing red color. Yet they are not wild in the sense of predomesticates. A trained botanist can tease out their real identity by examining the peppers' anatomy (see pages 13 to 16) and by the fact that the ripe pods don't detach from the pedicel as easily as do their wild cousins. (This means that they cannot seed themselves without human help.) To an untrained eye and palate, they generally look and taste indistinguishable from the minuscule chiltepines of Mexico and the US Southwest, *C. annuum* var. *glabriusculum*. To indigenous peoples everywhere, from the South American to the Mesoamerican tropics, these tiny firebombs still are an indispensable seasoning. In contrast, the Spanish colonists and their descendants have tended to prefer the larger, domesticated phenotypes, with their complexly developed interplay of flavors.

Five Strong Individualists

The five domesticated capsicums have as much individuality as the five major domesticated alliums—garlic, chives, globe onions, leeks, and shallots—each marked by the secretion of distinctive sulfur compounds corresponding to the capsaicin secreted by capsicums, all related but not interchangeable.

For generations, cooks and food lovers in the United States had no chance to appreciate the real richness of the different domesticated pepper species. The only kinds available were *C. annuums*, and only in the Southwestern states were there more peppers to choose from than bell peppers and a few gentle siblings. Hot peppers came into vogue in other parts of the country during the late 1960s. But the cultivars of fashion were also annuums, though ones with heavier doses of capsaicin. Intoxicated with the rush of sheer chile heat, new converts rediscovered Scoville's measurement system and started comparing favorite peppers on the basis of how many Scoville units—that is, how much capsaicin—they contained. When the habanero, a newly popular pepper that happened to be a *C. chinense,* enjoyed an ecstatic reception in the early '70s, the first leader of taste to point out its different botanical lineage was Mexican cooking expert Diana Kennedy.

Even now, discussions of cooking with peppers don't always make species distinctions clear, but the species have real culinary importance. I learned this during the many years I spent becoming acquainted with different peppers through the cuisines of the lands where they are grown. It was an education to my palate. To go back to the allium analogy, it was like coming to understand that leeks cannot be judged by how garlicky they taste.

While I was researching this book, the US pepper scene began changing along with emigration from many parts of Latin America. For instance, Peruvians settling into new homes soon demanded their favorite peppers, which were previously unknown in US retail stores. Today, all cooks willing to search in the right neighborhoods can find flash-frozen baccatum and pubescens peppers and taste for themselves how different they are from the usual suspects in supermarkets or even most gourmet shops. The fact that I was able to obtain seeds or seedlings of several hundred *Capsicum* cultivars from all five species and grow them in one small New Jersey garden is a further sign of permanently enlarged horizons.

For me, nurturing many different annuums, chinenses, and others from infancy to harvest led to another dimension of knowledge: It deepened my desire to learn more about the unknown peoples who brought them into being, working to harness the heat of each and develop its delicate nuances and subtleties. Each of the five domesticated species has its own intricate story, bound up with particular ecological or cultural contexts.

Capsicum annuum

In many ways *C. annuum* is the most mystifying of all domesticated *Capsicum* species, as well as the one that has contributed most to the spread of peppers from the Latin American tropics to the rest of the planet. The Spanish found it in Mexico already developed by pre-Hispanic peoples into an incredible profusion of cultivars, and being eaten with corn and beans much as it is today. Each kind had its preferred uses in cooking, whether fresh, dried, or both. To this day, the word "chile" or "chilli," which the invaders picked up from the Nahuatl (Aztec) language, is the generic name for any hot pepper in English-speaking countries.

The mystifying question is what brought *C. annuum* to Mexico in the first place. It, or its closest ancestors, initially evolved in east-central Bolivia or perhaps eastern Amazonia. Plant researchers are at a loss to explain how and when it became naturalized in Mexico, three or four thousand miles to the north.

Of all pepper species, *C. annuum* displays the greatest physical diversity, or phenotypical variation. An annuum can be a round berry less than 0.5 inch/1.3 centimeters

C. annuum (chile huacle negro)

THE ANNUUM-CHINESE-FRUTESCENS COMPLEX

The habanero, as the name indicates, was reportedly brought to the Yucatán Peninsula from Havana. In colonial times, travel between Havana and Yucatán was so constant, and *C. chinense* was so widespread throughout the islands, that a useful cultivar may well have been carried to Campeche and spread from there. But *C. chinense* had already done some traveling from its native South America before habaneros landed on the Yucatán Peninsula. And here we reach mysteries involving not just one species but the two other members of the *annuum-chinense-frutescens* complex.

At best guess, the three genetically linked species were jointly conceived but later underwent some process of incomplete divergence that left each one capable of interbreeding with the others, but more likely to produce sterile crosses than viable seeds.

C. annuum became the dominant capsicum of Mesoamerica, *C. chinense* of the humid South American tropics from Bolivia eastward to the Caribbean. The less prolific *C. frutescens* figured only selectively in the general picture.

Where and when did the common ancestor originate, and where and when did the splitting-off process take place? It is possible that the story involved a primary and a secondary center of dispersal, the first near the birthplace of all capsicums, in the Bolivian piedmont, and the second farther east in northern Amazonia. Both of these areas lie at the intersection of different topographies and habitats, allowing important plants to penetrate into diverse ecosystems where they would later figure in many cultures and cuisines.

The northeastern Brazilian state of Roraima may have been a major vector of dispersal. It sits close to the Guiana Shield,

an ancient geological formation that partly covers areas of Brazil, Colombia, Venezuela, Guyana, French Guiana, and Suriname. In this general area, researchers have found what seem to be primitive forms of chinense and frutescens peppers with a few annuums.

At the same time, scholars have made significant progress against another crucial roadblock to tracing the dispersal of peppers and many other plants in the hot, moist tropics. The very conditions that make the region ideally suited to nourish a certain range of plants like capsicums also guarantee that most physical evidence of their existence will be wiped out in a very few years. In contrast, the arid climates found in some parts of Mexico and the Pacific Coast have faithfully preserved remnants of the peppers that reached those places—*C. annuums* in dry Mexican caves, and several *Capsicum* species on the Peruvian coast and a few high Andean caves.

Only in the last decades have archaeologists begun conquering the limitations of evidence in rain forests and cloud forests. The modern chemical techniques of analyzing plant microremains now allow us to zero in on microscopic starch grains or capsaicin residues that can conclusively demonstrate the presence of peppers—and, just as important, tell us what other foods they were cooked and eaten with. As a result, the classic yuca-pepper association that I have seen in indigenous communities throughout the Amazon and Orinoco basins can now be traced back into the remote past.

By careful comparison of genotypes and some external traits, researchers hope to learn more about the genetic events that split one ancestor into three incompletely differentiated species.

in diameter, a blocky sphere the size of a large apple, a carrot-shaped object more than 8 inches/20 centimeters long, a minute fingerling, or dozens of other shapes. It ripens to a brilliant spectrum of different colors. It and *C. chinense* are the only two species whose capsaicin content can range between sky-high and zero in different cultivars. The most familiar heatless annuums are "sweet peppers" or bell peppers.

For sheer visibility on every continent of the eastern and western hemisphere, *C. annuum* eclipses all others. Annuums are found in every region of Mexico, having adapted to an incredible range of climatic conditions from rain forest to semi-desert. The parent form is thought to be the small, fiery bird peppers or chiltepines, generally classified as *C. annuum* var. *glabriusculum* or *aviculare*, that seed themselves like weeds throughout northern Mexico and the US Southwest. It is difficult to distinguish between bird pepper bushes that have long been growing wild and "escapees" from gardens.

Luckily for US gardeners, any annuum cultivar, whether hot or "sweet," will tolerate conditions in all of our growing zones. The best-known fresh and dried peppers in the United States are all annuums, from poblanos, serranos, jalapeños, Anaheims/New Mexicos, and minuscule bird peppers to bell peppers, cubanelles, Italian frying peppers, and piquillos from Spain. Ground dried peppers from Mexico are always *C. annuum*. So are chipotles (which are really smoked jalapeños) and the Guatemalan *ululte* (a smoked bird pepper). I have to say that no one can appreciate the sheer richness of this one species without traveling through Mexico and Central America.

Capsaicin heat is usually clean and direct in both fresh and dried annuums. Depending on the degree of heat, the underlying annuum flavor may be hard to perceive. But it is there underneath any amount of fiery capsaicin. Cultivars in their green state have a straightforward flavor suggesting cut grass and leaves, with an aroma contributed by volatile methoxypyrazines (especially characteristic of green bell peppers). Ripening brings out a satisfying interplay between developing sugars and organic acids, including citric and ascorbic acid. The effect is intensified by drying.

Toasting and soaking dried Mexican chiles before using them introduces varying degrees of fruitiness, sweetness, and caramelization. The reconstituted chiles lend body as well as flavor to all kinds of sauces. Mexicans often use combinations of several different kinds for a depth and complexity that one dried chile variety alone could not create.

The range of pepper shapes, sizes, and colors that annuums possess means that they can look like members of almost any Capsicum species. There are few conclusive identifying signs. The flowers are usually white, less often purple. As in other species, the number of petals can be between five and seven. The calyx, like the fruit, can take too many possible shapes to furnish positive clues about identity. Only the seeds are a real giveaway. The pale yellow seed coat is smooth; the shape resembles the outline of a round, fat kidney bean; and in cross section, the seed does not thin markedly between the center and the edges.

C. baccatum

ANDEAN PEPPERS: A SIXTEENTH-CENTURY ACCOUNT

"They put on everything they eat, whether stewed, boiled or roasted, something which they call *uchu*, and the Spaniards, Indies pepper, even though there they call it *ají*, which is its name in the language of the Barlovento islands [Greater Antilles]. Those from my country are so fond of *uchu*, that they eat nothing, not even a few greens, without it. Because of the intense flavor it gives to everything to which it is added, they prohibit its consumption during times of fasting, so that the fast may be true in form, as mentioned earlier. This pepper comes in three or four varieties; the most common of which is fat, somewhat oval and without a tip, called the *rocot uchu*: which means fat pepper; they eat it yellow or green, before it is completely ripe and takes on its final color of red. There are other peppers that are yellow and purple, although in Spain I've only seen the red ones. There are other peppers that are long, thin as the baby finger and are found in homes of somewhat more luxury, and even in the royal household and among the aristocracy; the name is somewhat different and escapes memory; they also call it *uchu*, like the aforementioned; but the adjective is what I cannot remember. Another pepper is very small and round, no bigger than a cherry with its stem; they call it *chinchi uchu*, it is much hotter than the others, by far, and they grow little of it, and thus is it greatly valued. Poisonous bugs flee from this pepper and its plant. From a Spaniard who had come from Mexico, I heard said that it was very good for eyesight, and so for dessert and even at every meal he ate two of these peppers, roasted. Generally speaking, all of the Spaniards who have visited the Indies and who return to Spain, eat it regularly and prefer it to the spices from Oriental India. The Indians value it so much that they eat it more than any other of the fruits I have mentioned."

—Inca Garcilaso, sixteenth-century Peruvian writer, in *Comentarios reales de los Incas* (*Royal Commentaries of the Incas*)

Capsicum baccatum

Capsicum baccatum is named or misnamed for the resemblance that some early botanist saw to a berry (*baca* in Latin), though few cultivars have that shape. The species originated in the general Bolivian center of first dissemination and spread out in various directions. It has reached other South American countries, including Brazil, Bolivia, Colombia, Ecuador, and parts of Argentina. But its most important journey was across the Andes to coastal Peru.

Because *C. baccatum* has difficulty adapting to locations far from the equator, it never had *C. annuum*'s opportunities to cross the Rio Grande border. It requires a long growing season, never ripening to peak flavor in climates where frost comes early. I have had fairly good luck with some of the smaller, more quickly ripening cultivars in New Jersey. One commercial grower, Happy Quail Farms, is producing larger peppers

C. chinense (datíl)

of excellent quality near Palo Alto, California. In my opinion, baccatums are bound to become a sensation when leading US chefs and writers understand why Peruvian cooks regard them as the soul of their cuisine.

It is always a joy for me to watch somebody who has never encountered these wonderful peppers taste them for the first time. Don't expect volcanic blasts of capsaicin. Baccatums are never hellishly hot or completely mild. Their great charm is a graceful balance of fire, sweetness, and fruitiness unlike anything that exists in other peppers. I never recommend substitutes in my recipes. They are bound to falsify the true flavors.

They are also very beautiful peppers, usually varying in color from lemon yellow to fire-engine red. They do not differ in size as dramatically as annuums, but can take assorted shapes, resembling tapered fingers, carrots, stubby torpedoes, miniature pumpkins, or blobby Chinese dumplings. The names of two Brazilian cultivars, starfish and bishop's crown, make sense when you see them.

The chief baccatums of Peru are long, robust, pointed peppers in different yellow, red, and orange hues, with firm, meaty pulp. The most important, the *ají amarillo*, or "yellow pepper," is actually a rich apricot shade. To make things more complicated, people sometimes call it *ají verde*, meaning not "green" but "fresh." When it is used to spice vinegary *aderezos* (*sofritos*, or flavoring bases, for pickling sauces), it is called ají escabeche. You can find it flash-frozen in Latin neighborhood supermarkets.

The *ají amarillo* is equally delicious dried, when it is called *ají mirasol* (not to be confused with the *chile mirasol* of Mexico). To me, the copper-colored Peruvian mirasol is a bit of Andean sunshine captured in a pod. It is to *amarillos* what very good sun-dried tomatoes are to fresh San Marzano tomatoes.

Fresh or dried, this favorite Peruvian pepper is the backbone of many sauces. No dedicated cook would be without a batch of reconstituted *mirasoles* ground to a paste and another of pureed fresh *amarillos*. Mirasol paste is imported to US markets in jars, but it lacks most of the winey, smoky flavor I love. I prefer to use the dried ground powder (which is very nice) or make *mirasol* paste myself from soaked dried peppers (see page 248).

Capsicum chinense

When the habanero chile came on the US hot pepper scene in the 1970s, it was the first time that a *C. chinense*—indeed, anything other than a *C. annuum*—had ever attracted a local following of its own. Knowledgable cooks from many parts of Latin America must have rejoiced at this long overdue expansion of the US perspective on peppers. New initiates gasped in pain, joy, and sheer disbelief, and *C. chinense* began building of its US fan club.

The newcomer peppers were small and dainty, with a shape suggesting miniature lanterns, usually orange but sometimes red or yellow. They were soon joined by the chubbier and more robust Scotch bonnet pepper, a chinense found in Jamaica, the Lesser Antilles, and parts of Central America like Panama (where it is called *ají chombo*). Slightly larger and with a more crumpled shape, it packs an impressive firepower just short of the fiercest habaneros. The two shared another quality that at the time did not attract equal attention: a complex, slightly musky perfume—one that's familiar to me from my Cuban childhood. It is music to the soul of cooks in all the lands of chinenses, from Brazil to Puerto Rico. I think it is a more telling badge of chinense identity than Scoville units. In fact, these are the most complexly flavored and delicately nuanced of all peppers—if you think delicacy can't go with startling heat, you don't know *C. chinense*. It is indeed a clan filled with surprises.

Chinense Heat and Fragrance

The two most distinctive qualities associated with *C. chinense* are extreme heat and a varied, fascinating bouquet of volatile compounds. But strangely, only the second of these is found in all cultivars. Like *C. annuum* and unlike all other members of the *Capsicum* genus, *C. chinense* often shows a genetic variation that suppresses the production of capsaicin. The mutation does not affect the wonderful aroma.

In Venezuela, Colombia, Puerto Rico, and the Dominican Republic, a heatless chinense is known as *ají dulce* ("gentle" or "sweet" pepper). In Cuba we adore it and call it *ají cachucha*. It may be the most delicious of all nonhot peppers. At the opposite extreme, the capsaicin-secreting *chinenses* are the hottest of all peppers on the Scoville scale or by any other method of measurement. In fact, pioneering horticulturalist Paul Bosland has found that a few superhot chinenses have the ability to secrete capsaicin ectopically, or not just in the placenta, but in the tissues of the pericarp—that is, the meaty part of the fruit. Tasting the smallest particle of the flesh can take your breath away. Bosland is also the chief developer of a delightful reduced-heat cultivar called the NuMex Suave (see pages 164 to 165), which he specifically bred to let the true chinense flavor shine through.

Capsaicin secretion is a *Capsicum* trait that food chemists and plant geneticists have analyzed with zeal. A single gene controls it. The secretion of the volatile compounds that make chinense peppers so unique is a more complex affair involving the interaction of several genes and has received far less attention. I see this gap in research as an opportunity beckoning researchers who share my fascination with the enchanting chinense perfume and are willing to stop and smell the roses (or other flowers). The beauty of chinenses goes far beyond Scoville tallies. It rests on that elusive fragrance and a tantalizing complex of flavors that can be drowned out by the scorching flames of really hot cultivars.

I taste citrus with notes of pineapple, ripe papaya, and other tropical fruits in my favorite chinense peppers. They can also have a hint of peach or apricot. The aroma harmonizes with these flavors. Both arise from several different methylbutanoates (esters responsible for a cluster of fruity scents and tastes) together with beta-ionone (a member of the so-called rose ketone group that helps create the odors of violets and roses). If you smell the chinenses closely, you will also detect disturbing aromas like turpentine, wood, sweat, and frying oil. The production of distinctive chinense aromas and flavors is a heat-sensitive trait expressed to the fullest when they are grown in warm, steamy climates.

Identification Clues

When I began growing chinense peppers in my garden, I was amazed to see how many different sizes and shapes they can take. Reading South American culinary and scientific accounts, I found that I'd hardly scratched the surface. The Roraima investigations in Brazil had uncovered a wealth of forms ranging from little golden teardrops and lumpy cream-colored caterpillars to scarlet quail's eggs and pale parsnips. And the Roraima gallery didn't even touch on the globular, Peruvian Amazon member of the group, as large as a *rocoto*, or the long, curving brownish maroon pepper that reached the Peruvian coast to be used in dried form as the beloved *ají panca*. Only the annuum species shows a bigger range of *Capsicum* phenotypes. You wouldn't necessarily know that you were seeing a chinense from a cursory glance at the outside.

When the aroma is well developed, it is a dead giveaway. Otherwise, identification can be tricky. The flowers are usually off-white or greenish white but occasionally purple. The anthers (pollen-bearing tips of the stamens) are violet colored. The rounded waxy petals usually end in a slight point. The calyx is not conspicuously *dentate* (toothed). The most distinctive feature is an annular constriction of the calyx where it joins the pedicel, and often thick, corrugated leaves. The seeds are smooth and straw colored, and you can see a deep indentation on one side of the margin—called a "fish mouth" by the researchers who pioneered *Capsicum* seed identification—marking the scar where the seed detached from the placenta.

C. frutescens (ají guaguao)

No pepper species better rewards the curiosity of cooks who are willing to investigate its inexhaustible possibilities. But you must realize that cooking with the hottest chinenses requires forethought. You will defeat your own purpose if you do not temper a small handful of hot peppers with a large allowance of *cachuchas* or a newer cultivar like NuMex Suave, to preserve the beautiful perfume while preventing sheer heat from obliterating all other flavors. And you will miss a real pleasure if you do not try cooking with *ají cachucha* or *ají dulce* on its own, in a Caribbean-style stew or soup, for example.

Capsicum frutescens

Discussions of pepper species never have as much to say about *C. frutescens* and there is a reason. In pepper terms, the *annuum-chinense-frutescens* complex born in South American jungles and savannas is a bit like a litter of three with two sturdy pups and a runt.

Not that *C. frutescens* is unimportant. But for whatever reason, it has refused to grow along the prodigious lines of its siblings. Some researchers think that it is an incompletely domesticated form, closer to a primitive forebear than either *annuum* or *chinense*. Certainly it never developed into a great range of phenotypes. And its uses in cooking are extremely limited compared with other peppers. Because of their small size, *frutescens* peppers cannot be used as a vegetable, and they do not present a varied flavor palette.

Virtually all members of the species bear brilliant red or red-orange fruits in the same shape: narrow, straight, and pointed. They are not perfectly symmetrical, having a small bulge on one side close to the point of intersection with the calyx. One interesting exception, the *wiri-wiri* of Guyana, has round, button-shaped pods. The more usual skinny frutescens seldom grow beyond about three inches long, and most are closer to one inch. Instead of hanging, the pods stand upright on the pedicel like miniature bristling spears. At maturity they tend to separate easily from the calyx rather than clinging. Both these traits are usually associated with undomesticated pepper species.

The flavor, too, suggests that *C. frutescens* has undergone less genetic intervention at the hands of humans than other species. It is not so much a flavor as a sting—a needle-sharp jolt of capsaicin without the fruitiness, sweet-sour interplay, or wininess that are the great charms of some hot peppers. The fruit has a penetrating odor that reminds me of vinegar and sometimes of Tabasco sauce. Perhaps it's only coincidence that this pepper pairs so well with vinegar but in the lands of its birth, it often figures in vinegary condiments. Where peppers are combined with yuca, people like to infuse it in vinegary sauces of fermented yuca juice. Brazilians pickle their tiny, lethally hot green or red *malagueta* peppers in strong vinegar, and Cubans do the same with their fiery frutescens, *ají guaguao*.

In the United States, the form in which most people have encountered frutescens peppers is also vinegar-based: the famous Tabasco sauce of the McIlhenny Company in Louisiana. The red peppers used with distilled vinegar in the sauce may or may not have actually come from the southern Mexican state of Tabasco, but they are a frutescens cultivar that apparently reached New Orleans in the 1850s with claims of "Tobasco" origin. Other American hot sauces based on the same general idea, though not necessarily on frutescens peppers, have hit the market since. Some are fairly fancy. The original, however, relies on a clean, basic simplicity that makes it more versatile than many competitors.

Frutescens peppers crave humid tropical climates. They can be grown in the northern United States, but they will never have the broad appeal of their *annuum-chinense* relatives. When *C. frutescens* accompanied seventeenth-century Portuguese and other voyagers sailing to the Old World, it stuck close to the equator. The peppers were adopted by cooks and gardeners everywhere in the tropics, and often escaped into the wild successfully enough to be taken for weeds that had been there since the dawn of creation. The *piri-piri* or *pili-pili* of many African nations is a frutescens, though of course nobody was asking about botanical certificates of identity when it arrived. Many of the skinny little bird's-eye peppers of India, Southeast Asia, and southern China are also frutescens, but only a knowledgable observer can tell them from similar-looking (and similar-tasting) annuums. On the other hand, the renowned Filipino *siling labuyo* is certainly a frutescens.

The fruit of *C. frutescens* has few marks to distinguish it from other thin, tapering peppers. When you can see the whole plant, the upright position of the fruits is a strong clue. The flowers are usually white or greenish white, and the pointed tips of the petals may be slightly curled back. Like *C. chinense*, it has blue- or violet-colored anthers. The straw-colored seeds have a distinctive, slightly pointed teardrop shape.

C. pubescens (rocoto)

Capsicum pubescens

Like the otherwise very different *C. baccatum*, the beautiful and fascinating *C. pubescens* has been slow to attract the notice of cooks north of the Andes. On its home territory it has a distinguished history stretching back to (and undoubtedly beyond) the Inca civilization. Today it is sold in all Andean markets and in popular restaurants called *picanterías*, particularly in highland towns like Cusco and Arequipa, often stuffed with meat and baked in milk with a cheese topping.

The environmental limitations of the species—fairly cool temperatures combined with a long frost-free growing season—kept *C. pubescens* at home in high Bolivian and Peruvian mountain valleys. About a hundred years ago enterprising growers managed to establish it in some fairly similar Mexican locations, where it achieved some success as the *chile manzano* or "apple pepper," from the chubby shape of many cultivars. (For some reason it was also carried to Indonesia, as the *cabe gondol*.) But despite a few experiments in the Rockies, the Cascades, and the San Francisco Bay Area, it is likely to be some years before we see the species commercially established in the United States.

I am one of many who can hardly wait for *C. pubescens* to be widely available. I first met the genus in South America under the local names *rocoto* (Peru) and *locoto* (Bolivia) and was smitten. Pubescens peppers can be longer or shorter, fatter or thinner, but the type that speaks to my imagination as a cook looks a little like a small, gleaming red, yellow, or orange bell pepper. Any misunderstanding vanishes at one bite: This innocent-seeming customer has quite a kick. It is not one of the all-time record-breaking hot peppers, but it packs a solid capsaicin wallop. And its particular combination of shape, size, and sturdy meatiness makes it absolutely ideal for using as a stuffed vegetable. It cooks through more quickly and less soggily than a bell pepper.

C. pubescens is not one of the endlessly versatile species like *C. annuum* or *C. chinense*. It does not have "sweet" (that is, heatless) mutations, and has not been bred to bring out an exciting range of qualities. Though it is not especially aromatic, it has green bell pepper notes with a hint of cucumber and a pleasant vegetable greenness. It is just itself—a juicy, clean-flavored little vegetable that happens to be a neat and very attractive parcel for enclosing any filling of your choice. It also makes wonderful table sauces and would be good discreetly slivered onto something like a potato salad. The golden *manzano* is delicious cooked in sugar syrup until it caramelizes and becomes almost translucent. Though fresh *rocotos* are not yet widely available in most of the United States, pan-Latin supermarkets carry several brands of flash-frozen *rocotos* that are more than satisfactory. Fresh golden *C. manzanos* from Mexico are now becoming more widely available.

Despite some cultivars' resemblance to bell peppers, *C. pubescens* is beyond question the easiest of all species to distinguish from others. The slightly fuzzy leaves justify the Latin name *pubescens*, which literally refers to the sprouting down on an adolescent youth's chin. (The little hairs may produce an aphid-repelling substance.) The flowers are a rich purple, often with a white border, never white or greenish white like those of other species, and the calyx is markedly dentate, with long toothlike projections. But the biggest surprise comes when you cut into the fruit and find yourself confronting rows of rough-coated black or brownish seeds.

All these traits point to the uniqueness of a species that evolved in complete isolation from other capsicums and cannot be crossed with them to produce any sort of offspring. It has been the least known of all peppers outside its native region, and researchers have hardly begun to explore its genetic possibilities. I suspect that its culinary future will be at least as bright as its long past.

PEPPERS INTO WORDS

On January 15, 1493, Columbus was preparing to set sail for Spain and report on the three months he had spent exploring the "Indies," a region of incredible beauty that he still thought might include Japan. He now felt hopeful about the success of the expedition, after some dark moments. The darkest had been the loss of his flagship, the *Santa María*, when she ran aground on a shallow reef off the island of Hispaniola just after midnight on Christmas morning. But tragedy turned to unexpected good fortune. At daylight, the Taíno people of the immediate locale—who already had impressed Columbus as the finest human beings imaginable—rushed to the Spaniards' aid at the orders of their hospitable, warmhearted chieftain, Guacanagari. With their help, all the ship's stores were safely off-loaded. The two leaders, who had taken a great liking to each other, each made ready to play host the next day, December 26.

After dining with Columbus aboard the *Niña*, Guacanagari had a great feast prepared on shore. The Spaniards had had repeated encounters with Taíno foods in the previous few months, but this was the first Taíno banquet in their honor. Briefly describing the menu, Columbus mentioned two or three kinds of root vegetables, shrimp (probably some kind of spiny lobster), game, "and other victuals" that they had, together with "some of their bread that they call *cazavi*." But perhaps the most important item for the future was one that Columbus did *not* mention: hot pepper, known as *ají* in the Taíno language. (Other romanizations include *agi* or *axi*.)

We now know that Columbus and the crew tasted *ají* along with every food that the Taínos shared with them because, as he himself would soon comment, nobody ate without it. By January 1, having decided to leave a few dozen crew members as a shore party on Hispaniola, he specifically told them to collect as much as they could of the abundant local *especeria*, or "spicery," as being more valuable than peppercorns or the prized African *melegueta* pepper. And two weeks later, on the eve of his return voyage, the admiral gave the Spanish monarchs a glowing report of the new spice's large-scale commercial

SORTING OUT SEMANTIC CONFUSION

Columbus had his first taste of hot peppers in the Hispanic Caribbean, where Spaniards dubbed the plant *pimiento*, no doubt because its piquancy reminded them of the (unrelated) Old World black pepper (*Piper nigrum*) known as *pimienta* in Spanish.

It was the Spaniards who started the Babel-esque confusion with pepper names. When they marched on to Central America and Mexico, where they found an even greater number of peppers belonging to the *C. annuum* species, they became familiar with the generic Nahuatl word for all peppers—"chilli," which they translated as the Hispanicized *chile*. Curiously, however, the Spanish carried the Taíno word *ají*, rather than the Nahuatl-derived *chile*, to other parts of the Americas, such as the Andean region, where *ají* replaced the native Quechua and Aymara words for peppers.

For Spanish-speaking cooks like me who were raised using the word *ají*, the popular US usages—chile, chili, chilli, or the redundant chile pepper, chili pepper, or chilli pepper (literally "pepper pepper," the equivalent of saying "minestrone soup")—reek of an illogical Aztec-centrism. Using the words "chili" or "chilli" as a qualifier for hot peppers is also misleading since the Nahuatl *chilli* was a generic name for all peppers, sweet and hot. The British could teach the rest of us something about clarity here: They've adopted the term "capsicum" for all peppers. Granted, US pepper lovers are most familiar with Mexican chiles, but that's no reason to impose a culturally narrow label on every pepper from Latin America or other parts of the world. I much prefer to use the more neutral English word "pepper" with flavor qualifiers, such as hot or sweet, and appropriate regional labels. For this reason, when I write in Spanish I use the same terms used in the countries I'm writing about (that is, *chile*, *ají*, *pimenta*, and *pimiento*, to name a few).

I don't propose to ban the useful word "chile," but I'd like to restrict its use to peppers from Mexico and Central American countries, such as Guatemala, Honduras, El Salvador, and Nicaragua, where "chile" supplanted various native words at an early date.

---

possibilities. After mentioning local resources of gold, copper, and "fine cotton," he added: "There is also much *ají*, which is their pepper, which is worth more than [black] pepper, and the entire populace won't eat without it, as they find it extremely healthful. It would be possible to load an annual fifty caravels with it in Hispaniola."

These glimpses into Taíno *ají* and Columbus's first voyage mark a lucky alignment of the stars. It isn't merely that two different civilizations that were destined to play a part in the global journeys of capsicums met in the Greater Antilles. It's that at precisely this point, a society able to write down its impressions for posterity came looking for precious spices in time to stumble on a totally different but highly marketable spice—a plant that had reached a major culmination in the Caribbean through the genius of a culture with no writing system. With Columbus's scanty notes about something better than Old World pepper, a centuries-long silent capsicum history began to find a still-echoing voice.

Though the Spanish conquests were marked by great cruelty, they also brought to the Indies (today's West Indies) a number of chroniclers to whom we owe an immeasurable debt. Unlike the British in North America, the early Spanish colonists came without wives or families and generally depended on local women to cook for them, which speeded up their introduction to the use of peppers at every meal. Instead of families, the conquerors were accompanied by monks, friars, and, a little later, Jesuits—all dedicated missionaries who (unlike most English Protestants) took the job of converting the Indians seriously enough to study the local languages. Not only did they learn to preach in the tongues spoken by their congregations, but some of them also patiently inquired into vanishing beliefs and traditions, setting down minutely detailed accounts. Many Spanish expeditions also included at least one medical botanist eager for knowledge of local plants. The first of these was Dr. Diego Alvarez Chanca, who sailed with Columbus on his second voyage in 1494 and took note of "a spice called agi" being used to season foods, including yuca bread (the *cazavi* mentioned by Columbus), sweet potatoes, and fish. But he did not have long enough opportunities of observing local foodways to see how vitally *ají* was linked with yuca (*Manihot esculenta*, also called manioc or cassava in English), a spindly, narrow-leafed shrub that he described as "a grass that is between tree and grass."

Not until the late twentieth century would the discipline of archaeobotany catch up with the insights into the pre-Hispanic capsicum story that Spanish colonial chroniclers have left us. An important truth now understood by archaeologists who have excavated pre-Hispanic sites, and also previously noticed by many of the chroniclers, is that peppers were never grown in isolation. People always raised and ate them with other foods, especially bland starchy foods with satisfying texture but without marked flavors of their own.

The Caribbean and Amazon-Orinoco Basin Region

Three great culinary cultures dominated the neotropics when the first Europeans arrived, and in each, peppers were planted as part of a particular crop system centered on one paramount starchy crop, with others playing supporting roles. Of the three, the two that received the most abundant early documentation revolved around maize; they were based in Mesoamerica and the Andes.

The third, which originated in the Amazon-Orinoco basin region, was the most scantily described despite the fact that it covered by far the largest geographical area and—through its outer fringes in the Antilles—was the first system of foodways to introduce the Spanish to peppers. The core staple throughout the interior and the islands was yuca. Compared to maize-based food complexes, systems that depend on

Wooden mallets for grinding cooked ingredients, including peppers, in the Ecuadorian Amazon.

yuca have received comparatively little attention from culinary historians. But these food cultures are at least as old as their better-known maize-centered counterparts (possibly older), and it is important to remember that their home territory on the South American continent was also the first home of peppers.

As explained earlier, the wild ancestors of all peppers originated not in the lands of maize but on the western margin of the Bolivian Amazon, close to the Andean foothills. Three of the five domesticated species, *C. chinense*, *C. frutescens*, and *C. annuum*—which are so closely related to each other that they can sometimes interbreed—had traveled through the hot, humid tropical lowlands to reach the northeastern seaboard of South America in pre-Hispanic times. They occur together in the region of the Guiana Shield, an area of great biodiversity. *C. chinense*, *C. frutescens*, and possibly *C. annuum* had been carried together to the islands of the Caribbean under the general name of *ají* by peoples rooted in the cultures of the Amazon-Orinoco basin region, including the Taínos who greeted Columbus. The major staple food that shared the journeys of these species was yuca, which the chroniclers saw the islanders eating with *ají* and a complex of less central starchy foods.

The Spanish universally agreed that *ají* was the natives' *pimienta*, meaning their equivalent of peppercorns from the Far East. Several chroniclers also remarked that this one seasoning was their entire *especeria*, or spice supply, able to replace a shelf of different Old World spices. It took no time for the invaders to start eating *ají* as enthusiastically as the natives. Already during the 1490s, Ferdinand and Isabella's Italian-born court chaplain Peter Martyr had personally interviewed Columbus and members of his first crews and recounted of the pepper called *axi* in the New World: "Where it is used there is no need of Caucasian pepper." (I completely understand this claim. As a Latin American, I can attest that I seldom feel the need to use black or white pepper in my own cooking, while seasoning food with hot capsicum peppers is second nature.)

The remarkable Bartolomé de las Casas, who preserved for posterity the log of Columbus's voyages by transcribing a copy from a manuscript that has since disappeared, was also a great champion of the native peoples and one of the most painstaking observers of New World plants and foodways. In his *Apologética historia sumaria* he reported that there were two domesticated forms of *ají*, one very red and as long as a finger, the other hotter and resembling a cherry. A third, the size of "the peppercorn that we know," grew uncultivated everywhere in the mountains, just as tiny wild peppers do today throughout all New World capsicum habitats. The chronicler Gonzalo Fernández de Oviedo singled out many more different kinds in highly varied shapes and sizes, including one with black pods that turned a parti-colored dark blue and another "that can be eaten raw and doesn't burn." He also commented that the leaves of the plant could be used in something like a Spanish parsley sauce or put into a cooking broth with meats (something still seen in the Filipino chicken stew *tinolang manok*).

By the time Cortés's expedition sailed from the recently conquered Cuba to Mexico in 1519, the Spanish occupying the islands were perfectly familiar with *ají* in different sizes, shapes, and colors. It grew wild in many places and was also cultivated as part of a polycultural farming system that seemed strange and primitive to the invaders. Taíno farmers grew a rich array of plants close together on small mixed-use plots called *conucos*. Yuca was the core crop, but several other root vegetables and maize shared the densely packed space along with peppers, which according to Oviedo were sown and raised "with great diligence and attention." He thought them "better with meat and fish than very fine [black] pepper." For the Taínos, they were good with everything, but particularly important in bringing the starchy staples to life on the palate—especially yuca, the most revered of plants. It was sacred to the god Yucahu, one of the greatest deities of the Taíno pantheon.

The Spaniards, who were not used to placing high agricultural value on root vegetables, nonetheless recognized that yuca was a remarkable plant. They were amazed at the skill with which Taíno women peeled the long, thick tuberous roots and removed the potent poison found in many varieties through a lengthy grating and draining process followed by cooking. Two major articles of the Taíno diet were obtained through these methods. One was a vinegary, pungent condiment made by fermenting and boiling down the squeezed-out juice with a lacing of hot peppers. It was a ubiquitous accompaniment to virtually all foods, but especially to the second result of the grating-draining procedure: *casabe*, an enormous, thin, griddle-cooked flatbread made from the grated meal—the same *cazavi* previously served to Columbus on Hispaniola, and also destined to be familiar to all Spanish colonists by the time of Cortés's expedition. Casabe was the cornerstone of the Taíno diet as well as the chief ritual offering to Yucahu.

The perceptive Bartolomé de las Casas did not fail to note the excellence of *casabe* (second only to Spanish wheat bread, in his estimation) or to mention the combination of yuca-based vinegar and the local *pimienta* (*de las Indias*) in an all-purpose condiment: "more usual than any other delicacy was cooking a great deal of the aforesaid pimiento [of the Indies] flavored with salt and the juice of yuca (or the roots from which they made *cazabi* bread), which we have previously noted to be their vinegar, and they ate it as someone might eat well-cooked kale or spinach."

Ethnobotanists now know, though the first chroniclers could not have guessed, that the overall culinary culture of the Taínos had been transplanted to the islands from the Amazon and Orinoco river basins on the mainland. Yuca-centered agriculture, the skills for processing the roots, and the association with hot peppers attested to the people's origins in northern South America. Large, heavy rectangular slabs of hard tropical wood studded with tiny stone teeth were the original graters used to reduce the yuca flesh to a mass ready for draining; their use in the islands certainly dates back more than five hundred years before Columbus, and graters of this type are still used by peoples in remote parts of Brazil and Venezuela. The draining apparatus was (and among yuca-dependent tribes remains) the *cibucán*, a long, flexible cylinder of woven palm fibers that was packed full of grated yuca and hung up in such a way that it could be wrung and twisted to help expel the juice—a process that some chroniclers compared to the Spanish way of squeezing almond milk from grated almonds.

Fortunately for scholars interested in the culinary-cultural history of yuca, the mainland societies where Taíno foodways had largely originated put up fierce resistance to the Spanish. They were assisted by difficult, dangerous local terrain that allowed unfriendly natives to easily overmatch badly prepared expeditions of invaders. Until fairly recent times, large parts of the lowland forests in the Amazon and Orinoco basins remained somewhat sheltered from cultural and ecological disruptions, preserving very ancient intertwined uses of yuca and peppers that the Spanish conquerors first witnessed on Hispaniola in 1492. *Capsicum* peppers were and are the great spice of many mainland tribes, the animating factor that makes the difference between a collection of cooked ingredients and a cuisine. This is also true to an extent in the islands, but Spanish colonial policy swiftly introduced many other complications.

Taíno civilization in Hispaniola, Cuba, Puerto Rico, Jamaica, and some smaller islands was rapidly marginalized under Spanish rule. The Taíno economy depended on subsistence farming on the *conuco* system, supplemented by fishing and hunting small game and birds. It had been completely sustainable until Columbus returned to Hispaniola in 1493 with a larger fleet and more grandiose colonial ambitions. From then on, the Spanish had great difficulty in feeding themselves, since their wheat could not be raised on the islands and they resented not having other pleasures of their own table. The larger the numbers of the invaders, the more they had to willingly or unwillingly depend on Taíno foods whenever they ran out of supplies from Spain. Unfortunately, the Taínos had no surplus food production to feed more hungry mouths, especially the mouths of armed intruders who by various chroniclers' accounts demanded anywhere between four and ten times more food per day than the natives. Almost at once, the Taínos' control of their own food supply was wrested from them.

The coup de grace to the islanders' way of life came a few years into the conquest, with optimistically planned Spanish gold mines and large *encomiendas* that resulted in the de facto enslavement of the Taínos. In theory, *encomiendas* were agreements between an individual and the Spanish crown by which the recipient was granted the labor of a stipulated number of Indian families to work a particular allotment of land. In fact, if not in law, these arrangements usually amounted to land grants with the added bonus of extorted Indian labor. The great hope of the settlers who set themselves

Orinoco wooden grater with quartz teeth to process yuca.

up as *encomenderos* was to raise sugarcane on a plantation scale, as a cash crop destined for European markets. Mine owners benefited from equally favorable policies.

Encomienda contracts, like those governing mine labor, were also supposed to include some boilerplate about work schedules and food rations for the helpless Taínos. What we know about the food side of the situation makes it clear that malnutrition was normal and expected. So was death from sheer overwork. Many people were driven to suicide by, among other means, drinking poisonous unfermented yuca juice.

Bartolomé de las Casas was the most prominent and vocal of many horrified Spaniards—official colonial overseers as well as members of religious orders—who repeatedly documented abuses by mine owners and *encomenderos*. A soldier turned priest and (later) Dominican friar, las Casas was shaken by the sight of enfeebled human beings enduring hours, weeks, and months of hard labor on almost nothing except *casabe* softened in water boiled with hot peppers—a brutal caricature of the pre-Hispanic diet. From time to time, royal decrees capitulated to protesters, at least on paper, by occasional additions to the usual concentration-camp rations. The extra allowances might include meat or fish as well as fresh root vegetables with more *casabe* and, tellingly, hot pepper—the grace note that might have helped the people endure a monotonous diet had it not been for other unbearable living and working conditions.

In any case, it is not clear how far the liberalized decrees were actually enforced. Ravaged by oppression and European infectious diseases, the Taínos of the islands were reduced to a few thousand in the course of the sixteenth century. But the Spanish mine owners and *encomenderos* were prepared with an alternative labor source: African slaves. Las Casas strongly supported this idea for some years before recognizing that it was as wicked as the first system and then praying for divine forgiveness of his mistake.

The slave trade opened a whole new chapter in the story of Latin American food, including peppers. The Spanish considered it a great success, since the Africans had even fewer legal rights than the Taínos and did not die as fast. Without excusing this mentality or the horrors of the transatlantic passage, I must point out that Caribbean culinary traditions, including pepper-based traditions, would have been much poorer without the resourceful Africans, who were brought as slaves into the increasingly depopulated islands.

At first, efficiency-minded Spanish administrations planned to feed the slaves on imported rations. But the colonists' original hopes of untold wealth from gold or sugar soon faded. The local gold resources turned out to be small, and the logistics of large-scale sugar production were more demanding than they had foreseen. Within a few decades many Spaniards had headed to the more promising mainland. The island colonies were left in comparative neglect (except Cuba, still useful because of the strategic location of Havana). The Africans, who proved more resilient than the natives, soon became a majority population on most of the islands. The administrators eventually allowed them to grow their own food, supplementing or actually supplanting imported items like rice and salt cod. Many became runaways, successfully fending for themselves far from coastal towns.

The Africans profited from the example of Taíno agriculture, and they supplemented their meager plantation rations with the bounty of small *conuco*-style plots where they grew yuca (which they learned to make into *casabe*), other native vegetables, plantains (which arrived from the Canary Islands early in the sixteenth century), and peppers—often the hottest of hot peppers, for which they developed a passion. It is no accident that so many of the fiercest superhot chinense cultivars originated in the Caribbean.

After the most avid fortune seekers had departed for the mainland, thousands of humbler Spanish immigrants came to the islands with lesser ambitions. A certain division developed everywhere between those who settled in coastal towns and those who headed into the mountainous interior to found small farms. Much interchange and even intermarriage took place among rural Spaniards, Africans, and the remnants of the Taíno population. A hardy mixed-race peasant class (known as *jíbaros* in Puerto Rico and *guajiros* in Cuba) kept alive subsistence farming traditions derived from *conucos* as well as the ancient fondness for capsicum-fired condiments eaten with the beloved starchy vegetables.

In my own homeland, Cuba, successive waves of other Spanish newcomers arrived after the former colony won independence in 1898. Preferring to settle in coastal cities and towns, they kept apart from *guajiro* culinary traditions, especially the love of untamed capsicums. The two kinds of peppers that they most happily adopted were *ajíes cachuchas*, the small, fragrant, heatless cousins of superhot chinenses; and the *pimiento morrón*, the Spanish name for what US cooks call bell pepper. *Cachucha* is obligatory in many favorite Cuban stews, soups, and bean dishes; under the name of *ají dulce* it is equally important to Puerto Rican and Dominican cuisines. The *pimiento morrón* became a frequent element in Cuban *sofritos*, those tasty, savory cooking sauces of carefully sautéed onion, garlic, and tomatoes that exist in local variations throughout Latin America. In the form of red pimiento strips from jars, it also became an almost inevitable garnish for nearly any dish imaginable. Otherwise, hot peppers are conspicuous for their absence from bourgeois twentieth-century Cuban cuisine.

The Spanish were the first Old World colonists to "discover" the peppers of the Caribbean. They would not be the last, though it took a while for other nations to break a Spanish monopoly on shipping between the Old World and most of the neotropics. For all practical purposes, until the mid-sixteenth century, "the Hispanic Caribbean" meant the entire Caribbean, to the vexation of France, the Netherlands, and Great Britain. All three openly sponsored piracy along Caribbean coasts and in the region's waters.

It was not until 1655 that a British fleet conquered Jamaica, the first Caribbean possession that any European power had managed to wrest from Spain. Meanwhile, British mariners waged war by piracy against Spanish ships and ports. We owe the first known mention of "bell peppers" to one of these adventurers, Lionel Wafer, who for a time was surgeon on a pirate ship in the West Indies. In 1681 he took part in a land expedition on the Isthmus of Panama, where a wound forced him to spend some months recuperating among the Cuna Indians of Darién. (When he again found his companions, he was so convincingly covered with body paint that they first took him for an Indian.) More than fifteen years later he wrote an account of his travels with many descriptions of local plants. Food historians have often pointed to his book, *A New Voyage and Description of the Isthmus of America,* as proof that he was the first to come across the bell peppers that are familiar to all US supermarket shoppers.

Wafer's remarks on peppers are frustratingly brief: "They have two sorts of Pepper, the one called Bell-Pepper, the other Bird-Pepper, and great quantities of each, much used by the Indians. Each sort grows on a Weed, or Shrubby Bush about a Yard high. The Bird-Pepper has the smaller Leaf, and is by the Indians better esteemed than the other, for they eat a great deal of it." There are no further details, though later he gives *cah* as the people's word for peppers and comments that "they never forget to have in their Plantations some of their beloved Pepper." I am not sure that the Cuna, whose farming and cooking have much in common with those of the Taíno, used only two kinds of pepper; many others grow on the Isthmus. And it is almost certain that Wafer's "bell peppers" were unrelated to anything we know by that name.

In 1688, Hans Sloane, a young British physician, traveled to the newly conquered colony of Jamaica and made copious notes on the properties of local plants, incorporated into a remarkable work of natural history published eighteen years later as *A Voyage to Jamaica.* Describing half a dozen kinds of local capsicums with many citations from other naturalists, he gives "bonnet pepper" as an alternative name for "bell-pepper," and provides other details about the fruit's fragrance, pungency, and "sinuated or furrowed" surface that are consistent with nothing except the very hot Jamaican *C. chinense* now called "Scotch bonnet." (The *ají chombo* of Panama is sufficiently similar to make me suspect that under some Cuna name it was Wafer's "bell pepper.")

Edward Long, a renowned eighteenth-century chronicler of Jamaica, mentions bell peppers among "about fifteen varieties of the *capsicum* in this island" and says that when gathered slightly immature they are considered the best kind for pickling. He gives directions clear enough to be followed by a modern cook. There are other fascinating sidelights on uses of hot peppers in the British West Indies in Long's *History of Jamaica* (1774). He describes pounding sun-dried bird peppers to a powder with salt to use as "cayan-butter," esteemed "for the excellent relish it gives to soups, turtle, and other dishes." He says that infusing very hot peppers in "spirits of wine" (distilled alcohol) partly tames their sting. (The reason, as we now know, is that capsaicin is soluble in alcohol.) He provides a sketchy but clear recipe for *man-dram,* a cucumber relish involving mashed bird peppers and minced shallots or onions, mixed with lime juice and Madeira wine. This entered English cookbooks in slightly altered form during the nineteenth century. Eliza Acton's classic *Modern Cookery for Private Families* (1845) gives a version using powdered cayenne and another made with "chili" vinegar. In fact, for generations, West Indian ways with hot peppers had a greater impact on English tables than any kind of curry from India because commerce with British possessions in the islands was faster and more reliable.

The North American colonies, and later the young United States, also owed an early familiarity with hot peppers to trade with the Caribbean, more specifically an Afro-Caribbean culinary strain that reached such ports as Philadelphia and New York. A fact that Hans Sloane pointed out about the smallest and "most biting" of the Jamaican capsicums (probably close to the north Mexican *chiltepines*) was repeatedly noted by Spanish and other British observers on the islands: very hot peppers were "much used by *Indians, Negroes,* and *Europeans,* who have liv'd here any time."

Peppers in Mesoamerica

The Spanish colonists did not reach Mexico as complete newcomers to the capsicum tribe. They had become familiar with New World *pimienta* (pepper of the Indies) or *pimiento* in the islands, particularly Hispaniola and Cuba, and promptly recognized it when they again came across it on the mainland. The Mexican picture, however, proved to be different in many regards.

In the first place, only one *Capsicum* species— *C. annuum*—had become really important in the Aztec empire. But this sole species had been developed into an extraordinary range of different cultivars used with a complex artistry unlike the simpler achievements of the Taínos. This had happened long before Columbus or Cortés. As in the case of the Taínos and their Amazon-Orinoco forebears, the beginnings of the story are silent except for scattered archaeobotanical evidence that researchers are only now piecing together.

In pre-Hispanic Mexico, as in the lands of yuca, peppers were always an accompaniment. They were never themselves the core food of any civilization, but went hand in hand with the great core food of all Mesoamerica: maize (*Zea mays*). Over a long period of time, the peoples of the region brought the breeding and culinary uses of both maize and *C. annuum* cultivars to remarkable heights.

Domesticated maize was likely created from the wild grass known as *teosinte* 8,000 to 9,000 years ago. Mesoamerican pepper domestication

Chile diety, by Catalina Delgado, New Mexico.

seems to have been much more recent. Again, a wild plant was bred into a multiplicity of forms for many uses. But the wild pepper ancestor is still exuberantly visible—*C. annuum* var. *glabriusculum*, the tiny, very hot chiltepín that Mexicans still happily gather and use, dried and crushed, as a superb all-purpose condiment.

The shrubby perennial plant, which hasn't undergone true domestication, grows widely as a weed and is easy to cultivate (that is, to encourage to seed itself). For this reason, establishing a definitive date for the first appearance of domesticated *C. annuum*s in Mexico is not easy; domestication may have happened independently in more than one location.

Some of the earliest evidence for use of peppers comes from Coxcatlán Cave, an important site in the Tehuacán Valley of Puebla State. It was occupied or used for many millennia and contains remains of many food plants, including peppers, at different pre- and postdomestication stages. Pepper seeds and other evidence have been recovered from some of the oldest as well as more recent levels at Coxcatlán. The earliest (possibly from as early as 7700 BP) appear to be wild, but eminent botanist Barbara Pickersgill believes that the size of seeds from layers dated at roughly 3000 to 2200 BP definitely points to domestication. Linda Perry and Kent V. Flannery, studying much later specimens from the sites of Guilá Naquitz and Silvia's Cave in the Valley of Oaxaca, found well-enough preserved material—sometimes whole fruits—to show the use of several different domesticated *C. annuum* cultivars (and possibly one *C. frutescens*) in both fresh and dried form, perhaps as early as AD 600. Recent excavations at Chiapa de Corzo in Chiapas State have discovered capsaicin residues on Mayan cooking pots dated between 400 BC and AD 300, showing that hot peppers were being cooked along with other ingredients, though it is not known whether they were wild or domesticated. Traces of capsaicin also have been identified in pots where turkey was cooked with cacao at Copán in Honduras (also a Mayan site), anticipating later pairings of chiles and chocolate in pre-Hispanic as well as colonial Mesoamerica.

The most "silent" aspect of the story is the process through which Mexican peoples learned to purposefully exploit the genetic potential of wild chiltepines, developing the ancestral plant into a huge range of specialized cultivars that could almost be thought of as "designer" chiles by virtue of their perfect tailoring to individual niches. The perennial shrub was reinvented as many annuals that might have individual qualities, such as being suitable for sowing in late summer in order to bear through winter and spring; tasting best when dried, toasted, and ground; or having fleshy enough fruits to use as a vegetable. Unfortunately, we have no timeline to trace the stages by which prehistoric peoples accomplished all this. The work had been done before any Spaniard set foot in Mexico, but how long before, we do not know.

Arriving on the mainland from an archipelago where yuca reigned over all other staple foods and sharp pepper condiments over all other seasonings, the 1519 invasion force carried with it the *casabe* and *ají* that Spaniards had learned to eat in the islands. Cortés provisioned the voyage from Cuba to Mexico through a still unexplained mixture of legitimate planning and furtive ruses to bamboozle the Cuban governor Diego Velázquez, who did not trust Cortés and wanted a tighter control of the expedition. There is a story about Cortés surreptitiously raiding the principal butcher shop in Santiago de Cuba by dead of night and making off with the town's entire meat supply. One incontrovertible fact is that he made sure to acquire large amounts of *casabe*. It is possibly the lightest, most portable form of bread ever invented, and after more than twenty-five years in the Antilles the Spaniards knew that it would last almost indefinitely if kept dry. Cortés's secretary, Francisco López de Gómara, also states that the fleet's stores included six thousand *cargas,* or "loads," (each equating to roughly fifty pounds) of maize, yuca, and *ají.*

The invaders thus hoped to march on rations partly borrowed from a Taíno diet that they had modified with a heavy dependence on herds of European meat animals, especially pigs for salt pork, their chief protein. But something new greeted them after they reached the mainland near Cintla in Tabasco and quickly overcame local resistance. They had left one culinary culture behind and entered another. As Gómara relates, as a token of surrender the Cintla townspeople offered the victors gifts, including twenty women to cook the army's meals and prepare bread—not *casabe* from grated yuca, but tortillas made out of maize, which the Taínos ate fresh but did not use for bread.

Ignorant of mainland foodways, Cortés's army found that, as in the islands, hot peppers were eaten with all meals but that everything else bespoke a new cuisine, or array of local cuisines. Dough (masa) for the maize tortillas that were the Mexican bread had to be prepared, shaped into flat cakes, and griddle-cooked daily by the women who joined the party at Cintla because, unlike *casabe*, the masa was highly perishable. Only women were thought to have the proper knack for handling and cooking tortillas. Vinegar from yuca juice was absent; the acid element in cooking came from tomatoes or tomatillos. The Spaniards, who had grown accustomed to the word *ají*, now heard hot pepper being called *chile*, and learned that it was cooked with tomatoes and salt in many different stewed dishes that they called *cazuelas*, for the pots that held them. In Spanish-language documents, *ají* and *chile* came to be used interchangeably.

La Malinche or Doña Marina, one of the women handed over by the Tabascans, turned out to be a captive whose birthright language was the Nahuatl spoken by the Aztecs, though in childhood she had learned the Mayan language of her captors. Working together, Marina and Gerónimo de Aguilar (a Spaniard shipwrecked among the Maya eight years earlier), capably translated for Cortés's army as it traveled inland to the Aztec capital of Tenochtitlan.

Through the presence of women cooks, the invaders were introduced to the sights, smells, and flavors of the cuisine much sooner than they could have been on their own. At almost every stage of the journey they were greeted by townspeople with "maize cakes" (tortillas) and other foods that the two interpreters understood well. Since the welcome also included offers of *tamanes* (porters) to carry heavy paraphernalia, lugging stone metates for grinding would have been no problem. But the Spaniards also knew of dreadful, un-Christian native practices like human sacrifice and cannibalism. By the time they reached the city of Cholula and met a shifty reception that made them suspect an ambush, Cortés had enough grasp of both local intrigues and local cookery to stage a loud, theatrical showdown denouncing his hosts' traitorous plot, reporting "they wanted to murder us, and eat our flesh, so that they already had the pots ready with salt, and peppers, and tomatoes." He gave the Cholulans a foretaste of Christianity by massacring several thousand of them before moving on to the capital.

Almost from the moment they disembarked, the Spaniards knew that they had come upon a civilization of great power and refinement, and had been told that in Tenochtitlan the exalted monarch Moctezuma II reigned over a world of wonders. But the reality surpassed anything they could have imagined. The capital city was actually the linked twin cities of Tenochtitlan and Tlatelolco. They stood on an island in a vast and beautiful chain of lakes, surrounded by what the Spanish thought were floating gardens (in fact, they were elaborate raised beds) of plants and flowers. Pyramids and temples rose before the invaders' eyes like enchantments in a book of knightly romance. Moctezuma's gleaming palace plainly represented the zenith of a high culture.

Just as obviously, the meals served to the ruler and his household reflected a high cuisine founded on both plenty and elegance. The soldier Bernal Díaz del Castillo, the best-known chronicler of the expedition, could say only, "I don't know where to begin, but we were awestruck at the superb organization and provision that prevailed in everything."

The city, the palace, and the principal market in Tlatelolco were the hub of an immense tributary system that brought food and other wealth from every town and district in the Aztec empire. Records of tribute, showing stipulated amounts of different articles, figure largely among surviving Aztec documents. Much fresh food came from the nearby "floating gardens," or *chinampas*, on the lake. Peppers were grown there along with maize, beans, tomatoes, squashes, and a wealth of different flowers, which the Aztecs held in great esteem. But the records also show chiles—represented by the stylized image of a red pod and some symbol indicating a specified number of loads—arriving on a large scale from various tributary regions. Some or most of these were sent in dried form. (The Spaniards eagerly perpetuated the tribute system for their own purposes, encouraging provincial functionaries to "tax" local communities through levies of chiles, maize, beans, cacao, and other foods.)

The oldest documents containing accounts of tribute are Aztec books, or codices, composed of mingled pictorial and glyphic elements painted on pages made of processed bark. Hundreds of such books probably existed at the time of the conquest; nearly all were burned by Spanish authorities who thought they were works of devil worship. But among the Catholic missionaries dispatched from Spain to convert the natives were some who cared enough for the Aztec people and their civilization to study the Nahuatl language and its written documents. Some also recognized that invaluable knowledge would die with the last inhabitants old enough to recall life before the conquest unless they could dictate their memories to scribes.

Most of the chroniclers touch on food only incidentally in the course of relating other events. But here and there details about peppers appear, such as Fray Diego Durán's account of the revolt by the province of Cuetlaxtla against Aztec demands for tribute under Moctezuma I, ancestor of the unfortunate namesake deposed by Cortés. Having assassinated the Aztec governor, the Cuetlaxtlans graciously received the royal officials sent to inquire about the missing tribute and invited the visitors to rest in the governor's house while he was sent for. They then "closed the door of the chamber where the Aztec emissaries rested and set fire to a great pile of dried chiles that they had placed next to that room so the smoke would penetrate it. The smoke from the chiles, flowing into the chamber, was so great and so pungent that the Aztec envoys, trapped inside, unable to defend themselves, were suffocated."

Food is more central to other chronicles. Two sixteenth-century documents in particular are responsible for most of what we know about daily life and commerce in Moctezuma's Mexico on the eve of the conquest. One was the work of the Franciscan friar Bernardino de Sahagún, who was sent from Spain as a young man to preach to the Indians and ended by asking them to help him compile an encyclopedia of their customs and beliefs. He put together a textual-pictorial codex— now owned by the Laurentian Library in Florence—after the Aztec model, written in both Spanish and phonetically transcribed Nahuatl, and painted by Indian artists on European paper. Antonio de Mendoza, the viceroy of New Spain, is thought to have been the official who commissioned another codex (with Spanish and Nahuatl annotations as well as Aztec glyphs) containing much detail about Aztec life, for the information of Emperor Charles V and the colonial overseers in Spain.

The Codex Mendoza provides many insights into food in Aztec times. The section on bringing up well-disciplined children is the source of the famous illustrations that show parents making a son and daughter inhale the fumes of burning chiles—though stopping short of what the Cuetlaxtlans did to the Aztec envoys. Other passages depict specified amounts of chiles paid as tribute (in woven wrappings topped with stylized images of a chile) to Tenochtitlan from individual pueblos and provinces, or fill in useful details, for example, in regard to *chiles secos* or dried chiles. One of the tribute-paying towns actually appears in the codex as "Chiltecpintlan," indicating that it was a major supplier of the tiny, much-prized chiltepín.

Sahagún's Florentine Codex is even more revealing. His informants told him about the uses of chiles in medical remedies for ailments ranging from cough to toothache. They supplied him with vast amounts of information about the sacred Aztec calendar and religious observances, including many fasts during which people were commanded to eat their meals without either chiles or salt—a sign of how necessary people considered chile heat to the enjoyment of food. (Bartolomé de las Casas, who also wrote about abstention from "chilli" for Mexican fasts, remarked, "This is something without which they don't think they're eating.")

The codex also painstakingly described the great market of Tlatelolco in its heyday, with its vendors and wares. It listed many kinds of peppers sold by "the chile dealer," some now unidentifiable: "He sells yellow chile, cuitlachilli, tenpichilli, and chichio-achilli. He sells water chiles, conchilli, smoked chiles, very tiny chiles, tree chiles, slender chiles, those that look like beetles. He sells hot chiles, those sown in March, those with a hollow base. He sells green chiles, pointed red chiles, a later variety, those from Atzitziucan, Tochmilco, Huaxtepec, Michoacan, Anahuac, the Huasteca, the Chichimeca. Separately he sells chiles strung on cords, chiles for cooking in a pot, chiles for cooking with fish, chiles for cooking with white fish. He who is a bad chile dealer sells fetid chiles with an acrid taste, nasty-smelling damaged [chiles], chile refuse, chiles that failed to develop. He sells chiles from the wet land, incapable of being burnt, insipid in flavor, those that have not finished forming, unripe, limp, and ones shaped like buds."

The markets also sold many dishes made with chiles, and even today any cook who loves Mexican food might want to try re-creating some of them from the descriptions in Sahagún—for instance, tortillas with ground *ají* inside or spread with *ají* or *chilmole* (a sauce with ground chiles); or *cazuelas* that involve "ají, green tomatoes [tomatillos] and chiles, and large tomatoes, and other things that made a good stew"; or some kind of mole "from avocados mixed with chile that burns a lot, called chiltepín." There were various sauces made with different-colored chiles, in half a dozen degrees of hotness from *picante* to *picantisima*. His informants also went into great detail about dishes formerly served to the Aztec lords, including many *cazuelas* of "hen" (*gallina*, probably meaning turkey), fish, frogs, or shrimp with different kinds of chiles. In fact, a whole Aztec chile cookbook could be compiled today just from the accounts in Sahagún.

Did Dr. Francisco Hernández de Toledo, the Spanish naturalist dispatched by King Philip II to study the possible medical or other uses of plants in New Spain, ever learn of Sahagún's immense research project or exchange thoughts with him on such subjects as chiles? It's a tantalizing question. Probably Sahagún began to systematically collect information during the early 1540s and completed an initial draft in 1579. Dr. Hernández arrived at the port of Veracruz in 1572 and returned to Spain in 1577 after lengthy travels through Mexico, so that at least theoretically the illustrious botanist could have met the friar and been shown his life's work. But their approaches could not have been more different.

Sahagún has been called the first modern anthropologist or ethnographer. He went to immense lengths to put down his informants' own comments in their own language, and the great numbers of chile-related terms that he records, as well as the painstaking descriptions of dishes made with them, are typical of his concern for detail in the fabric of pre-Hispanic Aztec life.

Hernández spent less than six years in Mexico. As a sixteenth-century scientist, he was fascinated by the stunning wealth of local flora. He worked hard to place New World medicinal and food plants within an existing medical context, ranking peppers high on the scale of "heat" and "dryness" according to the theory of humors. He also paid attention to the distribution of *ají* and "chilli" on Hispaniola as well as the mainland, and drew an interesting distinction between the curious plant's roles as *mantenimiento* (sustenance) for the Indians, and *cundamiento y salsa* (condiment and sauce) for Spanish living in the Indies. He distinguished six principal varieties, listing the Nahuatl names of each, and tossed in a few more for good measure. After that, Hernández frankly declined to try categorizing all the chiles found in New Spain: "I fear that such a long recital would be more work than benefit." His was essentially a European perspective focused on contributions to state-of-the-art science, a strong contrast to Sahagún's decades-long immersion in the historic Aztec perspective.

It is a pity that despite Cortés's original landing in Maya territory, the lands of the Maya did not receive nearly as much attention from colonial Spanish chroniclers as the Aztec empire and Moctezuma's capital. But it is not illogical. Aztec civilization was at its height of power when Cortés arrived, while decline had set in in the Maya world some six centuries earlier. There was also a language barrier for visitors like Hernández, who might have wished to collect information in the Mayan-speaking south: For some decades after the conquest few of the invaders learned any native language except Nahuatl or had access to interpreters in other languages. For these reasons, we know much less about local uses of hot peppers (*ik* or *ich*, in Mayan) than about the corresponding picture in and around the Aztec capital. This is especially disappointing since both the lowland and highland habitats of the Maya (respectively, in the Yucatán Peninsula and the Chiapas State–Guatemala upland plateau) are thought to be regions of great biodiversity containing capsicum varieties not found elsewhere.

The Maya communities—which extended from Chiapas, the Yucatán, and Guatemala through parts of today's Honduras and El Salvador—were comparatively disunited and had not been fully absorbed into the Aztec tributary system. The people also waged a fierce fight against being absorbed into "New Spain," putting up local resistance until about the start of the eighteenth century and retaining a strong cultural independence in the tropical hinterlands to this day.

The colonial experience left Maya society less radically altered by *mestizaje* (hybridization) between conquering and conquered peoples than most of the former Aztec empire. Sizable pockets managed to remain surprisingly untouched, with people continuing to live in small, scattered communities, speaking their own branches of the several Mayan languages. Especially in forested highland regions of Chiapas State and Guatemala, survival of pre-Hispanic Maya foodways can be found to this day. An example is the use of hot peppers with cacao, as shown in the findings at Chiapa de Corzo and Cobán. The pairing is not unique to the Maya homelands, but it originated there because cacao—though beloved by the Aztecs—could not be grown as far north as their strongholds in the Valley of Mexico; it had to be imported from the Maya regions.

There are no records of market displays rivaling those of Tenochtitlan, with dozens of different chiles. Pepper landraces would not be attributed to the Maya; it would seem that specialized breeding of peppers for retail sale was not of equal importance to them. Landraces of *C. frutescens*—seldom or never found in Aztec pepper-growing regions—are less rare in the south than the north, and the process of domesticating

Dedicatory text on a sauce vessel at the Museum of Fine Arts in Boston, which contains the phrase *i=chi=li ja=yi*, interpreted by archeologist David Stuart to mean "its chile vessel."

wild chiltepín probably also resulted in some local *annuum* landraces unique to Yucatán, Chiapas, and points farther south. (Habaneros, the orange *chinense* peppers that today are familiar in parts of coastal Yucatán, arrived there not in pre-Hispanic times but during the great era of colonial traffic between the ports of Campeche and Havana. This is clear simply from the Spanish name and the fact that chinense peppers have no name of their own in Mayan.)

Historian Sophie Coe suggested in 1994 that chile infusions of either toasted or untoasted dried peppers boiled in water were the basic stock of Maya cooking, an endlessly versatile base for anything from a minimalist sauce for tortillas to the liquid in stewed feast dishes. More recently, archaeologist David Stuart has deciphered inscriptions containing the Maya glyph for peppers on a beautiful pottery bowl as well as the name of an owner together with *ich*, meaning that this was an actual individual's chile sauce bowl. Perhaps it was the ancient prototype of such a bowl that figured in a famous episode of the sacred Maya creation-myth book the *Popol Vuh*, where the Hero Twins Hunahpu and Xbalanque persuade their grand-mother to make them tortillas with a bowl of chile sauce. In a scene that I love to recall, the twins then gaze on the surface of the sauce as a mirror reflecting the actions of a rat hidden in the rafters of the house, who will restore to them their dead father's belong-ings for playing the sacred ball game. What a wonderful image: a dish of Maya chile sauce as a magic mirror.

The Andean World

The third great region of New World pepper cultivation encountered by Spanish invaders was the long north-south expanse of western South America lying astride the Andean cordillera for more than three thousand miles. The heart of the Inca civilization that ruled this vast territory was in today's Peru and Bolivia. When Francisco Pizarro's army reached the Inca strongholds of Cajamarca and Cusco in 1532, every member of the conquering force was already familiar with peppers under the Taíno name of *ají,* which is still used throughout the Andean countries instead of the native words *uchu* (Quechua) or *huayca* (Aymara). But almost everything else about the empire—for instance, the reversal of seasons south of the equator—was new and unexpected. The food system within which peppers held a major role left the Spaniards awestruck.

In every aspect Inca life was the model of a centralized and minutely planned economy. The Inca himself (the name of the ruler as well as the people) and his court governed from the lofty capital of Cusco at an altitude of more than eleven thousand feet above sea level. A form of collectivized agriculture supplied food to all. The conquerors noted with surprise that hunger, as known in Europe, did not exist. Food planning—from dictating what could be grown in individual areas to distributing specific shares of harvests to every member of society—was a cornerstone of state regulation.

This accomplishment was not completely original, since the Inca had finished absorbing the customs of earlier societies only a century or less before Pizarro arrived in the middle of a dynastic war that he promptly used to his own military advantage. But rigorous mastery of details seems to have been part of the Inca character. The food system as the Spanish encountered it brought into play every gradation of an ecological spectrum filled with extreme contrasts, all of which were exhaustively exploited by the planners in Cusco.

The arid, rainless coastal strip furnished seafood to everywhere else. The hill country that began a short distance inland held a prodigious complex of irrigated terraces for many different crops, also destined for assigned segments of society. Farther east, a steep ascent brought the Spaniards to the thin air breathed by the ruling classes in the high, dry, and, at first sight, barren *altiplano* (upland plateau), as well as many mountain valleys lying between towering snowcapped peaks. And on the eastern side of the cordillera lay the *ceja de montaña* or *ceja de selva,* the "brow of the highland" or "brow of the forest," a warm cloud-forest region sloping downward into the hot, steamy Amazon river basin.

Though lacking any writing system, government record keepers accounted for every bit of food produced throughout the empire's dizzying range of environments. (In lieu of written numbers they used a system of knots tied along different-colored strings, the *khipu* or *quipu.*) Food was carried along a vast, scrupulously maintained network of roads whose engineering the Spaniards thought dwarfed anything since the Roman Empire. Stone storehouses, built at intervals along the roads, were stocked and periodically restocked with supplies of food (including peppers) to be distributed to local households as needed. In contrast to reliance on yuca in the Caribbean and maize in Mexico, potatoes and other tuber crops stood out as the core food of the Inca diet. What one historian has called the "vertical archipelago" of the Inca food system involved an array of starchy vegetables. Peppers were the default seasoning for all dishes.

Thanks to the roads and an imperial corps of runners, fish from the coast reached the emperor's palace at Cusco not only dried but also alive and flapping. The terraced hillsides supplied various local squashes, beans, and a kind of maize with gigantic

Woman selling assorted Andean peppers at a market in Piura, Peru.

kernels unfamiliar to the conquerors. The windswept highlands had herds of llamas along with what the Spaniards described as some kind of "small rice" (quinoa) and, more surprising to the invaders, many kinds of knobby roots dug out of the ground (potatoes and half a dozen other tuber crops, including *oca* and *ulluco*).

The *ceja de montaña* and the Amazonian lowlands were not as tightly integrated into the Inca food system (though the *ceja* was the source of one major necessity, coca). But these two ecologies are of great importance, since it was close to the transitional zone between them that all capsicum species originated.

Though peppers are intrinsically plants of moist, warm climates, several species were carried up into the highlands, and eventually as far as the coast, as early as 6,000 years ago. We are lucky that these latter environments were dry enough to preserve vital evidence. Some of the earliest identifiable remains of *C. baccatum* and *C. chinense* were discovered at the archaeological sites of Guitarrero Cave high in the cordillera and at Huaca Prieta on the bone-dry Pacific coast (see pages 3 to 8). It seems likely that the Guitarrero specimens had been grown at a lower altitude, since as Jesuit missionary José de Acosta wrote about the New World pepper in the late seventeenth century, "it does not appear in cold regions like the sierra of Peru; it is found in warm irrigated valleys." However, a third species—the *rocoto* pepper, *C. pubescens*—somehow evolved to fit a unique niche somewhat higher than the usual pepper habitats. Alone among capsicums, it requires a chilly climate and cannot be grown in warm regions.

It was no surprise to Spanish chroniclers to find that hot peppers were a prominent— indispensable, even—part of the Andean food scene. As in the Antilles and Mexico, people simply could not imagine a meal without them. The Spanish did not understand that the local larder included two species unique to the Inca Empire (*C. baccatum* and *C. pubescens*) as well as another that they had already eaten in Hispaniola and Cuba (*C. chinense*). But they did understand part of the reason that Andean peoples placed such a high value on peppers: By comparison with the Aztec capital, the local cuisines were somewhat austere.

The subjects of the Inca did not go to the marketplace to buy a rainbow of different pepper cultivars that lent subtle nuances to dishes. Cash transactions did not exist. Neither did marketplaces where food changed hands between private buyers and sellers. Nobody went hungry, but displays of status through food seem to have been unknown. In a micromanaged society where the essentials of the diet were strictly doled out, peppers—always included in these distributions—were the spice of life.

The Spanish had first encountered *ají* as a spice particularly suited to cuisines of torrid, steamy climates. Now it appeared that peppers had equally adapted to the coldest inhabited zones of the Inca Empire. Another seventeenth-century Jesuit chronicler, Bernabé Cobo, commented that in the dish called *locro* (a soup-stew involving potatoes, maize, and probably some form of *charqui*, or dried llama meat) "the Indians and even some Spaniards, throw in so much ají that people unaccustomed to it cannot eat without shedding tears drawn forth by the strength of the ají."

Peru, which for centuries was the general Spanish name for the former Inca Empire, never elicited an ethnographic description to rival Sahagún's portrait of Aztec society. But luckily we have some fairly early descriptions by people of Inca blood who spoke both Quechua and Spanish. One was Garcilaso de la Vega, called El Inca, who was born in 1539 as the son of a Spanish officer and an Inca princess. Raised by his mother's family until the age of ten but also given Spanish-language education, he traveled as a young man to Spain and remained there for the rest of his life. His *Comentarios reales de los Incas* (*Royal Commentaries of the Incas*), composed solely from memories of his childhood and youth in Peru, was the first Spanish-language account of pre-Inca as well as Inca history, with voluminous commentary on all aspects of society. He described peppers as "the seasoning that [the people] put in everything that they eat—whether stewed, boiled, or roasted, there is no eating without it. As among the Aztecs, the fact that abstention from peppers is mandated during a fast showed "the pleasure that it confers on whatever they eat." He recalled a few different kinds of Peruvian peppers, including *rocotos* in several colors; long, slender peppers that were considered more aristocratic but whose name he had forgotten; and the small, highly prized, cherry-shaped *chinchi uchu* that "burns incomparably more than the others."

Another window on the Inca world was presented by the slightly younger Felipe Guaman Poma de Ayala, a full-blooded Inca nobleman who had learned enough Spanish to compile a manuscript titled *El primer nueva corónica y buen gobierno* (*The First New Chronicle and Good Government*), which was never published in his lifetime. It contains nearly four hundred illustrations, making it virtually the equivalent of an Aztec-style codex. Like the Inca Garcilaso, Guaman Poma gives the names of a few different kinds of peppers, such as the *rocoto, asnac* (fragrant) *uchu, puca* (red) *uchu,* and *cachuma* (sweet) pepper. His text and drawings also convey much insight into farming practices and timetables, with details about when particular crops were planted. But his work also had a more general polemical aim: to protest the havoc that the conquerors had wreaked and were wreaking on the entire Inca way of life. After a takeover marked by murderous struggles between partisans of different Spanish leaders, the victors had quickly started deporting Indians from their former villages to new settlements, turning them into a conscripted workforce in the great silver mines of Potosí, and destroying much of the infrastructure that had made Inca agriculture and food exchanges possible. From their new capital at Lima, Spanish fortune seekers engineered the switch to a cash economy completely unlike the old forms of exchange, generally leaving the Indians in impoverished dependence and creating vast landholdings for themselves. Guaman Poma wrote out of undisguised anger at this state of affairs, while Garcilaso more dryly noted that nobody had starved under Inca rule.

Markets now became places where more goods changed hands. But even so, the people retained a pre-Hispanic dependence on exchanges instead of cash purchases. Bernabé Cobo, writing probably in the 1650s, recalled women coming to town plazas on feast days to swap their own goods with someone else's: "one woman giving a plate of fruit for one of stew; such a one buys salt with *ají*, such a one meat with maize. . . ." In completely wordless staring matches that might take half an hour, one party to a transaction would approach another and carefully measure out a small pile of an article such as maize with which she meant to "buy" something being "sold" by the second woman. The "seller" would silently and impassively look at the offered maize until the "buyer" slowly added a little more, a few grains at a time. At last the "seller" reached out to gather up the maize in token of acceptance.

Cobo's is the most detailed description of Andean *ajíes*. He mentions dishes in which they figure, such as *locro* and *motepatasca*, a soupy dish of *mote* (Andean hominy), ancestor of the contemporary *motepata* of Cuenca in southern Ecuador cooked until the kernels burst. He comments that the plants bear better when sown annually than when allowed to continue from year to year. Like Oviedo, he points out that the leaves are good in stews (such as locro) or green sauces. He also says that people like to take peppers *en escabeche* (cooked in acid) on sea voyages. (Possibly the vitamin C content made them useful against scurvy.) On the medical front, he recommends ground dried peppers boiled in wine or vinegar—the first for earache, the second for toothache.

Cobo made the claim that there were forty kinds of *ají*. He accurately notes that the leaves of *rocotos* (the unique *C. pubescens*) differ from all the others in being larger and less smooth, while the fruit can be as large as a lime or medium-size orange. Though he mentions no other individual names, he talks about some that are "long and thick, bigger than the longest finger of the hand, others pointed or less pointed," a kind "of the size and shape of a date," and another resembling an olive. "The most beautiful to sight is one so similar in color, size, and shape to cherries (*guindas*) that a person can easily be deceived into thinking that's what it is. There is another very hot ají as small as pine nuts."

The Colonial and Post-Colonial Legacy

When Father Cobo wrote in the 1650s, close to a hundred fifty years had elapsed since Christopher Columbus had died in Spain, still convinced that he had found his way to the coast of Asia. He did not live to see that he had started a conversation between Spain and the Indies that would expand to embrace the whole planet. Peppers are only one part of that dialogue, but one that kindles the imagination.

The first meals at which Columbus and his crew tasted peppers on Hispaniola started ripple effects in two hemispheres. Of course Spanish gold seekers rushed to the New World expecting to make every newly explored territory a colony of an empire. Spanish armies established themselves in the Caribbean, which furnished their formative experience of peppers. They arrived in Mexico to be greeted by the most brilliantly developed of all pepper cultures. And they invaded Peru to find peppers acting as the cementing flavor principle in a food system encompassing about 3,000 miles/4,800 kilometers, spanning north to south and 3 miles/5 kilometers high.

But while they were doing all this, the so-called pepper (pimiento, or *pimienta de las Indias*) that Columbus, Cortés, and others had carried back from the new possessions was winning another victory: the conquest of Spanish tables. Explorers returned from the Indies and New Spain having acquired a taste for the local *pimienta* or *ají*. Gardeners found that it grew like a weed. In a generation or less after Columbus, new waves of Spaniards were sailing for the colonies as preestablished fans of a naturalized Spanish spice.

The invaders and the conquered New World peoples—at least those who were not killed by brutal maltreatment or European diseases—underwent a slow, very uneven process of mutual acculturation that happened more rapidly in large colonial cities. Indigenous women cooked for a largely male influx of Spaniards, bore their children, and (especially in the former Inca Empire) married them in Christian weddings. Of course we know that the cuisines of all the colonies were enriched by the importation of Spanish livestock, Spanish field crops (from wheat to chickpeas), and Spanish vegetables. But it's easy to forget that nothing stopped peppers born and bred in Spain from showing up with the vegetables.

We must also remember that Spanish journeys to the Americas did not come to an abrupt halt the minute that the Hispanic Caribbean, and the Central and South American colonies declared their independence. A fluctuating but never completely disappearing flow of Spanish newcomers over the centuries was responsible for a certain taming of pepper heat in postcolonial cuisines. The reason is that Spanish cooks and diners in Spain liked their peppers a good bit milder than people in the Americas— meaning the indigenous peoples, the millions of African slaves who had been brought in to grow sugar, and the Spaniards who had gone half native for long enough to become addicted to a capsaicin rush.

The New World pepper scene today is a complexly layered one in which a post-colonial Cuban-style *sofrito* (cooking sauce) with the gentle herbal accent of bell peppers or cubanelles plays as much of a part in the spread of capsicum as does a sharp pepper-laced Venezuelan vinegar, a complex Mexican mole rooted in the viceroyalty of New Spain, or a sauce of fruity Peruvian *ají mirasol*. In their different ways, all of these peppers hark back to the first contact between Taínos and Spaniards in late 1492. That encounter launched American-born peppers on a Spanish-bound journey that would prove to be the first stage of a global capsicum conquest.

Hand-colored ceramic bowls by the women of Chazuta, a small town in the province of San Martín on the Peruvian Amazon.

THE WORLD TRAVELS
OF PEPPERS

It is startling to think that peppers had been unknown in Spain until 1493, when Columbus returned from his first voyage and presented a sampling of New World foods to Queen Isabella and King Ferdinand.

Francisco López de Gómara, Hernán Cortés's secretary, later described the monarchs' first taste of several novelties: "They tried *ají* [hot pepper], a spice of the Indians, which burned their tongues, and *batatas* [sweet potatoes], which are sweet roots, and *gallipavos* [turkeys], which are better than peacocks and hens." I've always wished that someone had recorded the appearance of the *ají* they tasted, or even whether it was dried or fresh from a live plant carried over on the ship. But we will never know.

Nevertheless, the glowing report that follows from Nicolás Monardes, a physician born and raised in Seville (the entry point for new foods arriving in Spain from the Americas in the sixteenth century) shows that by Monardes's time, peppers had already become commonplace in that country.

What had happened in the eighty-plus years between that first exposure to the burning hot *ají* and a wholehearted Spanish embrace of the beautiful peppers described by Monardes? Obviously, a lot—including the start of a Spanish pepper gardening tradition and the appearance of other peppers that the conquistadors found in Mexico or other New World territories under their control.

Many events were set in motion as soon as Columbus took his leave of the Catholic monarchs in Barcelona and embarked on a devout pilgrimage to a shrine of the Virgin Mary. (The cult of the Virgin Mary had become the galvanizing force of integration since Ferdinand III and his son Alfonso X had taken Andalusia from the Muslims in the thirteenth century.) At the time, travelers often vowed to worship at some particular site if they returned home safely, and Columbus had a debt to pay to Mary for having survived a fierce storm on his homeward voyage. His destination was the shrine of Our

Lady of Guadalupe at the Real Monasterio de Nuestra Señora de Guadalupe, a monastery of Hieronymite monks—"Jerónimos"—in Extremadura. Guadalupe and other monasteries of the Jerónimos would be bound up with subsequent pepper history.

In a political-religious climate marked by cutthroat jockeying for influence among religious orders, the Jerónimos enjoyed royal favor and great power. They had been allowed to found monasteries surrounded by vast landed estates with extensive farms and gardens. Apparently, useful New World plants and seeds carried back by returning conquistadors often were presented to the Jerónimos during pilgrimages like Columbus's and planted in monastery gardens. The order seems to have taken the lead in the early dissemination of peppers in Spain. Several major varieties became widely cultivated in the neighborhood of two other Hieronymite monasteries, Yuste in the Jerte Valle de of Extremadura and San Pedro de la Ñora in Murcia.

Probably not all the peppers spread by the monks were identical to the kind that burned the royal tongues in 1493. In the Bahamas, Cuba, and Hispaniola, where Columbus first encountered the Arawaks (Taínos) and their food, several *Capsicum* species shared favor under the name of *ají*. There is no way now to tell whether what he brought back from his first voyage was a *C. chinense*, *C. frutescens*, or *C. annuum*. But as the Spanish New World adventure continued, a clearer picture emerges. The pepper destined to conquer Spain was *C. annuum*, the principal *Capsicum* that the invaders "discovered" as their chief ambitions shifted from the islands to Mesoamerica. The new colonial focus began after Columbus's third voyage when he sailed as far south as the mouth of the Orinoco River in today's Venezuela and on his fourth voyage when he reached the Central American mainland and traveled along the coasts of today's Nicaragua, Costa Rica, and Panama in 1502.

Spaniards quickly followed up with explorations of the coast that were to culminate in Hernán Cortés's 1519 invasion of Mexico. Both before and after Cortés's conquest of the Aztec Empire, settlers of newly founded outposts in the Antilles returned at intervals to the Spanish court bearing further shiploads of promising island or mainland bounty. In 1528, Cortés briefly returned to Spain and made his own journey to the Extremaduran Guadalupe shrine where he stayed for nine days and presented an ex-voto, or votive offering: a golden, jewel-encrusted image of a scorpion whose bite he had miraculously survived in Mexico. It is likely, though not documented, that by the time of this event, the Spanish monastery and other gardens already housed the first *C. annuum* specimens.

Of the five domesticated pepper species, only three would have careers in the Eastern Hemisphere: *C. chinense*, *C. frutescens*, and *C. annuum*. It was the last species that would account for the lion's share of peppers' global adventures for the subsequent five centuries. The other two can only sometimes adapt to conditions outside of their neotropical birthplace. Annuums, however, are the chameleons of the *Capsicum* genus. They have a phenomenal talent for taking root and flourishing in any region where they happen to alight, including tropics, subtropics, and a huge range of temperate latitudes, either cool or warm. They also display a dazzling range of both size and shape, from minuscule chiltepines to big blocky bell peppers, and capsaicin content, again represented by the same two extremes. Geneticists attribute this capacity for variation to the great number of transposons—tiny DNA segments that can switch positions on a chromosome—in the *C. annuum* genome. Only with the arrival of the many-faceted *C. annuum* in Spain did the real story of peppers' Old World travels begin.

Peppers already had a lot going for them in Spain. When the conquerors were introduced to different *Capsicum* species everywhere from Mexico to the Andes, their general reaction was love at first or second bite—a love that suggests some unrecognized hunger or yearning for a hot sensation waiting to surface. Every chronicler writing about the foods of the New World sang the praises of peppers, using local names like *ají* (the Caribbean), *uchu* (the Andes), and *chile* (Mesoamerica). Once planted in Spanish gardens, annuums won cooks over for another aspect of their immense variability: Alone among major world food plants, this amazing species can be equally valuable as a vegetable as it is as a spice.

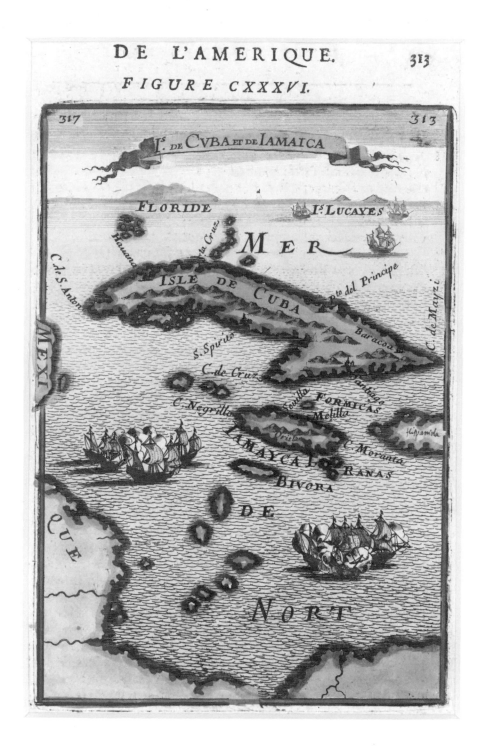

Peppers in Today's Spain

There are two main culinary uses of peppers in the wide rage of cuisines around the world: fresh and dried. Generally speaking, annuum peppers are eaten fresh as vegetables when mature and either unripe or fully ripe—sometimes cut into convenient-sized pieces to make cooking sauces like *sofrito* and sometimes used whole (in which case they are often roasted and stuffed with savory fillings). When used as a spice or pre-prepared seasoning they are usually (not always) dried before being added to dishes, either whole or ground to powder or flakes. Additionally, fresh peppers, hot or otherwise, are often chopped or pureed to make relishes. Large peppers for vegetable purposes are most often mild or only moderately hot. Ground dried peppers can be mild, semihot, or very hot, depending on local culinary preferences.

Through selection and breeding, growers in every region of Spain would gradually develop local types (landraces) that became known for many of the aforementioned uses. Those that are small and eaten when fresh and green include the stubby and thin-skinned Padrón or Herbón peppers (*pementos* in Galician) with their notoriously unpredictable levels of heat, and the consistently sweeter pimientos de Couto, which are good for panfrying. Both were brought to Galicia by missionaries and were first planted in the Franciscan monasteries of San Antonio de Padua in Herbón and San Martiño de Couto in the A Coruña Province. The iconic fresh pepper of the Basque country is the Guernica pepper, known in Euskera, the Basque language, as *Gernikako piperra*. The Guernica grows more in length than the Padrón pepper but is equally succulent and thin-skinned; it is ideal for panfrying and grilling.

All fresh Spanish peppers are called *pimientos* whether or not they are large or small, sweet or hot. The distinction between pimiento (heart-shaped) and bell pepper pod types that botanists often make to describe the shape of large sweet peppers does not apply to Spanish cultivars. A Spanish pepper might look like a Bull Nose bell, ending in well-defined lobes, but it is still called pimiento, though an accompanying descriptive adjective like *morrón* or *hocico de buey* (oxen snout) paints a clearer picture. Likewise, the sweet, heart-shaped piquillo pepper of Navarre, another iconic Spanish landrace, is called *pimiento de piquillo* (little beak) because it tapers into a pointy end.

Though imported sweet pepper types that were developed in the United States, France, and Italy are now grown commercially in Spain, there are still fascinating and delicious landraces that evolved from smaller and perhaps hotter American ancestors that arrived in the country centuries ago to become larger and sweeter peppers loved by Spaniards today. Some are little known outside of their ecological niches but have loyal local followings, like the pimiento de Oimbra in Orense, Galicia, and the impressive pimiento Fresno-Benavente grown in northeastern Castille, with its long, rectangular shape ending in a sturdy snout. Among the most famous outside of its traditional terroir, besides the *pimientos de piquillo* from Navarre, is the pimiento Najerano or Pimiento Riojano. In La Rioja, a fertile region in northern Spain and a crossroad of history and culture as it is bordered by the Basque Country, Navarre, Aragon, and Castile and León, this long, conical pepper is king. Cooked when ripe or fire-roasted with onions and garlic (and often tomatoes), the Riojano is the flavor base of the region's famous *chilindrón* (in the Rioja context, a sauce) for many succulent regional dishes. Roasted in wood-fired ovens and canned, the pimiento Riojano is as popular and as valuable as an export item as the fire-roasted piquillo pepper in Navarre.

Through the centuries, Spaniards developed a preference for sweet pepper cultivars, a taste that they brought back to the Americas, particularly to the Hispanic Caribbean. That the islands that gave Spain its first taste of hot peppers became large importers and consumers of sweet Spanish roasted pimientos speaks volumes of Latin America's deep connection with Spain and the curious ways in which peppers became harbingers of flavor change across continents.

Among the best-known dried varieties of Spain even now are ones first disseminated through the Jerónimos at the monasteries of Ñora in Murcia and Yuste in Extremadura. The eponymous *ñora* peppers (the name comes from a kind of waterwheel introduced to Spain along with Arab irrigation systems) are round, meaty, and sweet-flavored. Spanish cooks reconstitute dried *ñoras* in water to soften them and then scrape the meat from the flesh to add flavor and color to cooking sauces for rice dishes like *caldero murciano*; Valencian *pericana* (salt cod skin seasoned with a sauce of peppers and tomatoes); fish soups, braises, and stews; and table sauces, such as Catalan *romescu* (romesco).

In Murcia, the dried *ñoras* are ground into a sweet paprika (pimentón) while Extremadura is nearly synonymous with a more famous kind of paprika, the pimentón de la Vera. Careful selection of sweet and hot cultivars best suited for drying from landraces growing for centuries in this historic region, practically next door to the Valle de Jerte where the Monastery of Yuste is located, has contributed to the quality and worldwide fame of the pimentón de La Vera. Based on mixtures of several different milder and hotter cultivars—*Jeromín* and *Ocales* (hot), *Jaranda* (sweet), and *Jariza* (mildly hot)—the peppers are smoked-dried over wood fires before grinding and combined in different proportions to make sweet, sweet-sharp, and hot versions. Other regional versions of pimentón are made throughout Spain. It is almost as important as the meat in the many incarnations of chorizo, which would lose half their character without the intense flavor and rich, warm color imparted by the paprika. Together with the taste for sweet peppers, the reliance on pimentón as a seasoning traveled back to the Americas with every wave of Spanish settlers.

These developments were far in the future during the new plant's early sixteenth-century debut in Spain. But peppers were an instant hit. People took to them not with caution but enthusiasm. This pattern was repeated everywhere that peppers were fully integrated into local cuisines on their global journeys. They seemed to satisfy some deep need, a physical or perhaps more than physical craving that eaters hadn't been conscious of before. The beautiful appearance and ornamental value remarked by Nicolás Monardes (see page 67) can only have helped peppers' rise to stardom. And the fact that this lovely vegetable could also be enjoyed as a spice was perhaps the most important fact of all in its Spanish adventures. Peppercorns, previously the most popular spice among those who could afford them, reached Spain only through long sea voyages from India or the Spice Islands, as did other classic spices such as cinnamon, nutmeg, cloves, and ginger. No humble family's kitchen could be stocked with those imported luxuries year-round—while, as Monardes observed, the new spice "costs no more than the sowing" in anybody's garden.

In only a few decades, Columbus's tongue-burning novelty was poised to become the great democratizer of Spanish cuisine. The seventeenth-century Baroque poet Francisco de Quevedo pointedly commented, "con rojos pimientos y ajos duros/tan bien como el señor, comió el esclavo" (with red peppers and hard garlic, the slave ate as well as the master). A whole flavor palette had changed for good without people realizing it. It was easy to forget that peppers hadn't always existed in Spain. Similar memory lapses have marked many of the most passionate love affairs with capsicums throughout the Old World.

The kind that became most widely important in Spanish cooking was the *guindilla*, a spice or seasoning pepper with a long, narrow shape conforming to the overall type that botanists call *cayenne*. Broadly speaking, it is *the* hot pepper of Spain whether used fresh, pickled, or milled into pimentón. The speed with which capsicums took over Spain can be judged from two of my favorite paintings by the Sevillian Diego Velázquez. Both date from 1618 and show guindillas in ordinary kitchen settings. In *The Old Woman Frying Eggs*, an elderly cook is tending to a couple of eggs in an earthenware pot set over an *anafre* (brazier). The table at which she sits holds a typical Spanish brass *almírez* (mortar and pestle), along with an onion and two dried guindillas—familiar, comforting sights to this very day for so many people in Spain and Latin America. A guindilla also figures in Velázquez's *Christ in the House of Martha and Mary*, on a table where a glum-faced servant is pounding something in an *almírez*. This time the other ingredients are some garlic, a couple of whole eggs, and a plate of fresh fish waiting to be cooked. How natural for dried capsicums to be sharing space with anything as commonplace as an onion, how naturally they would fit into one of the classic pounded sauces made in an *almírez* and used for seasoning fish or fish stews and soups—possibly what is called *all i pebre* (garlic and pepper) in the cooking of Valencia, Alicante, and Murcia, or something like a French aioli or rouille, where peppers lend spice to a garlicky emulsified sauce. And how clearly we can see that the New World gift had already ceased to be a newcomer and joined the list of humble, affordable everyday Spanish foods.

Long before the two Velázquez paintings, a knowledge of peppers had started to spread among the pioneer botanists of Europe. In 1542, Bavarian physician Leonhart Fuchs published a treatise with illustrations of three widely different types of peppers, including one of the cayenne or guindilla type. Further descriptions by Dutch, English, and other botanists followed. We can see that peppers were on the move not only in Europe but also in the rest of the Old World—thanks not to the Spanish but to the Portuguese and the Ottoman Turks.

The Expanding Diaspora: Africa and Eastern Europe

Having brought New World foods across the Atlantic, Spaniards were content to explore their possibilities in the mother country, along with the Spanish dependencies in Italy. By contrast, Portuguese merchants and voyagers tirelessly carried them from Brazil along expanding trade routes to Africa, the Indian Ocean, and the Far East. Possibly as a result of armed Portuguese-Turkish naval encounters in the vicinity of the Persian Gulf and the Indian Ocean, the Turks became acquainted with peppers early in the seventeenth century and succumbed to the new attraction as rapidly as the Spanish. Peppers (*C. annuums*) went with them as they annexed a succession of Balkan states and finally Hungary.

As in Spain, local landraces tended to spring up wherever the newcomers were planted, becoming symbols of a nation's or region's cuisine. In Hungary, several strains of peppers were developed to be sun-dried, ground, and combined in varying proportions to make many types and grades of beautiful burnished-red paprika, the spice that today nearly defines Hungarian cooking. Other varieties appeared after the Turks carried peppers to North Africa, the Near East, and Western Asia as far as the Caucasus.

One strikingly fertile breeding ground was a swath of territory just north and south of the Turkish-Syrian border. The climate was ideal for bringing either sweet or hot peppers to succulent ripeness and sun-drying them to concentrate every iota of flavor before crushing and milling them to flakes, sometimes with small amounts of oil and salt to round out the effect. In Turkish marketplaces today, pyramidal mounds of pepper flakes roasted to intense shades of red or purplish black catch the eye, casting ancient Near Eastern seasonings like dried mint, sumac, and nigella into the shade. The areas around the cities of Antep, Maraş, and Urfa in Turkey and Aleppo in Syria became especially famed for their own versions of dried pepper flakes from particular landraces. Their differing balances of pleasing fruitiness, tartness, and sweetness with moderate heat are the subject of patriotic debate. Some people swear by the dark, intense Urfa peppers that take on a winey richness through being alternately exposed to the open sun and tightly covered to make them sweat. Others adore the brighter, more tart Aleppo peppers (endangered by the political turmoil in Syria). Such debates make it clear that, as in Spain, capsicum peppers didn't just arrive here and seamlessly join a company of other spices and herbs. They gave a startling new cast to the whole scene—a break with the past.

North Africa and the Caucasus acquired a Turkish-inspired legacy of seasoning pastes made by chopping and pounding fresh peppers with varied bouquets of herbs and aromatics. *Harissa*, containing a strong red pepper kick together with garlic, coriander, and caraway or cumin seed, used to be made regularly in all Tunisian homes. Even in commercial form, it still sounds the keynote of innumerable dishes. Other versions are popular in Algeria and Morocco. The hot pepper paste idea also took root in the Caucasus, with red or sometimes green peppers married to a whole complex of fresh herbs in the famed *adjika* of Georgia and Abkhazia. It would be hard to convince local cooks that peppers are not native to their region.

Even more dramatic transformations overtook the cuisines of many African and Asian regions that were touched by Portuguese commerce, either directly or through some further relaying step. Astonishingly, some Old World eaters would come not just to tolerate but to demand, crave, and positively depend on pepper heat at levels completely unknown in the Caribbean, Mexico, or South America.

On both the western and eastern coasts of sub-Saharan Africa, incredibly hot local *C. annuum* and occasionally *C. frutescens* varieties turned regional stews and soups into something that can make foreigners gasp in agony at a single taste. Here the preferred kinds were often small, thin *C. annuum* or *C. frutescens* varieties generically dubbed bird peppers. They are the piri-piris of Angolan and Mozambican cuisine, which lend their name to many dishes based on these scorchingly hot peppers. At the Portuguese colony of Goa, Indian cooks rapidly replaced—or sometimes supplemented—the familiar heat of black pepper and "long pepper" (a close relative of peppercorns) with the cheaper and more intoxicating *Capsicum* stimulus. Goan vindaloo dishes (the name started out as *vinha-d'alhos*, referring to a particular kind of Portuguese wine-vinegar marinade, but took on a life of its own in Goa) became synonymous with the most blistering fire that Indian cuisine has to offer. It took several centuries for the new spice to travel across the subcontinent and reach the northern Indian regions of Punjab and Kashmir. Historians attribute their northward journey to protracted military campaigns by the Maratha, a coalition of Hindu warrior castes who battled the Mughal Empire and the invading English until the early nineteenth century.

On to Asia

Peppers also reached the farthest eastern end of India—that is, Bengal and several neighboring provinces. The Portuguese are reported to have brought peppers to Calcutta, the greatest city of the region and later the capital of the British Indian Empire. It is likely—though just when has not, as far as I know, been documented—that from there peppers were carried up through the tea-growing foothills of the Himalayas into the handful of nations that literally share the top of the world—Tibet, Nepal, and Bhutan.

Astonishingly, this pepper journey involved not just the expected *C. annuum* with one or two frutescens outliers, but some of the explosive chinense peppers. The searing *Bhut Jolokia*, also known as ghost pepper (a *C. chinense* showing introgression of *C. frutescens* genetics), apparently originated in some of the hilly provinces near today's state of West Bengal. What *C. chinense* was doing in this part of the world would be a fascinating detective story for some future historian.

Hot *C. annuums* were the conquerors of Bhutan and were made even hotter by the high altitude. If anyone can love pepper heat more than cooks in Africa and Southeast Asia, it is the Bhutanese. People insist that they literally cannot live without constant doses of hotter-than-hot peppers. Children are praised when they graduate from bland foods to full participation in pepper-mania. Crushed dried pepper is a ubiquitous spice. Fresh green cayenne-type peppers—the more inflammatory the better—appear as a vegetable in many vegetarian or other dishes. One taste of *ema datshi* (often translated as "chiles and cheese,) and I recognized a mountain-bred cousin of a Latin American and Spanish *sofrito*: onions, peppers, and sometimes tomatoes simmered together to make a sauce enriched with cheese, such as for the family of pepper dishes called *picantes* in Peru and Bolivia. (Both cows and yaks

are highly valued as dairy animals in Bhutan.) There are other versions with potatoes added, and ones made with whole dried peppers. I have found these dishes appearing on restaurant menus even in my part of New Jersey and suspect that they are about to win over many diners beyond the Bhutanese community.

It was also the Portuguese who took hot peppers to their outposts in Southeast Asia—Macao in southern China and Malacca (Melaka) in peninsular Malaysia—from where they spread like wildfire, becoming prominent in a number of cuisines from Vietnam to Thailand and from Malaysia to Indonesia. In these countries there are a very small number of cultivars, the most popular being the tiny bird pepper (*C. frutescens*) and some cayenne types like the red finger hot or Holland red finger hot pepper (*C. annuum*). These deliver a punch of heat when needed and they are usually combined with flavorful ingredients in table salsas and cooking sauces (such as the Malaysian *sambal belacham* made with hot peppers and a toasted pungent shrimp paste). They do a great job, providing a baseline of heat that intensifies the interplay of sweet, salty, bitter, and sour sensations that Southeast Asians favor in their food. There is no doubt that peppers awakened eaters from these regions to a nearly unappeasable desire for the unique, galvanizing capsaicin rush—a sensation produced by no other food.

Some societies remained fairly untouched by the new thrill. The peppers brought to Japan by the Portuguese joined the ranks of garden vegetables but did not become a prominent seasoning until much later. But when they were taken from Japan to Korea at the start of the seventeenth century, hot peppers in the form of *gochugaru* (milled flakes of dried red pepper) and *gochujang* (the rich, spicy red seasoning paste made from the flakes)—soon took off as the chief propellant of Korean cuisine.

The logical next stage of the Far Eastern journey was China. Unfortunately, we have only scattered documentation of how peppers got there. The centuries when they reached the rest of coastal Asia were marked by repeated imperial Chinese attempts to stop or at least curtail any incoming flow of Europeans and their goods. Even though the Portuguese had reached Chinese waters by about 1500 and were granted a small trading outpost at Macau in 1557, it is far from certain that they played any role here.

However, the historian Caroline Reeves has been able to glean some crucial facts by examining local county gazetteers covering a period of several centuries. The new peppers are recorded in the coastal province of Zhejiang, south of Shanghai, as early as 1671 and intermittently throughout the eighteenth century, but apparently they disappeared with no immediate influence on Chinese cuisine. They have a much more persistent track record in the far northeastern Liaoning province, from 1682 until the founding of the People's Republic in 1949. Liaoning, however, belongs to the area of the former Manchuria long marked by contact (and conflict) among peoples of Siberia, Korea, and northeastern China, somewhat insulated from the rest of Chinese culture. Orthodox Chinese culinary authorities paid the Northeast (Dongbei) region no attention at all until ten or fifteen years ago.

This history makes it is all the more unexpected that China would eventually emerge as the world example par excellence of all the paradoxes, contradictions, and surprises in the entire *Capsicum* story. By some unknown route or routes—perhaps overland from the Silk Road or the Yunnan Province borders with several Southeast Asian countries, perhaps from the South China Sea—fierce *C. annuum* and possibly some *C. frutescens* cultivars arrived in the southwestern provinces of Hunan (1684) and Sichuan (1749). And during the nineteenth century, hot peppers roared off on a blazing trajectory surpassing anything in the New World lands of their birth.

Sichuanese cooks married dried-pepper firepower to the curious mouth-tingling effect of the local spice *Zanthoxylum spp.* (the so-called Sichuan pepper and sansho pepper in Japan) to create a host of now classic *ma la* (numbing-hot) dishes. They pan-seared fresh green cayenne types over high heat to blister their skin and create a showstopper called tiger-skin peppers. Hunanese cooks carpeted the famous dish Chongqing chicken with literally hundreds of dried hot peppers, and chopped up brilliant fresh red peppers for sauces and relishes. They also poured what seems to be a scarlet blanket of hot peppers over an equally renowned steamed fish-head dish.

For generations, other Chinese marveled at the fiery ways of Hunan, Sichuan, and their near neighbor Guizhou Province. But prolonged twentieth-century political upheavals would throw people from different regions into unexpected kinds of contact, starting in home and restaurant kitchens on the island of Taiwan, the seat of the

Nationalist government-in-exile after the 1949 Communist victory on the mainland. Later, the death of Mao Zedong—a product of Hunanese upbringing who famously declared that hot peppers were the food of the true revolutionary—opened mainland China's path to a strange amalgam of Communism and robber-baron capitalism.

The pepper situation in China has been greatly shaken up because everything imaginable has been shaken up. First of all, forced and voluntary labor migrations redistributed regional populations and ethnic groups everywhere in the People's Republic, along with their local cuisines. Meanwhile, the cyber age arrived with a bang in China's new money-mad consumer society. The Internet enabled food fashions from overseas Chinese communities like Vancouver's Richmond neighborhood, New York's Flushing neighborhood, or California's San Gabriel Valley to reach Beijing, Shanghai, and other great cities, and then return to North America with new tweaks. A new class of ambitious Chinese restaurant chefs acquired a sense of freedom beyond boundaries. So did a new class of aggressive entrepreneurs who had set their sights on the international market for peppers.

Pepper Agribusiness

Racing to match the agribusiness dominance of industrialized nations, Chinese growers are now raising many dozens of pepper cultivars on an industrial scale and importing them back to the lands of their birth. Mexico is only one example. A few years ago I visited the Central de Abasto, the great Mexico City wholesale market. I was stunned at what I saw. Side by side with Mexican-grown chiles at prices that made sense to me stood burlap bags stamped all over with Chinese characters, brimming with guajillos, *chiles de árbol*, and more, at bargain basement prices. The wholesale buyers know just what they're getting. But what of retail customers in little *tiendas*, or diners who order moles in restaurants, or buyers of dried chiles here in the United States? The cheap imported chiles now threaten to crowd out the genuine articles and put thousands of Mexican farmers out of business.

Such stories could have multiplied on every continent. Koreans have to search for versions of their beautiful milled red *gochugaru* flakes made from Korean-grown rather than cheaper Chinese-grown peppers. In my local Korean market, a kilo of freshly milled pepper flakes from Andong, a historical and rich agricultural region in the Gyeonsang Province of South Korea, costs three times as much as a bag of the same weight of pepper flakes made from peppers grown in India or China and packaged in Korea. In another startling twist, Dutch greenhouses distribute many kinds of bell peppers, and more recently a range of hot peppers, to markets everywhere. (A couple of weeks ago, I found superhot Trinidad Moruga Scorpions grown in the

Netherlands at my local whole foods store.) Here is history repeating itself! Dutch gardeners were pioneer specialists supplying improved vegetables to all of northern Europe in the sixteenth and seventeenth centuries—also just the time when the Dutch East India Company and Portuguese commercial interests were battling for possession of Southeast Asian colonies. Now China—which claims to be the world's greatest producer and importer of peppers—also imports Dutch bell peppers.

Peru, an ancient cradle of South American peppers, is also looking to hit the international jackpot. Until now, Peru has had to export its own special peppers, such as the *ají amarillo* and the *rocoto*, to the United States only in flash-frozen form. But in 2016, it was granted permission by the US Department of Agriculture to send fresh Andean peppers as well as US standbys like bell peppers and jalapeños. In a clause that is troubling, the agreement specifies that the peppers must be grown in approved greenhouses under pest-resistant conditions. This will benefit the largest growers while creating insuperable barriers to the thousands of small farmers who cultivate Peru's many landraces on tiny plots that average less than twelve acres.

Dried peppers also figure in Peruvian agribusiness equations. The huge Pomalco firm, formerly known as a sugar producer and rum distiller, is branching out into growing and drying guajillo chiles in the hot, arid climate of Lambayeque Province, in northern Peru, for export to Mexico and the United States. It seems all too likely that in the future, Peru and China will be competing to see which will sell the most dried Mexican chiles to the homeland of chiles.

A huge factor driving an ongoing worldwide increase in pepper production has been the highly visible "chilehead" vogue in the United States. Already in the 1970s and '80s, aficionados were swapping news about which Sichuanese or Southwestern restaurants delivered the most blistering heat, or how one bottled hot sauce stacked up against others. The movement has never paused since. (The Xi'an Famous Foods, a popular Flushing restaurant with a Chinese Muslim slant, has evolved into a successful chain of eateries with menus entirely composed of pepper-powered dishes, including lamb ribs that have spawned a fan club in China.) Echoing earlier African and Asian developments, the insatiable yen for a capsaicin fix eventually became a prominent enough feature of the US food landscape to inspire Chinese producers looking for a market.

Pepper fandom doesn't stop with China and the United States. Superhot is supercool in all world capitals that are influenced by American food trends. And developing nations in both hemispheres are joining the rush to compete with the mass-market Chinese pepper agro-industry and the Dutch specialty pepper market. With the help of their governments, farmers in Nigeria, Ghana, and Uganda have invested much acreage and effort in growing peppers to export to Europe. In fact, it can be hard to sort out just who is selling to whom, since peppers seem to be moving around the globe in so many directions at once. Many nations now boast pepper research institutes determined to emulate the plant-breeding success of New Mexico's pioneering Chile Pepper Institute.

Japan has finally joined the ranks of hot pepper eaters and, lately, of pepper exporters. *Ichimi togarashi*, a Japanese version of dried hot pepper flakes used as table condiment, has become ubiquitous. Japanese chefs, US chefs, and many others regularly use beautiful Japanese-bred green peppers for grilling or panfrying in the same style as the hard-to-find Spanish Padrón peppers, which they closely resemble. The name shishito is now as familiar to American food-lovers as Wagyu beef or wasabi. Today US-grown shishitos from Mitsuwa, a Japanese market with a branch in New Jersey, are my go-to pepper for many uses, and I've even been lucky enough to find a special Kyoto strain grown on a Maryland farm—the sought-after *manganji* with thin skin, a wonderful balance of sweet and "green" flavor, and just enough resistance to the bite when grilled. I'm equally dependent on the gorgeous long red Korean peppers, a very smooth-skinned and brilliant variant of the cayenne type that I use all the time in fresh or lightly pickled relishes. Korea, it turns out, is now a leader of world pepper research, constantly improving on the strains most important to Korean cuisine. (Yet their favorite red peppers are often imported into the US from the Netherlands!)

Leave it to the Chinese to outdo everyone else. The People's Republic has launched peppers on the most extreme world travels of all—rapidly circumnavigating the planet, at heights far above the Himalayas. In 1986, Chinese scientists began sending crop seeds into space on rockets and high-altitude balloons in order to study the effects of cosmic radiation on rates of mutation. What was an experiment is now a multimillion-dollar program that involves recovering space-voyager seeds, planting and harvesting them over several generations, and selecting the most promising specimens for desirable qualities like fast growth, color, or nutrient content. By 2009, *China Daily* reported that more than half the peppers sold in north-central Gansu Province were "space peppers." A few years later, seeds of cayenne-type space peppers were appearing in American seed catalogues as numbered variants of Hangjiao (voyaging pepper) or under fanciful English names like Comet's Tail, Super Nova, and Total Eclipse. If the first manned Mars expedition finds some rocket-propelled capsicum waiting for it, this would be a fitting next adventure for the humble plant that started out evading predators to survive and multiply in tropical South America and ended up forever influencing human appetites and changing flavor the world over.

Gallery *of* Fresh Peppers

The brilliant beauty of the ripe capsicums must have fascinated the pre-Columbian people who first explored their possibilities. When I walk through my pepper garden and dozens of cultivars are at peak ripeness, every plant seems to be a living display of jewels. No other fruit found in nature achieves such glowing intensity. It doesn't take much imagination to deduce that this is what originally incited people to touch and taste peppers.

The same quality undoubtedly was a major reason for Spain's enthusiastic adoption of peppers, by which time five domesticated species were flourishing throughout the conquered territories. Early botanists commented on the peppers' beauty and on how they could adorn anyone's garden at no cost.

The red of a red pepper is really as unusual as the capsaicin heat that is peppers' best-known attribute. The two pigments that create it—capsanthin and capsorubin—are synthesized by no other fruits and vegetables. While red pepper fruits are developing and growing to maturity, they appear green to the eye because large amounts of chlorophyll mask all other pigments. As the peppers ripen, the chlorophyll breaks down, allowing the full effect of capsanthin and capsorubin to become evident.

The brilliant pigments do not stay fixed after the ripe fruit is harvested, but gradually become oxidized and break down in their turn. The process can be hastened in the presence of heat, sunlight, and air. But careful drying (see pages 233 and 236) can convert the original pigmentation to a spectrum of muted colors that are lovely in their own right.

Ají Amarillo (also Ají Escabeche)

If I were pressed to choose only one Andean pepper for cooking, this would have to be it. The intensely fruity, flavorful, and colorful all-purpose *ají amarillo* has it all: perfectly balanced heat and flavor, succulence, delicious aroma, and stunning color. Ripening from green through lemony yellow to bright apricot orange, this brilliant baccatum is believed to have originated in central Bolivia, though it now grows throughout Bolivia and Peru and even in Argentina and Brazil. Curiously, Peruvians often refer to it as *ají verde*, or "green pepper," which does not mean immature but simply fresh. In northern Peru, cooks call it *ají escabeche* because it is often used to spice vinegary *sofritos* for the pickling sauce *escabeche*. Among the native peppers of Peru, the *ají amarillo* surpasses all others in internal consumption, whether fresh, dried, pureed, or ground into powder. This wonderful pepper comes to US markets flash frozen, dried, and processed in various ways. The bright orange cultivar known as *escabeche* is grown commercially from Lambayeque in the north to Tacna in the south. A larger type, called *pacae* because it resembles the pod of the "ice cream bean" plant (*Inga edulis*, also called *pacay*), grows mostly in the southern regions of Arequipa, Moquegua, and Tacna. Occasionally one finds huge specimens the size of a zucchini in markets, but savvy cooks, particularly in the north of the country, think the shorter ones are tastier. Andean cooks like perfectly ripe *ajíes*, which are sweeter. Ground or cut into strips, the *ají amarillo* is sautéed with onions and garlic to flavor braises like *sudado* or in *escabeches*. Ground into a paste, it is the fundamental seasoning for marinades and the cooking sauce called *aderezo*, a cousin of *sofrito*. Some cooks blanch the pepper briefly in boiling water and peel it afterward before grinding it to a paste for cooking sauces. When dried,

Ají Amarillo

the *ají amarillo* is commonly known as *ají mirasol* (not to be confused with the Mexican pepper of that name). Colored like old copper, it has a lovely fruitiness and a winey, smoky flavor.

3.4–4.5 IN/8.64–11.43 CM LONG BY 1.5–1.75 IN/3.81–4.44 CM WIDE (*C. BACCATUM*)

Ají Ambato

Ají Ambato, Red

Ají Ambato (also Ají Ambateño)

This native of the Ambato region in the Ecuadorian central highlands is a long, slender pepper that ripens from green to light yellow to deep orange. Smooth-skinned with firm, crunchy flesh, it has a refreshing flavor suggesting mingled tropical fruits dominated by guava peel. It can be used in cooking when mild heat and bright color are needed. It is particularly good raw in salsas.

3.75 IN/9.62 CM LONG BY 0.8 IN/2.03 CM WIDE
(*C. BACCATUM*)

Ají Ambato, Red (also Ají Ambateño)

This bright red version of the Ambato cultivar is nearly identical to the orange in all but color. I find that it tends to be deeper flavored, but the two can be used interchangeably.

4.25 IN/10.79 CM LONG BY 1 IN/2.54 CM WIDE
(*C. BACCATUM*)

Ají Aribibi Gusano

Ají Benito

Ají Aribibi Gusano

This is an unusual pepper from the Amazonian town of Aribibi in the Santa Cruz region of Bolivia. The small pods hang in pairs like tiny, segmented caterpillars (*gusano* means "worm"). The crinkly-skinned fruit ripens from light green through shades of yellow to creamy white. The name *aribibi* is local slang for a loud, tantrum-throwing person, which fits the heat profile of this cultivar, intense enough for a single pod to flavor a full pot of food. The pepper surpasses the floral and fruity complexity expected of some chinenses. It is also lightly citrusy. In Bolivia, they grind it to a paste for vinegar-based table sauces. I like to preserve the charming shape by using it whole in a pickled vegetable medley (see page 258). The bushy plant is a beautiful ornamental, and the dangling "caterpillars" never fail to arouse curiosity.

1.75 IN/4.4 CM LONG BY 0.6-0.7 IN/1.5-1.8 CM WIDE
(*C. CHINENSE*)

Ají Benito

This sturdy Bolivian pepper bears as many as 7 pretty fruits per nodule, ripening from light green to shades of yellow and orange to deep vermilion. This thick-skinned and mildly hot *baccatum* has a slight tomato acid tang, a guava flavor, and a light herbaceous scent that is more characteristic of the *chinense* species.

2-3 IN/5.1-7.6 CM LONG BY 0.75-1 IN/1.9-2.5 CM WIDE
(*C. BACCATUM*)

Ají Bola

Ají Cacique

Ají Bola (also Ají Bola Criollo de Piura)

This is one of the many members of the diverse *ají limo* group. It is a small, round, smooth-skinned pepper that ripens to shades of orange and deep red. Typical of Peru's northern coastal region, particularly Piura, it often adds heat and color to *cebiche*, *tiraditos*, and the iconic pepper-laced stew called *seco de chabelo*.

0.75-0.8 IN/1.9-2 CM LONG BY 0.75 IN/1.9 CM WIDE
(*C. CHINENSE*)

Ají Cacique (also Ají Ratón)

This Ecuadorian pepper, shaped like a small toy top, ripens from apple green to yellow to brownish orange. In Manabí, a coastal region of Ecuador north of the province of Guayas, it is used in a table sauce called *ají* that also calls for a tasty regional type of vinegar made from banana peel (*vinagre de guineo*). Though the *cacique* is a *chinense*, it is less aromatic than other peppers of this species.

0.8 IN/2 CM LONG BY 0.75 IN/1.9 CM WIDE
(*C. CHINENSE*)

Ají Cajamarca

Ají Cajamarca

From Cajamarca, a region in northern Peru that straddles the Andes and stretches down to the Amazon, these small pods, similar in shape to *ají limo*, are stunningly beautiful, with almost translucent yet firm white skin and splashes of purple that turn bright red as they ripen. The region and its capital city, Cajamarca, are famous as the place where conquering Spaniards led by Francisco Pizarro subdued the last Inca emperor in 1512, but the look of these peppers alone is another claim to fame. Not particularly complex, they have medium heat, a sour green taste, and a pleasant *chinense* aroma. Use in any recipe that calls for *ají limo*. Mexican hot peppers like the *chile Tuxta* of Oaxaca and the *chile blanco* of Chiapa de Corzo, in Chiapas, have a similar coloration.

2.25 IN/5.7 CM LONG BY 0.75 IN/1.9 CM WIDE
(*C. CHINENSE*)

Ají Cereza

Ají Cereza

This plant is a pretty sight, with round, lightly tapering thin-skinned pods that grow pointing upright like upside-down triangles. Ripening from green to a deep cherry red, they are intensely hot bordering on bitter with a taste that reminds one more of a *baccatum* or *chinense* than an *annuum*. This Peruvian pepper, sold as ají cerezo in the US, can be used whenever heat and straightforward flavor are needed.

1-1.75 IN/2.5-4.4 CM LONG BY 0.4-0.75 IN/1-1.9 CM WIDE
(*C. ANNUUM*)

Ají Cerezo

Popular in the Lambayeque region of northwestern Peru, this mildly hot pepper is extremely seedy (a pod can hold as many as 120 seeds). It is thick-skinned and juicy, round or triangular in shape, and has a smooth fire-engine red skin when ripe. Beyond the heat, which varies considerably, there is a distinct bell pepper flavor and subtle herbal and fruity notes. Though not as complex in flavor and aroma as the local *chinense* and *baccatum* species, it is widely used fresh and raw as an accompaniment to specialties of three northwestern provinces—Lambayeque, Chiclayo, and Ferreñafe—including *espesado* (a kind of grated corn polenta), *arroz con pato* (duck with rice), and braised goat.

1 IN/2.5 CM LONG BY 1.1 IN/2.8 CM WIDE
(*C. ANNUUM*)

Ají Cerezo, Triangular

Unlike the *ají limo* peppers, which exhibit great phenotypical diversity, there are two main types of *ají cerezo*: round or triangular. The triangular cultivar has medium heat like its round counter-part but it is less fleshy.

1.5 IN/3.8 CM LONG BY 0.75 IN/1.9 CM WIDE
(*C. ANNUUM*)

Ají Cerezo

Ají Cerezo, Triangular

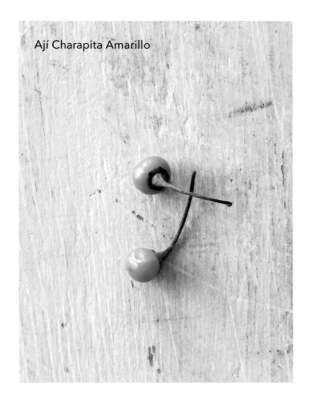

Ají Charapita Amarillo

Ají Charapita Rojo

Ají Charapita Amarillo

If I were to choose a favorite Amazonian *chinense* from Peru, it would have to be this tiny round pepper packed with potent scent and heat to match. A mainstay in the Amazonian region, it ripens from green to yellow or green to red. *Charapita* smells like ripe peaches and strawberries (some say apples), crushed herbs, and cut grass, with hints of wood and turpentine. (I have tasted *charapitas* from different regions in Peru and find marked differences in the intensity of the aroma and fruit shape. For instance, the rounder fruits from the Loreto region are sharper in taste and aroma than the more conical *charapita* from San Martin.) It is mostly used in tart table sauces, particularly one made with the local fruit *cocona*, another member of the Solanacaeae family, which is closely related to the tomato. Just one *charapita* pod, crushed with broad-leaf cilantro (called *sacha culantro* in the Peruvian Amazon) will give incomparable aroma to a rum, pisco, or cacao liquor cocktail, like the Tropical Sour that I serve at my restaurant Cucharamama.

0.2 IN/0.5 CM LONG BY 0.25 IN/0.6 CM WIDE
(*C. CHINENSE*)

Ají Charapita Rojo

This pepper is as delicious as the *ají amarillo*, but slightly less aromatic.

0.35 IN/0.9 CM LONG BY 0.4 IN/1 CM WIDE
(*C. CHINENSE*)

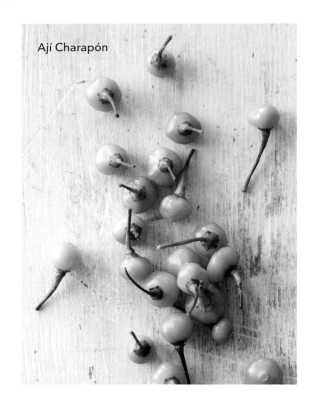

Ají Charapón

Ají Chombo, Red

Ají Charapón

As its name indicates, this is a chubbier cultivar of the tiny *ají charapita*. Though not as tart, it is also deeply perfumed and can be used in any recipe calling for *charapita*.

0.25 IN/0.6 CM LONG BY 0.4 IN/1 CM WIDE
(*C. CHINENSE*)

Ají Chombo, Red

A feature of Panama's Afro-Caribbean cuisine and the key ingredient of a favorite Panamanian vinegar-based hot sauce often laced with mustard and turmeric, which is also called *ají*, this handsome, bright-red *chinense* (there is also a yellow variant) delivers intense heat and complex flavors and aromas like its Caribbean relatives, the Scotch bonnets and the Yucatecan habaneros. In the mixed-race society of Panama, *chombo* is a colloquial term for a black man, and when applied to peppers it signifies "powerful." The province of Chiriquí now leads the country in *ají chombo* production.

2.25 IN/5.7 CM LONG BY 1 IN/2.5 CM WIDE (*C. CHINENSE*)

Ají Cito

Ají Colorado

Ají Cito

The plant bears pendant pods ending in a tiny, sharp tip with a thin and almost translucent skin, growing 6 to a nodule on delicate stems and ripening from light green to dark yellow and mustard yellow, for a beautiful contrast with the broad green leaves. Containing few seeds for its size (about 10 or 11 per pod), it is delicately fruity with medium heat, a hint of sweetness, and a citrusy tang. When green, it has a deep, musky aroma, reminiscent of the fragrance of the Brazilian *pimenta-de-cheiro*.

2.25 IN/5.7 CM LONG BY 0.6 IN/1.5 CM WIDE
(*C. BACCATUM*)

Ají Colorado

This Bolivian *baccatum* has a compact habit of growth and long slender leaves. The calyx is dentate and the pods resemble cayenne-type pods but with narrower shoulders. Sweet with just a touch of heat, it is also pleasantly fruity.

5.5 IN/14 CM LONG BY 0.7 IN/1.8 CM WIDE
(*C. BACCATUM*)

Ají Cristal

Dubbed *ají cristal* for the smooth, almost translucent greenish white to ivory color of the skin at an intermediate stage of ripening, this well-known pepper plays a versatile role similar to that of a medium-hot jalapeño or serrano in Mexican cooking. In Chile, it is used in favorite table salsas like *pebre* (a type of chimichurri), and the curiously christened *chancho en piedra*, literally "pig in a stone," a mixture of tomatoes, onions, cilantro, and fresh hot peppers crushed in a stone mortar (see Chilean "Pig in Stone" Salsa, page 263). It ripens from a light apple green to greenish white, a lovely bright orange, and then to orange-red. But the heat and the flavor notes of fresh grass and cucumber are most pronounced when it is unripe, and that is how people commonly use it. It is crunchy and delicious in salads.

3 IN/7.6 CM LONG BY 1.25 IN/3.2 CM WIDE
(*C. BACCATUM*)

Ají Cristal

Ají Dulce
(Puerto Rico No Burn Pepper)

Puerto Rican No Burn Pepper is the commercial name of this island chinense. A touch of heat gives this sweet, herbaceous, and fruity Puerto Rican *ají dulce* (also called *ajícito dulce*) extra appeal. Green pods growing from thick stems next to corrugated leaves mature to deep red. This is a lovely pepper for *sofrito*, the base of Puerto Rican cooking sauces, and the fresh table sauce *ajilimójili*. Tastier and more aromatic when green, it is a good substitute for the Cuban sweet chinense *ají cachucha*.

0.8 IN/2 CM LONG BY 1 IN/2.5 CM WIDE (*C. CHINENSE*)

Ají Dulce (Puerto Rico No Burn Pepper)

Ají Dulce, Bolivia

Ají Dulce, Bolivia

This Bolivian cultivar has the characteristic bonnet or pattypan squash shape of the emblematic sweet Cuban *ají cachucha* and the *ají dulce* of Puerto Rico and the Dominican Republic, but with a pointed tip like a tail. Thin-skinned with about 40 seeds to a pod, it ripens from pale green to shades of orange and rich, bright red. The small pods hang from sturdy stems, and the calyx shows the typical chinense constriction. It is mildly hot and intensely aromatic.

0.8 IN/2 CM LONG BY 0.6 IN/1.5 CM WIDE
(*C. CHINENSE*)

Ají Dulce, Venezuela

This Venezuelan *ají dulce* cultivar has oval to elliptical pods with small tips. They are about the size of the Yucatecan habanero, but less crumpled looking. The fruit usually becomes lightly ridged as it ripens. The plant can bear as many as 3 pods to a node, and the fruit ripens from the dark green of some jalapeños to crimson. This is a delicious cooking pepper, mildly hot with pronounced floral notes reminiscent of violets and fresh-cut grass. Venezuelans are justly proud of their aromatic *ají dulces*, particularly cultivars from Margarita island (*ají dulce margariteño*), which have achieved iconic status among chefs and the pepper cognosenti.

1.25 IN/3.2 CM LONG BY 0.85 IN/2.2 CM WIDE
(*C. CHINENSE*)

Ají Dulce, Venezuela

Ají Ecuador Hot

This plant is marked by striking, unusual coloring. The graceful lanceolate leaves are a dusky purple; the flowers are the same shade. Even the stems are dark purple. It bears small, thin-fleshed oval pods that ripen from solid dark purple through stages of purple-streaked and gold-streaked dark green to shades of vermilion. More beautiful than flavorful, it delivers a delayed but subdued punch of heat.

0.5 IN/1.3 CM LONG BY 0.1 IN/0.3 CM WIDE
(*C. ANNUUM*)

Ají Ecuador Hot

Ají Guaguao

The *ají guaguao* is a legacy of the pre-Columbian Taíno people on the islands of Cuba and Hispaniola. A tiny and very hot frutescens that grows wild and as a semidomesticate throughout the two islands, it is synonymous for "hot" in local parlance, but it is probably the least understood of the local peppers. In Cuba, it is used in the religious rituals of Afro-Cuban Santería and as a natural remedy for ailments. In my native Oriente region, it is used as a condiment for traditional foods, such as *chilindrón* (goat stew) and *enchilados* (land crabs or other shellfish cooked in a peppery sauce), and in spicy vinegars (see pages 254 and 256). The Taíno name is first mentioned as *huarahuao* by the sixteenth-century naturalist Dr. Francisco Hernández, who reports that it was so named in Hispaniola. It resurfaces in several nineteenth-century botanical or linguistic works. Estéban Pichardo's dictionary of Cuban words, first published in 1836, gives the name *ají guaguao*. Pichardo describes it as having small leaves and pods the size of peppercorns that ripen from yellow to red. He notes that these are mainly used in *tierradentro* (the island's interior), adding that "mockingbirds, thrushes, and wild pigeons eat the fruits, while cattle eat the whole plant." Pichardo also observes that the pulverized pods are used in *sinapismos* (chest poultices) and considered an efficacious cure for *masamorra* (athlete's foot). Interestingly, capsaicin is now known to have antifungal properties.

A Cuban friend brought me a few pods from Yara, a small rural town in eastern Cuba. The plants grew happily in my backyard, though they did not bear fruit until the end of the season. The plant is vigorous, bearing numerous tiny erect pods similar in shape to Tabasco and *pimenta malagueta*, ripening from apple green to shades of orange and red. Like wild chiltepines, *ají guaguao* pods are tender-skinned and detach easily from the calyx when ripe, making it easy for birds like the *sinsonte* (the Cuban mockingbird) to feed on the fruit and propagate its seeds. It sprouts opportunistically on any patch of vacant ground. The plant is a perennial in Cuba, where it begins to fruit between March and April and continues vigorous production for at least two years. People in Yara pick *ají guaguao* when green and ripe to make a spiced vinegar called *mojito* (see Cuban-Style Wild Pepper Vinegar, page 254), which is reminiscent of Tabasco sauce.

0.4–0.5 IN/1–1.3 CM LONG BY 0.15–0.2 IN/0.4–0.5 CM WIDE (C. FRUTESCENS)

Ají Guaguao

AJÍ LIMO

In northern Peru, a large number of chinense cultivars bear the generic name of *ají limo*, though they are also known by regional names such as *bola* (round), *paringa* (white pods), or *picante* (hot). These small peppers come in a plethora of different shapes and are held in great esteem for their intense yet pleasant heat and characteristic fruity taste reminiscent of guava peel, laced with a subtle musky floral fragrance. The fruits often ripen to different colors (red, yellow, purple, ivory white with streaks of purple) on the same plant. Mixed limos like these are regionally called *miscuchos*. When you buy a batch of *ajíes limos* in the market they are usually *miscuchos*, a name that may come from the Quechua word *misk'i uchu* (*misk'i* meaning "sweet," "tasty," or "succulent," and *uchu* meaning "pepper"). In northern Peru *ají limo* is used mostly fresh as a favorite seasoning for *cebiche*. I have also seen people adding it whole to fish soups and taking bites of fresh unripe pods as they eat.

Ají Limo 1

Ají Limo 1 (also Ají Miscucho)

These multicolored *limos* or *miscuchos*, ranging from translucent white with purple streaking to shades of red, come from La Libertad Region in northwestern Peru. While the yellow pods are preferred to add heat to *cebiches*, the less flavorful purple *miscuchos* are often used as garnish.

1.75-1.8 IN/4.4-4.67 CM LONG BY 0.75 IN/1.9 CM WIDE (*C. CHINENSE*)

Ají Limo 2 (Paringa)

A small, pointed pepper in shades of white-streaked purple or purple-streaked white. Mildly hot, pleasantly sweet, and deeply fruity. The slightly turpentine-tinged flavor reminds me of the sweet-and-sour, faintly astringent tropical fruit called hog plum in English (*Spondias purpurea*), also known as *ciruela verde* in Cuba, *jocote* in Mexico, or *mombin* in Brazil.

1.8 IN/4.6 CM LONG BY 1.25 IN/3.2 CM WIDE (*C. CHINENSE*)

Ají Limón

A small, fairly seedy Peruvian pepper with thin, somewhat bumpy skin that ripens from green to yellow-green and finally banana yellow. The shape is an irregular oval with a bulge around the middle, a shallow depression below that, and a lightly pointed tip. Moderately pungent and subtly citrusy, with an underlying bitterness, it lacks the complex flavor of other *baccatums* but looks lovely as a garnish.

1.25 IN/3.17 CM LONG BY 0.6 IN/1.52 CM WIDE (*C. BACCATUM*)

Ají Limo 2

Ají Limón

Ají Moche

Ají Moche (also Ají Mochero or Mocherito)

The *ají moche* is a pepper landrace that takes its name from the Moche River, also the namesake of the small town of Moche in La Libertad Region and the ancient Moche civilization that gave this fascinating part of Peru a distinct identity. It grows on small bushes that thrive in the region's sandy, well-drained soils. A favorite in people's home gardens and on small farms, it was on the verge of disappearance a few years ago when prominent Lima chefs like Gastón Acurio brought attention to its cultural importance and delicious flavor. Ripening from green to a deep yellow with traces of green, the small, tapering, oval pods have flesh of medium thickness. This pepper tastes like a very ripe fruit, with heat that grows gradually and allows subtle floral notes to emerge. Sliced and tossed into *cebiches*, ground into a paste to make a table sauce for grilled chicken, or chopped and combined with a bit of water, lime juice, and salt to make a simple table salsa called *ají soltero* (bachelor sauce), this is the signature pepper of the Moche region. It is my *ají* of choice to flavor Peruvian *cebiches* (this is a popular Peruvian spelling of the word, spelled differently in other parts of Latin America), to season *cangrejos reventados* (cracked crabs with scrambled eggs), to pickle in vinegar, and to eat raw as a fruit.

2.75 IN/7 CM LONG BY 0.8 IN/2 CM WIDE
(C. CHINENSE)

Ají Norteño

As its name indicates, this Peruvian pepper grows in the north of the country, particularly in the fertile valleys of Virú in La Libertad Region and neighboring Lambayeque, which have proven ideal for large-scale commercial pepper cultivation. Despite the exchanges between regions that are bringing many varieties across boundaries, it has remained a strictly local specialty. A large plant with large broad leaves, it bears small, broad-shouldered peppers with a pointed tip, hanging from very long, curved pedicels, ripening from greenish yellow to hues of orange and red. With a pleasant slowly developing, lingering heat, it tastes like apple and guava peel; it is used raw to season seafood, primarily cebiche.

2.5 IN/6.4 CM LONG BY 1.1 IN/2.8 CM WIDE
(*C. BACCATUM*)

Ají Norteño

Ají Omnicolor

This prolific Andean pepper is both a lovely ornamental and a terrific cooking pepper. The pods grow upright on the stems, ripening from yellow with splashes of purple to shades of orange and red. The pods are thin-skinned; the flesh is crunchy and firmly packed with juice, mildly hot, and deeply flavored, with refreshing notes of guava and cucumber.

1.75 IN/4.4 CM LONG BY 0.5 IN/1.3 CM WIDE
(*C. BACCATUM*)

Ají Omnicolor

Ají Panca

Ají Trompito

Ají Serranito

Ají Yellow 2

Ají Panca

This is a robust Andean pepper with large leaves and long, slightly curved pods, showing the characteristic *chinense* constriction of the calyx and bottleneck shoulders. Like the Mexican poblano, it is classified according to the different colors that the pods may acquire when fully ripe—*negro* (very dark), *rojo* (bright red), *colorado* (reddish). Grown intensively along the central and southern coast of Peru, it is usually sun-dried, as its name *panca* ("dried" in Quechua) indicates, and turns a deep burgundy shade. This is the quintessential all-purpose dried pepper of Peru and Bolivia. Ground to a powder to season a wide variety of dishes or soaked in water, reconstituted, and ground to a paste to be used like Mexican chiles in cooking sauces, it lends food a rich reddish plum or deep cherry color. The flavors deepen in drying. Though it is a *chinense*, it is unlike the more assertively hot peppers of that species. Fresh unripe panca is pleasantly mild tasting, with a lightly herbaceous undertone and an overriding fruity effect that blends the tart sweetness of guava with the freshness of cucumber—flavors usually more associated with *baccatum* peppers.

4.5 IN/11.4 CM LONG BY 1.25 IN/3.2 CM WIDE (*C. CHINENSE*)

Ají Serranito

This is an unusual hybrid between a Mexican serrano (*C. anuum*) and a Peruvian *ají amarillo* (*C. baccatum*) grown in Tampico and obtained by the Chile Pepper Institute from a Mexican grower named Octavio Pozo. A small, slender pepper ripening from green to yellow to orange-red, it is mildly hot with the lovely fruitiness of a *baccatum* and some of the herbal greenness of a serrano.

3 IN/7.6 CM LONG BY 0.5 IN/1.3 CM WIDE (*C. BACCATUM*)

Ají Trompito

Shaped like a tiny, deep-red child's toy top when ripe, this pretty pepper from Ucayali, in the Peruvian Amazon, has mild heat and little flavor.

1.1 IN/2.8 CM LONG BY 1.05 IN/2.6 CM WIDE (*C. CHINENSE*)

Ají Yellow 2

Ripening from green to bright yellow, this small late-season chile from Peru stings with bitter heat but seduces with an enticing fragrance. It keeps its color well when pickled in vinegar.

2.5-3.5 IN/6.4-9 CM LONG BY 0.5-0.75 IN/1.3-1.9 CM WIDE (*C. CHINENSE*)

Amazon

Anaheim

Amazon

A lush and vigorous plant bearing 2 or 3 pendant peppers per nodule. It is a late-season pepper in New Jersey, ripening from green through yellow to a slightly mustardy yellow-orange. Fragrant and deliciously herbaceous, it tastes like a ripe, deeply scented apricot. It seems mildly hot, but the heat increases gradually. I got it as a seedling from a nursery that lists it as being of unknown origin, but it looks very much like an *ají pucunucho* from Pucallpa in the Peruvian Amazon.

2 IN/5.1 CM LONG BY 0.4 IN/1 CM WIDE
(*C. CHINENSE*)

Anaheim (also Long Green)

This long, tapering, smooth-skinned pepper can be found in most US markets almost throughout the year, though it is harvested ripe only in August. It originated in New Mexico but was subsequently taken to California by entrepreneur Emilio Ortega, who marketed it as the Anaheim chile. Most of the crop is harvested fully grown but unripe, when the skin is the color of a Granny Smith apple. The flavor also reminds me a little of apples, but with a light, grassy edge; green bell pepper notes; and a hint of dried legumes being soaked for cooking. It is an excellent all-purpose cooking pepper for those who prefer mild-mannered capsicums.

6.25-6.75 IN/15.9-7.1 CM LONG BY 2.25 IN/5.71 CM WIDE
(*C. ANNUUM*)

Antillais

Bell, Ace Hybrid

Antillais

Sweet, floral, and very fruity, with a moderate but pleasurable blast of heat, this is another great all-purpose cooking pepper from the Caribbean. Ridged like a box-pleated skirt, the pods ripen from yellow to orange to crimson. The skin seems a bit leathery, but it is not without crunch.

1.5 IN/3.8 CM LONG BY 1.3 IN/3.3 CM WIDE
(*C. CHINENSE*)

Bell, Ace Hybrid

I adore this small bell pepper. It ripens from dark green to bright red and has a subtle heat that is unusual in bell peppers. It also peels easily when roasted, making it ideal for stuffing. The thick flesh is delicious and crunchy.

3 IN/7.6 CM LONG BY 2.25 IN/5.7 CM WIDE
(*C. ANNUUM*)

Bell, Bull Nose

Bell, Bull Nose

As my use of bell peppers normally exceeds the few pods that I can get from a handful of plants in my garden, I prefer to grow hot peppers because, in the case of some cultivars, just one pod is enough to season seven pots of food. But I can't resist a pretty bell with the perfect shape for stuffing, like the Ace Hybrid, or one with a historical pedigree like the Bull Nose pepper. Though it is unassuming looking, garden and seed catalogs describe it as an heirloom whose claim to fame is to have been planted by Thomas Jefferson at Monticello. Compact and rather small, it has three well-defined lobes, resembling a bull's snout, and a stocky look. William Woys Weaver, my go-to source for heirloom US vegetables, writes about this pepper in his esteemed book *Heirloom Vegetable Gardening*. He explains that a painting of Bull Nose peppers by Philadelphia painter Raphael Peale showed that these were rather small, which explains why historical recipes call for as many as six peppers for a dish. He also believes that the early Bull Nose peppers had a certain degree of heat, pointing to a recipe for "mangoing" (pickling) Bull Nose peppers in Mary Randolph's *The Virginia House-Wife*, where she instructs cooks to remove the seeds and veins to prevent their heat from permeating the entire pod. I grew these peppers from seeds that I sourced from Seed Savers Exchange, and in my garden they have grown into sweet, juicy little pods, heatless with a nice crunch.

2.6 IN/6.6 CM LONG BY 2 IN/5.1 CM WIDE (*C. ANNUUM*)

BELL PEPPERS (*C. ANNUUM*)

These workhorses of the international pepper kitchen are often disparaged as uninteresting cousins of hot peppers. If you judge them as seasoning elements, of course they are boring. The point is that they are vegetables—the great vegetable triumph of the *Capsicum* genus.

Bell peppers are among the largest of all capsicums, and one of several mutant versions that lack the capsaicin-secreting gene. But they are delicious in their own right. They are interesting in every regard except Scoville scores. The green bell pepper has a delightful juicy crunch and a curious taste so characteristic that even wine tasters commonly reach for green bell pepper similes to describe some wines. At one time the only ripe cultivars in stores were red, but those are not to be sneezed at either. Red bell peppers are a textbook example of how sugars develop in a ripening pepper to create a beautiful fruitiness.

Modern growers have learned to exploit the capsicum talent for producing different-colored specimens, as shown by many entries in this gallery of fresh peppers. (For instance, take a look at the multicolored *ají limo* on page 96.) Yellow, orange, purple, and white bells began appearing in specialty shops a couple of decades ago and have now made their way to supermarkets everywhere. Today the great center of bell pepper production is the Netherlands, where they are grown in special controlled-atmosphere greenhouses and shipped around the globe, including to China. We have some excellent sources in the United States, too. (I ordered most of the colored bell pepper cultivars pictured in this book from Happy Quail Farm in Palo Alto, California.)

The different-colored cultivars are all bright-flavored, firm, and beautiful. Many people love eating them raw, to preserve their jewel-like colors. To me, however, bell peppers of all colors cry out for cooking— for being married with other vegetable flavors in the context of a Latin-style sofrito, sizzled in a wok as part of a Chinese stir-fry, or roasted over a flame to bring out a rich, rounded, slightly caramelized flavor with the faintest charred edge. The green version is an indispensable foil to other elements in Cuban dishes, such as stewed black beans or *moros y cristianos* (black beans with rice). And of course they are the stuffing vegetable par excellence, the perfect edible envelope for any number of fillings.

The name "bell pepper" sounds as if it was dreamed up by a modern marketer. But their history goes back to 1699, when an Englishman named Lionel Wafer published an account of his adventures living among the native peoples of Panama. He suffered an injury in the course of his duties as ship's surgeon on a privateer and was abandoned by the crew near Darién. The Indians, according to Wafer, knew "two sorts of Pepper," of which they preferred the "Bird-pepper" (presumably some tiny chiltepín-like hot pepper or a devilish *C. frutescens*) to the "Bell-Pepper."

Was Wafer's "Bell-Pepper" as devoid of heat as today's versions? Probably not. It sounds as if bell types arrived in the eastern United States during the eighteenth century under various names, including "bull nose pepper," and there are unmistakable references to the heat of the bull nose in some early recipes. By the end of the nineteenth century, however, it is clear that bell peppers were one of the capsaicin-free mutations that would enjoy worldwide popularity.

Bell, Admiral

Bell, Blocky Jumbo Colossal

Bell, Chocolate

Bell, Giant Colossal, Red

Bell, Giant Spanish from Reus

Bell, Lavender

Bell, Orange

Bell, Striped Holland

Bell, White

Bell, Admiral

Much admired by growers for its productivity, resistance to disease, and bright golden color, the blocky Admiral cultivar is an industry standard. It is stunningly beautiful, though less sweet and flavorful than ripe red bell peppers.

3.5 IN/8.9 CM LONG BY 3.5 IN/8.9 CM WIDE (*C. ANNUUM*)

Bell, Blocky Jumbo Colossal

This squarish bell, as wide as it is long, is grown from Spanish seed. It is picked red-ripe, when the flesh is deliciously crisp and juicy but sweet. *Colossals* are named for the great size they can attain in commercial plantings.

3.5 IN/8.9 CM LONG BY 3.5 IN/8.9 CM WIDE (*C. ANNUUM*)

Bell, Chocolate

The seed for this handsome "Hershey" bell came from Enza Zaden, a large international seed company based in the Netherlands. It is an early pepper when grown in the western United States, starting out purple in May and darkening to a Hershey's Kiss brown as it ripens. From the outside, the color seems much like a *poblano mulato*. But when you cut it open you will see that the flesh of the pericarp, right under the skin, is red. It has the sweetness of a ripe red bell, with little green pepper flavor.

4.5 IN/11.4 CM LONG BY 2.75 IN/7 CM WIDE (*C. ANNUUM*)

Bell, Giant Colossal Red

A thick-fleshed Colossal with a longer shape than the blocky jumbo, picked red. With pleasant sweetness and crunch, it is excellent for roasting.

5 IN/12.7 CM LONG BY 3 IN/7.6 CM WIDE (*C. ANNUUM*)

Bell, Giant Spanish from Reus (also Pimiento Largo de Reus)

This handsome Catalan pepper takes its name from its size and the twelfth-century city of Reus, the capital of the the fertile Baix Camp region in the province of Tarragona. This is a good example of one major bell type, heavily fleshed and sweet but longer in shape than the blocky peppers that we usually see in US supermarkets. It is roughly rectangular, tapering gently to a narrowed end with 3 or 4 well-defined lobes. Weighing as much as 1 pound/455 grams, it is picked when fully ripe and is much prized for roasting, as it is sweet, succulent, and easy to peel.

6 IN/15.2 CM LONG BY 3 IN/7.6 CM WIDE (*C. ANNUUM*)

Bell, Lavender

Like the chocolate bell, this lovely violet-purple cultivar originally came from Enza Zaden seed, though the strain has now been discontinued by the Dutch giant. Happy Quail, in Palo Alto, California, is probably the only company still growing this pepper in the United States, from their own seed treated against tobacco mosaic virus. In central California, it is an early pepper, picked in May when fully purple, along with other spring peppers like white bells and cubanelles.

3.25 IN/8.3 CM LONG BY 2.55 IN/6.5 CM WIDE (*C. ANNUUM*)

Bell, Orange (also Queen)

As large and square as lavender and chocolate bell peppers, the Queen is picked at an intermediate stage of ripeness, when it has developed a level of sweetness much higher than a green bell but less than a fully ripened red pepper. Crunchy and fresh when raw, it is delicious and showy in salads, but also terrific roasted, cut into strips, and simply seasoned with salt and extra-virgin olive oil.

3.25 IN/8.3 CM LONG BY 2.55 IN/6.5 CM WIDE
(*C. ANNUUM*)

Bell, Striped Holland (also Enjoya)

This new bell pepper cultivar from the Netherlands was found at Wilfred van den Berg's Gelderland nursery in 2013 and officially introduced in 2015 by van den Berg and the Dutch pepper producer 4Evergreen. It was quickly picked up by US specialty produce dealers and is now carried by Whole Foods Market, where I discovered it in early 2016. Striking without being garish, it has alternating sunrise-yellow and warm reddish pink streaks running lengthwise from top to bottom. It is meaty and mildly sweet, with thick walls and very crunchy flesh. The gentle flavor, and the fact that the lovely color contrast isn't destroyed in cooking, make it great for my pepper "steaks" (page 280), which involves roasting, trimming off the tops and bottoms, and unfolding the body of the pepper into a beautifully variegated strip the size of a skirt steak that is ready for panfrying. It's also an excellent stand-in for eggplant in a pepper parmigiana.

3-4 IN/7.6-10.2 CM LONG BY 3-4 IN/7.6-10.2 CM WIDE
(*C. ANNUUM*)

Bell, White

This sturdy, thick-walled, prolific bell was developed in the Netherlands for Eastern European and particularly Hungarian cooks, who traditionally used pale greenish-ivory kinds like the Hungarian wax pepper to make stuffed peppers. It is picked when it has reached full size and lost the original bright green color but not yet started to turn red. In the Northwest United States, it is harvested in early May.

3.75 IN/9.5 CM LONG BY 2.75 IN/7 CM WIDE
(*C. ANNUUM*)

Beni Highlands

Beni Highlands

This is an intensely aromatic *ají* from the Alto Beni (Upper Beni), a rich agricultural area in Bolivia's northern lowlands. It is reminiscent of the northern Peruvian *ají limo,* only hotter, with a more pronounced herbaceous chinense flavor and the tropical guava scent of a baccactum. It is a vigorous plant bearing small, chubby pendant pods that ripen from green to yellow.

1.3 IN/3.3 CM LONG BY 0.75 IN/1.9 CM WIDE
(*C. CHINENSE*)

Bhut Jolokia, Red

This is the famous ghost pepper of India, holder of the *2007* Guinness World Records award for hottest pepper, but dethroned by the Trinidad Scorpion Butch T in 2011. It is thought to be a naturally occurring fluke—*C. chinense* showing some introgression of *C. frutescens* genetics. Hailing from a hilly area of northern India, the part of the world that is closely associated with the hottest peppers and includes part of the neighboring Indian states of Assam (of tea fame), Manipur, and a tribal state called Nagaland, this pepper was brought to the Chile Pepper Institute in 2001 and tested genetically and for heat level in 2005. Once it won Guinness recognition, it became the stuff of legend and a favorite of chileheads worldwide. In one feat of daring in 2013, Anandita Dutta Tamuly, an Indian woman from Assam, ate 51 Bhut Jolokias in 2 minutes and smeared more peppers over her eyes. In Nagaland the pepper is known as *Naga Jolokia* (*naga* for "cobra," and *jolokia* for "pepper") or the *King Naga Chili* (king cobra pepper), for its fierce bite. Chileheads from India and all over the world make the trek to Nagaland's famous Hornbill Festival in Kohima to watch pepper daredevils gulp down the fiendish pepper and writhe in pain. The plant has more *C. chinense* than *C. frutescens* qualities, with the wrinkly, bumpy texture; multiple fruits per node; greenish flowers; and slight constriction of the calyx typical of a chinense. Rough-textured, the long pods ripen to green, then orange with traces of green near the threadlike tip at the end, and finally vermilion red. It is a superhot pepper with a very intense chinense floral aroma and the notes of cut green grass. In India it is used for curries and pickles. Worldwide it appears as a flavoring for many foods, even chocolate bars and truffles.

2.75 IN/7 CM LONG BY 0.8 IN/2 CM WIDE
(*C. CHINENSE*)

Bhut Jolokia, Red

Bishop's Crown (also Chapeu de Frade and Pimenta Cambuci)

This Brazilian pepper is almost too beautiful to eat, though it has lovely flavor reminiscent of guava and cucumber, herbal notes, and a pleasant crunchy texture. The complex, sunken folds of the tip reminded early growers of a bishop's miter or a friar's hat. The apple-green fruits, which dangle from long hook-like curved pedicels, turn light vermilion when ripe.

1.35 IN/3.45 CM LONG BY 3 IN/7.6 CM WIDE
(C. BACCATUM)

Black Cuban

I am smitten with this showy, bushy ornamental from Cuba for its purple foliage and small upright pods with glossy skin, ripening from dark purple to shades of orange and vermilion. Though the pods are seedy (about 48 seeds each), I use them when looking for clean heat and bell pepper flavor with a touch of bitterness.

1.5 IN/3.8 CM LONG BY 0.3 IN/0.8 CM WIDE
(C. ANNUUM)

Bolivian Rainbow

I always find a place for pretty pepper ornamentals in my garden, and I use them whenever I need a hot pepper. True to its name, this Bolivian cultivar bears pods in a rainbow of colors—yellow, purple, orange, mustard, and red—throughout the season. Though not complex in flavor, they deliver a range of heat sensations, from mild to hot, with an edge of bitterness.

0.6 IN/1.5 CM LONG BY 0.4 IN/1 CM WIDE
(C. ANNUUM)

Bishop's Crown

Black Cuban

Bolivian Rainbow

C. baccatum Gold

Bonda Ma Jacques

C. baccatum Gold

This tall, slender Peruvian *baccatum* plant has lovely long, slender pods like small, skinny pea pods that ripen from green to lemon yellow and mustard yellow (like small, skinny pea pods). Fruity like most baccatums, it is also sweet and medium hot. I use it when I can't get ahold of the fleshier *ají amarillo*.

3 IN/7.6 CM LONG BY 0.5 IN/1.3 CM WIDE
(*C. BACCATUM*)

Bonda Ma Jacques

The cuisines of Martinique and Guadeloupe owe their heat and aroma to robust but perfumed chinenses, generically dubbed "piments." A good example is the Bonda Ma Jacques, a Caribbean landrace that sports the smooth and slightly elongated latern-shape of a habanero rather than the crumpled shape of a Scotch bonnet pepper. Ripening from green to yellow, this is a beautiful and moderately fleshy pepper with an intensely herbal, fruity aroma. Use it raw in table salsas or braises.

2 IN/5.1 CM LONG BY 1.25 IN/3.2 CM WIDE
(*C. CHINENSE*)

Brazilian Starfish

This Brazilian pepper really is shaped like a tiny starfish growing upright on a long pedicel. It is pleasantly hot with a crisp, medium-thick flesh that ripens from green to shades of orange and red. When I first planted it, I thought it was a *C. chinense*. But when it blossomed, the green-yellow flecks on the white petals firmly identified it as a *C. baccatum*. The flavor also was that of a baccatum, with tart green guava notes. The pod type is similar to that of the Brazilian Bishop's Crown (see page 112), but less intricately creased.

0.75-1.35 IN/1.9-3.4 CM LONG BY 0.75-3 IN/1.9-7.6 CM WIDE (*C. BACCATUM*)

C. chacoense

Gardeners who love working with the five domesticated *Capsicum* species sometimes hanker to experiment with a wild species. I was especially curious about two: *C. galapagoense* for its mysterious island origin, and *C. chacoense* for its very different birthplace, the Gran Chaco. This is a huge plain stretching from just east of the Bolivian Andes to the border of Paraguay also including parts of western Argentina and a corner of Brazil. It was one of the great regions of prehistoric plant dispersal between South American ecosystems. *C. chacoense* grows wild from the Andean foothills into the main plains area and still is occasionally used by local cooks. It is thought to have been a key player in the history of the *Capsicum* genus— the ancestor of other species including *C. baccatum*. Its remarkable ability to ramp up or suppress capsaicin production, depending on the presence or absence of natural enemies (see the description of Joshua Tewksbury's research on page 18), points to a very old evolutionary strategy that we are just beginning to understand. My *C. chacoense* plants had a Christmasy look, like berry-spangled holly boughs. The small fruits, borne upright, ripened from green to bright red. They were somewhat seedy and a little bitter, but not at all unpleasant, with moderate heat. It was a thrill to have one of the oldest known links with pepper prehistory growing alongside all kinds of modern cultivars in my garden.

0.6 IN/1.5 CM LONG BY 0.4 IN/1 CM WIDE
(*C. CHACOENSE*)

Brazilian Starfish

C. chacoense

C. galapagoense

C. galapagoense (also Wild Galapagos)

This is the real rarity of my collection, a wild *Capsicum* species that somehow traveled from South America to two of the Galapagos Islands. It would have excited Darwin had he known about it. It is what students of plant origins and distribution describe as a narrow endemic, meaning a species that is confined to a single habitat. A curious plant with a creeping habit and a conspicuous light fuzz covering stems and leaves, it bears minute fruits ripening from dark green to matte red, with a pronounced bitterness that overwhelms all other flavors. You will not be able to cook with it, but like me, you may want to grow it for its unique genetic status and peculiar beauty.

0.3 IN/0.8 LONG BY 0.25 IN/0.6 CM WIDE
(*C. GALAPAGOENSE*)

CAYENNE

"Chilli" peppers made a big hit in upper-class English gardens and botanical society collections as hothouse or "stove" ornamentals. ("Stove" was the term for a forcing-room or hothouse.) Just how early cayenne began to enjoy this popularity is not known, but it was certainly well before the late eighteenth century. The beauty of the peppers, especially those belonging to one long, thin, lightly curved type (see Cayenne, Long Slim on page 119), was the big attraction at first. So they were there when people started paying more attention to their uses in cooking.

Cayenne pepper, also spelled "cayan," "chyan," and "kian," was well established in English cookbooks by about the middle of the eighteenth century. It was made by drying the pods set on layers of flour before bashing them to a powder with the flour, moistening the mixture, making it into small loaves, drying them in the hot sun or an oven, and grinding the loaves to powder. Clearly there would have been some thickening action when this type of ground cayenne was used in sauces.

A persistent habit of using cayenne pepper in fish dishes developed in the late eighteenth and early nineteenth centuries, in English as well as English-influenced US cooking. Cayenne was often used in conjunction with vinegar or lemon juice.

I think two factors may have been involved. First, *melegueta* peppers from Africa had a reputation for being a good defense against shipboard plagues, such as dysentery, that killed thousands of African slaves being transported to the New World. This reputation was transferred to New World hot peppers. For a long time, they were reported to be good for digestion and to counter yellow fever and other contagious diseases. Second, in the early nineteenth century an idea took hold among some British and US cooks that vinegar, lemon juice, and other acids were good to eat with fish and seafood. Part of the idea was that they retarded "putrefaction."

In 1830, Dr. William Kitchiner wrote, in the influential cookbook *The Cook's Oracle*, that many people otherwise unable to eat fish found that they could tolerate it if served with cayenne vinegar. This passage was borrowed by Mrs. Beeton and at least one influential US cookbook. It should be no surprise that thereafter cayenne vinegar recipes turned up all over.

Cayennes are bitingly hot, which explains their early use in sauces and as a condiment in powdered form in the United States, particularly in Louisiana. The ground hot pepper powder called "cayenne" is no longer made exclusively with cayenne peppers, but from a range of suitably pungent *C. annuum* cultivars.

Cayenne, Long Gold

Cayenne, Long Thick

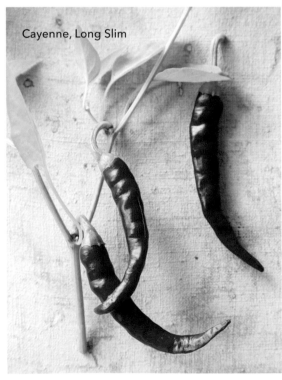

Cayenne, Long Slim

Cayenne, Long Gold

Most of the cayennes developed in the United States are red, not golden yellow like this pretty cultivar. Its clean, direct sharpness works well in Peruvian *cebiches* when I can't find Andean baccatum peppers like the *ají amarillo*. According to food historian William Woys Weaver, a specialist in heirloom North American plants, yellow cayenne-type peppers were most likely brought into the United States through the nineteenth-century sugar trade. Pleasantly hot and clean tasting, it also has a citrusy tang.

3.5 IN/8.9 CM LONG BY 0.6 IN/1.5 CM WIDE (*C. ANNUUM*)

Cayenne, Long Slim

This is a reliable and productive cayenne with vigorous foliage and pendant thin-skinned pods that ripen to a gorgeous red color. Fresh and clean tasting like a vegetable and moderately hot, it seems less acidic than the long gold cayenne, with a very subtle tinge of eucalyptus or bay leaf. Ideal for fresh and fermented salsas.

3.5 IN/8.9 CM LONG BY 0.75 IN/1.9 CM WIDE (*C. ANNUUM*)

Cayenne, Long Thick

Cayenne's origins are shrouded in mystery, though it probably got its name from the capital of French Guiana in South America or a river in that region. It is thought that the Portuguese found a long, slim hot pepper growing at an undetermined location in South America and took it with them on voyages of exploration across the world, allowing them to naturalize in many different spots. Today the term "cayenne type" is unsystematically applied to nearly any kind of hot pepper with a long, slender, slightly curved shape. This long and thick cultivar does beautifully in my New Jersey garden, growing to almost 8 feet/2.4 meters with pods sometimes reaching a whopping 10 inches/25.4 centimeters in length.

8-12 IN/20.3-30.5 CM LONG BY 1.5 IN/3.8 CM WIDE (*C. ANNUUM*)

Chile Cobán

Chile Cochiti

Chile Cobán

This very hot, small *piquín* is named after the town of Cobán in Guatemala's Alta Verapaz region, the heartland of the Kekchi (also spelled *Q´eqchi´*) Maya. When young it puts out lots of small, tender and thickly clustered leaves, many growing out of the central stem and similar to the growth habit of some wild chiltepines. The tiny 5-petaled flowers grow 2 or 3 per node, developing into oval pods that vary in size depending on the cultivar. They grow erect, ripening from lime green to bright vermilion. Called *chile cobanero* in Alta Verapaz, they are used fresh when they taste as complex as some chiltepines, as well as dried and smoked. This chile gives heat and flavor to a beloved local turkey dish called *K´ak´ik,* a soupy stew colored brick red with achiote.

0.5 IN/1.3 CM LONG BY 0.2 IN/0.5 CM WIDE (*C. ANNUUM*)

Chile Cochiti

One of the heirloom landraces of New Mexico; the *chile cochiti* comes from the Keresan Pueblo Indian community of the same name, not far from Santa Fe. Warm days and cool nights don't bother this feisty chile, which is usually grown at an altitude of about 5,200 feet/1,600 meters. These sweet peppers, which ripen from green to bright red, are mildly hot, tasting a bit grassy like a green bell pepper. A versatile pepper good for stir-frying, roasting, or stuffing.

2.75-3.5 IN/6.7-8.9 CM LONG BY 0.75-1.25 IN/1.9-3.2 CM WIDE (*C. ANNUUM*)

Chile Costeño Amarillo

The *costeño* is one of the most commercially important peppers of Oaxaca State, with both yellow and red versions. As the name indicates, it usually comes from the coastal region (*la costa*), where it is used both fresh and (more commonly) dried. The largest town of the region, Pinotepa Nacional, is the main center of production and distribution. For local cooks, the dried chile of choice for *mole negro* is *costeño*, not the rarer *chile huacle negro* from the north. The costeño is also popular inland in the Mixteca, the land of the indigenous Mixtec people, which extends over the state border into Puebla and Guerrero. The Mixtec cooks of Putla District grind dry-roasted *costeños* with garlic and tomatoes to make fresh salsas. Other Oaxacan dishes in which they figure include iguana mole from the coast as well as *guaximole* (made with the strong-tasting seeds of the *guaje* tree) and versions of the soup-stews *chilate* and *chilecaldo*.

This yellow *costeño* strain has slender, pendant cayenne-type pods with curved tips, ripening from green to intense orange-gold. When dried, it becomes translucent like amber. The flavor is lightly fruity and citrusy, with pronounced green pepper notes, high but pleasant heat, and some residual bitterness.

0.75 IN/1.9 CM LONG BY 2 IN/5 CM WIDE (*C. ANNUUM*)

Chile Costeño Amarillo

Chile Costeño Rojo-Amarillo

Chile Costeño Rojo-Amarillo

These beautiful red and yellow *costeños* were grown by Happy Quail Farms in Palo Alto, California. Milder in heat than their Oaxacan and New Mexico counterparts, they can be used in lieu of jalapeños and serranos in table salsas, or be chopped and sautéed in cooking sauces to flavor stews and braises.

2.5 IN/6.4 CM LONG BY 0.8 IN/2 CM WIDE
(*C. ANNUUM*)

Chile de Agua

This popular Oaxacan chile, with a tapered heart shape reminiscent of an especially slender poblano, but a much hotter flavor, is used mostly fresh, either green or when it ripens to a bright red. Oaxacans stuff it like a poblano with a savory pork hash or with cheese and epazote. A combination of pungent *chile de agua* and the more herbal and moderately hot poblano, both cut into strips and sautéed with onions and epazote, and enriched with milk and fresh cheese, is a marvelous first course with hot tortillas, as in Chile Rajas with Epazote, Milk, and Cheese (page 282).

2-2.75 IN/5-7 CM LONG BY 0.8-1.2 IN/2-3 CM WIDE
(*C. ANNUUM*)

Chile de Agua

Chile de Árbol, Green to Red

Chile de Árbol, Purple to Red

Chile de Árbol, Green to Red

Medium-long, lightly curved, and very narrow, with a pointed tip, this wonderful Mexican chile grown in Aguascalientes, Jalisco, Nayarit, and Zacatecas is exceedingly hot. The thin, smooth skin has the attraction of remaining bright red when dried; the color and its very clean taste make it a favorite in table sauces with tomatoes and tomatillos. This is my dried chile of choice to spice hot chocolate because it gives the drink a direct pungency without distracting flavor notes.

2.5 IN/6.4 CM LONG BY 0.5 IN/1.3 CM WIDE
(*C. ANNUUM*)

Chile de Árbol, Purple to Red

Chiles de árbol that are greenish purple when fresh will turn a darker color when ripe. It has sharp, bitter heat and can be used interchangeably with the red-ripening *chile de árbol* when color is not a consideration.

1.75 IN/4.4 CM LONG BY 0.55 IN/1.4 CM WIDE
(*C. ANNUUM*)

CHILE HUACLE

This extraordinary pepper is one of the world's most rarefied, expensive ingredients, in the same class as beluga caviar and white truffles. Its three cultivars are the pride of Oaxaca State in Mexico—more precisely, one tiny region close to the state's northern border called La Cañada (the ravine). La Cañada is a steep river gorge that in colonial times linked Oaxaca's Central Valley with the Tehuacán Valley of neighboring Puebla State. The *chile huacle,* or just *huacle,* is unique to the particular terroir of the gorge, especially the district of Cuicatlán and the township of San Juan Bautista Cuicatlán.

The three *huacle* cultivars—*amarillo* (yellow), *rojo* (red), and *negro* (black)—are delicate, thin-skinned peppers with moderate rather than fiery heat, mostly grown for drying. Despite the frequent claim that *huacle* comes from a word meaning "old" in Nahuatl, the language of the Aztecs, it's clear from dictionaries of the language that the real meaning of *huaqui, uaqui,* and several other forms is "dried." In La Cañada, the fresh peppers sometimes are roasted and cut into *rajas* (strips) for serving like poblanos. They also appear in a robust meat and vegetable soup called *chilecaldo* that used to be eaten in the pepper harvest field. But their status today is too precarious for the region's farmers to make any kind of fresh *huacle* a frequent sight at their own meals.

I grow the three cultivars of the extraordinary Oaxacan *chile huacle* in my garden to feel the pulse of their living history, but when the plants bear fruit my small victory against the fickle garden gods is bittersweet. Outside of their unique terroir and the cultural context that gives them meaning, they are beautiful garden specimens. The truth is that yellow, red, and the especially prized black *chiles huacles* are on the verge of extinction—despite the fact that all of them in dried form were long considered indispensable for some celebrated moles. Oaxaca is the nation's citadel of mole traditions. But do not believe the old saw that it is "the land of the seven moles." An accurate estimate would number over one hundred. The elaborate ones are feast foods for the Day of the Dead, Christmas, New Year's Eve, weddings, christenings, and other special occasions. But the *huacles* that virtually defined some of the state's iconic moles can no longer be counted on.

The members of the Cuicatec and other north Oaxacan indigenous groups who used to grow and dry *huacles* for markets in other parts of Oaxaca—sometimes Puebla and even Mexico City—are an aging, dwindling handful. At present the number of producers stands at five. The plots that they work, where *huacles* share space with other peppers, like the *chilcostle,* or tree crops like limes, are seldom larger than an acre or two. The farmers allow the fruits to ripen on the plants before harvesting and spreading them on open surfaces—the bare earth, cement slabs, or *petates* (straw mats)—exposed to the sun. The peppers are turned every few hours to promote even drying, which may take as long as fifteen days depending on the variability of the weather. It's a lengthy, labor-intensive process that severely limits production. Meanwhile, climate change is hitting La Cañada's tiny fields hard. Hurricanes and heavy rain are an increasing problem, making the seasons for germination and postharvest drying more unpredictable. Plant diseases carried from neighboring states have caused heavy losses in recent years. All these factors drive the prices of real *chiles huacles* higher and higher, especially the most coveted of all: the *huacle negro*—the soul of the *mole negro,* which is often considered the summit of the Oaxacan mole maker's art. In the future it may be a lost soul.

The middlemen who sell peppers at the market in Oaxaca City and in the prosperous Central Valleys generally grade them by size and condition. Premium *huacle negro* specimens can command very high prices. (In the United States, I pay about $150 per pound.) The well-deserved *huacle negro* mystique fosters a tendency for growers to focus on them more intensively than their red and yellow cousins, which consequently become even scarcer. It's not surprising that budget-minded cooks turn to cheaper substitutes for the *huacle negro* and replace the other two with somewhat similar peppers that are easier to find.

Huacles aren't the sole base of the great Oaxacan moles. The most elaborate have traditionally involved combinations of different peppers—mulatos, guajillos, anchos, or others, along with carefully judged amounts of special regional cultivars such as the different *huacles* from La Cañada. But in the past, the art of mixing and matching peppers for moles didn't usually involve deception. Today, on the other hand, even celebrated restaurants are rumored to tout their moles as bona fide *chichilo, mole negro, mole amarillo,* and so forth, with only broken morsels or scarcely an iota of any Oaxacan *chile huacle.* Substantial amounts of burned corn tortillas and pepper seeds ground together with the other ingredients of the mole paste now contribute more heavily to the blackness of *mole negro.* (The burned seeds and tortillas have been used for a long time, but historically they weren't meant to be a crutch.)

Meanwhile, farmers in Zacatecas State, six hundred miles away, managed to acquire seeds from La Cañada more than a decade ago. Since then they have flooded Oaxacan markets with inferior-tasting *huacle negro,* sold as the real thing at a fraction of the very lowest price that local farmers can manage even when selling at a loss. Lovers of premium-quality *huacles* consider this rank piracy.

In recent years concerned Oaxacans have been coming together to call attention to the plight of La Cañada growers and the threat to a unique Oaxacan patrimony. The Universidad Tecnológica de los Valles Centrales (UTVC) has formed an alliance with the remaining Cuicatlán growers and local representatives of Slow Food México and Oxfam México to create a strategy. One major priority is seeking protected denomination of origin status for La Cañada *huacle negros* and the black *mole negro* of Oaxaca. Another is sheltering the plants and the harvested fruit from the elements at crucial stages. UTVC is working to develop drying platforms that can be covered if needed. A UTVC project is also underway to make *huacle* cultivars less susceptible to disease. Local chefs and journalists have pitched in, urging the state and federal government to take a role.

An initial *huacle* festival, La Primera Feria Internacional del Chile Huacle, was held in October 2014 at San Juan Bautista Cuicatlán to publicize the rescue effort. I applaud the friends of Oaxacan moles and La Cañada *huacles* for their mission, which deserves to be taken up by champions of Mexican cuisine in the United States.

At my New Jersey latitude, no kind of *chile huacle* reaches its biggest size or real flavor potential. But they certainly are stunning garden plants. The fruit usually has a somewhat stubby tapered shape, though there is a wide range of conformations. Some kinds can be as long as a small cubanelle. Shorter ones often resemble broad-shouldered poblanos or triangular versions of a small, thin-skinned bell pepper, with a sunken stem attachment and pointed apex.

Chile Huacle

Chile Huacle Amarillo

The specimens I planted have borne long, thin-skinned pendant pods ripening from green to an intense salmon-orange color. They are even more beautiful when dried, a translucent amber like red agate, carnelian, or Chiapas red amber. The flavor is discreet and neutral, neither sharp nor fruity. It reminds me less of other Mexican peppers than of the crumb of a fresh loaf of country bread, but with a slight tinge of bitterness and the moderate heat typical of *huacles*. When reconstituted and ground in seasoning pastes, it lends an earthy raw sienna color that not surprisingly is characteristic of the traditional Oaxacan *mole amarillo*.

3.1-3.5 IN/7.9-8.9 CM LONG BY 1-1.25 IN/2.5-3.2 CM WIDE
(*C. ANNUUM*)

Chile Huacle Negro

This cultivar has been called the king of the *moles*, those iconic pinnacles of Oaxacan cuisine. A black mole made with *huacles negros* is one of the world's great luxuries. For best quality the peppers are picked at the peak of ripeness, when the fruit is just a bit soft to the touch. If harvested sooner, they may develop an ashy gray color on drying. But when properly handled, they turn deep black with a gorgeous dull sheen like unpolished ebony, with the texture of ancient parchment. A paste made from grinding unroasted black *huacles* is dark mahogany with reddish and olive green undertones. The roasted and ground peppers yield a glossy, rich black paste, necessary for the right effect in Oaxacan *mole negro* and *chichilo negro*. But even more crucial is the flavor. It is the most complex and intensely fruity of the three *huacle* cultivars. Its sweetness and delicate herbal acidity remind me of a mixture of prunes and raisins with subtle notes of bell pepper and artichoke, all

playing against a pleasant backdrop of moderate heat. The plant is beautiful and graceful. When the pods ripen, it looks like a little Christmas tree with chocolate-colored ornaments hung on the branches.

2-2.5 IN/5.1-6.4 IN LONG BY 2 IN/5 CM WIDE
(*C. ANNUUM*)

Chile Huacle Rojo

The pods, like those of the other *huacles*, can vary a lot in shape. They ripen from deep green to different reddish brown shades—sometimes a mahogany brown like a *mulato* poblano. When dried, they look more reddish bronze, but the flesh brightens up to something between rich cherry red and orange after soaking and reconstituting. The flavor is subtle rather than intense, with little of the sweetness found in the *huacle negro*. They have moderate heat and slightly acid background notes suggesting unripe papaya. In *moles*, the *huacle rojo* contributes beautiful color and is often used in combination with other peppers.

2.1 IN/5.3 CM LONG BY 2.1 IN/5.3 CM WIDE
(*C. ANNUUM*)

Chile Jalapeño

Chile Jalapeño

I think of the jalapeño as the chicken of the pepper world, since US cooks who need a substitute for any other hard-to-find hot pepper routinely turn to it as a safe backup. Mexicans might prefer the sharper, cleaner heat of serranos to make *salsas crudas* (uncooked table sauces), but they love the fleshy, larger, and somewhat sweeter fresh jalapeño as a vegetable. Green jalapeños have a distinct green bell pepper flavor contributed by pyrazines and the signature subtle apple flavor of alcoholic esters like (Z)-3-hexenyl 3-methylbutanoate, which jalapeños share with *C. chinense* and the *C. frutescens, pimenta malagueta*. In Mexico and many Central American countries, green and red jalapeños are pickled in vinegary escabeches or cut into *rajas* (strips) to give mild heat to a variety of foods, including the fillings for tamales. Full-sized jalapeños (usually ripe, but sometimes still green) are often dried and smoked, becoming wrinkled and turning a rich burgundy or ashy light brown. In that form they become the hotter, infinitely more interesting smoky chipotle, which assumes many names—*meco, tamarindo, morita*—depending on the specific cultivar or region. The chipotle is a powerhouse of concentrated hammy flavor like a good Spanish smoked paprika. In the United States, both green and ripe jalapeños are canned, pickled, and also fermented in brine to make hot sauces. Red jalapeños are preferred to other, less fleshy red peppers for the ever-popular Sriracha sauce (see page 260 for Miracha, my take on Sriracha sauce).

3.5 IN/8.9 CM LONG BY 1.25 IN/3.2 CM WIDE (*C. ANNUUM*)

Jumbo jalapeños on display at a Mexico City street food market.

Chile Jalapeño, Jumbo

Chile Macho

Chile Jalapeño, Jumbo

Everything about the jumbo jalapeño is vigorous, even the way the seedlings tower over other plants a couple of weeks after sprouting. This large, plump jalapeño ripens to a lovely red. It is thick-skinned and very mild, with a strong bell pepper aroma. I like to add it to dishes as *rajas* (strips) when I want to keep heat to a minimum. It is also a good, meaty chile for a savory stir-fried dish like Tiger Skin Peppers (page 279) or cut into slices as a garnish for salads.

**2.75 IN/7 CM LONG BY 1.1 IN/2.8 CM WIDE
(*C. ANNUUM*)**

Chile Macho

This semidomesticated Mexican *chiltepín* type lives up to its name, *macho* which means just what it sounds like. The plant is stunningly vigorous, with stubby conical pods that have a rounded point and grow erect on strong, long pedicels. Maturing from deep green to shades of orange, the *chile macho* is burning hot, with an assertive and unexpected flavor that reminds me of menthol, eucalyptus, or bay leaves when green. Crush a couple of pods and add to a soup, a cooking sauce, or a salsa for a touch of red-blooded macho heat and a bit more.

**0.75 IN/1.9 CM LONG BY 0.6 IN/1.5 CM WIDE
(*C. ANNUUM*)**

Chile Manzano
(also Rocoto, Yellow)

Because of its unique climatic requirements, *C. pubescens* did not travel outside of the Andean range. However, yellow cultivars were taken to Central America and Mexico under the names *chile manzano*, *chile perón*, and *chile caballo*. (*Manzano*, which means "apple," refers to the shape; the color must have reminded someone of a pear, which is *perón* in Spanish. *Caballo*, or "horse," is more puzzling, but it certainly kicks like one.) Since my local Latin market started carrying Mexico-grown fresh *manzanos*, I have become an admirer and prefer them to the frozen red Andean *rocotos*—which, however, are easier to find and can be very good. *Manzanos* have firm flesh and a gorgeous golden color. Less complex in flavor than a baccatum, they have sharper heat, little acidity, and an underlying sweetness with bell pepper notes. Because of their medium size and round shape, they are perfect for stuffing with savory Peruvian-style meat fillings before steaming or baking. Cooked either whole or quartered in syrup, they become the best possible candied fruit to eat with a Latin *queso blanco* or a creamy fresh chèvre. I also adore *manzanos* in fermented Sriracha-style salsas (see Miracha, page 260) or fresh savory salsas calling for tart Andean fruits like tamarillo (see Rocoto and Tree Tomato Sauce, page 270).

2.5 IN/6.4 CM LONG BY 2 IN/5 CM WIDE (*C. PUBESCENS*)

Chile Manzano

Chile Mirasol

Chile Pasilla

Chile Mirasol

In Spanish, *mirasol* means "sunflower," or more literally, "sun gazer," an apt name because the pods grow pointed upright on the plant. Not to be confused with the dried Andean pepper called *ají mirasol*, it is the source of the popular dried guajillo. It is a shame that more cooks are not familiar with fresh *mirasol* in its own right. It is a beautifully shaped pepper, one of the ancestors of the New Mexico pod type. It ripens from green to shades of brown to a bright red and has crunchy, medium-thin flesh and a slightly tart taste with a pleasant underlying bitterness that is reminiscent of red currants. I like it in salads and as a garnish.

2.2 IN/5.6 CM LONG BY 0.4 IN/1 CM WIDE
(*C. ANNUUM*)

Chile Pasilla (also Chile Chilaca)

This Mexican chile is known as *chilaca* in many parts of Mexico, but commercial nurseries often list the seedlings only by the name the pepper acquires when dried: *pasilla*, which means "little raisin" in Spanish. Long and narrow, the fresh peppers mature from a deep olive green to a dark mahogany with a purplish tinge. They can be thinly sliced crosswise and added to stir-fries as an accent. The taste of my fresh chilacas reminds me of a mixture of cucumber and bell pepper, with mild heat. When dried, the pods turn wrinkly like ancho chiles, but much darker, almost black. Then they become infinitely more interesting: sharply hotter with deep, tannic notes. Dried pasillas are important in moles, but when smoked they are usually stuffed.

6-12 IN/15.2-30.5 CM LONG BY 1 IN/2.5 CM WIDE
(*C. ANNUUM*)

Chile Petenero

Chile Poblano

Chile Petenero

This is one of the most important traditional chiles of Guatemala—the others are the *guaque* (guajillo), *cobanero* (a type of chiltepín), and the dried chile chocolate, which are *C. annuum* and *C. frutescens*. Chinense types, including the handsome yellow *petenero*, were most likely introduced into the country in the postconquest period. They now thrive in the Petén Department on Guatemala's Caribbean coast, where they are known generically as habaneros and grown commercially as an export crop. Very hot, with thin skin and few seeds (about 5), the *petenero* is highly perfumed; just a couple of slivers can season a pot of food or a table sauce. In Petén, it is also processed by farming cooperatives into commercial sauces with seasoning vegetables such as onion, garlic, and carrots.

1.1 IN/2.8 CM LONG BY 1 IN/2.5 CM WIDE (*C. CHINENSE*)

Chile Poblano (also Ancho Gigantea)

If you are looking for a large poblano with medium-thick flesh and mild heat, this is a good choice. It ripens from dark green to red and can be easily peeled when roasted to make *rajas* (strips) or to use for stuffing.

3.25-3.75 IN/8.3-9.52 CM LONG BY 1.8-2.25 IN/4.6-5.7 CM WIDE (*C. ANNUUM*)

Chile Poblano

Chile Poblano (also Ancho)

Having the same elegant heart shape as the piquillo pepper, the poblano is the quintessential pepper for stuffing in Mexico and is also delicious cut into *rajas* (strips) and sautéed with onions. There are several poblano cultivars distinguished not only by their shape but also by color. Some are a glossy deep green maturing to a reddish mahogany, while some ripen to an almost chocolate brown. They can be used fresh at all stages of ripeness. The name under which I bought this cultivar is somewhat confusing. Strictly speaking, the terms *ancho* (broad) and *mulato* (literally, mulatto) are used only for dried versions of the poblano. Anchos are made from cultivars that ripen from green to bright red and turn wrinkled and dark brown in drying. Chocolaty-brown ones become the almost black mulatos.

2.5 IN/6.4 CM LONG BY 1.8 IN/4.6 CM WIDE (*C. ANNUUM*)

Chile Poblano, Mulato Isleño

Chile Poblano, Mulato Isleño

This beautifully shaped poblano ripens from deep green to reddish brown to a glossy chocolate brown. It is delicious for stuffing but tastes even better when dried. It is medium hot with a pronounced prune flavor that deepens with drying, developing notes of star anise that are lovely in any mole.

3 IN/7.6 CM LONG BY 1.8 IN/4.6 CM WIDE (*C. ANNUUM*)

Chile Serrano

Widely available in the United States, the Mexican serrano ("mountain" pepper) is a small, pungent chile with a clean, sharp flavor. Mexicans favor it over jalapeños for guacamole and fresh salsas. It is delicious in a textured salsa made in a stone *molcajete* (see Serrano Chile and Tomato Salsa, page 266).

2.8 IN/7.1 CM LONG BY 0.6-0.8 IN/1.5-2 CM WIDE
(*C. ANNUUM*)

Chile Serrano Tampiqueño

This Mexican serrano hailing from Tampico is moderately hot with a pronounced green bell pepper taste. Use it in fresh table salsas when you want a tempered heat.

1.75 IN/4.4 CM LONG BY 0.6 IN/1.5 CM WIDE
(*C. ANNUUM*)

Chile Serrano

Chile Serrano Tampiqueño

CHILTEPÍN (*C. ANNUUM* VAR. *GLABRIUSCULUM*)

The *Capsicum annuum* species is both the greatest world traveler of all peppers and the one found in the most incredibly diverse forms. It is also the domesticated species whose origin is least well understood. By rights you'd expect the oldest link with wild annuum ancestors to exist in or near the western Amazon, close to the known precursors of the four other domesticated *Capsicum* species. Instead, the great stronghold of this ancestral link lies thousands of miles away in Mesoamerica and North America. It grows there like a rambunctious weed, along with numberless domesticated *annuum* descendants that the genius of Aztec, Maya, and other pre-Hispanic civilizations created over many centuries without benefit of research centers.

The weed-like predecessor of all domesticated annuums goes by a host of names, including *chiltepín*, *tepín*, or *tecpín* (all from the Nahuatl word *tecpin*, for "flea"), as well as *chile pequín* and *chile piquín*. Botanists call it *C. annuum* var. *glabriusculum*, with *glabriusculum* meaning "smoothish little object." You have only to see a container full of round, ripe chiltepín fruits, which look like shiny scarlet buckshot, to understand why it is so named.

Wild chiltepines are endemic to a wide range of ecosystems from southern Mesoamerica to north of the Rio Grande. The lives of people and chiltepines are most deeply interlinked in the swath of desert running from the Mexican states of Sonora and Chihuahua into Arizona, New Mexico, and Texas. One of the best descriptions of the area was written in the eighteenth century by Ignaz Pfefferkorn, a German Jesuit missionary who had spent eleven years working among the Indians of Sonora. After describing a cultivated chile variety that was a great favorite with Spanish settlers in the area, he goes on to say,

"A kind of wild pepper that the inhabitants call chiltepín is found on many hills. It grows on a dense bush about an ell in height [slightly less than 4 feet/1.2 meters] and is similar in shape and size to the thick juniper berry, except that it is not black, but all red, like the Spanish pepper. It is more bitingly sharp than the latter, yet it is manna to the American [Indian] palate and is used with every dish with which it harmonizes. It is placed unpulverized on the table in a salt cellar and each fancier takes as much of it as he believes he can eat. He pulverizes it with his fingers and mixes it with his food."

Father Pfefferkorn's account rings true in every detail. The plant is indeed a dense bush that grows throughout the region, and the fruits are about the size of juniper berries. When dried in the open air, they are light and brittle, easy for diners to crush between their fingers and sprinkle over food. People in Sonora still eat chiltepín with every meal and feel cheated when they can't get it.

No plant on Earth is a better argument for intelligence in the plant kingdom than this little wild chile in its Sonoran habitat. The chiltepín can thrive under many conditions, with scattered populations at high or low altitudes, in jungles or grasslands. But it really seems to come into its own in the high Sonoran Desert. There the pepper bushes grow to great height and size, becoming a magnet for birds during the fall ripening season. At that point the intelligence of the chiltepín comes to the fore, expressed by an amazing range of features.

First of all, the fierce bite of the capsaicin lurking under the berries' attractive surface is a repellent to all marauding animals—but not to birds like the mockingbird, which are unaffected by the fiery substance. At the same time, the vine-like chiltepín stems have the habit of becoming so closely entwined with other bushes and vegetation that it can be hard for any creature without wings to get near the fruit. It's the perfect setup for hungry birds to feast on peppers before flying off to another roosting spot and dispersing the seeds to form future bushes. Another clever strategy involves the need of the pepper bushes to avoid strong sunlight. They do best when they take root in the shade of taller trees—and the fact that some of the big local shade trees, such as hackberries, happen to have berries somewhat resembling chiltepines in shape and size increases the chances that feeding birds will be attracted and then will excrete pepper seeds in favorable spots.

Despite the difficulty of harvesting chiltepines in the wild, determined gatherers, called *chilteperos,* trek out to the pepper bushes every year during a roughly one-month window in (usually) late September and early October. They bring in the early crop bright green, then wait for the rest to ripen to brilliant red. The exact timing and the size of the harvest depend on just when any summer rains arrive. The plant likes desert conditions as long as it can enjoy shade and at least one good dose of well-timed moisture. Prolonged drought can mean no harvest at all, while sudden floods can wipe out a whole crop. Experts seriously worry that unpredictable events in recent growing seasons may augur long-term derangement of the wild plant's growth cycle.

Not surprisingly, people in chiltepín territory have long been interested in less chancy and labor-intensive ways of obtaining the fruit. In some corners of the region, the bushy weeds share commercial attention with semidomesticated or domesticated varieties. But Sonoran fans are convinced that there is no substitute for the flavor of wild chiltepín. Naturally it commands higher prices than any alternative.

Chiltepín, Sonora Wild

The wild Sonora chiltepín can be recognized by a warm fragrance like sun on dry grass together with a sharp, clean, refreshing bite—a quick burst of strong heat that doesn't build in the mouth or unfold into lingering complexities. The appearance of the berry is also a giveaway. The rounder the shape, the closer it is to the true wild form. An oval or oblong shape indicates some degree of domestication.

0.4 IN/1 CM LONG BY 0.3 IN/0.8 CM WIDE
(*C. ANNUUM* VAR. *GLABRIUSCULUM*)

Chiltepín, Sonora Amarillo

Similar in growth pattern to the wild Sonora chiltepín, the plant's stems branch off close to the ground to produce a spreading shape. The leaves are tender and almost heart-shaped. The round upright pods grow on long pedicels, sometimes 2 per node, ripening from apple green to yellow. A student of chiltepines, ethnobotanist Kraig H. Kraft, explains that in Sonora, the yellow chiltepines are considered an anomaly and not commercialized. When green, it is sharply hot with a flavor reminiscent of bell pepper and tomato leaves laced with a touch of bitterness.

0.4 IN/1 CM LONG BY 0.3 IN/0.8 CM WIDE
(*C. ANNUUM* VAR. *GLABRIUSCULUM*)

Chiltepín, Tarahumara

This wild chiltepín is named after the Tarahumara, a native American people living in northern Mexico's Sierra Madre Occidental in the state of Chihuahua. In my New Jersey garden, it is a tallish plant with a strong stem that rises without branching and then spreads with a bushy habit of growth and larger leaves than other chiltepines. The pods seem pendular when they first emerge, but they grow erect, ripening from deep green to greenish brown and then to a bright orange-red at the end of the growing season. The tiny, erect pods are elongated, almost conical, fairly thick-skinned, and full of seeds (about 10 to a pod), with an unusual tomato leaf aroma reminiscent of a *chinense* and a clean, intense heat. Delicious pickled in vinegar, this is also the kind that I like to simply crush when green to add to food at the end of cooking for clean heat and flavor, along with beguiling aroma.

0.5 IN/1.3 CM LONG BY 0.25 IN/0.63 CM WIDE
(*C. ANNUUM* VAR. *GLABRIUSCULUM*)

Chiltepín, Pima

My *Pima chiltepín* bore conical fruits similar to those of the Tarahumara chiltepín and not the rounder pods that I was expecting. Another surprise was the taste of the fresh pods, bitingly hot but markedly fruity, with the taste of soursop (*guanábana*) leaves.

0.7 IN/1.8 CM LONG BY 0.2 IN/0.5 CM WIDE
(*C. ANNUUM* VAR. *GLABRIUSCULUM*)

Chiltepín, Sonora Wild

Chiltepín, Tarahumara

Chiltepín, Sonora Amarillo

Chiltepín, Pima

Chimayo

Chimayo

Pungent and delicious, this pepper is the pride of the beautiful Chimayo district of New Mexico, not far from Santa Fe. Scientists describe it as a local landrace that was developed from Mexican chiles brought to the region by early Spanish settlers through a combination of human nurture and natural adaptation to their new terroir.

4.5 IN/11.4 CM LONG BY 1.3 IN/3.3 CM WIDE
(*C. ANNUUM*)

Chinchi Uchu

This tiny Peruvian chinense, a late-season pepper, has the distinction of having been mentioned by sixteenth-century Peruvian chronicler Garcilaso de la Vega in his *Royal Commentaries of the Incas and General History of Peru*. He describes it as follows: "Another small round pepper resembles a cherry with its stalk. It is called chinchi uchu. It is incomparably stronger than the rest and only small quantities of it are found wherefore it is the most esteemed." Compared to other Peruvian peppers like the *ají amarillo* and *rocoto*, and even *ají panca* (another *C. chinense*), the *chinchi uchu* packs a mightier punch, combined with the characteristic intense floral chinense aroma and fruity qualities. In the Vilcanota Valley of the Cuzco Region, a stronghold of pre-Hispanic traditions, it is commonly dried for use as *chaki uchu* (from Quechua ch'aki, meaning "dried" or "withered").

1 IN/2.5 CM LONG BY 1.4 IN/3.6 CM WIDE (*C. CHINENSE*)

Chinchi Uchu

Congo, Nicaragua

In Latin America, particularly in Central America and the Caribbean, when a pepper is known by the name of Congo, it is understood that is very strong and hot, as the word evokes the reputed strength of Africans brought from the Congo to this region as slaves in colonial times. In the case of this very hot Nicaraguan cousin of chiltepines, it might also refer to the strong Congo monkeys that roam the forests of the country. The small conical pods are borne erect on bushy plants and ripen from green into shades of red. As hot as their name indicates, they are also very fruity and pleasantly floral and herbal. They are a favorite condiment for the yuca and pork crackling salad *vigorón* and the large meat-filled *nacatamal* (a large *tamal* made with a silky strained *masa*), and are commonly used to make *chileros* (peppers pickled in vinegar).

2.5 IN/6.4 CM LONG BY 2 IN/5 CM WIDE
(*C. ANNUUM* VAR. *GLABRIUSCULUM*)

Cubanelle

Cubanelle peppers mature to red but are normally sold when they are pale green. They are long and glossy, with a tapered shape. Mild, thin-fleshed, and low in water content, they are ideal for frying, which explains their generic name Italian frying pepper or *pimiento de cocinar*. This is the sweet fresh pepper of choice in Hispanic Caribbean cooking.

6.15 IN/15.6 CM LONG BY 2.75 IN/7 CM WIDE
(*C. ANNUUM*)

Congo, Nicaragua

Cubanelle

Criolla Sella

Cumarí (See Pimenta Cumari)

Criolla Sella

This is a Bolivian pepper with pendant pods ripening from green to deep orange-yellow and mustard yellow. Lightly ribbed and thin-skinned, this small pepper has a small placenta bearing many seeds (about 31 per pod). Fruity, perfumed, and sweet like a Caribbean guava, it stings with sharp but modulated heat at the back of the tongue.

1.75-2.75 IN/4.4-7 CM LONG BY 0.4 IN/1 CM WIDE
(*C. BACCATUM*)

Dátil, Hot

The *dátil*, whose name means "date" in Spanish, is the only US landrace of the *Capsicum chinense* species. When I first managed to acquire seeds and start growing this pepper in my garden, I had heard of its adoptive home of St. Johns County, Florida, and the accounts of its origin that circulated for generations in St. Augustine, the county seat. It's quite a tangled tale, starting in the eighteenth-century settlement of New Smyrna, 60-plus miles/100-plus kilometers south of St. Johns County.

In 1768, an ambitious New Smyrna plantation owner tried to import a mixed Old World work-force, including a large contingent from Minorca, to grow indigo and other crops on a vast scale. The scheme failed, and by 1777 the Minorcans had headed north to St. Augustine, where their descendants still proudly claim to be the only Minorcan immigrant community in the United States. Today their name is linked with various dishes, including rice pilaus and seafood stews or chowders that local "experts" long touted as age-old classics of Minorcan cuisine. And the signature touch that was said to prove the relationship was the use of blazing hot *dátil* peppers—there were various theories about how they acquired the name—carried to Florida from Minorca.

I was fascinated with the story. But the details didn't quite ring true. For one thing, the food connections didn't sound at all like Balearic Islands cuisine as I understand it. Minorca does have its celebrated seafood stew, the *caldereta* made with the local spiny lobster, but it has no resemblance to the Florida chowders. Nor does the Minorcan climate seem suitable for growing chinense peppers, which generally favor humid conditions. Besides, the rich floral perfume of the *dátil*—one of the most aromatic chinenses—is essentially foreign to the Old World Minorcan kitchen, no matter how beloved it may be in Florida.

Dátil, Hot

It all didn't add up. So I was glad to learn that patriotic St. Johns County Minorcans have recently started backing off their earlier insistence that the *dátil* came with their ancestors to New Smyrna and were carried to St. Augustine. Local historian David Nolan has unearthed a 1937 article in the *St. Augustine Record* by an earlier city chronicler, Edward W. Lawson, who was an indefatigable sifter through Spanish- and English-language records. Lawson traced the local arrival of *dátil* peppers to one Stephen (or Esteban) B. Valls, who was manufacturing jams and jellies in St. Augustine during the 1880s when he sent to Cuba for seeds of *dátil* peppers—and not just Cuba, but my hometown, Santiago de Cuba in Oriente province!

In today's Cuba it is rare to find cooks using hot peppers except for the tiny semiwild *ají guaguao*. But before the Spanish conquest, all three species of the annuum-chinense-frutescens complex grew on the island. Though the taste for hot peppers was largely tamed by demographic changes that brought many Asturians and Galicians to Cuba after the war of independence, those capsicums had thrived for centuries before that under colonial rule. If Valls (a Catalan name still common in Santiago) was able to order *dátil* seeds in the 1880s, these very hot and fragrant peppers must still have been going strong in eastern Cuba.

My curiosity had already been stimulated by the name *dátil*. To anyone who has seen real dates being grown and harvested, applying the name to similarly shaped capsicums needs no explanation. Sure enough, when I turned to the pepper entry in Esteban Pichardo's authoritative nineteenth-century dictionary of provincial Cuban words, I found that under "Agi" in the original 1836 edition he listed the *dátil* "for its resemblance to its namesake." The expanded 1849 edition (with the revised spelling "ají") gives the further information that "the aroma is strong and arousing" and that it "is among the most used" of Cuban peppers.

A small but illuminating 1947 newspaper article by Mrs. E. W. Lawson in the *St. Augustine Record* clearly shows that the *dátil* continued to be associated with Caribbean influence in St. Augustine. It describes two dishes supposedly brought there from Old Spain, "gundinga" and "mondonga." Any Cuban or Puerto Rican will know at once that these are actually *gandinga* and *mondongo*—respectively, a robust dish of braised pork kidneys, heart, and liver; and an equally fortifying tripe and vegetable stew. To me, the most telling details of Mrs. Lawson's account are the mention of *dátil* peppers in both dishes and the fact that Minorca isn't mentioned at all.

Only one conclusion makes sense to me: *Dátil* peppers reached St. Augustine not through some eighteenth-century route from Minorca, but much later through a Cuban who got the seeds from my own birthplace, Santiago. And a Cuban culinary connection—perhaps unrecognized by Minorcan descendants determined to call attention to their own colorful heritage—persisted in the area for many decades.

In any case, the long-established St. Augustine Minorcan community eagerly took to the new arrival. By the early twentieth century their cuisine had absorbed many elements of the southeastern US cooking styles found from southern South Carolina to northern Florida, and they were used to claiming versions of local dishes as their own without applying rigorous tests of authenticity. In the same accommodating vein, they easily fell into the assumption that they had been responsible for bringing *dátils* to the New World from Minorca and introducing them into St. Augustine kitchens, one hundred years before Stephen Valls placed his order for seeds.

The *dátil* pepper is so good that I can't blame anyone for wanting to claim credit for introducing it to Florida. With a dangling pod type more blocky and elongated than most *chinenses*, it bears more than a passing resemblance to a freshly harvested, not yet dried date. It ripens from green to deep yellow and is so aromatic that just cutting open one pepper fills the room with a flowery, slightly musky perfume startling even among the fragrant tribe of chinenses. It is extremely hot by most chinense standards, though nowhere close to the record-eclipsing heat of Trinidad Scorpion or Carolina Reaper. The flavor is also delightfully fruity, with a refreshing note of acid.

2-2.25 IN/5-5.7 CM LONG BY 0.75-1 IN/1.9-2.5 CM WIDE (*C. CHINENSE*)

Dátil, Sweet

These are bright red fruits with a pointed and slightly crumpled shape. Not unlike the Venezuelan *ají dulce* in taste and aroma, this *dátil* sibling is a fantastic cooking pepper, marrying a delicious mild heat with the latent sweetness and fruitiness masked by the fiery heat of other *dátils*. Use in any dish calling for great aroma and complex flavor like Puerto Rican or Dominican-style soups, stews, braises, and rice dishes.

1.25-1.5 IN/3.2-3.81 CM LONG BY 0.75-1.1 IN/1.9-2.8 CM WIDE (*C. CHINENSE*)

Dátil, Sweet

Diente de Perro

Earbob

Diente de Perro

Found growing as a semidomesticate all over Guatemala from scrubland and pastureland to home gardens, this tiny but colorful *C. frutescens* has erect pods like the *ají Cajamarca* that change color from greenish ivory with purple streaks to shades of orange and red. This "dog's tooth" (the meaning of the name comes from the peppers' shape) bites hard, with a clean intense heat.

1 IN/2.5 CM LONG BY 0.4 IN/1 CM WIDE
(*C. FRUTESCENS*)

Earbob

I love this rare *baccatum* with a bulbous squash shape more reminiscent of the *chinense* species. Pronouncedly thick-skinned, with very tough but crunchy and juicy flesh like a green hog plum, it ripens from green to brownish orange to orange-red. It is the kind of pepper that I like to eat like as fruit, but beware; though the crunchy flesh has no heat, the closer to the placenta that you bite into, the hotter it will feel.

0.8 IN/2 CM LONG BY 1 IN/2.5 CM WIDE
(*C. BACCATUM*)

Finger Hot Pepper
(also Holland Red Finger Hot Pepper)

I buy these skinny, glossy red peppers by the kilo at my local Korean market, and every spring I also get them as seedlings to plant in my garden. The plants look delicate, with some purplish coloring on stems around the nodes. The fruit is borne erect at first, becoming pendant and ripening from deep emerald green to a bright scarlet that shines like lacquer. Long, narrow, and tapering somewhat only about 1 inch/2.5 centimeters from the tip, the shape is usually quite straight or only slightly curved. These peppers have certain qualities— perfect color, medium heat, and a fruity, tomato-like flavor—that make them ideal for fermented sauces like Sriracha (see Miracha, page 260). Usually sold as finger hot pepper or Holland red finger hot pepper, chances are they have come from a greenhouse in the Netherlands. Though this part of the world is better known as the source of different colored glossy bell peppers, hot peppers for the Asian market have become big business in recent years.

5.5 IN/14 CM LONG BY 1 IN/2.5 CM WIDE (*C. ANNUUM*)

Finger Hot Pepper

Fish Pepper

Fish Pepper

What I know of this fascinating US-bred pepper's story comes from the culinary historian and heirloom vegetable gardener William Woys Weaver. African-American painter Horace Pippin gave seeds to Will's grandfather in the glory days of the Philadelphia-Baltimore fish houses, oyster houses, and other popular eateries specializing in seafood. Terrapin dishes, snapper soup, oyster stew, and similar dishes reigned supreme in this segment of the Mid-Atlantic restaurant trade, and gardeners in black communities used to supply much of the necessary produce.

Pippin believed that fish peppers had first been grown around Baltimore and had been adopted by chefs in this class of restaurants. (It is possible that the plants' forebears originally reached the area from the Caribbean, via the slave trade.) They are a striking-looking cultivar with variegated green and white leaves and pods that start out green-and-white striped and mature through other striped stages to solid red. The story goes that restaurant chefs used to order fish peppers at the unripe green-and-white stage, either fresh or dried, in order to use them in white sauces that had to be kept white. I ordered them from a nursery catalog knowing nothing of this history and was delighted by their gentle but lingering heat, accompanied by a green bell pepper edge and a strong herbaceous quality that would go beautifully with seafood.

**1.8 IN/4.6 CM LONG BY 0.8 IN/2 CM WIDE
(*C. ANNUUM*)**

Fresno

Grenada Hot Seasoning Pepper

Fresno

This dependable *annuum* developed in California has enough heat to sharpen any sauce and the deepest red color to make it irresistible. The pods have a beautiful tapering cone shape and ripen from green to orange and then to a smooth, glossy, and vibrant red. Though not as juicy and pulpy as a red jalapeño, Fresno is still a good option for fresh table salsas and fermented garlicky Sriracha-style sauces (see page 260). They are mildly hot and tart, with just a hint of sweetness.

2.9 IN/7.4 CM LONG BY 1.05 IN/2.6 CM WIDE
(*C. ANNUUM*)

Grenada Hot Seasoning Pepper

This bulbous pepper from the island of Grenada in the Lesser Antilles seduces with a fruity, intense tropical aroma. It is milder than the name indicates, similar in flavor to the *ají dulce* of Venezuela. It is an excellent choice for cooked sauces, stews, and bean dishes.

2 IN/5 CM LONG BY 1.25 IN/3.2 CM WIDE (*C. CHINENSE*)

Grenada Pimiento Seasoning Pepper

Grenada Pimiento Seasoning Pepper

When Caribbean cooks talk about a seasoning pepper, they usually mean a very flavorful chinense with no sting or just enough residual heat to make flavors sing, like this Grenada cultivar. One of my favorite cooking peppers, it is herbal, musky, and deeply perfumed (cut open one pod and it will scent the whole kitchen). The deep perfume is reminiscent of a Venezuelan *ají dulce* from Margarita Island; the flavor recalls guava and other tropical fruits. Bulbous and sensuously chubby, the pods ripen from apple green to intense yellow. Use it in cooking sauces and table sauces based on tropical fruits.

1.3 IN/3.3 CM LONG BY 2.25 IN/5.7 CM WIDE (*C. CHINENSE*)

Guindilla

This is the quintessential Spanish hot pepper. It is most probably one of the earliest introductions from the New World into Spain, arriving at the end of the fifteenth century. The plant looks like Leonhart Fuchs's 1542 botanical drawing of what he called "Long Indian Pepper," with lots of curved pendant pods of a cayenne type. When beginning to ripen from green to fire-engine red, the guindilla has the fresh flavor of an Anaheim pepper with the medium heat of a cayenne. Though they sprang from a narrow genetic foundation, there are several guindilla cultivars throughout Spain. In the northern province of Gipuzkoa Spain, part of the Basque Country, there are narrow, thin-skinned guindillas known as *Ibarrako piparrak*. The small and skinny pods growing on long curved stems are light greenish yellow and are picked young for pickling. They are prized for their soft texture, delicate flavor, and lack of heat, which reflect the right growing conditions in the area of Ibarra, not the plant's genetics. They are the favorite accompaniment to a hearty Tolosa black bean stew. The small and very hot guindilla called *pebrera* in the Mediterranean region of Spain might be a *C. frutescens*. It is used dried and is the hot pepper of choice for the Valencian fish dish *all i pebre*.

6 IN/15.2 CM LONG BY 1 IN/2.5 CM WIDE (*C. ANNUUM*)

Guindilla

Habanero

Habanero

The best-known *C. chinense* in the United States is the Yucatecán habanero, a scorching hot, aromatic, and deeply flavored pepper that has a characteristic lantern shape and, when ripe, smooth orange skin. Because it has no Mayan name, it is believed to have reached the Yucatán via Cuba, perhaps as late as the Colonial period.

This is the habanero most likely to be found in any North American supermarket. Though it delivers a punch, it is aromatic and herbal—ideal for enlivening fresh fruit salsas, pickling in vinegar, and adding to braises, soups, and stews. A few slices will lend heat and flavor.

1.5-2.5 IN/3.8-6.4 CM LONG BY 1-1.5 IN/2.5-3.5 CM WIDE
(*C. CHINENSE*)

Habanero, Francisca

This very hot *chinense* was developed by Frank García of GNS Spices in California, the same man who gave us the Red Savina habanero of Guinness World Record fame. Until 2011, it was a protected variety sold only by a small number of licensed growers, like Cross Country Nurseries, where I got mine as a seedling. The large, almost globular pendant pods (about 10 seeds per pod) ripen from green to yellow. Despite its intense heat, this is a delicious and very aromatic pepper with musky notes, tropical fruit flavors, and a mild acidity.

1.35 IN/3.4 CM LONG BY 1.3 IN/3.3 CM WIDE
(*C. CHINENSE*)

Habanero, Francisca

Habanero, Red

Habaneros also ripen to a brilliant red, but I find that they are then less floral and aromatic than their orange-skinned counterparts. However, their vivid hue is an asset in raw salsas.

1.75-2 IN/4.4-5.1 CM LONG BY 1.25-1.4 IN/3.1-3.6 CM WIDE
(*C. CHINENSE*)

Habanero Red, Belize

This glossy, red chinense comes from Punta Gorda in Belize. Like *ají dulce,* it is deeply aromatic and surprisingly mild. It makes a colorful and flavorful addition to any cooking sauce.

1.5 IN/3.8 CM LONG BY 1.2 IN/3 CM WIDE
(*C. CHINENSE*)

Habanero, Red

Habanero Red, Belize

Habanero Red, Dominica

Habanero, Red Savina

Habanero Red, Dominica

Like its French Caribbean neighbors, Martinique and Guadeloupe, the island nation of Dominica is home to very hot and tasty *chinenses*. Lantern shaped and delicately pleated, the pods of this cultivar are very fruity, with aromatic notes of musk and jasmine. Though only mildly hot at first bite, it has the kind of heat that keeps growing in the mouth. Use judiciously in cooking and fresh table sauces.

1.75 IN/4.4 CM LONG BY 1.25 IN/3.2 CM WIDE
(*C. CHINENSE*)

Habanero, Red Savina

Developed during the 1990s from Costa Rican seed by Frank García at the California-based GNS Spices, this was the first habanero protected by the USDA's Plant Variety Protection Act. Its claim to fame was blistering, outrageous heat. Though since surpassed in the Guinness World Records by the criminally fiery Indian *Bhut Jolokia*, the Trinidad Moruga Scorpion, and more recently the Carolina Reaper, this is still one of the hottest habaneros in existence.

1.5 IN/3.8 CM LONG BY 1.6 IN/4.1 CM WIDE (*C. CHINENSE*)

Habanero, White

This unusual habanero from the Yucatán bears conical, smooth-skinned ivory-colored pods that look like delicate Christmas lights hanging from festive lime-green foliage. Surprisingly mild for a habanero, the juicy seed-filled pods (approximately 66 to a pod) are aromatic, with a distinct Caribbean guava flavor and a not unpleasant residual bitterness. I like to use this pepper in a milk-based hot pepper sauce, as a garnish for salads, and pickled in delicate champagne vinegar.

1.1-1.6 IN/2.8-4.1 CM LONG BY 0.8-1 IN/2-2.5 CM WIDE
(*C. CHINENSE*)

Hijueputa (also Hijo de Puta)

When Latin American eaters get more than they bargained for in a hot pepper, they have the habit of unprintably cursing the pepper's mother. Since many of us born in pepper country do not have the endurance of true chileheads, we curse hot peppers a lot even when they are not that hot—as is the case with this Ecuadorian *frutescens*. Tiny, with many seeds for its size (approximately 38 per pod), it ripens from apple green to red. Yes, it is hot, but it is not a killer. What makes it interesting is its intense pine aroma, a characteristic of some *frutescens* that can be attributed to particular terpenes and other organic compounds.

1.1 IN/2.8 CM LONG BY 0.7 IN/1.8 CM WIDE
(*C. FRUTESCENS*)

Inca Red Drop

Inca Red Drop

Perfectly suited to New Jersey's warm summers, this is a prolific plant of Peruvian ancestry. It bears a bumper crop of gorgeous, fleshy little pods that look like crimson water droplets when fully ripe. Like most *C. baccatums*, it is deliciously fruity and tastes terrific raw in Peruvian *cebiches* and fresh salads.

1.2 IN/3 CM LONG BY 0.6 IN/1.5 CM WIDE (*C. BACCATUM*)

Jamaican, Hot Chocolate

A handsome plant with gorgeous plump, thin-skinned pods, borne 2 to a nodule, ripens from green to an attractive reddish chocolate brown. A Scotch bonnet type, it has the tropical fragrance and the intense heat that characterizes Caribbean *chinenses*.

**1.75 IN/4.4 CM LONG BY 0.8 IN/2 CM WIDE
(*C. CHINENSE*)**

Jamaican, Hot Chocolate

Jamaican Hot Red

Lemon Drop

Jamaican Hot Red

This Jamaican Scotch Bonnet bears pods ripening from apple green to bright vermilion. It has a curious shape, with bulging shoulders that form a thick, irregular rim above a stubby pointed or rounded tip. For a Jamaican *chinense*, the heat is surprisingly mild and the delicate perfume somewhat subdued. Chop it up and sauté with garlic and onions in cooking sauces, or use it liberally in fresh salsas.

0.85-1.3 IN/2.2-3.3 CM LONG BY 1.2-1.55 IN/3-3.9 CM WIDE
(*C. CHINENSE*)

Lemon Drop

This attractive and prolific Brazilian *baccatum* bears irregular-shaped pendant pods showing constriction at the top beneath the dentate calyx, and ripening from green to lemon yellow. The thin-skinned, mildly hot pods are crunchy, and the flavor recalls a lightly acidic Asian guava. I love it thinly slivered in *cebiches* and seafood salads.

1.75 IN/4.4 CM LONG BY 0.6 IN/1.5 CM WIDE
(*C. BACCATUM*)

NEW MEXICO GOLD

My favorite time of year in New Mexico is the fall when a cool breeze sways the *piñon* pines and the air is filled with the aroma of green chiles roasting in large, gas-fueled drums by the side of every road, in parking lots, and in front of markets. The chiles, blistered, charred, and piping hot, are peeled on the spot and sold, often by the sackful, to waiting throngs who cherish this seasonal treat and appreciate the convenience of an essential ready-to-cook ingredient only hours from the field.

From Hatch and Mesilla in the southwestern corner of the state to Chimayo, north of Santa Fe, chiles of the New Mexico pod type, maturing from green to red and with varying levels of pungency, are the cornerstone of the regional cuisine and a big business, garnering the state millions of dollars and employing thousands of farmers.

The green chile harvest reaches its peak around Labor Day, when Hatch, the self-proclaimed Chile Capital of the World, holds its famous chile festival. The green chiles are sold fresh, processed for canning and freezing, dehydrated into flakes, or ground into a seasoning powder. By the middle of September, the chiles start turning red, and farmers get busy stringing them into long *ristras* (garlands) for sun drying.

Splashes of red against the muted terra-cotta brown of adobe walls, *ristras* are emblematic of New Mexico—as unforgettable as the desert landscapes immortalized by Georgia O'Keefe and as attractive as Pueblo Indian pottery and concho belts.

I bought my first *ristra* of dried New Mexico chiles years ago from an old man named Fidel who claimed to be a descendant of one of the twelve Spanish families who settled in Chimayo way back at the end of the seventeenth century. The chiles were pungent and delicious, and I used them lavishly in every conceivable dish, from red enchiladas to cooked salsas.

The Chimayo chiles that I so cherished belong to a distinct landrace of the *Capsicum annuum* species that developed through time by a combination of natural adaptation and human ministration in this lovely part of New Mexico from chiles brought from Mexico by the early Spanish settlers. They are only a small fraction of the state's booming chile industry, which is dominated by varieties like NuMex Heritage 6-4, NuMex Heritage Big Jim, Sandia, NuMex Joe E. Parker, and NuMex R Naky (a paprika cultivar), among others.

Like the Chimayo chiles, these are also cultivars of *C. annuum*, but rather than being the result of adaptations to a particular terroir, they are all descendants of the so-called New Mexican pod type developed by Mexican agronomist Fabián García at the beginning of the twentieth century at what is today the New Mexico State University (NMSU) at Las Cruces.

Born in Chihuahua, Mexico, in 1871, Fabián García came to New Mexico as an infant with his grandmother, settling in the town of Mesilla. A member of the first graduating class of the New Mexico College of Agriculture and Mechanical Arts in 1894, García went on to Cornell University for postgraduate work. Hired by his alma mater as a professor of horticulture, he later earned the distinction of being the first director of the college's Agricultural Experiment Station and the first Hispanic to occupy such position in the United States.

Plant breeder Dr. Paul Bosland, the director of the Chile Pepper Institute at New Mexico and a García fan, explains, "Though García worked in a number of important horticultural projects, including pecan farming, his call to fame was his pioneering work in chile breeding." Starting around 1898, García began collecting chile specimens, primarily pasilla cultivars, from several parts of New Mexico with the goal of developing a milder chile with a standard pod size. After years of careful pod selection, he succeeded in creating the New Mexico No. 9, the genetic base of all future New Mexico–type chiles, including the widely popular Anaheim chile (a California cultivar developed by Emilio Ortega).

The standard prototype for New Mexico chiles until the 1950s, New Mexico No. 9 was meaty with a long, tapered shape that facilitated roasting and peeling, and moderate heat, both attributes that made it attractive to Anglo farmers. Because of his enormous contribution to the food industry in New Mexico, a research center at NMSU and a campus residence hall have been named in García's honor.

Since the 1950s, García's successors have created varieties that better meet the needs of the industry, addressing important issues such as flesh thickness (the meatier the better for canning), a smooth skin and tapered shape for ease of peeling, more uniform levels of pungency, sweet cultivars destined for the making of paprika, and varieties destined for specific consumption in green or ripe form. Dr. Roy Harper, for instance, developed a variety with rounder shoulders and more uniform shape that largely superseded the New Mexico No. 9. In its milder form it was renamed NuMex 6-4, becoming the most widely planted chile in the state. NuMex Big Jim, a chile developed by Dr. Nakayama in 1975, has the distinction of being the world's longest pepper, according to the Guinness World Records.

Unlike chiles of the *C. chinense* family, which are scorching hot and deeply herbal, even the hottest New Mexico chiles have a broad heat that does not linger and a noticeable apple peel flavor. In most varieties, Dr. Bosland also detects "a hint of pear and a spicy sharpness in the midpalate that dissipates quickly."

In any form, green or red, fresh or dried, New Mexico chiles are terrifically versatile ingredients. Thanks to researchers like Fabián García and his successors at the New Mexico State University at Las Cruces, they all have the meaty succulence of a bell pepper, the sleek tapered shape that makes peeling a breeze, a sharpness that is never too assertive, and a fresh, delicious taste that always pleases.

Dr. Paul Bosland, Regents professor of horticulture at New Mexico State University and director of the Chile Pepper Institute in Las Cruces, New Mexico.

NuMex Bailey Piquin

This tiny and very pungent pepper owes its success to the work of agronomists at the Chile Pepper Institute at New Mexico State University. It is well-known that the pods of wild peppers typically detach from the calyx and fall to the ground when fully ripe—a smart adaptation tailored to dispersal by birds. In the 1980s, researchers at the institute began investigating ways to exploit this trait for machine harvesting. After collecting likely candidates from the Caribbean coast of Mexico and conducting greenhouse trials over several generations of plants, a team including the distinguished agronomist Alton L. Bailey selected one individual for field trials. The NuMex Bailey Piquin, released in 1992, has the distinction of being the first of its kind to be marketed for harvesting by machine; the harvester shakes the plant so that the peppers fall onto a conveyor belt. Most of the crop is commercially dried and sold ground into powder. This strain of *piquín* peppers grows straight up, with long and very narrow leaves, and bears erect, thin-fleshed fruits that ripen from green to red.

0.8 IN/2 CM LONG BY 0.4 IN/1 CM WIDE
(*C. ANNUUM* VAR. *GLABRIUSCULUM*)

NuMex Española, Improved

This is an early producer developed by New Mexico State University in 1984 to suit the state's short growing season. It bears mature green fruit in 70 days. Either green or ripened to red, this is a meaty, pleasantly hot chile with relatively thin skin and succulent flesh that roasts well and lends itself to both stuffing and stir-frying.

4.5 IN/11.4 CM LONG BY 1 IN/2.5 CM WIDE (*C. ANNUUM*)

NuMex Heritage 6-4

In 1947, Dr. Roy Harper, an agronomist at New Mexico State University in Las Cruces, began working with a locally selected pepper and launched it three years later as New Mexico No. 6. Up to that time, the hotter New Mexico No. 9, developed by Dr. Fabián García and released in 1921, had been the standard-bearer of the chile industry in the state. No. 6, a meaty, much milder pepper that had more versatile appeal in cooking, was a rapid success. An even gentler incarnation released in 1957 and dubbed New Mexico 6-4 came to dominate the industry, partly because of its attractiveness to the state's commercial canners with its mild heat, even green color, and medium-thick flesh.

Through the years, however, genetic degradation brought about a decline in the original flavor of the legendary 6-4. To restore it to its former glory, Dr. Paul Bosland of the Chile Pepper Institute went back to the original 6-4 seeds that had been kept in cryogenic storage for more than forty years at the USDA's National Center for Genetic Resources Preservation at Colorado State University in Fort Collins, an important long-term repository of agricultural seeds. He was able to recover about 200 New Mexico 6-4 seeds and put twenty-seven breeding lines through several years of trials. Of these, six were chosen for a combination of flavor qualities and conformity to the standards set by the state's chile industry, such as ease of processing, uniformity in heat levels from plant to plant, and high yield. The result of the painstaking process was NuMex Heritage 6-4, successfully released in 2009—meaty, smooth-skinned, easily peeled, and as delicious as an apple.

5.5-7.5 IN/14-19.1 CM LONG BY 1.4-1.55 IN/3.6-3.9 CM WIDE
(*C. ANNUUM*)

NuMex Bailey Piquin

NuMex Heritage 6-4

NuMex Española, Improved

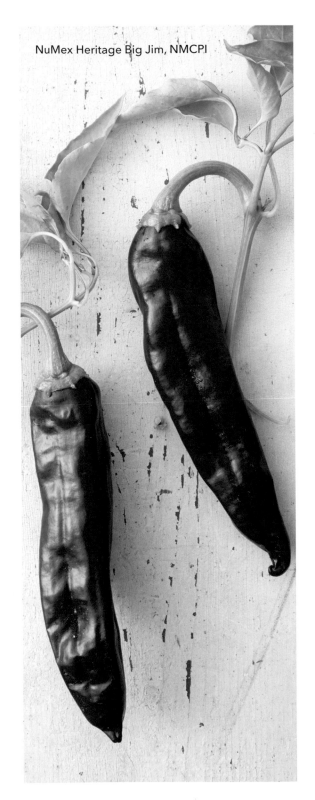

NuMex Heritage Big Jim, NMCPI

NuMex Heritage Big Jim, NMCPI

Allegedly the longest pepper in the world, this broad-shouldered pepper with a hooked pointed tip can grow to about 13 inches/33 centimeters—though in my garden it reached only a little more than half that length. A stunning, meaty chile, it is easy to peel and has a pleasant medium heat. The size makes it ideal for stuffing. I also like fire-roasting it and serving the charred, peeled peppers in salads with a simple sprinkling of olive oil and sea salt.

7 IN/17.8 CM LONG BY 1.6 IN/4.1 CM WIDE (*C. ANNUUM*)

NuMex Joe E. Parker

Released in the 1990s, this is an improved selection of the ubiquitous NuMex Heritage 6-4 (see page 160) with medium heat and thicker flesh that is ideal for stuffing. Selected in an open-pollinated field of NuMex Heritage 6-4 in the late 1980s and released after greenhouse and field trials in 1993, it was named after Joe E. Parker, an alumnus of NMSU's School of Agriculture and Home Economics, who was involved in the selection process.

6.55–6.75 IN/2.8-4.4 CM LONG BY 1.1-1.75 IN/16.6-17.1 CM WIDE (*C. ANNUUM*)

NuMex Joe E. Parker

CHILE HABANERO GETS SUAVE

Unlike most Cubans, I adore hot peppers of every kind, an infatuation I attribute to a certain genetic predisposition for spicy foods and to my trips through pepper-loving regions of the world. I firmly believe that hot peppers are essential in cooking. If you use them judiciously, not only will they add their incomparable flavor, color, and aroma to any dish, but their heat will bring sweet, sour, and salty flavors into sharper focus.

After years of cooking with peppers, I have concluded that nothing beats the amazing flavor of the *Capsicum chinense* peppers. Of the five species of domesticated peppers, the chinense combines an amazing range of piquancy (some have no trace of heat, while others are so devastatingly hot that just a bite can send you howling to the hospital) with a beguiling depth of flavor and aroma that is the signature of the species as a whole.

The first time I saw mounds of habanero chiles on display at a Mérida market, I fell in love with their shiny smooth skin and bright orange color. But it was their flavor that made me a convert. Beyond their scorching heat, I detected notes of citrus and tropical fruits ranging from pineapple to ripe papaya and the same deeply herbal flavor of the sweet Caribbean *ají cachucha* or *ají dulce,* one of my favorite cooking peppers.

But while you can swirl dozens of sweet *cachucha* peppers into sofritos and salsas, you need to use restraint with habaneros.

Habanero cultivars are the hottest peppers in the world. For me, the excessive heat gets in the way of flavor, and I have always lamented having to use only a few slivers in my cooking.

Luckily for lovers of the habanero flavor, help is on the way. Dr. Paul Bosland and his team of researchers at the Chile Pepper Institute have developed the NuMex Suave habaneros, new cultivars that have the intense flavor of the Yucatecan habanero with little of its heat. After several years of careful pod selection, the Suave Red and Suave Orange, measuring a meager 300 to 800 Scoville units, are even milder than the mildest commercial jalapeño. What this means to cooks is having the luxury to benefit from their intense herbal and citrusy flavor and lovely color (orange and red pods) without fear of third-degree burns. For a shrimp ceviche (see Tropical Shrimp Ceviche with Yuca, page 296), for instance, I can use as many as six pods of Suave habanero without running the risk of overwhelming the dish or my palate.

This is the most recent chapter in the history of *Capsicum chinense*; a fascinating journey of transformation from growing in the steamy jungles of South America to meeting the varied needs and penchants of New World cooks.

NuMex Suave Orange

NuMex Suave Red

NuMex Suave Orange

In 2004, the Chile Pepper Institute released two remarkable chinenses, one orange and one red, both dubbed NuMex Suave (from the Spanish for "gentle" or "delicate"). Their exact ancestry is not known. The institute grew them from seed obtained from W. D. Adams, who was unable to say more than that he had gotten them from someone who called them *ají*. Several years ago I received a sampling of the peppers from Dr. Paul Bosland at the institute and was smitten. Beautifully shaped, they were mildly hot (at only 700 to 800 Scoville units, milder than the mildest commercial jalapeño) but as intensely perfumed and complexly flavored as the best *ají dulce* from Venezuela, with the mellow but tart taste of a stone fruit.

2.5 IN/6.4 CM LONG BY 1.5 IN/3.8 CM WIDE
(*C. CHINENSE*)

NuMex Suave Red

This is the red sibling of the NuMex Suave Orange, with the same perfumed and delicate qualities.

1.75 IN/4.4 CM LONG BY 1.1 IN/2.8 CM WIDE
(*C. CHINENSE*)

Peanut Chile

Peruvian Serrano

Peru Yellow

Peter Orange

Peanut Chile

Though commercially sold by the name *chile*, this really ought to be an *ají*, due to its Andean ancestry. Shaped like a peanut in the shell with a lightly lobulated tip (though I have gotten pods with pointed tips) and ripening from green to vermilion red, it reminds me of the pimiento de Padrón and the thicker-skinned Japanese shishito, except that it has less heat. The fruits are at first borne erect but become pendant.

1.6 IN/4.1 CM LONG BY 1.6 IN/2 CM WIDE (*C. BACCATUM*)

Peru Yellow

This Peruvian *baccatum* bears five fruits per nodule. The thin-skinned, almost translucent pods ripen from an iridescent greenish yellow to shades of yellow and brown. They are very seedy (approximately 47 seeds per pod), with moderate heat. To showcase the herbaceous but fruity flavor (reminiscent of peach and guava) and delicate peach-like aroma, it is best to use this delicious pepper raw in salads, fresh salsas, and as a garnish.

2.25 IN/5.7 CM LONG BY 0.5 IN/1.3 CM WIDE (*C. BACCATUM*)

Peruvian Serrano

This one is a vigorous plant with attractive foliage, bearing ridged slender pods with thin, flexible skin that ripen from green to vermilion red. The heat starts out moderate but gains in intensity as you continue to taste; the floral fragrance is similar to Brazilian *pimenta-de-cheiro*. Delicious in citrusy fresh salsas.

2 IN/5.1 CM LONG BY 0.5 IN/1.3 CM WIDE (*C. CHINENSE*)

Peter Orange

The startling shape and jocular name of this pepper will always elicit comments. The hanging pod, emerging from abundant foliage, looks like a penis. Ripening from apple green to dark green to orange, and from brown to dark orange, the peter is a thick-skinned, mildly hot pepper with a large placenta, tart and fruity flavor, and a subtle herbaceous scent. It is more a curious ornamental than a cooking pepper.

3.5 IN/8.9 CM LONG BY 1.25-1.4 IN/3.2-3.6 CM WIDE (*C. ANNUUM*)

Piment Doux Long des Landes

Piment Doux Long des Landes (also Basque Fryer)

This delicious pepper is at home in the Landes department of southwestern France as well as the Basque regions. Shown here as grown by Happy Quail Farms in Palo Alto, California, it has a fruity taste reminiscent of apple and guava. It ripens from green to bright orange-red and has the long, slim cayenne-type shape with an extra curly twist. Thin-skinned and mildly hot, it is ideal for fire-roasting and panfrying.

0.8–0.9 IN/2–2.3 CM LONG BY 1 IN/2.5 CM WIDE
(*C. ANNUUM*)

Pimenta Biquinho

Pimenta Cumarí

Pimenta Biquinho (also Pimenta Chupetinho)

Ripening from light green to lovely shades of orange and vermilion red, this prolific Brazilian *chinense* is named for its distinctive shape, with a nipple-like tip resembling a child's pacifier. A lovely ornamental, it is also a handy kitchen resource. The juicy, flavorful pods are delicately floral and herbal, with mild heat and a tart tomato tang laced with sweetness. This is a favorite cooking pepper in the southeast of Brazil, particularly in Minas Gerais, where it is used in salads, jellies, and cooking sauces and even eaten whole as an appetizer. I simply love it pickled.

1.1 IN/2.8 CM LONG BY 0.75 IN/1.9 CM WIDE
(*C. CHINENSE*)

Pimenta Cumarí (also Pimenta Passarinho, Comarí, or Combari)

I came to know this tiny but potent and deeply aromatic Brazilian Amazon pepper in Salvador, the capital of the state of Bahia, where I learned to pickle it in vinegar and crush it lightly to give amazing heat and flavor to *molhos* (table sauces). The plant is beautiful, leafy and bushy, a bit similar to the Bolivian *Quintisho*, bearing bullet-shaped and lightly pointed pods that ripen from green to light and sunny lemon yellow. I like to display it as an ornamental, but it is also one of my favorite cooking peppers and the one closest in aroma to the Peruvian yellow *charapita*. I simply adore its herbal and green notes, which remind me of the scent of tomato leaves.

1.25 IN/3.2 CM LONG BY 0.6 IN/1.5 CM WIDE
(*C. CHINENSE*)

Pimenta-de-Cheiro

Pimenta-de-Cheiro

In Brazil, the collective name *pimento-de-cheiro*—
"smelly" or "perfumed" pepper—embraces a
spectrum of *chinense* peppers in many shapes,
sizes, and colors. They range from large lantern-
shaped, salmon-colored specimens to this cultivar
from my garden—a tiny, roundish pepper that
ripens from green or light yellow to dark yellow,
orange, or red. Their Portuguese name is justified
by a potent aroma of apricots and freshly cut grass.
Moderately hot, with thin but resilient skin and
no acidity, members of the clan are prized mostly
for their excellent flavor and extraordinary floral
perfume. They are usually pickled in vinegar and
added to table sauces.

0.75 IN/1.9 CM LONG BY 1.25 IN/3.2 CM WIDE
(*C. CHINENSE*)

Pimenta-de-Cheiro, Round

This *pimenta-de-cheiro* cultivar has small blocky
fruits that ripen from green to purple to deep
mustard yellow. The pods, seedy for their size
(approximately 26 seeds per pod), are much hotter
than most other peppers in this group. The flavor
evokes guava, with little of the usual *C. chinense*
musky quality. Use like any *pimenta-de-cheiro*.

0.4 IN/1 CM LONG BY 0.5 IN/1.3 CM WIDE
(*C. CHINENSE*)

Pimenta-de-Cheiro, Round

Pimenta Dedo-de-Moça

This Brazilian *baccatum* grows wide and lush in hot New Jersey summers, bearing pods the length of a young girl's index finger (the literal meaning of its poetic name). This is one of the favorite hot peppers for *molhos* (table sauces) in the state of Bahia in northeastern Brazil. It has a clean, moderate heat, less overpowering than that of other popular Brazilian peppers like the tiny *pimenta malagueta* and the perfumed *pimenta-de-cheiro*. More flavorful green than ripe, this *pimenta* has an herbal and green flavor with an earthy, mushroomy undertone, all courtesy of monoterpenes.

2.5 IN/6.4 CM LONG BY 0.75 IN/1.9 CM WIDE
(*C. BACCATUM*)

Pimenta Guampinha de Veado

Literally, "deer's horn pepper," this prolific early season *baccatum* from southern Brazil has erect pods that ripen from green to an orange-red. Flavorful and fruity with medium heat, it is a lovely pepper for table salsas like citrusy Brazilian *molho* and is delicious pickled.

1.5 IN/3.8 CM LONG BY 0.4 IN/1 CM WIDE
(*C. BACCATUM*)

Pimenta Dedo-de-Moça

Pimenta Guampinha de Veado

PIMIENTO DE PADRÓN

When my cooking becomes too elaborate, memories of a dish as simple and satisfying as the blistered pimientos de Padrón I have eaten in Galicia bring me back to my center. These petite green peppers, a specialty of Spain's humid northwestern region, require no embellishment. All that you need to bring out their refreshing grassy flavor reminiscent of freshly picked asparagus are the warm caress of olive oil and the rugged kiss of coarse sea salt.

I first tasted the peppers at a tapas bar in Santiago de Compostela back in the early 1970s, and I was seduced for life. They came to the counter whole, blistered and softened from frying. I grabbed them by the stem, as everybody else was doing, and popped them into my mouth between sips of Albariño, which I drank from a white porcelain cup.

Like a hungry child greedy for candy, I reached out for more and then some more until I was ready to fight with my husband for the last scrawny pepper on the plate. Later I realized that in the process of munching and craving hundreds of peppers in this and other summer visits to Galicia, their green purity had gotten imprinted in my mind as an ideal of true pepper flavor; this flash of memory comes to me every time my mouth needs relief from sensory overload or from eating too many hot peppers.

Like many New World peppers that found a home in Spain, the Padrón pepper is a member of the *Capsicum annum* family. Popular lore has it that one of the friars at the Franciscan monastery of San Antonio de Padua in Herbón, a parish of the municipality of Padrón in the province of A Coruña, brought the pepper seeds from Mexico and planted them in the monastery's *huerta* (vegetable garden).

A few years ago, I interviewed seventy-seven-year-old Friar Lamela, one of three Franciscans who were living in the monastery. He told me that the *huerta* was lovingly tended by a gardener named Manuel. A lively feast celebrating the peppers (Festa do Pemento), where cooks fry the peppers by the thousand next to the monastery, is held yearly on the first Saturday of August.

The Franciscan connection rings true. Many New World plants that are now part and parcel of Spanish cooking, like potatoes, first found a home in monasteries. Besides, it is a lovely creation story for a thriving pepper industry that has brought fame to the region. Now pimientos de Padrón are sold throughout Spain and are grown in other regions such as Mallorca, Murcia, and even Morocco to supply the increasing demand, to the chagrin of Galicians, who are justifiably proud of the quality of their peppers in season.

I imagine that the early peppers grown in Herbón were hot, becoming tamer through human manipulation. The genetic memory of their fiery ancestors kicks in when the growing season is excessively warm or when the peppers are left to ripen for too long on the plant or after picking; it is not uncommon to find a few peppers in a bunch that are hot enough to make you gasp.

For many Padrón pepper lovers, the unexpected jolt is an added bonus. My Galician assistant Paloma Ramos, who adores them, says, "Uns pican e outros non. E a gracia do pimento (Some bite, some don't. It is the beauty of the pepper)." For milder-tasting peppers with the grassy freshness and subtle herbal quality that make them unique, the rule of thumb is to pick them small and eat them as fresh as possible—if you keep them past their prime they'll get hotter.

Because of their small size (about half the size of a jalapeño), thin skin, small seeds, and generally mild flavor, the peppers make an ideal tapa. To my knowledge the one pepper that comes close to Padrón's thin skin and taste is the Japanese shishito pepper. Shishito peppers are forgiving of excessive heat and sun and they grow beautifully in my New Jersey garden. For my restaurant, I buy them by the hundred from my local Japanese and Korean Markets and pan-roast them in our wood-burning oven with some olive oil and sprinkled with sea salt.

Though shishitos are terrific in their own right, they lack the romantic associations that make pimientos de Padrón endearing. Lucky for all of us with an appetite for these Galician marvels, David Winsberg, a Florida-born farmer who relocated to East Palo Alto, California, close to thirty years ago, now grows about six thousand pounds of them organically every season at his two-acre Happy Quail Farms. Production starts in May and continues through December. By October amounts dwindle and Winsberg has enough supply for only a few select faithful customers.

The process is not without complexity, Winsberg sends the seeds to Florida in November and the seedlings are sent back to Palo Alto in January. "By March when the danger of freezing is over, the plants are planted in beds inside a greenhouse where they are protected from excessive sunlight on warm days," Winsberg explains. "The climate in this part of northern California is similar to that of Galicia," he adds. Here the cooling marine breeze that comes from the San Francisco Bay tempers the dog days of summer. The peppers grow as tall as seven feet in their protective environment producing an average of one hundred pods per plant, but warm days and cool nights keep them from developing too fast and becoming hot.

Winsberg tried to grow the pimientos de Padrón at his family farm in Delray Beach, Florida, but found that the high temperatures and high humidity were detrimental to the flavor of the peppers. Then came Hurricane Wilma, which wiped out the 2005–2006 winter crop.

When he first started growing the peppers in California from seeds he had gotten from a friend in Spain, he sold his crop locally at farmers' markets. When production increased, he began to establish contact with Spanish restaurants throughout the United States and sending out samples. Now everyone wants pimientos de Padrón.

As Winsberg says, "calling pimientos de Padrón 'peppers' is like calling truffles 'mushrooms.' I am glad that North Americans now have the opportunity to find out the difference on their home turf.

Dave Winsberg, of Happy Quail Farms.

Pimenta Malagueta

Pimenta Malagueta

This Brazilian *frutescens* is not to be confused with the unrelated African *melegueta* peppers sometimes called grains of paradise. The small, oval-shaped pods are borne upright, with 2 or 3 pods per node. The nondentate calyx indicates that the fruit can be easily detached from the calyx when ripe. Ripening from green to orange to vermilion red, they make a beautiful sight in Brazilian markets where you'll find mountains of tiny *malaguetas* in all stages of ripeness. Cooks crush them lightly to season their *molhos* or pickle them in vinegar (see Cuban-Style Hot Wild Pepper Vinegar, page 254). *Malaguetas em vinagre* is a staple of the Brazilian table. But one pod will add a lot of heat to any food. The *malagueta*, despite is minute size, delivers the kind of heat that feels like a lingering burn on your tongue. As in other *C. frutescens* like Tabasco, of the over 83 volatile compounds identified in *malagueta*, esters and alcohols predominate, lending fruitiness and a green herbal kick to this tiny and seemingly unassuming pepper.

0.8 IN/2 CM LONG BY 0.25 IN/0.6 CM WIDE
(*C. FRUTESCENS*)

Pimenta Peito-de-Moça

This pretty Brazilian pepper has a pronounced nipple-like tip to which it owes its Portuguese name "girl's breast." Shaped much like the *pimenta biquinho* but much hotter, it contains many seeds per pod (approximately 76). Ripening from green to orange to shades of brilliant red, it is a stunning ornamental as well as a delicious cooking pepper with fruity flavors, delicate perfume, and scorching heat.

0.75-0.8 IN/1.9-2 CM LONG BY 1.05-1.1 IN/2.6-2.8 CM WIDE
(*C. CHINENSE*)

Pimenta Peito-de-Moça

Pimenta Piaozinho

Pimiento de Padrón

Pimenta Piaozinho

From the northwest of Brazil, here is a pepper that—like the *pimenta biquinho* and the *pimenta peito-de-moça*—has a pronounced nipple. Very hot like the latter, it is pretty, ripening to a vivid red. Good in citrusy *molhos* (fresh salsas), it is also used in fish dishes, regional dishes like *ximxin de galhina* (a braised chicken dish thickened with ground nuts), and pickled in vinegar.

1.25 IN/3.2 CM LONG BY 0.6 IN/1.5 CM WIDE
(*C. CHINENSE*)

Pimiento de Padrón

These peppers are expensive because they need special growing conditions and constant pampering to develop their characteristically delicate, grassy flavor.

1.5 IN/3.8 CM LONG BY 1.05 IN/2.6 CM WIDE
(*C. ANNUUM*)

PIQUILLO PEPPERS

When a batch of fresh *pimientos del piquillo* I had ordered from California first arrived, I was mesmerized. Heart shaped with a pointy tip and a glossy vermilion hue that dazzles, these peppers were so beautiful to look at that I was torn between cooking them or piling them on a decorative plate for an edible still life. Finally, my appetite and curiosity won the day and I sacrificed them to the heat of my grill. They blistered without splitting and I marveled at how easy it was to peel them. Their parched skin, thin and translucent, came off like a glove; one of the reasons these peppers, a specialty crop of Navarre, Spain, are normally roasted on embers and canned as soon as they are picked, often by the same people who grow them.

Fresh or canned, piquillos are the ultimate sweet pepper for cooking. They are two-lobed fruits with a juicy thin flesh that does not tear easily, a sweet and tangy flavor, and the perfect shape for stuffing. Spanish cooks like to stuff them with seafood preparations, from cod to tuna. At my restaurant Zafra, I fill them with a combination of refried black beans scented with avocado leaves and grated Manchego cheese, then broil them in a pool of vanilla-scented chipotle-tomato sauce until the cheese is bubbly (see Zafra's Piquillo Peppers Stuffed with Refried Beans on Chipotle-Vanilla Sauce, page 286). Simply sautéed in olive oil with garlic slivers, piquillos also make a delicate side dish for grilled meats.

Developed from a pepper strain brought to the Ebro River Valley from the New World, the piquillo pepper is a distinct landrace of *C. annuum* that developed through time by a combination of natural adaptation to a particular terroir and human manipulation. There are two main types, distinguished primarily by size and weight: the small traditional piquillo and the larger *pico*,

which boasts thicker flesh. Each type has several varieties, but you would not know because they are never listed on the can or jar. What features on the label is the origin of the pepper.

The piquillos from the small community of Lodosa in Navarre, which are considered to be the finest, are protected by a denomination of origin since 1987. Only the small piquillo-type peppers grown in Lodosa and seven nearby municipalities have the right to bear the Lodosa denomination of origin label.

From a product only known to locals less than twenty years ago, piquillos have become superstars in both Spain and the United States in recent years. To satisfy growing national and international demands, they are now grown in areas of the Ebro River Valley not included in the Lodosa denomination of origin, such as La Rioja, as well as in other parts of Spain, and in countries as far away as China, Turkey, and Peru.

The farmers of Navarre have nothing to fear from Palo Alto, California farmer David Winsberg of Happy Quail Farms. He sells them to restaurateurs and chefs like me who are curious about the experience of working with the fresh product but don't hesitate to use the canned peppers imported from Spain, which are always of excellent quality and available year-round.

The Navarre growers have bigger worries now that countries like China and Peru are growing piquillos, as well as other specialty crops they once considered their birthright, as part of a campaign to diversify their economies with export crops destined for Spanish and European Union markets.

A few years ago Peruvians found that their northern coastal valleys, a stark land sandwiched between the Andes and the Pacific Ocean, have the perfect climate to produce luxury crops such as white asparagus, artichokes, and piquillo peppers. The seeds of the piquillo peppers came from Spain, and so did technical assistance.

Pedro Chinchón, an agricultural engineer with Gandules S.A.C., a large producer of peppers and other agricultural products in Chiclayo, Peru, told me that the dry conditions and moderate temperatures of this region during winter are kind to peppers, which enjoy warmth during the day and cooler temperatures in the evening. In the district of Jancalla, they plant the piquillos directly in the ground without the protective shelter of greenhouses. The one problem they face is sunburn, but a healthy canopy of leaves usually takes care of that problem. Yields in Chiclayo are usually high and the harvest takes place in August, the height of the Peruvian winter, 100 days after planting.

This is a desert land, but farmers tap into aquifers to irrigate their crops by the drip method. Farther north, in warmer Piura, major producers of piquillos irrigate their fields with water from the ponds where they raise freshwater langoustines.

Peruvian agronomists and entrepreneurs see specialty export crops, such as piquillos, as a new frontier in areas where traditional crops, such as rice, are being abandoned because of competition from cheaper imports from Asia and places where there is plenty of fallow land. Although piquillos are being planted in several regions of Peru, like Lambayeque (where Chiclayo is located) and Virú in La Libertad, Piura is emerging as ideally suited for this crop. Piquillos are now also grown in Lima, an important region for other peppers, such as *ají amarillo*, and in Ica to the South.

According to ADEX, the national association of Peruvian exporters, acreage for the cultivation of piquillos and export profits

from that continue to increase. Peruvian piquillos are roasted locally and usually exported in unlabeled jars and cans, primarily to Spain and the United States. By Spanish law, imports should be identified on labels, although that has not always been the case.

That piquillo peppers are now grown far from their country of origin and imported back to it is an example of how, historically, foods and plants have found ways to spread through human ministrations. It also shows how our global economy works.

Consumers are now guaranteed abundant supplies of the coveted piquillo; and have more options to choose from. For the farmers of Peru, this new export crop presents welcome opportunities for economically depressed areas. Ironically, most Peruvians don't eat piquillos, preferring their own hot peppers. Will their traditional crops suffer as a result of the new emphasis on export crops? For the farmers of Navarre, who are justifiably proud of the quality of their product but who face high production costs and shrinking arable land, piquillo imports may threaten their livelihood.

In the end, I hope that variety can be assimilated as long as quality prevails and traditional crops are not completely abandoned.

Piquillo de Lodosa

Piquillo de Lodosa

Squarish with no pronounced tip, this is a thick-skinned piquillo that takes longer to roast than other cultivars.

5.5 IN/14 CM LONG BY 2.5 IN/6.4 CM WIDE
(C. ANNUUM)

Piquillo Grueso de Plaza

This is a large, thin-skinned piquillo cultivar with a mild taste.

5.75 IN/14.6 CM LONG BY 3.5 IN/8.9 CM WIDE
(C. ANNUUM)

Piquillo Pico

As tart as a fruit, this piquillo cultivar is easy to peel after roasting.

4.75 IN/12.1 CM LONG BY 1.8 IN/4.6 CM WIDE
(C. ANNUUM)

Piquillo Grueso de Plaza

Piquillo Pico

Piquillo

Piquillo Tradicional

Piquillo (also Piquillo Seasoning Pepper)

This perfectly oval, thick-skinned piquillo has no heat and lots of aroma.

2.25 IN/5.7 CM LONG BY 1.4–2 IN/3.6–5.1 CM WIDE (*C. ANNUUM*)

Piquillo Tradicional

This nicely shaped long piquillo has smooth, hard skin with no ridges and a lovely tart, fruity flavor. It takes a long time to roast.

4 IN/10.2 CM LONG BY 1.45 IN/3.7 CM WIDE (*C. ANNUUM*)

Piri-Piri

Piri-Piri

Piri-piri is the melodic Swahili name (meaning "pepper pepper") for a small *frutescens* pepper introduced to Africa from the Americas by the Portuguese in the sixteenth century. It probably arrived first in West Africa before becoming established in East Africa, where it became and remains wildly popular. The plant has abundant leaves and produces several pods per node, thickly clustered and bigger than the Brazilian *pimenta malagueta*. They start out erect, but become heavy enough to dangle a bit as they mature. As hot as the *malagueta* or the Louisiana Tabasco pepper, the pods ripen from a lime green to a bright red and have a sharp, acidic quality. When overripe, they begin to smell like a vinegary Tabasco sauce.

1 IN/2.5 CM LONG BY 0.4-0.5 IN/1-1.3 CM WIDE
(*C. FRUTESCENS*)

Quintisho

This is a sturdy Bolivian pepper with a lovely spreading habit of growth and small, blocky hot peppers borne erect on long pedicels, 1 or 2 per node, ripening from green to gold. I have seen it listed as a *C. baccatum* or *C. annuum*, but the greenish-white petals and dark purple anthers of the flower identify it as *C. chinense*. Though not quite aromatic as the Brazilian *pimenta*, *cumarí* has a strong fruity fragrance and enough acid to balance the sharp sting.

0.5 IN/1.3 CM LONG BY 0.75 IN/1.9 CM WIDE
(*C. CHINENSE*)

Quintisho

Rocotillo, Red

Despite its name, this small, dimpled Peruvian pepper is not a *rocoto*. The lack of a smooth-skinned surface and the clear engorgement of the calyx gives it away as a chinense. It more closely resembles a Caribbean *ají dulce* or Scotch bonnet. But perhaps it was dubbed *rocotillo* because it has a short bottleneck like that of the small *rocoto de chacra* or *rocoto de monte,* which probably preceded the apple-size commercial *rocotos* grown in some parts of Peru. The plant is vigorous, with crinkly leaves, and produces abundant fruit from green to deep crimson. Moderately hot, it is deeply perfumed and fruity with an acid and slightly bitter undertaste.

1.75 IN/4.4 CM LONG BY 1.75 IN/4.4 CM WIDE (*C. CHINENSE*)

Rocotillo, Red

Rocoto, Red

Rocoto, Red

The luscious *rocoto* (called *locoto* in Bolivia) is the best-known representative of *C. pubescens*, a species that has very few pod types and that failed to move beyond the Andes in pre-Columbian times. Unlike all other peppers, *rocotos* have black seeds, purple or white-and-purple flowers, and thick leaves that have a downy surface. The pod is about as wide as it is long. Grown at higher altitudes than most of the Andean baccatums (as high as 10,800 feet/3,000 meters in Bolivia), they cannot thrive without cool nights and sunny, not excessively warm mornings. Andean cooks love *rocotos* because of their sturdy conformation and thick flesh. They are not as hot as the fiercest chinense peppers but have a piercing bite that permeates every bit of the flesh. I adore *rocotos* and use them in Peruvian *cebiches* and in table sauces with tree tomatoes (see Rocoto and Tree Tomato Sauce, page 270). They are easy to seed while leaving the shape whole, which makes them perfect for stuffing; I love them filled with meat, topped with cheese and baked, as is done in Arequipa, Peru. These are the small *rocotos* that do well in my New Jersey garden, a type known in Peru as *rocotos de chakra*.

1.25 IN/3.2 CM LONG BY 1.25 IN/3.2 CM WIDE
(*C. PUBESCENS*)

Rocoto, Yellow (see Chile Manzano)

Rooster Spur

I discovered this lovely pepper at the Union Square Greenmarket, the largest farmers' market in Manhattan, and fell in love with its history. It is an heirloom pepper that has been grown by the Ainsworth family of Laurel, Mississippi, for over a century and used to season the family's eponymous Rooster Spur Sausage. Virgil T. Ainsworth donated seed to Seed Savers Exchange, an organization dedicated to preserving heirloom plant varieties. It is a showy pepper with upright, thin-skinned pods that ripen from brownish green to vermilion red. Its biting heat registers as a needle sting laced with a pleasant bitter edge.

1.5-2 IN/3.8-5.1 CM LONG BY 0.3-0.4 IN/0.8-1 CM WIDE
(*C. ANNUUM*)

Rooster Spur

Santa Fe Grande

This mildly pungent pepper, of a conformation known as wax pod type, was developed at the University of California, Davis, in 1966. It matures to various shades of orange, red, or (like the ones I grew) sunrise light yellow. It can be used in much the same way as a mild jalapeño: pickled in escabeche, or finely chopped in cooking sauces and fresh salsas.

3.5 IN/8.9 CM LONG BY 1.25 IN/3.2 CM WIDE
(*C. ANNUUM*)

Santa Fe Grande

SCOTCH BONNET (*C. CHINENSE*)

Named after the Scottish tam-o'-shanter, this is a *chinense* clan typical of Jamaica and the Lesser Antilles. Slightly flattened like their namesake but more bulbous, these Caribbean peppers ripen from green to vermilion and are usually corrugated and pleated, in contrast to the lantern shape and smooth skin of their habanero cousins. They are also less aromatic than Yucatecán habaneros and not as scorching hot as they look. Use in Jamaican jerk sauce and fresh hot salsas.

Shishito

This Japanese cultivar has an uncanny resemblance to the Padrón pimiento and is often passed off as Padrón at US tapas bars. Despite the peppers' similarity in appearance and flavor, people in the know can always tell the difference because of the tougher skin of shishitos. The name comes from the words *shishi* for "lion" and an abbreviation of *togarashi* for "peppers." Like Padróns, some shishitos pack some heat, but they are generally sweet, tasting a bit like a green bell pepper.

3-4 IN/7.6-10.2 CM LONG BY 0.5-0.75 IN/1.3-1.9 CM WIDE (*C. ANNUUM*)

Shishito

Siling Labuyo

When the Philippines were a Spanish colony, they became an important intermediary in the exchange of goods between Asian markets and Spain's colonies in the Americas. Some American staples brought by the conquering Spaniards found a receptive home in the islands, including cacao and peppers (for example, this unusual *frutescens*). The name means "wild pepper" in Tagalog. Grown in kitchen gardens, it has tiny, thin-skinned pods with pointed tips, borne upright 2 or 3 to a nodule and maturing from green to shades of red. They are sweet, lightly tart, scorching-hot, and assertively scented like most *frutescens*. As in parts of Latin America, the leaves are cooked as a vegetable in dishes like *tinolang manok* (a chicken and green papaya stew scented with ginger) and *monggo guisado* (a rich mung bean soup-stew). The pods are pickled in vinegar like the Cuban *ají guaguao* and crushed to make fresh salsas. In 2000, Eriberto Gonzalez of the Bicol Region, where this pepper is widely popular, landed in the hospital after eating 350 *siling labuyo* pods, a feat that also earned him a Guinness World Record.

0.4 IN/1 CM LONG BY 0.3 IN/0.8 CM WIDE (*C. FRUTESCENS*)

Siling Labuyo

Tabasco

Tabasco

The Tabasco pepper is the best-known domesticated variety of *C. frutescens*. The plant can reach over 4 feet/1.2 meters in the right conditions and is prolific, producing abundant small and slender erect pods with narrow shoulders under the round calyx, widening slightly before tapering into a point. They ripen from yellowish green to orange to vermilion red. The ripe pods have soft skin and are seriously hot with an acid edge. Unlike green bell peppers, Tabasco has no pyrazines (the specific aroma compound that produces the distinct smell of green bell peppers), but it has both the aroma of freshly cut green grass and the greenness of lettuce stalk, brightened by tropical fruit notes that recall pineapple and guava, with an underlying oniony aroma.

The exact date at which peppers of this type arrived in Louisiana is uncertain. It has been claimed that Louisiana banker Maunsell White brought seeds from the southern Mexican state of Tabasco, and gave fruits and a sauce of his own making to Edmund McIlhenny. The company's story explains that Edmund McIlhenny found these tiny, very hot peppers growing at his family farm on Avery Island around 1865 and turned them into a sauce that he named Tabasco after the putative origin of the peppers. *Frutescens* peppers of several strains are now grown in Central America and the Dominican Republic to supply the McIlhenny factory. The making of Tabasco-like sauces is becoming a big business in many countries, creating a market for the tiny peppers. Peru, which has an important pepper-producing tradition of its own, is now growing Tabasco peppers as an export crop. I adore Tabasco peppers in vinegar (see Cuban-Style Wild Hot Pepper Vinegar, page 254).

1.05 IN/2.6 CM LONG BY 0.4 IN/1 CM WIDE
(*C. FRUTESCENS*)

Taviche

Tobago Seasoning Pepper

Taviche

From Oaxaca's Central Valleys, the *taviche* bears pods of the *chile de agua* type—elegantly tapered to a pointy end, ripening from green and greenish maroon to a bright vermilion red. Prolific, with many long, pendant green pods, *taviche* is thin-skinned and appears almost translucent when dried, with a color like red amber verging on brownish maroon. This is a hot pepper whose heat intensifies with drying.

6 IN/15.2 CM LONG BY 1.5 IN/3.8 CM WIDE (*C. ANNUUM*)

Tobago Seasoning Pepper

Lantern shaped like a habanero and ripening from apple green to deep vermilion, this handsome *chinense* from Tobago closely resembles the Trinidad Perfume Seasoning pepper in its mixture of floral notes, fruity flavor, and grassy freshness with a backbone of pleasurable heat.

1.75 IN/4.4 CM LONG BY 1 IN/2.5 CM WIDE
(*C. CHINENSE*)

Trinidad 7-Pot Jonah, Red

Trinidad 7-Pot Jonah, Red

The island of Trinidad, located close to the Orinoco Delta, scarcely 6 miles off the Venezuelan coast, has been a gateway for the dispersal of Orinocan and Amazonian foods throughout the Caribbean for millennia. Peppers are among the most important. Trinidadian peppers are some of the hottest in the Americas—and the world. This handsome example of the crumpled Scotch bonnet pod type from Trinidad's Chaguanas region is said to be flavorful and powerful enough to season seven pots of food. The Jonah strain pictured here, ripening from Granny Smith green to orange to vermilion red and producing 1 or 2 fruits per node, is among the superhots in heat, with 800,000 to 1,200,000 Scoville heat units, but trails behind the Trinidad moruga scorpion. What I love about this deeply ridged, interesting pepper is the intense floral perfume that permeates my kitchen when I cut open just one pod. The 7-pot is delicious, exuding an herbal aroma laced with the scent of violets, geranium, and wood. The apple and berry flavors are detectable even if you also feel that a blast of fire has torched your mouth at first bite. The plant is large and sturdy, with strong leaves

2.4 IN/6.1 CM LONG BY 1.75 IN/4.4 CM WIDE
(*C. CHINENSE*)

Trinidad 7-Pot, Yellow

Just as aromatic and beguiling as its red counterpart, this 7-pot, ripening from green to yellow on a tall gangly plant, is not scorchingly hot, but rather mild, with a bitter lingering heat and tropical fruit notes.

1.1 IN/2.8 CM LONG BY 1.25 IN/3.2 CM WIDE
(*C. CHINENSE*)

Trinidad 7-Pot, Yellow

Trinidad Congo, Red

This sturdy, vigorous chinense with textured leaves and 1, 2, or 3 blossoms per node bears large, bulbous, pendant fruits ripening from green to orange to a bright vermilion red. Perfumed like most Trinidad chinenses, with a hint of tomato leaves, it lives up to its name, packing a fiery heat that lingers.

2 IN/5.1 CM LONG BY 1.8 IN/4.6 CM WIDE (*C. CHINENSE*)

Trinidad Congo, Red

Trinidad Moruga Scorpion, Red

If an odd shape can be taken as an indication of danger, then the Trinidad Moruga Scorpion pods flash a warning sign while still hanging from the plant. Ripening from green through shades of greenish orange to orange-red, the crumpled-looking fruits are thin-skinned and almost translucent, covered with a strange pebbly-textured skin that seems reptilian. The fleshy upper part of the pod bulges over the blossom end, from which an ominous stinger-like tip protrudes from some cultivars, giving the impression of a coiled reptile ready to attack.

In 2012, chile sleuth Paul W. Bosland and his team at the Chile Pepper Institute in Las Cruces, New Mexico, confirmed that two fruits from Trinidad Moruga Scorpion plants growing at the center's Leyendecker Plant Science Research Center field plots had been measured at an unprecedented 2 million Scoville heat units, beating the celebrated *Bhut Jolokia* from northern India, which had been crowned as the hottest pepper in the world in 2007. The plants had been tested against a number of superhot cultivars like *Bhut Jolokia* and Trinidad relatives such as the Trinidad Scorpion, Douglah Trinidad 7-pot Chocolate, and Trinidad 7-pot Jonah. The results made "hot pepper" history and turned Jim Duffy, the San Diego pepper farmer who had donated the seeds to the Chile Pepper Institute, a revered figure among chileheads. Concomitant analyses of the test subjects showed that all the Trinidad peppers examined were genetically related—naturally enough, since they were open-pollinated landraces growing on the same small island.

The day I harvested and tasted my homegrown Moruga Scorpion, I braced myself for the incendiary blast with a gallon of milk and a pint of creamy yogurt as antidotes standing by my side. I cut the pepper open, relishing the chinense aroma though it made me sneeze. I observed that the seeds (28 in this specimen) were clustered high on the placenta. I then chewed a single thin sliver of the pepper and immediately was overwhelmed by a severe case of hiccups. But as with all chinenses, beneath the flames and the feeling that my mouth would be on fire for the rest of my life, I was masochistically drawn to the beguiling perfume—wood, turpentine, alcohol, sulfur, and herbaceous greenness laced with peach notes. Would I dare cook with the fiery beast? Absolutely, but in such minute proportions that a sliver would be enough to set an entire pot of stew or a table salsa on fire.

1.3 IN/3.3 CM LONG BY 1 IN/2.5 CM WIDE (*C. CHINENSE*)

Trinidad Moruga Scorpion, Yellow

The superhot yellow cultivar of the celebrated red Moruga Scorpion was created by a self-taught farmer, Wahid Ogeer, in the Moruga district of Trinidad. My plants produced a few pods very late in the season when I was just about ready to give up on seeing any fruit. They were wrinkly with pronounced pleats tucked above a broad dimpled tip. Ripening from green to a bright sunny yellow, this cultivar is lightly tart, fruity, and extremely hot, but not as incendiary as the red Moruga Scorpion.

1.25 IN/3.2 CM LONG BY 1.3 IN/3.3 CM WIDE (*C. CHINENSE*)

Trinidad Moruga Scorpion, Red

Trinidad Moruga Scorpion, Yellow

Trinidad Perfume Seasoning Pepper

Wild Honduras

Wild Brazil

Yellow Hot Wax

Trinidad Perfume Seasoning Pepper

What this pepper lacks in heat it makes up for in flavor and aroma. The beautiful pendant pods, maturing from green to yellow to red, have a lovely crunchy texture and a heady floral scent that lingers. They are absolutely fantastic in raw or cooked salsas, or a goat or pork stew.

1.8 IN/4.6 CM LONG BY 0.75 IN/1.9 CM WIDE
(*C. CHINENSE*)

Wild Brazil

This prolific Brazilian chinense bears small, light-yellow pods with very few seeds (about 4 per pod). It is extremely hot but seriously delicious, with an intense, lingering, seductive perfume.

0.2-0.3 IN/0.5-0.8 CM LONG BY 0.25 IN/0.6 CM WIDE
(*C. CHINENSE*)

Wild Honduras

This mildly hot Honduran pepper ripens from green through yellow and light orange stages to a pretty bright red. The flesh is deliciously meaty and crunchy, with a flavor suggesting green guava.

1.9-2.1 IN/4.8-5.3 CM LONG BY 0.75 IN/1.9 CM WIDE
(*C. CHINENSE*)

Yellow Hot Wax
(also Hungarian Hot Wax)

Once American peppers made it to the Iberian Peninsula with returning conquistadors, they traveled all over Europe and beyond. The Turks are credited with introducing peppers to Hungary, where they were received with enthusiasm from the sixteenth century on. This reliable early-season pepper is said to hail from Hungary. Though it ripens to an orange red, it is used mostly when it is light green and starting to turn yellow. I turn to this pepper when I am looking for a replacement for a Latin American pepper of similar color like the Yucatecan xcatic. Not as flavorful as a jalapeño, it is slightly less hot, with a fresh apple flavor reminiscent of a New Mexico Anaheim. I like to cut it into long thick slices and eat it simply panfried, sprinkled with sea salt and a bit of olive oil. It is also delicious cut into rounds and pickled.

3.2-4 IN/8.1-10.2 CM LONG BY 1-1.25 IN/2.5-3.2 CM WIDE
(*C. CHINENSE*)

Gallery *of* Dried Peppers

I have always been captivated by the romance of peppers dried in gorgeous garlands: red pods of pimiento Riojano strung on cords and hung from the eaves of Spanish cottages, or brilliant *ristras* of Chimayo chiles dangling in the September sun against weathered adobe walls and at market stands in New Mexico. These sights are still seen in the lands of peppers where the climate makes it easy to dry the harvest in perfect condition. The thought of them always makes me wish I could do the same with my harvest. But the real options are very different for me and most other pepper lovers.

The commercial dried peppers we get from Latin American countries, such as Mexico and Peru, are not handled in the same way. The time when simple artisanal methods could get the crop to market and allow growers to turn a profit is long past. As buyers of dried peppers, we are on the receiving end of a huge, swiftly evolving industry. The rules of the game are being rewritten, as I write this, by many major players, including agriculture-school researchers, government policy advisors, and factory-scale growers and processors. The technology of growing, harvesting, drying, transporting, and packaging has been drastically reshaped. But even in today's ever-changing global economy, small farmers may still have a part to play. In fact, some state governments are eager to work with them, seeking means to help small-scale artisanal producers confront twenty-first-century challenges.

"Artisanal," it turns out, doesn't always mean "more eco-friendly" or "more pristine." What if using local wood for smoke-drying chipotles contributes to deforestation? What if spreading out the harvest on the ground for days or weeks of sun-drying may expose it to *E. coli* contamination by marauding animals? Paradoxically, technological innovations driven by the interests of megaproducers may also be selectively brought to bear on the situation of struggling small growers. Those who value the beauty and subtleties of these remarkable fruits in the dried state aren't necessarily witnessing a triumph of soulless agribusiness; rather, I'd say that many different possibilities are being explored on huge and very small regional scale both as generally trending toward increased availability of high-quality dried chiles.

Anyone who cooks often with dried peppers knows that all dried peppers are not created equal. There is the question of origin—where they were grown and whether it's the ideal spot. Devotees of local chiles that once were synonymous with this or that valley in one corner of some Mexican state now complain that growers in the state of Zacatecas are in effect hijacking them to completely different soils and microclimates where the right flavor can never develop. The truth-in-labeling situation is much like that for Italian olive oils. A package may list the address of a distributor in one location even though the fruit got there only after being picked three hundred miles away. There is a good chance that this problem can be addressed through a denomination of origin system. In my opinion, the pleasure of tasting and cooking with dried chiles can only be enhanced by an appreciation of the different terroirs that produce them. This is one reason that I like to buy from serious online distributors; I'm willing to pay a premium because I know I can expect detailed information about the sourcing of their peppers.

It is also crucial to appreciate that what you get is the end result of a long, painstaking production process. From the moment that the pods ripen to their full physiological maturity and optimum color, all kinds of variables—the stage of ripeness at which the pods are picked from the plant, the particular drying technique that is applied to them (sun-drying, hot air tunnels, and infrared heat lamps, among other methods), and how they are stored after drying—can affect the quality of the processed fruit. As the global pepper industry gears up for vastly expanded production of dried chiles, intense attention is being focused on optimum conditions of temperature, time, humidity or dryness, air circulation, and other aspects of quality control. Food scientists are working toward a more nuanced understanding of how to preserve nutrients, flavor, color, pungency, and texture. It is a swiftly developing scene, as shown by the evolution of packaging methods and materials over the last decade.

Ají Guaguao

Ají Guaguao

In Cuba we have nothing like the Mexican or Andean tradition of drying peppers. But when my friend Amanda Viltrez Pérez brought me a cache of searing-hot green *ajíes guaguao* from the municipality of Yara, her home in my native Oriente region, I thought at once of how to preserve them.

The *ají guaguao* is a minuscule wild frutescens that grows everywhere in the Sierra Maestra mountain range inland from Cuba's southern coast. People there pick it from the plants sprouting in fields and backyards or on roadsides. The seeds are dispersed by the *sinsonte,* the same mockingbird that is a friend to chiltepines in northern Mexico. This probably was one of the first peppers that Columbus and his crew were given to taste on Cuba by the Taíno or Arawak people during the 1492 to 1493 expedition.

Amanda tells me that the *ají guaguao* had never been seen in her hometown until floods caused by the devastating Hurricane Flora in 1963 apparently washed the seeds down the River Yara from the Sierra Maestra. Now it is a common sight. I used some of Amanda's gift for Yara-style *mojito* (see Cuban-Style Spicy Wild Hot Pepper Vinegar, page 254) and dried most of the rest to use in the same way as wild Sonoran chiltepines. The tiny, blazing-hot dried peppers turned out to be a great kitchen resource. They are wonderful crushed and added to cooking sauces or sprinkled over a dish at table. I kept some for seed, and the plants grew vigorously in my backyard, though they bear only very late in our New Jersey season. I will miss my lovingly tended *guaguaos* when the first frost comes.

0.4-0.5 IN/1-1.3 CM LONG BY 0.15-0.2 IN/0.4-0.5 CM WIDE
(*C. FRUTESCENS*)

Ají Mirasol

The name *mirasol* means "sun gazer." Confusingly, it also belongs to two very different peppers. One is the Mexican annuum *chile mirasol*, which grows erect on the plant and then is dried to produce the chile guajillo. The Andean *mirasol*, on the other hand, is the dried form of the wildly popular *ají amarillo*. It and the *ají panca* are the quintessential dried peppers of Peru and Bolivia. To add to the semantic confusion, the *ají mirasol* is also sometimes called *ají panca* in parts of Peru (for instance, in La Libertad Region on the north coast) because the Quechua word *panka*, meaning "dried corn husk," survives as a general term for "dried."

Grown mostly along the Peruvian coast from Piura in the north to Tacna in the south, the *ají amarillo* overshadows other local ajíes; it is the only pepper grown in Huaral and Chancay near Lima. Farmers usually harvest the peppers at maturity, when they have reached their brilliant orange-yellow color. Sometimes, they cut corners by picking the crop while still green and letting it ripen covered, sorting out peppers as they ripen and leaving the rest covered until they are ripe. The ripe peppers are spread out on mats of reeds from the local bulrushes (*totoras*), turned every three days, and dried for thirty days or longer. Large exporting companies have more sophisticated methods, but sun-drying is still the practice of choice.

Drying changes the bright color of the *ají amarillo* to a tawny orange and intensifies the natural sweetness, giving it a complex, refined, winey flavor with deeper notes of dried prune or apricot. The pureed pulp is the color of mashed sweet potatoes with brown sugar. In the United States, I often prefer to use *ajíes mirasoles* in sauces instead of the flash-frozen fresh *amarillos*. They enrich whatever they touch.

5.25 IN/13.3 CM LONG BY 1.25 IN/3.2 CM WIDE
(*C. BACCATUM*)

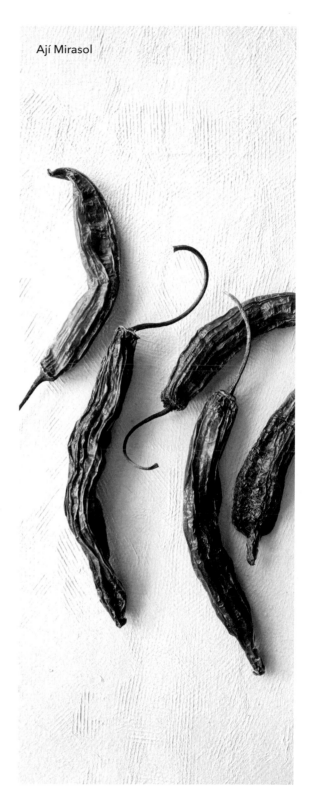

Ají Mirasol

Aji Panca

The contrasting hues of two different dried peppers are the opposite color poles of Peruvian and Bolivian cooking. The *ají mirasol*, the dried version of the pepper called *ají amarillo* in its fresh state, lends a burnished copper shade to many dishes. The *ají panca* yields an equally beautiful color, often deep maroon, depending on the handling of the harvest.

Unlike the *ají amarillo*, the *panca* is almost never eaten fresh. In fact, it doesn't develop strong character in its fresh form. Chances are that you will never meet it undried in Peru unless you go to a field where it is grown. (The name *panca* comes from a Quechua word meaning "dried corn husk.") It is a very unusual *Capsicum chinense* that, unlike most members of that species, develops only moderate rather than burning heat. It lacks the perfumed quality of chinense cousins like the tiny, scorching *charapita* from the Peruvian Amazon. In appearance, it belongs to the longer type of chinenses that can easily be mistaken for baccatums if you don't know the signs. When fresh, *pancas* have the distinctly engorged calyx of a chinense along with thick, faintly ridged skin, a narrowed neck, and a slightly paunchy middle tapering gently toward a pointed (or sometimes blunt and lobular) tip.

The Peruvian names can be confusing. In the important centers of production along the central and southern coast and as far inland as Cajamarca in the northern sierra, it is variously known as *ají especial, ají colorado,* or *ají negro,* the last two referring to the color of the fruit of different cultivars at peak ripeness. (Mine is an *ají colorado.*) The peppers are allowed to ripen on the plant to different stages of color development. They start out bright or sometimes yellowish green and ripen through a brownish green to either a deeper brownish red like a chile ancho or maroon like a chile mulato.

When the peppers dry, these differences are amplified, resulting in a dark reddish- or purplish-brown appearance. Peruvians and Bolivians usually pick the fruit when ripe but sometimes somewhat green. In Peru, it is spread on reed mats, covered, and allowed to mature to peak color. The ripest peppers are selected for further sun-drying as they change color. In parts of Bolivia, like Chuquisaca, the peppers are dried on the ground in open fields or in covered sheds and turned every three days for even drying.

Dried *pancas* are incomparable. Their fragrance resembles the smell of a grass field under the sun after a brisk rain. They are a multipurpose condiment that enhances food with beautiful color and mild heat—while, some can pack a fairly hefty punch, I have yet to find one that is scorching hot. Peruvian cooks often adjust the heat level by removing the seeds and veins and boiling the peppers with two or three water changes. But I think heat is becoming to the panca, an energizing counterpoint to the deep, rich sweetness that is the keynote of flavor along with a hint of green vegetable notes and little acidity. Andean cooks grind *pancas* into powder or flakes (at Cucharamama, we sprinkle these on the flatbreads and pizzas made in our wood-burning oven), or soak them and grind the reconstituted peppers into a puree the color of mulberry jam. When cooked in oil, it turns a brighter carmine shade, similar to that of homemade tomato paste. The pureed peppers are used in *adobos* (marinades) for pork or *anticuchos* (Peruvian beef-heart kebabs), or to add body and color to *aderezos,* the basic cooking sauces of Peruvian and Bolivian cuisine.

4.5 IN/11.4 CM LONG BY 1.25 IN/3.2 CM WIDE
(*C. CHINENSE*)

Ají Panca

Chile Ancho

The chile ancho, the workhorse of the Mexican kitchen, is the dried form of the chile poblano, a beautiful and shiny *C. annuum* cultivar. The fresh chile owes its name to Puebla, where preparing poblanos for the famous dish *chiles en nogada* is an art. (The picadillo-stuffed peppers are blanketed with a creamy walnut sauce and colorfully decorated with pomegranate seeds.) Immensely popular for stuffing or to roast and shred into *rajas* (strips), most of the poblanos grown in Mexico are consumed fresh. Only 20 to 30 percent of the total production is destined for drying.

Fleshy chiles like the poblano require careful drying. Key to the quality of the dried pepper is first allowing the fruit to reach complete ripeness on the plant, changing from green to bright red. But poblanos often require as much as 15 days after full maturity to reach peak color, and the great variations in size, shape, and fleshiness found in different local landraces can make uniform, even drying difficult. Farmers sometimes pick the fruit green or when it begins to show signs of red and let it ripen in the sun, which can compromise the full drying process.

In parts of Mexico, such as Zacatecas, where dried chiles are big business, anchos and their darker relative, the mulato, are dried in hot air tunnels powered by diesel engines at temperatures ranging from 140°F/60°C to 175°F/80°C for thirty to forty hours, or in the open air spread out on *paseros* (metal mesh stretchers covered with straw and tilted at a slight angle to help water run off when it rains). A third method involves placing the chiles on *paseros* and covering them with clear plastic sheets anchored with stones at 3-foot/91 centimeters intervals, to allow some circulation of air while protecting the chiles from the elements.

Once dried, anchos have a flattened heart shape and very wrinkled, leathery dark blackish-brown

Chile Ancho

skin with a hint of reddish undertones. Their real color emerges more fully when they are soaked and pureed to a deep oxblood-red paste that is the backbone of many moles and adobos. In fact, the anchos are used for nearly everything. They are especially popular in the Mexican central highlands, or altiplano. The ancho has only slight heat, with a bright flavor incorporating dried fruit sweetness and a slight tomato-like acidity. By comparison with the other main Mexican chiles, it also has a higher fat content that rounds out the basic sweetness. Usually it is combined with other chiles, such as guajillos, for more complexity, and sometimes with *chiles puyas* for added heat.

4 IN/10.2 CM LONG BY 2 IN/5.1 IN WIDE (*C. ANNUUM*)

Chile Chilcostle
(also Chile Costle or Chile Coxtle)

The first European Spanish expedition to the New World began in 1570 when Philip II of Spain appointed the Toledo physician and botanist Dr. Francisco Hernández to gather information about useful plants of New Spain and compile illustrated descriptions. Hernández traveled throughout Mexico and other Spanish domains from 1571 to 1577 with an entourage including Spanish translators and three Aztec painters. He recorded about three thousand new plants, including seven kinds of chiles that he carefully identified by Nahuatl names.

One of these was the *chilcoztli*, from "chile" and "coztic" (yellow): "The fourth type is called chilcoztli because of the saffron color it gives to the pottages and stews seasoned with it, and called saffron pepper, for the same reason, among the Spaniards living in the island of Hispaniola. It is six to seven fingers long and moderately thin. At times it turns from white to red; at others it approaches the color of a raisin. It is planted in December and is harvested from August to the end of the year."

Today it is still known as chilcostle in La Cañada, the same region of Oaxaca State famous for the elusive *chiles huacles*. Conical, slightly curved, and tapering to a point, it ripens from green to red and becomes a deep mahogany color when dried. It calls out to be teamed up with other complementary or contrasting chiles. The flavor is hotter than *guajillos* or *puya chiles*, with vegetable notes and only a bare hint of sweetness. Because chilcostle is as expensive and endangered as the *huacles*, it is often replaced with the cheaper guajillos. When they can, Oaxacan cooks enjoy combining it with milder chiles, such as the *huacles*, to give a boost of heat to iconic dishes like *mole amarillo* (yellow) or *mole coloradito* (red). When soaked, reconstituted, and ground into a paste, it

Chile Chilcostle

turns a rich, deep red somewhat like achiote paste. And like achiote, it takes on a different yet equally intense color when you add it to hot oil with other sauce ingredients and cook it over lively heat. After a while, you begin to see the oil separating out, now dyed a vivid orange-yellow like saffron. Beware of splatters at that point unless you're wearing an apron! Chilcostle has that same ability to get daubed all over everything that led cooks to christen one famous mole *manchamanteles* (table-cloth stainer).

3-5 IN/7.6-12.7 CM LONG BY 1.2 IN/3 CM WIDE
(*C. ANNUUM*)

Chile Chipotle Morita

Wonderful things happen to peppers when they undergo not just drying but a controlled process of smoke-drying over wood fires, in ovens designed for the purpose. This technique was well known in Mexico before the Spanish conquest. Fray Bernardino de Sahagún, the sixteenth-century Spanish chronicler who recorded surviving Aztec foodways in stunning detail, described smoked chiles being sold in the great Tlatelolco marketplace. At about the same time, the naturalist Dr. Francisco Hernández, who was trying to sort out the varieties of Mexican chiles, described a pleasant-tasting kind by the name of *texochilli* that "is called pocchilli when it is dried by smoking in order to keep it all year." The two halves of the word, from the Nahuatl *poctli* for "smoke" and *chilli* for "pepper," gave rise to the modern "chipotle" when combined in reverse order.

I do not know for certain that Dr. Hernández's *texochilli* was identical to the modern jalapeño. However, it makes sense that it would have been a similarly versatile, adaptable cultivar. Though named for Xalapa, the capital of Veracruz State, jalapeño chiles in larger or smaller, hotter or milder subvarieties flourish everywhere in Mexico. Even at their most pungent they never approach the pain threshold, and their fairly neutral flavor responds well to smoking—though for some reason the practice wasn't adopted everywhere. Among the handful of areas where chiles are smoke-dried, Veracruz State in the south and Chihuahua State in the far north are the most important today.

The business is much older in Veracruz. The state's cooks take chipotles so much for granted that they simply call them *chiles secos* (dried chiles), which is confusing to outsiders but no problem for anyone else. Most production is from the Papaloapan River basin in the southwestern corner of the state or Misantla in the central north.

Misantla lies close to the old trade routes that historically connected the great port city of Veracruz with Mexico City and the central highlands. At one time it was a major center for chipotle distribution to many regions. A 1900 manual of Veracruzan agriculture, *Perfíles del suelo veracruzano*, by Joaquín María Rodríguez, describes the simple ovens in which the harvested jalapeños were placed on latticed platforms over fires carefully managed to ensure proper drying, and identifies the *capón* (literally, "castrated rooster") as the most coveted kind of *chile seco*. Still produced on a limited scale today, it is made from good-sized, meaty jalapeños that have had the seeds carefully removed before smoking. The resulting chipotles are unusually large and succulent, with discreetly tamed heat—the best kind for stuffing.

Two other principal types of jalapeños are used for smoke-drying in Veracruz. The only one I have grown in my garden is the *morita*, or "small *mora*" (literally, blackberry or mulberry), which ripens to a luscious, slightly dark red. I have dried it without smoking and been rewarded with beautifully fruity chiles in rich shades from deep orange-red to burgundy. But smoke-drying shrinks them more drastically and turns them almost maroon-black while keeping largely the original fruit notes. Veracruzans much prefer a larger chipotle type called *meco*. This starts out a brighter red and is slowly smoke-dried to a freckled mouse-brown color sometimes shot through with a reddish undertone (the name means "mottled"). The flavor is more intensely smoky, with less sweetness than the *morita*. Cooks in Veracruz use soaked and reconstituted *mecos* in a large range of table sauces or cooking sauces.

Chipotles of any kind did not register with the US market until the 1980s. Mexican food then began to reach a large mainstream audience, while the Southwestern American cuisine movement was at its height. Mexican producers eagerly realized that jalapeños were marketable both in mature green form and when turned into chipotles—especially canned chipotles *en adobo*. The sauce that coats canned chipotles of all brands is a textbook example of an *adobo*, in the sense of a thick, savory sauce laced with vinegar, tomatoes, garlic, and several herbs and spices. In Veracruz, cooks often had added chipotles to homemade *adobos*; the canned commercial counterpart was the form in which chipotles swept US shoppers and diners off their feet. For many, it was as if a Southern barbecue sauce had died and gone to heaven. I had a certain feeling of déjà vu a few years later when suddenly nobody's kitchen was complete without Sriracha sauce, a miracle ingredient fueled by—you guessed it—red jalapeños.

In the state of Chihuahua, growers near the city of Delicias began a heavy investment in raising jalapeños to sell both fresh and as chipotles. The favorite chile type there has been the *morita*, which US consumers prefer to the *meco*. They also prefer a lightly to a heavily smoked flavor. I think the triumph of canned *morita*-type chipotles en adobo—enjoyable though they can be—unfortunately means that few American fans of chipotles have ever tasted them in their own right without the overpowering *adobo* accent.

There are other troubling aspects of the Delicias jalapeño boom. This is really a desert or semidesert environment, but jalapeño peppers are not arid-climate plants. Water-management authorities on both sides of the US–Mexico border are concerned about the toll the crop takes on both reservoirs and underground aquifers. The toll on natural vegetation is equally grave. In a region of sparse tree growth, chipotle processors scoff at conservation laws, rapaciously feeding their smoke-drying ovens with any load of wood they can get their hands on. A huge black market thrives on cutting down giant elms and a rare species of fir. People will even destroy trees planted as wind

barriers—all because chipotles fetch far higher prices than unsmoked jalapeños.

I don't begrudge the Delicias growers and processors their living. But sometimes it's scary to realize how quickly a new culinary sensation can lead too many producers to put too many eggs in one basket. While feeling concerned for farmers in the path of danger, I also am relieved to know that jalapeños for the US market are now being successfully grown in several parts of the United States. They are a natural candidate for a double makeover: First of all, it's high time for fans of green jalapeños to understand how great they taste when red-ripe. And second, a few hardy pioneers on this side of the border are experimenting with small-scale chipotle processing. This is a cause that deserves to be taken up by a generation of artisanal producers.

1.2-2.5 IN/3-6.4 CM LONG BY 0.75-1 IN/1.9-2.5 CM WIDE (*C. ANNUUM*)

Chile Chipotle Morita

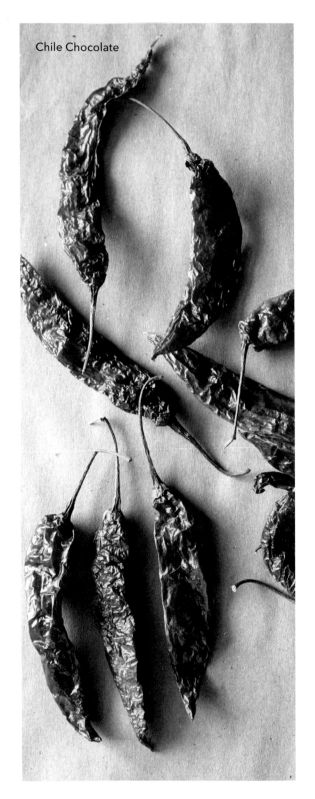

Chile Chocolate

Chile Chocolate

The Dominican friar Francisco Ximénez is best known for his translation of the Popol Vuh, the Mayan creation myth. But he also deserves to be remembered for his *Historia natural del Reino de Guatemala* (*Natural History of the Kingdom of Guatemala*), published in 1722, where he mentions the *chile chocolate*. Among about thirty cultivars that he says were then grown in Guatemala, he mentions the guajillo (under the name of *chile guaque*), the still-important *chamborote*, something called *Tactic*, and "another very thin one that they call de chocolate." The name has stuck, though I doubt that it has anything to do with chocolate. I got it from a market at Sololá in the cool Guatemalan highlands, though it is really at home in warmer regions where it ripens from green to yellow to orange-red. The small, skinny, thin-skinned chile dries to an almost translucent tawny orange. It is quite hot, with little fruitiness or acidity. Lacking the body and complexity needed for cooking sauces, it is toasted until brittle enough to be ground or crumbled over salsas and stews for a kick of heat.

3.5 IN/8.9 CM LONG BY 0.8 IN/2 CM WIDE
(*C. ANNUUM*)

Chile Cobán (also Cobanero, Cahabonero, or Ululte)

The *chile Cobán* is named for the capital of the Alta Verapaz department in Guatemala, high in the region's cool, moist, forested uplands. But the peppers themselves really belong to lower and warmer areas of Alta Verapaz, such as Lanquin, Cahabón, and Senahú.

This is the quintessential dried pepper of the Q'eqchi' (or Kekchi) Maya people in Guatemala, though it is also used fresh. The conical or oval-shaped peppers are usually tiny, like wild chiltepines, but can vary quite a lot in size. They grow erect on the plant, ripening from green to bright red, and are very hot with a tart undertone and the subtle notes of menthol that I find in some chiltepines. When fully ripe, they are gathered and ground to a paste and sold wrapped in cornhusks, a preparation called *mucul ik*. The rest are either sun-dried or hung in baskets over a wood fire to gradually dry in the smoke—virtually the same technique that I saw the Mapuche people of southern Chile using to dry the local *ají cacho de cabra* (goat-horn peppers) for the celebrated spice blend called *merkén*. Once smoked and ground, the *Chile Cobán* becomes a powerhouse of flavor and heat. It does not resemble other smoked chiles like chipotles. The smoky effect is less mellow and aromatic, with a more bitter edge. The smoked chiles are commonly ground with roasted cacao and salt and served in a small *huacal* (gourd) as a table condiment.

My favorite Alta Verapaz recipe is a version of this condiment made with smoked *chile Cobán*, roasted cacao beans, and salt, ground together into a coarse paste and sometimes shaped into balls to be dried and grated over the region's iconic turkey soup-stew, *kak-ik*. (*Ik* is the word for "chiles" in Kekchi Maya.) But these chiles have other uses, either fresh or dried. They are the preferred source of heat in the family of Guatemalan fresh table sauces called *chirmoles*, another variation on the Mesoamerican theme of crushed hot chiles and tomatoes.

0.5-0.8 IN/1.3-2 CM LONG BY 0.35-0.5 IN/0.9-1.3 CM WIDE (*C. ANNUUM*)

Chile Cobán

Chile de Árbol

This name of this potent pepper—literally, "tree chile"—probably reflects the plant's habit of growth, with tall upright stems branching out from the woody stem. Like many vernacular names, it may or may not correspond to similar-sounding designations found in historical sources. So it is a good but not definitive clue that the naturalist Dr. Francisco Hernández, who identified seven types of chiles in his travels throughout New Spain during the 1570s, pointed first of all to a hot pepper called *quauhchilli*, or "tree pepper," by the Aztecs. He describes it as "more burning" than any other and distinctly mentions that it was used as a condiment in place of black pepper, rather than as an article of sustenance. All this certainly points to today's well-known *chile de árbol*.

It is a small, slim, thin-skinned pepper with slightly bumpy contours, reminiscent of a petite cayenne-type chile. Curved and tapering to a point, the pods dangle delicately from the branching stems like ornaments that start out emerald green and eventually become a clear bright red, or in some varieties ripening from dark green to dark purple and finally purplish red. The fruit has the advantage of keeping a beautiful flamelike orange-red color when dried. It is my chile of choice when I want clean sharp flavor and an edge of bitterness without acidity or great complexity. I learned to appreciate the Mexican *chile de árbol* in Jalisco State when I saw an elderly friend use his thumb to mash together tomatoes and reconstituted chiles de árbol for the salsa that he dubbed "finger sauce" (*salsa de dedo*). It was so delicious that it stayed forever in my mind. In fact, it was the inspiration for the tart, bright-red Salsa Lulú, our most popular table sauce at my restaurant Zafra and our usual accompaniment to Cuban-style fresh corn tamales. The *árbol* is also the chile that I like to use in refried black beans (see Refried Black Beans with Chile de Árbol, page 284) and to give heat in the old colonial chocolate drinks that I have reinterpreted for my work on cacao and chocolate.

2.2-2.6 IN/5.6-6.6 CM LONG BY 0.4-0.5 IN/1-1.3 WIDE (*C. ANNUUM*)

Chile de Árbol

Chile Guajillo

The *guajillo* is among the three or four most important dried peppers of the Mexican kitchen, used everywhere in a plethora of salsas, braised dishes, moles, and marinades. Rarely the star of the show, it has moderate rather than blistering heat and low-key rather than arresting flavor. These qualities make it a reliable and versatile supporting player that supplies body and some pleasant flavors to combinations of several dried chiles.

In the fresh form it is known as *ají mirasol* or "sun gazer," because the pods grow pointing upright toward the sun. Ripening from green to yellow to bright red, with an unusually smooth, glossy skin, it dries to a darker carnelian red while keeping its satiny skin. Guajillos can be very pungent but usually have only a moderate sting. Grown commercially in Zacatecas, San Luis de Potosí, Durango, and Aguascalientes States, they are generally used in combination with other chiles that have some other distinctive quality, such as heat (*chile puya*) or sweetness and fruity acidity (ancho).

5-6 IN/12.7-15.2 CM LONG BY 1.75 IN/4.4 CM WIDE (*C. ANNUUM*)

Chile Huacle Amarillo

This is the only *huacle* to have a long rather than squat shape. Either pointed or blunt at the tip, it ripens from green to vivid orange, drying to a warm reddish-caramel color that reminds me of red agate, carnelian, or amber. The heat is moderate. The flavor when reconstituted and pureed has green vegetable notes along with a certain underlying bitterness and something suggesting the crumb of a loaf of country bread. This increasingly rare chile contributes beautiful sienna color and some fruit to the lively Oaxacan *mole amarillo*.

3 IN/7.6 CM LONG BY 2 IN/5.1 CM WIDE (*C. ANNUUM*)

Chile Guajillo

Chile Huacle Amarillo

DRIED CHILE HUACLE

The three *chile huacle* cultivars grown in La Cañada Region of Oaxaca State are inextricably associated with the great moles of the region. Today they face mounting problems that include changing rainfall patterns associated with climate change and competition from farmers in Zacatecas State who have acquired *huacle* seed to plant hundreds of miles distant from the unique La Cañada environment. Still, a handful of farmers persist in raising the *amarillo, rojo,* and *negro* strains of *huacle* and sun-drying them either on the ground (as is traditional) or on raised platforms to afford some protection against the elements. For more about *chiles huacles,* see pages 124 to 127.

Chile Huacle Negro

Chile Huacle Negro

The most legendary of all the Oaxacan *huacles* and the backbone of the classic *mole negro*, the chile huacle is a medium-size chile with a square, blocky shape. It ripens from deep green to a matte maroon and dries to a dark blackish brown with an almost parchment-like finish. The flavor is sweet, complex, and intensely fruity, conjuring a mixture of prunes and raisins, with bell pepper notes and the delicate herbal acidity of artichokes and moderate heat.

2-2.5 IN/5.1-6.4 CM LONG BY 2 IN/5.1 CM WIDE
(*C. ANNUUM*)

Chile Huacle Rojo

Medium sized and smooth skinned, with a blocky shape resembling the *chile huacle negro*, the huacle rojo it ripens from green to a bright vermilion red with a matte finish and becomes a slightly tawny reddish brown when dried. It is less complex in flavor than the *huacle negro*, with moderate heat and the delicate fruity acidity of a green papaya. It is the key chile in the Oaxacan *mole colorado*.

3 IN/7.6 CM LONG BY 2.25 IN/5.7 CM WIDE
(*C. ANNUUM*)

Chile Mulato

Like the ancho, the mulato starts life as a poblano, but with a slightly darker green color. It ripens to a rich maroon, not red, and dries to nearly black. When reconstituted and ground to a paste, it is a stunning glossy, rich dark brown with a tinge of reddish mahogany. The flavor is sweet, with the deep, mellow fruitiness of juicy prunes and raisins. It has less heat and acidity than the ancho and adds sweetness to any tomato-based sauce. The same quality makes it excellent for mellowing the flavors of hotter, tarter chiles in moles.

3.4 IN/8.6 CM LONG BY 2.5 IN/6.4 CM WIDE
(*C. ANNUUM*)

Chile Huacle Rojo

Chile Mulato

Chile Pasilla

The pasilla is the dried form of the fresh *chilaca*, which is widely grown in the states of Oaxaca, Aguascalientes, Nayarit, Jalisco, Zacatecas, and Michoacán (where it is called *cuernillo*). The peppers ripen from deep green to shades of maroon, dangling from the plant like thin obsidian knives. When dried, the pasilla lives up to its name, which means "little raisin," by creasing into a thousand wrinkles. Do not confuse it with the smoke-dried *chile pasilla de Oaxaca*; Oaxacans call the regular pasilla the *pasilla mexicano* to avoid mixups.

As with many other peppers, the chilaca becomes more versatile once dried. The pasillas can be used in their own right; there is nothing more delicious than a Tarascan bean soup with a garnish of fried pasillas or a shrimp stir-fry with thinly slivered pasillas. But most often they are reconstituted and ground to a deep brown paste with greenish undertones like walnut stain. Mildly hot, the pasilla is sweet with a distinct grassy flavor and a bit of acidity. Pureed pasillas are often combined with other chiles in moles and braised dishes.

6.5-7 IN/16.6-17.8 CM LONG BY 1.5 IN/3.8 CM WIDE
(*C. ANNUUM*)

Chile Pasilla de Oaxaca (also Chile Mixe)

Not to be confused with the regular pasilla (called *pasilla mexicano* in Oaxaca), this is one of the finest smoke-dried Mexican peppers. It is firmly identified with the cuisine and culture of the Mixe people, an indigenous group occupying nineteen municipalities in the farthest northeastern region of the Sierra Norte de Oaxaca close to the Veracruz border. They are the only growers and processors of the *chile pasilla de Oaxca*, and jealously guard the secrets of its production from non-Mixe neighbors who might set up as rivals. (The online distributor from whom I got my last batch explained that now he could find only one grower who was willing to sell to him, at any price.) The fresh chiles (*chiles verdes*) used for smoke-drying are handsome chilacas.

The long chiles can be picked either green on the verge of changing color or bright vermilion red. The smoke-drying is done in roofed sheds, over wood fires in "ovens" that really are open-topped frames in which wooden trays with mesh bottoms are set to absorb the smoke. When dried they are wrinkled, almost black, and flattened to blade thinness, having lost some 70 to 80 percent of the original weight in the smoke-drying process. Most are shunted through a series of distributors in nearby Tamazulapan who send them to the great Mercado de Abastos in Oaxaca City. Oaxacan cooks highly prize the large specimens for stuffing with savory fillings like picadillo. I tried this and was just blown away by the flavor. They are intensely smoky, with medium heat and a certain meaty or, rather, porky note. I have ground the reconstituted chiles to a paste to combine with other kinds in sauces, but they are so good stuffed that it seems a shame to use them any other way.

5.5-7 IN/14-17.8 CM LONG BY 1.2-2.25 IN/3-5.7 CM WIDE
(*C. ANNUUM*)

Chile Puya

The Spanish word *puya* means "goad" or "steel point," a perfect description for a skinny chile that packs a sharp sting. In Zacatecas, one of Mexico's largest producers of chiles, the entire plants are uprooted when the pods ripen to a bright red and then heaped on the ground until the chiles are dried. The pods are removed from the stems at processing plants where the chiles are packaged for sale.

The slender, thin-skinned chile resembles a smaller brother of the guajillo, with which it is sometimes used. From carmine red it dries to a smooth, glossy reddish brown. After soaking and pureeing it takes on a rich, brilliant hue somewhere between wine colored and orange-red. The pulp is a little thin-textured and acidic, with no fat and none of the sweet, full-bodied quality of the ancho. It has a straightforward, penetrating pungency that makes it good for boosting heat when combined in a sauce with guajillos or other mild chiles.

5.5 IN/14 CM LONG BY 1 IN/2.5 CM WIDE
(*C. ANNUUM*)

Chile Pasilla de Oaxaca

Chile Pasilla

Chile Puya

Chile Taviche

Chile Taviche (also Chile Tabiche)

One of the many chiles of Oaxaca, the *taviche* plant bears thin-skinned, elegant, slightly curved pods that ripen from green to reddish brown to fire-engine red. When dried—the form in which it is mostly used—it turns the color of Chiapas amber. Until very recently, it was practically impossible to get *taviches* fresh or dried in the United States. But Zocalito, a mail-order source in Denver, sells them dried, together with the three iconic Oaxacan *huacles* from La Cañada Region. The Zocalito pods were sourced in Ocotlán, a district in the southern Central Valleys (Valles Centrales) of Oaxaca that is also home to the *chile de agua*. The Ocotlán *taviches* are smaller and less curved than the ones that I grow in my backyard, but they deliver the powerful kick of heat and gorgeous orange-red color that Oaxacans expect from this terrific annuum. The name *taviche* comes from the Zapotec *tani viche* (hill of the prickly pears; in Spanish *cerro de Tunas*), as well as the names of two towns in the region, San Pedro Taviche and San Jerónimo Taviche.

3-3.9 IN/7.6-9.9 CM LONG BY 1.1-1.4 IN/2.8-3.6 CM WIDE (*C. ANNUUM*)

Chiltepín, Wild Sonora

I began to pay full attention to dried *chiltepines* when a Texan friend, food and chocolate blogger Scott Craig, gifted me a bag of dried wild chiltepines that he had obtained near Hermosillo in Sonora State. There, chiltepines are sun-dried on straw mats on the ground. They command high prices because of the labor involved in harvesting a desert plant that has the habit of getting tangled up in the thorny vegetation that protects it. Craig's peppers came with a handsome chiltepín crusher (*chiltepinero*) made out of desert wood and shaped like a curved chile. The tiny chiltepines were mostly round, with a lovely bright pinkish-red color that reminds me of South American pink peppercorns. Full of seeds but thin-skinned, they were easy to grind in the *chiltepinero*. But I ended up crushing the chiles between my fingers, as is done in Sonora, and sprinkling them over the Cuban beef and potato stew that I was eating. What a difference the chiltepines made, adding clean, bright heat and a grassy edge to the food, making all the flavors come together into a symphony. I am now addicted and know that I will be using chiltepines for cooking and as a table seasoning forever. The plants that I have grown from the seeds of my Sonora wild chiltepines and from seeds that I got from Native Seeds/SEARCH in Arizona were a bit slow to start but have thrived in my New Jersey garden since I learned to place bigger plants next to them to protect them from direct sunlight.

0.3 IN/0.8 LONG BY 0.3 IN/0.8 CM WIDE (*C. ANNUUM* VAR. *GLABRIUSCULUM*)

Chitepín, Wild Sonora

Ñora

Pimiento Choricero

Ñora (also Nyora or Pimiento de Bola)

The Ñora Monastery, located in a part of Murcia famous to this day for its pepper and paprika production, lent its name to this bulbous, meaty local pepper that ripens from green to a bright red and is mostly consumed dried. The word *ñora* comes from *noria*, a local variant of the Arabic term for the wheel used to lift water in the region's complex irrigation system, a legacy of the region's long Islamic occupation. Known also as *pimiento de bola* (round pepper), it looks like the Mexican chile cascabel, but is sweet and nonpungent. The smooth, very lightly ridged green fruits ripen to a shiny crimson, becoming rich reddish brown and leathery looking when dried.

Traditionally, the ripe peppers have been sun-dried on straw mats, though mechanical drying has become more common. Murcia and parts of Alicante, like the Vega Baja del Segura (fertile lands by the Segura River), are the largest producers of *ñoras* on the Mediterranean coast of Spain. *Ñora* lovers swear by the quality of peppers from the seaside town of Guardamar del Segura, a municipality of the province of Alicante. The local farmers dry their *ñoras* in solar tunnel dryers directly over hot sand, which retains heat and ensures even drying. In Murcia, *ñoras* are ground into a paprika that is sweet and flavorful, though without the smoky edge and heat of some types of pimentón de la Vera from Extremadura. But cooks in Murcia and Alicante also reconstitute the dried whole peppers in water, scraping the meat from the softened flesh (as is also done with *pimientos choriceros*) to stir into cooking sauces made with garlic, onions, and often tomatoes. This is the flavor base of several important local dishes like the hearty Murcian *calderos*, soupy rice and fish dishes typical of the Mar Menor and the famous Arroz a Banda (see page 289). In Catalonia, dried *ñoras* are the peppers of choice for the iconic romesco sauce (see Romesco Sauce, page 268).

2 IN/5.1 CM LONG BY 1 IN/2.5 CM WIDE (*C. ANNUUM*)

Pimiento Choricero

Much prized in the cooking of the Basque country and La Rioja in Spain, and primarily used dried, this pimiento has a somewhat oblong shape that tapers slightly toward its three-lobed end. If I were to compare it to other important *annuums* used in the Mediterranean region, I would say that it is similar in shape and dimensions to Turkish and Syrian types like the *Urfa* and *Aleppo* peppers. Strung into garlands to sun-dry, the peppers find their most important uses in regional *sofrito*-type sauces like *salsa Vizcaína*, iconic codfish dishes like *bacalo a la Vizcaína*, and braises and stews. Spanish cooks reconstitute them by soaking in water or boiling before carefully scraping the meat from the skin, which they then discard (I find this step unnecessary). I simply love this pepper because of its wonderful aroma and flavor, reminiscent of dried prunes coupled with the acidity of a home-made tomato paste.

4 IN/10.2 CM LONG BY 2 IN/5.1 CM WIDE (*C. ANNUUM*)

INTO THE PEPPER GARDEN

In their original tropical habitats, peppers are perennials. Like most kinds of fruit, they have seasonal cycles of flowering and bearing followed by periods of rest before the next flowering. But in my part of North America, the Northeast, peppers need to be treated as annuals with a limited spring-to-fall growing season. I prepare for the too-short window of time by starting some peppers from seed in late winter under artificial light and ordering others as seedlings from my favorite suppliers (see page 331).

Peppers are among the strongest and most generous of food plants, as well as some of the prettiest, bearing delicate flowers that remind me of jasmine blossoms, with fruits in spectacular colors (for more about the pigments that create these colors, see pages 25 and 81). When the plants reach their peak by mid- to late August (in my growing zone), the multicolored pods look like ornaments on miniature Christmas trees.

Peppers' brilliant pigments do not stay fixed after the ripe fruit is harvested, but gradually become oxidized and break down. The process is often hastened by the presence of heat, sunlight, and air, but careful drying (see pages 233 and 236) can convert the original pigmentation to a certain spectrum of subtly muted colors that are lovely in their own right.

Growing and processing peppers every year has taught me to appreciate their colors—a true painter's palette—and many other qualities in addition to their culinary merits. Every year I expand my collection to include cultivars that are not only tasty but beautiful as flowering ornamentals. I plant them in oversized decorative containers where they can grow to their full potential and place them in strategic locations throughout my garden to show off their striking individual features—strangely variegated foliage, flowers with unusual hues, multicolored or odd-shaped pods—against the background of established perennials, vegetables, and berries.

I have a soft spot for the iconic peppers of Latin America, particularly ones like the Andean *ají panca* and *ají amarillo* or the diminutive Amazonian *ají charapita*, which I learned to love during research trips. And I have developed a motherly affection for peppers that tell a story that I have a personal stake in, such as the *dátil* of St Augustine, which allegedly reached that central Florida town from my own hometown, Santiago de Cuba. Developing a close relationship with the plants through gardening has taught me to love peppers that I used to take for granted. Cayennes are a prime example. Years ago, I was about to discard a scrawny cayenne seedling that I had grown from seed but somehow ended up planting it—and promptly forgot about it. It grew into a vigorous bush of close to 8 feet/2.4 meters tall and produced gorgeous, 9-inch/23-centimeter peppers that looked like crimson daggers. The plant was so resilient that it kept bearing flowers and fruit long after a first wet snow one November. Now I always plant Long Thick Cayennes (page 119), in the center of the garden to serve as a visual anchor for a collection of slightly shorter pepper plants. At the other end of the size spectrum, I have begun to pay closer attention to diminutive pods like the chiltepín. I now treat the different chiltepín cultivars as if they were precious bonsai trees.

While I like to design my garden around peppers, I am also a practical kitchen gardener. The bulk of my collection is planted not far from my kitchen door, in large pots arranged on long, durable planks of tropical ipe wood set on sturdy trestles. It is a setup that allows me to study the behavior of each plant during the growing season. And it is at my backyard table that I like to sit with knife in hand to cut the peppers for tasting. Through trial and error I have learned to decode what my peppers want—which ones enjoy longer hours of full sun and which ones are shy beauties requiring shade, such as Sonoran wild chiltepines and the fuzzy-leaved Andean *rocotos*. Having my peppers close to the kitchen also means that during the growing season I am never without them for cooking. Without consciously engineering it, I have run a bountiful pepper kitchen for years, learning to extract every bit of color and flavor from these extraordinary fruits, whether fresh or dried.

If you are interested in the history of food plants in Latin America and want to get acquainted with the plant that forever rewrote the playbook of flavor for every region of the world, there is no better way than to become a pepper gardener. You will find yourself part of a timeless adventure.

Growing Peppers

For me the best way to learn about the life of peppers is to follow their progress from seed to fruiting. Engaging in their care is not only a way to get to know them as the extraordinary creatures that they are, but also a way to value nature's quiet work through the ages and the toil of the silent gardeners of prehistory—the ancient people of the Americas responsible for turning unassuming wild capsicums into domesticated, infinitely useful kitchen resources.

There are two ways to start a pepper garden: from seed or seedlings. Both are rewarding in their own way. For growers in the areas where it is too cold to plant outdoors until later in the spring, there is no choice but to start seeds indoors. (An excellent guide to plant hardiness by growing zone can be found on the USDA website: planthardiness.ars.usda.gov.) As a general rule, I plant the seeds indoors eight to ten weeks prior to the projected date of the last freeze in my zone. Even without the threat of freezing, it's best to start the seeds indoors and transplant the seedlings once they're viable, acclimating them gradually to outdoor conditions.

I have found some excellent books to guide me through the process of planting peppers, particularly David De Witt and Paul Bosland's *The Complete Chile Pepper Book: A Gardener's Guide,* as well as useful tips from dedicated growers online. Here is a general approach that works for me: Start by choosing seeds and seedlings from reputable breeders and setting realistic goals about the number of plants that your outdoor space can accommodate, bearing in mind that some seedlings can become 5 to 8 feet/1.5 to 2.4 meter bushes.

For Indoor Growing

Before you start planting, set up the right indoor growing conditions. My nursery is a sunny room with southern and eastern exposure, where the baby plants share space with two colorful macaws and an Amazonian parrot. My windows are old, so I keep the planted seeds away from cold drafts and grow the seedlings under artificial lighting.

Special grow lights for plants will deliver the necessary energy for your seedlings to thrive indoors until transplanting. They are available online, and some come in kits with a fixture for a 24-watt T5 6400K high-output fluorescent bulb and an adjustable stand to hang it. You can also purchase inexpensive fluorescent lamps of the same output in hardware stores; you just need to rig yourself a stand to hang the lights 2 to 4 inches/5 to 10 centimeters above the plants.

I use a greenhouse kit with a ventilated dome, available at my local garden center. It comes with everything I need: a seed tray that fits into another plastic tray to collect water, and an additional plastic tray to fit an electric mat. You can also buy small plastic pots or six-pack plastic cells and arrange them in a shallow baking pan.

Pepper seeds need a warm temperature to germinate and grow. A heating mat, available in most garden centers or online, should be placed under seed trays to keep the temperature of the soil at about 80°F/27°C. Here are some other specifics to help you get set up:

- Use any good-quality seed starter potting and planting mix.
- I use 4-inch/10 cm plant label stakes so that a planter dome can fit comfortably over them.
- I like a watering can with a narrow spout and a mister.
- I have had the best results with Jack's Classic professional water soluble plant food, an all-purpose fertilizer that stimulates root and shoot growth.

Starting from Seeds

Examine the seeds carefully, discarding any that show signs of physical damage or fungal infestation. If using seeds from your own garden, choose seeds from early, perfectly ripe pods. Many pepper seeds go into dormancy after being extracted; use those that have been allowed to dry undisturbed for a few months to increase the chances of germination. I like to soak older seeds in a bowl of warm water overnight. This is also a good idea for seeds that have a hard casing, such as *rocotos*, or that are challenging to grow, such as chiltepines. Discard any that float; they are not viable. Some growers recommend soaking the seeds in a saltpeter (potassium nitrate) solution (about ½ teaspoon of saltpeter to 1 quart/960 milliliters of water) for 4 to 8 hours before planting to stimulate growth. (If you decide to soak the seeds, be sure to keep each variety separate and carefully labeled so you don't end up with a mystery pepper garden.)

Before transferring the soil mix to the planting tray or individual pots, I place it in a large bowl and wet it a little, which makes it easier to handle. Plant two seeds per cell or pot at a depth of about a ¼ inch/6 millimeters. Note the variety, seed source, and planting date on the labels. Take a picture of the planter, with the labels in place, so you know which seeds are where in case the stakes get disturbed.

After planting, water generously but gently with a mixture of ½ teaspoon Jack's Classic professional water soluble plant food dissolved in 1 quart/960 millileters of warm water. Thereafter, water only when the top of the soil is no longer damp and feed with the fertilizer mixture once a week. Avoid overwatering at all costs. It can cause serious problems, such as the development of a fungal disease that rots the stems of the seedling at the soil level. I once overdid the watering only to wake up one morning to hundreds of seedlings that had looked perfectly fine hours before now toppled over and dead. As I pulled out a few, I observed that their stems were completely withered below the soil level. After researching the cause, I learned that the fungal disease is called damping-off and can be averted by avoiding excess humidity and providing adequate ventilation. I now remove the dome of my greenhouse kit as soon as the seedlings are about 1 inch/2.5 centimeters tall and keep an overhead fan on at all times.

The seeds should germinate in two to three weeks. They prefer to be kept at about 80°F/27°C under 12 to 16 hours of artificial light daily. I have my artificial lights on a timer.

You will need to thin the peppers, cutting the weaker seedling of each pair at the soil level and letting the strongest one thrive. The seedlings will be ready for transplanting when they have six to eight sets of leaves, depending on the variety of the pepper. Peppers like a hot, sunny environment, so keep them inside until the cold weather is over and harden them to withstand outdoor conditions by gradual exposure. (I'll explain how to do this shortly.)

Sourcing Seeds

I am a seed saver by nature and have kept seed samples from all the peppers that I've grown, mostly for identification (using a very simple digital microscope). To save seeds, I pick the best early pods at the peak of ripeness, as those that ripen earliest in the season are the most vigorous. I cut the pods open and carefully remove the seeds, extricating them from the placenta. I usually place them on a plate to dry in a warm place for several days, and then store them at room temperature in labeled seed envelopes. (Specialists often store seeds in tightly sealed containers in the freezer.)

When I collect seeds either on my travels or from commercial sources, I know I may not get an exact replica of the parent plant. The truth is that you will not be able to create a perfect duplicate of your pepper garden collection year after year just by collecting and planting seeds. If you grow only a few closely related cultivars, your seeds may be true to the parent plant. But if you grow different cultivars in close proximity, chances are they will cross-pollinate. The changes will not be apparent in the fruit, and will only be expressed when the seeds are planted the following year. Professional gardeners and horticulturists protect the delicate pepper flowers from cross-pollination by covering them with special translucent cage nets. I have improvised my own kind of chastity belt for special peppers, with reasonable results. But unless you work hard to preserve the genetic purity of your favorite cultivars, it is best to purchase new seeds from reputable sources (see page 331) each season.

Starting with Seedlings

Ordering pepper seedlings is faster and less nerve-racking than starting from seed. Identify serious local growers in your zone or promising online sources and begin studying their catalogs in late winter. Avoid falling for every gorgeous picture that you see in a catalog and instead choose only the plants best suited to your zone's growing limitations. That said, I have learned that these guidelines aren't always hard-and-fast, especially if you are willing to keep trying for more than one or two seasons while you manipulate growing conditions such as shade and sun exposure. Even if the odds are against you, remember that the beauty of what you can grow will outshine the picture in the catalog. Indulge your curiosity. I remember promising myself that I would never again try to grow *panca* peppers in my garden after two years of miserable luck with this important Andean variety. Breaking my vow to try a third time, I was rewarded with an amazing harvest.

Once you have made your choices, place your orders early in the spring and arrange for delivery once the danger of frost is past. In my growing zone, the safest date to transplant is the first week of June, but for some varieties that is already too late for them to fruit by the end of the season in fall. So I take my chances and schedule the delivery of my seedlings for the first week in May.

When they arrive, I inspect them for general condition, discarding any that are badly damaged. Then I pinch off any prematurely set buds, flowers, or small fruits, to allow the plant to concentrate energy on its vegetative growth. This is probably the most difficult decision you need to make, but by being ruthless you will ensure that your plants grow vigorously and set flowers and fruit at the proper time. To acclimate the seedlings to their new environment, I usually keep them outdoors, protected against wind and direct sunlight, for at least five days before transplanting.

If planting directly in the ground, the soil should be warm and prepared with the organic matter of your choice. A pH of about 6.7 is ideal, according to De Witt and Bosland. The best temperatures for peppers are 70°F/22°C to 80°/27°C during the day and 60°F/16°C to 70°F/22°C at night. A sunny patch of ground with 6 to 8 hours of direct sunlight makes the best planting bed. Be aware that some peppers, such as chiltepines and *rocotos* and other Andean peppers, do best in indirect sunlight.

Dig holes a bit deeper and wider than the seedling pots, 18 to 24 inches/46 to 60 centimeters apart, in rows 2 to 3 feet/60 to 91 centimeters apart. Get to know the growing habits of the peppers that you are planting. Some will spread out laterally, needing more space than others. Different growers have strategies for easing the trauma of transplanting. My favorite New Jersey pepper grower, Cross Country Nurseries, suggests soaking the seedlings in diluted fish and seaweed emulsion for about 5 minutes before transplanting. (I have done this with good results.) Pepper Joe, an online source, recommends adding 1 teaspoon of sulfur to each hole before planting the seedlings.

Mulch to minimize weeds and keep the plants moist. When the plants are firmly established, switch to an organic fertilizer that is higher in phosphorus and potassium, cutting back on the nitrogen.

A Container Pepper Garden

My small garden, faced with the constant menace of two energetic young dogs who love to eat pepper leaves and dig holes as deep as caves, has forced me to grow most of my plants in containers on sturdy planks of wood set on trestles, about 3 feet/91 centimeters above the ground. Sturdy 5-gallon/20 liter plastic pots have served me well through the years. The clay pots that I love don't work well for peppers because porous clay allows the soil to dry out too quickly. I plant especially large peppers in large containers like whisky barrels and oversized glazed ceramic pots from Asia, or place the plastic containers in nicer decorative pots. To prevent the pots from harboring pathogens and insects over the winter, every year I discard the old soil and wash all containers thoroughly with soap and water, followed by a rinse with chlorinated water.

I use a good-quality organic potting soil mixture mixed with some vermiculite and perlite to improve water retention and ensure proper drainage. I transplant the seedlings by the same procedure as for setting them in the ground, often after a good five-minute soaking in diluted fish seaweed and emulsion.

But even when placed high above the ground, container plants aren't always safe. I have found that seedlings I've grown from seed are a favorite target for squirrels, which dig up the tender plants for no apparent reason. One season I had to protect dozens of seedlings for weeks by locking them up in old bird cages and dog kennel crates. It was a strange sight.

Planting in containers will give you the flexibility to save your plants from animal marauders and to use them as ornamentals. You can place your potted plants, pot and all, in nicer decorative containers and arrange them strategically at various places in your garden. Or you can move any pepper to another spot in the garden if it doesn't seem happy with its location, and you can easily bring them indoors over the winter.

Caring for Pepper Plants

I inspect my plants twice a day and discard any leaves or fruits that look diseased. Under usual conditions, I water my plants only when the soil seems dry to the touch. But when temperatures rise above 90°F/32°C, I water them deeply to keep them moist. In stressful conditions, peppers may start to drop their blossoms before setting fruit. Spraying the leaves and blossoms with a solution of magnesium-rich Epsom salts and water helps encourage the setting of fruit. Through the years I have followed the advice of several pepper experts when it comes to organic fertilizers. Whether you use a liquid, slow-release pellet, or granular fertilizer, make sure that it is low in nitrogen, which accelerates growth but not flowering.

When your plants have fruit, check them daily to see which peppers are ready to be harvested. Be aware that picking the pods as they become ripe stimulates the plant to produce more. I harvest my peppers not only at the peak of ripeness but at different degrees of maturity, looking for different flavor sensations. Always harvest peppers by snipping them with garden shears rather than pulling the fruit off the stems, which can damage the delicate plant. The only exceptions are tiny chiltepines and *frutescens*, such as *ají guaguao* and *malagueta*, which detach easily from the calyx with just a gentle pull.

Some gardeners like to extend the growing season by pruning the plants before the first frost. This forces the plant to focus its strength on fruits already in the process of ripening rather than on new vegetative growth.

I would like to save my entire pepper garden when winter comes each year. But I would have to move to another house, as the peppers would take over. Realizing that I have no space for such an epic rescue has made me concentrate on a few special cultivars. These include ones collected as seeds during my Latin American travels, as well as plants like the Andean *ají amarillo* and *rocoto*—such late bearers in my New Jersey growing season that allowing them to winter indoors gives them a head start the next year.

Being too soft-hearted to prune back the plants severely before bringing them inside has hindered my rescue efforts in the past by admitting bugs and disease. Shortly before the first frost, prune back the plants and remove fallen leaves and fruits from the soil. If your pots are too big, uproot the plants, trim the roots, and transplant them to smaller, more manageable containers using fresh soil. This will diminish the danger of pathogens and insect infestation as the plants enter dormancy. Place the plants in a cool space at 55°F to 60°F/13° to 15°C, with some light. Water sporadically; twice a month will do. As the growing season approaches, increase the warmth and light exposure and begin to water more frequently, about once a week. Allow the plants to come out of dormancy and begin to develop new growth. Treat them like seedlings and bring them out after the danger of frost has passed.

No matter which peppers or growing methods you choose, once the plants are established, observe how they behave in your garden and write down what you learn. The unexamined pepper is not worth planting.

COOKING WITH PEPPERS

From nurturing so many peppers through the years, I have gained an immense appreciation for the fruits' beauty and their amazing range of sizes, colors, and shapes, as well as their endless culinary versatility. Tasting home-grown versions of peppers that I'd encountered only abroad or when imported and frozen has sharpened my insight into the minds of Latin American cooks who have known their own local species or cultivars almost from the cradle.

For millennia, peppers have been the backbone of New World cooking. We chop them and slice them to stir into our *sofritos*. We dry them, smoke them, roast them on hot griddles, reconstitute them in water, and grind them into pastes to enrich the marinades known as adobos. We use them to bring other foods' flavors—sweet, sour, salty—into sharper focus. At times we reach for a brilliant final splash of color in the sweet, bright, handy form of Spanish fire-roasted pimientos in a jar.

Over the years I have also come to understand that the most important lesson of peppers can be breathtaking simplicity. The more I travel in the lands of peppers, the more accustomed I have become to the sight of people digging into meals with an occasional nibble on a plain, unadorned hot pepper, or seasoning their food by simply mashing peppers into it at the table, as if the peppers were salt or pepper. In Huánuco, in the Peruvian Amazon, it is common to see people crushing tiny fresh *ajíes charapitas* into bowls of soup made from *carachama*, a local river fish, or following a mouthful with a tiny bite of another very hot pepper like the pukunuchu. I've also seen old women in Huanchaco, a Peruvian beachside town in La Libertad Region, biting into a hot *ají moche* while drinking flavorful *chilcano* (a fish soup). In the same spirit, Mexicans in Sonora put a dish of dried wild chiltepines on the table and reach for them at intervals, crushing the tiny nuggets directly over their plates with their fingers. The tradition of using whole fresh peppers as a table condiment traveled to the United States in colonial times, most probably from the English Caribbean, and became entrenched in dining rituals in parts of the South.

THE RITUAL OF THE BIRD'S-EYE PEPPER

The ritual of the bird's-eye pepper is still observed in the old-fashioned households where the soup comes on steaming in the big tureen, and the host helps it at the table. He asks each guest if he will have one or two of the little green peppers which are picked fresh just before the meal and he mashes it (or them, if the guest has a hardy palate) in the plate before putting in the soup, so that it permeates the dish. But woe be to the guest who fails to remove the innocent looking little green condiment, for its trail is hot enough for the "highest" taste, and a touch of the pepper itself is purgatory undiluted.

—Harriet Ross Colquitt, *The Savannah Cook Book* (1933)

Perhaps this should be the first pepper "recipe" you try: As you sit down to dinner, take a fairly hot fresh pepper of any preferred kind—jalapeño, cayenne, habanero, or any others—and set it by your plate. Slice it and crush a bit with a fork into your food or pause from time to time while eating and nibble a very small morsel of the pepper, preferably closer to the tip than the stem end. Let the direct jolt of capsaicin heat register on your palate along with the fruit's other grassy, bitter, sweet, or floral notes before continuing with your next mouthful of dinner. This is probably the oldest way of using capsicums to enhance the pleasure of food.

A second, equally revealing experiment calls for an habanero, Scotch bonnet, or other chinense pepper—even a superhot cultivar like a Trinidad Moruga Scorpion, if you feel adventurous. Use a small, sharp knife to score a tiny cross at the stem end, and set the pepper aside while you start making your preferred cooking sauce, soup, or bean dish. Partway through the cooking, take the pepper by the stem and briefly swish it around in the pot. Some of the fragrance and heat will infuse the soup or cooking liquid and meld with the other flavors. This is a favorite trick of cooks in the Yucatán, the Caribbean, and the Orinoco basin, and a less-is-more example of the power of peppers to transform a dish.

All the advice on purchasing, storing, drying, pickling, and fermenting in this chapter can be used as a flexible template for making the most of your fresh and dried peppers as you build your own pepper pantry. You will find it a vital guide as you cook from my recipes.

Tasting Dried Peppers

With dried peppers, the business of tasting is a little more complex. You can't just bite into one and get a sense of the real possibilities. I think that the best way to take their measure is to reconstitute them in water and process them to a paste—seeds and all—in a food processor or blender, without steps like griddle-toasting and straining that you would commonly use in an actual recipe. There is method in this madness. Toasting dried peppers caramelizes some of their sugars and introduces more variables than you want when assessing the intrinsic flavors.

The basic procedure is as follows: Take the chosen dried *ajíes* or chiles and rinse them well. Use enough to engage the blades of a blender or food processor (after they have been rehydrated). The minimum that I recommend is about 2 ounces/55 grams. Fill a medium saucepan with 3 cups/720 milliliters water and bring to a boil over high heat. Add the dried peppers, lower the heat, and simmer, uncovered, until they have swelled to the size of fresh peppers and a pepper is soft enough to squeeze between your fingertips. The time this will take varies drastically depending on the pepper and drying method. Drain, reserving a few tablespoons of the cooking liquid, and remove the stems. Place the peppers in a blender or food processor and process to a rough-textured paste, adding the reserved liquid as necessary to help the action of the blades.

Scrape out the pepper paste into a small bowl and note its color and shine. Bring the bowl to your nose and spend a minute or two sniffing the paste, since volatile compounds are key to a full understanding of a pepper's overall flavor. Only then, taste a small amount. The principal qualities that you are looking for are heat, acidity, sweetness, and suggestions of particular fruits, vegetables, herbs, or spices. Be careful not to jump to conclusions based on sight alone. A jammy, berry-colored puree is not a guarantee that the peppers' taste will be sweet or fruity. And don't let a powerfully hot pepper deter you from tasting it after that first jolt of insufferable heat that tells your lizard brain to run. Be sure to have a glass of whole milk or a little plain yogurt or sour cream on hand to tame the burn, and keep tasting.

With very aromatic or refined peppers, you may want to put the paste through a mesh strainer in order to sample the puree in its purest form. It is best not to introduce distracting flavors, but as an alternative to tasting the basic paste by itself you may try putting it on a plain cracker.

My final step is to make a very minimalist cooked sauce by sautéing the pepper puree, seasoned with some salt, in a bit of oil and then diluting it to the consistency of tomato sauce by adding a bit of water and letting the sauce come to a simmer. That will give you a good idea of a dried pepper's culinary possibilities.

The huge range of different pepper sizes and shapes makes it difficult to match them to standard cup measurements, so weight is the best measure to use. You will need a scale capable of registering ounces and grams. In most recipes I list the weight in ounces or pounds and grams or kilograms followed by the approximate number of peppers. When minuscule peppers, such as chiltepines are called for, it is a waste of time to count them by the dozens.

A Pepper-Handling Primer

The pleasure of working with peppers will be enhanced if you can start out with a basic perspective on using peppers. It used to be that few North American cooks had access to any other hot peppers than fresh jalapeños and (maybe) serranos. Now many of us have choices—actually, it can feel like a bewildering number of choices.

Buying and Storing Fresh Peppers

You can buy fresh peppers year-round from supermarkets (which nowadays may carry more than half a dozen kinds), ethnic markets (especially in Hispanic and Asian neighborhoods), and—my preferred venue—farmers' markets and farm stands. In northern states with short growing seasons, it's a good idea to keep track of the seasons at which different peppers ripen so you will know whether the produce you see at market is likely to have been locally grown. Seasonal limitations can be partly offset in some cases by imported peppers from large-scale greenhouse operations, with the Netherlands supplying different sweet or hot cultivars of quite high quality. A good rule of thumb is that the readily available jalapeños and serranos will always deliver clean, moderate heat and pleasant unobtrusive green notes, but there are other annuum peppers, like the Fresno, Santa Fe Grande, and several types of cayenne that have similar heat and flavor notes. If a recipe calls for the perfumed notes and intense heat of an exotic chinense that is only available in season (most likely grown in your garden), the go-to pepper is always the reliable habanero or a combination of a perfumed heatless chinense, such as the Caribbean *ají dulce* or *ají cachucha* (available in most Latin American markets) and a straightforward hot annuum.

Whenever possible, buy fresh peppers that are displayed loose. Shrink-wrap packaging has a way of accelerating undetected spoilage (this is especially true with small, tender peppers such habaneros or *ajíes dulces*). If shrink-wrapped peppers are your only option, inspect the peppers for moldy stems and try to detect any soft spots by feeling with your fingertips. Buy slightly more than you think you need and prepare to discard some that have gone bad. Whether bought or freshly harvested from your own garden, all fresh peppers should be promptly rinsed under cold running water and drained until dry before you cook with them.

If you apply the same good sense you use when buying other fresh produce, you will not go wrong. Choose plump peppers with glossy skin and firm stems. Avoid any that are wrinkled, have soft spots, or show marked discoloration. There are exceptions to the last rule: sun spots and uneven coloration do not always indicate poor quality, and corky-looking striations on jalapeños are fine (in fact, some Mexican cooks prefer such jalepeños).

Like tomatoes, fresh peppers taste best if stored at room temperature. They are so beautiful that I keep them in baskets on the kitchen counter. If storing them for longer than two days, refrigerate them in a paper bag or a loosely sealed, perforated plastic bag. Avoid using tightly sealed plastic bags or storage containers, as they will trap moisture and hasten spoilage. Change paper bags if they get soggy.

In some areas of the country, the only place to find Andean *rocotos* and *ajíes amarillos* is in the freezer case. As with frozen vegetables, you should feel the bag to make sure the peppers are not covered with ice crystals, which indicates poor handling and compromised quality. Defrost, rinse, and pat dry before using. Be aware that since frozen peppers tend to retain more moisture than fresh ones and the flesh is slacker after defrosting, they are best for braises, stews, and pureed sauces.

Preparing Fresh Peppers

If your skin is sensitive or you are working with especially hot peppers, it can be a good idea to wear protective gloves. After rinsing the peppers under cold running water, proceed as your recipe directs. If the peppers are to be diced or chopped, cut each one in half lengthwise and use the tip of a paring knife or a small spoon (a serrated grapefruit spoon works well) to remove the seeds and

THE COMAL

The *comal* (from the Nahuatl *comalli*) is a round griddle, sometimes made of clay, used by Mexican and Central American cooks to roast staple ingredients like peppers and tomatoes before further cooking or grinding; it is also used to cook tortillas. Clay *comales* give foods a very special flavor but need careful treatment. They have a short life span and must be brushed with a lime solution after each use to season the surface. I recommend buying the more convenient and popular carbon-steel *comales*, which should be cured and treated like other carbon-steel pan. This is my favorite pan for roasting chiles, both fresh and dried.

membranes, which are where most of the heat-generating capsaicinoids reside. Slice each half into strips, stack them together, and cut crosswise into pieces of the desired size.

If the peppers are to be used whole, cut around the stems to detach them. (With irregularly shaped peppers, it is simpler to slice off the top about ¼ inch/6 millimeters below the stem.) If you wish to keep the stem and top intact for presentation purposes, make a lengthwise slit down the side of pepper and carefully scrape out the seeds.

Roasting or Broiling Peppers

Precooking peppers contributes to a rich layering of flavors. In some recipes, peppers are sautéed with aromatics in a cooking sauce. In others, intense dry heat is applied to caramelize the peppers' sugars, bringing out their sweetness and complexity. Here are three methods:

Griddle-roasting: Heat a cast-iron skillet or a comal over medium-high heat until a drop of water sizzles on contact. Place the whole peppers on the hot surface and roast, turning occasionally with tongs, until they are blackened on all sides. The timing will depend on shape and size—a few seconds for small peppers; 1 minute or so for long skinny ones; and up to 3 minutes for large wrinkled ones.

Flame-roasting: Working with one pepper at a time, hold it with tongs over a gas burner or grill, turning it so it chars evenly.

Broiling: Position an oven rack so the peppers will be about 4 inches/10 centimeters from the heat source. Set the whole peppers on a baking sheet, and when the broiler is hot, slide the pan into the oven. Turn them from time to time until they are blistered and charred all over.

Whichever method you use, immediately place the blackened peppers in a paper or food-safe plastic bag, close it tightly, and let them steam to loosen the skins. When they are cool enough to handle, after approximately 10 minutes, remove the skin with a paring knife or your fingers. Do not rinse them or you will lose some of the wonderful caramelized flavor. Core and seed the peppers and proceed with your recipe.

Drying Peppers at Home

The five magical months when my many individual pepper cultivars start producing fruit according to their different internal clocks are from late July to early November. I nurse them religiously, sheltering them from sun glare, watering them judiciously during hot spells, and trying to protect them from storms, marauding opossums and squirrels, and my rambunctious dogs, as the peppers develop to harvesting stage. When I know that they have produced their full complement of fruit for the year, I am proud. It is always with sadness that I harvest the last peppers. I often leave some to dry on the plant, just to watch the slow changes in the fruit as the skin softens, some red cultivars begin to darken, and others, such as the *aribibi gusano* and the yellow *pimenta cumarí*, blanch to ivory white.

The truth is that to run a proper pepper kitchen in my New Jersey neighborhood, it is best to embrace the seasonality of peppers. I've learned I do not have to use peppers at their peak to extract every iota of flavor. From August to early November, I shift to freezing, pickling, and drying what I can't use immediately. For me, drying is important and not because it will keep me in peppers until next summer. (It won't. I'm continually ordering a wide array of dried peppers from all over the Americas and Spain.) It's important because it allows me to be part of a process that is as old as humankind. Even in the lands of perennial peppers, people dry poblanos, chilacas, *ajíes amarillos*, and many more for the sake of the flavorful changes they undergo. I do the same with my humble bounty, garnered from less than perfect environmental conditions because I derive great pleasure from witnessing—and tasting—the peppers' transformation.

Forever the romantic, I make garlands from tiny peppers and dry them on pot racks in my kitchen. I find that some small, thin-skinned peppers do well with this treatment. But in the humid, thunderstorm-prone summers of our local climate, sun-drying large meaty peppers is not an option. Another strategy is necessary. The two most practical options for successful drying are to use an oven or a countertop dehydrator.

MERKÉN: CHILE'S EDIBLE GOLD

A condiment of the Mapuche, Chile's largest indigenous group, *merkén* is a ground mixture of dried, smoked *ají cacho de cabra* (a Chilean pepper that looks a bit like the Mexican *guajillo*) and seasonings that include cumin, coriander seeds, and salt. *Merkén* is one of my favorite Latin ingredients; this paprika-like blend adds heat, intense smoky flavor, saltiness, and subtle aroma to everything from soups and braises to table salsas.

A whiff of this wonderful stuff takes me back to a trip with my Chilean friend Maria Eugenia to the land of the Mapuche, where I first encountered *merkén*.

Beginning in Valdivia, a coastal town at the confluence of three rivers, we drove inland past Temuco to visit the family of a Mapuche Indian woman named Sofia, who had taught us many traditional recipes while working as a cook for Maria Eugenia.

We found Sofia's family living in a *ruka*, a traditional straw-thatched hut where life revolves around a central hearth. Above the fire hung sturdy baskets of provisions, such as corn and dried *cacho de cabra* peppers. The heat kept these foods dry (an important consideration in this humid part of Chile), while the smoke gave the peppers a delicious, paprika-like flavor. The women of the household ground them to a coarse powder in a small stone mortar with toasted dried spices and salt. I soon learned to tell homemade *merkén* from *merkén* that is processed in large mills, and to recognize regional variations in flavor. In some areas, merkén is rich in coriander seeds, while in others, cumin dominates the mix.

These days, *merkén* is sold in Chile's elegant food boutiques in handsome spice containers with symbolic Mapuche brand names. *Merkén* exported by Origen Chilean Gourmet is produced by artisans in the Araucania region and has fair-trade certification. The gentrification of *merkén* coincides with both the global search for local flavors and a revalidation of the Mapuche's contribution to Chile's national discourse.

The relationship among Spaniards, criollos, and indigenous peoples has never been easy. When Spanish troops moved into Chile in 1541, they encountered the Mapuche, one of the few Andean societies to have resisted Incan control. Seminomadic hunters and gatherers who also practiced agriculture, the Mapuche lived in central and southern Chile and across the Andes in parts of today's Argentina. So fierce was their resistance that the Spaniards could only claim control of the north and central regions of Chile. The vast lands south of the Bío-Bío River remained in Mapuche control.

Though maintaining a measure of independence, they were not immune to European influence, keeping captive Spanish women as wives, learning to grow wheat, and becoming cattle growers and accomplished horsemen. *Merkén*, with its mixture of native American *cacho de cabra* pepper and aromatic Mediterranean spices, such as cumin and coriander seeds, is another example of this creative fusion.

In the post-independence period, the Mapuche were stripped of their land and lost the right to trade and keep their herds. They became poor farmers whose interests often conflicted with those of the criollo farmers who flooded Chile's heartland. In recent years, many Mapuche have migrated to urban centers, particularly Santiago, where they continue to voice their grievances over land disputes and cultural issues in protest marches and public rallies.

When I use artisanal *merkén* from the Araucanía, the Mapuche heartland, I am not only keeping alive the spirit of the *ruka* and its smoky hearth, but also the collective will of a tenacious people who have won the right to leave their mark.

GROUND PEPPER POWDERS

Having several dried ground pepper powders on hand is an indispensable resource in a well-stocked pepper kitchen. Store the powders in tightly closed containers in a cool, dark place. Stir them into cooking sauces, soups or stews or sprinkle them on finished dishes for instant heat and color.

Ground Ají Mirasol

Color: Yellow ochre like old gold.

Flavor: Delicious bright tropical fruitiness with underlying sweetness.

Heat: Mild heat that builds slowly.

17 dried mirasol peppers (about 3¼ oz/90 g) makes ½ cup/55 g.

Ground Ají Panca

Color: Dark burgundy brown.

Flavor: Berry acidity and cooked vegetable notes. Mild cacao notes and bursts of stone fruit.

Heat: Slow buildup of heat, spreading through the whole mouth in a comforting way like the first sip of hot chocolate when you come in out of the snow.

17 dried panca peppers (about 2 oz/55 g) makes ⅓ cup/50 g.

Ground Chile Ancho

Color: Dark brown like rich espresso, with specks of crimson.

Flavor: Very fruity with tangy notes of cooked rhubarb.

Heat: Mild heat that does not spread out but rolls over the tongue.

24 dried ancho chiles (about 12½ oz/355 g) makes ½ cup/55 g.

Ground Chile Guajillo

Color: Bright brick red.

Flavor: Tart, green tamarind.

Heat: Mild heat.

24 guajillo chiles (about 5 oz/140 g) makes ⅓ cup/50 g.

Ground Chile Mulato

Color: Muted black olive and taupe.

Flavor: Mellow but rich dried fruit notes.

Heat: Gentle heat.

24 mulato chiles (about 10 oz/280 g) makes 1¼ cups/190 g.

Ground Chile Puya

Color: Burnt orange, like Sedona's red rocks.

Flavor: Nutty with a bit of tang.

Heat: Direct assault of sharp heat that grows.

49 puya chiles (about 2½ oz/70 g) makes ⅓ cup/40 g.

Ground Chile Chipotle Morita

Color: Rich, dark-orange cinnabar.

Flavor: Smoky with a bitter edge reminiscent of cacao.

Heat: Sharp, searing, burning down the throat.

60 chipotle morita chiles (about 6⅜ oz/180 g) makes ½ cup/85 g.

Chile Pasilla Flakes

Color: Burnt sienna mulch with a tinge of black olive and specks of onyx.

Flavor: Vegetable acidity and nuttiness with underlying sweetness.

Heat: Pleasant heat that builds slowly.

24 dried pasilla chiles (about 7 oz/200 g) makes 1 cup/140 g.

Preparing Peppers for Drying

Pick peppers only when they are perfectly ripe and have achieved peak color. Discard any with blemishes, discolorations, or soft spots. Rinse them under cold water in a colander, pat dry, and set aside until you are sure that they are bone-dry.

You may leave the peppers whole, stem and all, or cut them into pieces. If they are large and meaty, they probably will take a long time to dry evenly and completely in either the oven or a dehydrator. In that case, it is wisest to remove the stems and cut the peppers lengthwise in halves or strips, depending on the size. If you plan to grind them into a powder (see page 238), seed and devein them now for a purer pepper taste and brighter color. Seeding before drying may also help if you are using a dehydrator; the seeds tend to collect on the bottom and can clog the machine's air vent.

Oven Method for Drying Peppers

To dry peppers in a gas or electric oven, place them, cut-side down, in a single layer on a baking sheet and set it on the lowest oven rack. I suggest setting the heat at about 200°F/95°C. If your oven has a lower setting, such as 150°F/65°C or 175°F/80°C, that is even better. Check the peppers periodically, turning every 3 hours for even drying. Remove the peppers from the oven when they have reached the desired degree of dryness, which will vary depending on their size and meatiness. A good rule of thumb is that with large, fleshy, thick-skinned peppers, you should stop when most of the moisture has evaporated but they still feel pliable to the touch. With smaller, thin-skinned peppers, I usually continue the process until they are dry enough to crumble between my fingertips.

Dehydrator Method for Drying Peppers

I use an inexpensive countertop dehydrator with stacking trays and vertical central airflow. For the most even drying, you might want to use a model with horizontal airflow. Monitor the drying process carefully until you have a good feel for how your dehydrator works.

Place the whole peppers (if they will fit) or pepper strips on the dehydrator trays. They can touch but should not overlap. Set the thermostat between 135°F/57°C and 140°F/60°C. Dry the peppers for 36 to 48 hours, rotating the trays every 6 to 8 hours. Check the peppers every 2 to 4 hours, and stop the process when they have reached the desired stage, as described in the oven method.

Buying Dried Hot Peppers

Sight and touch are the most important aspects of shopping for dried chiles in a market. If you are buying see-through packages of peppers, be sure to examine the contents carefully and avoid any with punctures in the wrapping. Try to feel the dried pods inside the package. The color, appearance, and texture should closely match the individual descriptions given in the Gallery of Dried Peppers (pages 195 to 217). The more you work with them, the more you will notice signs of peak or past-peak quality. For instance, if you get to know the pliant suppleness that a good-quality ancho or mulato should have, you will recognize that a stiff, woody feel indicates the peppers have been stored too long. Buy only as much as you need at a time. Dried peppers don't stay in prime condition for more than 6 months; and you cheat yourself when you try to work with stale ones.

I have to stress that for all the glory of fresh peppers, dried peppers deserve equal billing. Their beauty is of a different kind, evoking the colors of an autumn forest filled with deep reds, tawny browns, dusky oranges, and subtly muted yellows. Slow, controlled drying reveals dimensions not present in the fresh fruit. By way of comparison, think of the flavors brought out in fresh dates, grapes, figs, plums, and apricots by drying. If fresh Mexican chiles and Andean ajíes speak to our tastebuds with bright clarity, the dried versions offer something fuller, deeper, earthier, and more evolved. Yes, they can be added to cooking sauces. But they come into their own when used as the true foundation of the sauce, binding all other elements in pungent but balanced harmony.

The dried peppers you choose to buy may depend on how you mean to use them. Larger specimens are preferable for stuffing, while size doesn't matter as much when you use them for sauces. The firmer, more intact, and free of crumbled bits they are, the better. Contrary to my advice for fresh peppers, choose prepackaged over loose, dried peppers if possible.

Dried peppers show up for sale at a range of different venues. Years of experience have led me to a sobering realization: At many stages from field to display bin, dried peppers are left open to contamination by small animals or insects. I now think it is best to treat dried peppers from all commercial sources (including online sellers) as potentially unsanitary. I make sure to rinse them in plenty of cold water, drain them well, and spread them out to sit until bone-dry before going further. (If they retain any moisture, they will steam later on, instead of roasting.) Of course, these precautions are unnecessary if you do your own drying in a home dehydrator.

Preparing Dried Peppers

After cleaning, you can turn dried peppers into lively seasonings with four simple steps: seeding (for most large meaty peppers), toasting, reconstituting, and grinding.

Seeding: If your recipe calls for seeding, pull out the stems of large peppers and shake out the seeds. With skinny peppers, slice them open with a paring knife (or tear them lengthwise with your fingers) and wipe out the seeds with a paper towel. I like to butterfly large meaty peppers, such as ancho chiles, to ensure even roasting.

Toasting: Heat a cast-iron skillet or comal over medium to medium-high heat until a drop of water sizzles on contact. With seeded and butterflied peppers, press the cut side against the hot surface with a metal spatula for a few seconds. Turn the pepper over with kitchen tongs and press the second side against the skillet, taking care that the flesh toasts lightly but does not burn. A pleasant roasted pepper aroma is a good cue. Watch closely, especially with smooth, thin-skinned peppers such as guajillos and cascabels, and be prepared to snatch them from the heat if they begin to scorch. Meatier, more wrinkled peppers such as anchos and mulatos are less prone to burning and may take longer to roast evenly. Small whole peppers should be toasted for a few seconds and turned once with kitchen tongs.

Reconstituting: Mexican and Central American cooks typically reconstitute toasted dried peppers to facilitate grinding. In Bolivia and Peru where toasting is not considered a prerequisite, dried peppers are also soaked to soften. To do so, cover the peppers with warm water or broth and let them soak for 15 to 30 minutes or until soft. Alternatively, boil them in water or broth to cover for 20 to 30 minutes, until softened. Drain the peppers, reserving the soaking or boiling liquid for use in grinding or later cooking.

Grinding: Process the peppers in a blender or food processor or grind with a circular motion in a *molcajete*, the three-legged volcanic-stone mortar used by Mexican cooks. Add small amounts of soaking liquid to loosen as necessary, and grind until you achieve the desired consistency.

Making Dried Pepper Powders

Many Latin American recipes call for ground dried peppers of various textures; some are processed to a very fine powder, while others are as coarse as the hot pepper flakes that are sprinkled on pizza. Prepared ground peppers are available in markets, but nothing beats the pure flavor and freshness of home-dried peppers ground to your taste. If using already dried peppers, clean and prepare them as described on page 237. You can toast the peppers briefly if you want a bit of a smoky flavor (see above), but I prefer to skip that process to enjoy the essential flavor and color of the dried peppers.

HOW THE TURKEY AND THE CHILE MET IN A POT OF MOLE

Franciscan friar Bernardino de Sahagún, in his monumental *Historia general de las cosas de nueva España* (*General History of the Things of New Spain*), provides valuable information on turkeys under both the local names—*totollin*, for the female and *huexolotl* (root of the modern Mexican word, *guajolote*) for the male—and the default Spanish name, *gallina*. He describes various ways in which turkey was cooked, chiefly dishes that we would call braises or stews. To this day, cooks in Mexico and much of Mesoamerica usually bypass versions of roasted turkey, preferring it cut into parts and cooked in sauces seasoned with chiles and tomatoes and often enriched with pumpkin seeds—dishes that Sahagún's Aztec friends and informants would easily recognize.

Sahagún is also one of our earliest sources of knowledge about moles. To the Aztecs, *molli* or *mulli* was a generic word for sauces, most of which used chiles as a principal flavoring. But there was no clear distinction between the sauce and the finished dish in which it was used. (This is still the case today, giving rise to many misunderstandings about moles.) Sahagún makes it plain that some moles were associated with weddings and other important occasions, and that turkey could play a major role. He describes the marriage custom involving one particular molli called *tlatonilli*: after washing the bride's mouth, her mother-in-law would bring her a wooden platter of tamales and another of tlatonilli, and feed her and the bridegroom four mouthfuls each before sending them into the bridal chamber. (Tlatonile is still a traditional wedding dish in the Huatusco Region of Veracruz State.) Sahagún reported that when *pochtecas* (Aztec merchants), an honored class who transported valuable wares within the empire, gathered for a ceremonial banquet, they began by offering a dish of turkey heads "with its molli" to their patron deity Xiuhtecutli, the fire god. We know that links between some of the more complex moles and festive meals have persisted since pre-Hispanic times.

The best-known example of a mole is the elaborate mole poblano, surrounded by myths about its supposed invention in the seventeenth-century convent of Santa Rosa in Puebla de los Angeles. The nuns, led by a gifted cook, Sor Andrea de la Asunción, coped with a surprise visit by bishop Manuel Fernández de Santa Cruz and his guest, the ruling Spanish viceroy, by improvising a turkey mole out of some chiles, chocolate, and anything else in the larder.

The convent larders held an assortment of native and Old World ingredients that they used with great skill. Maize and achiote for thickening and coloring drinking chocolate were already essential, along with Mediterranean spices and pumpkin seeds, stale corn tortillas, and dried chiles, which were ground into thickeners for sauces along with the almonds, hazelnuts, and stale wheat bread that medieval Spanish cooks had used for the same purpose. The alleged sacrificial pot of charred turkey bones, excavated from a royal tomb at the western Honduran site of Copan, dates to about AD 450 and contains traces of cacao and capsaicin.

It is evident that as early as the seventeenth century, moles had been transformed into the pre-eminent fusion dish of Mexico, preserving the basic premise of a pre-Columbian *molli* with tomatoes, chiles, and cacao but also enriched with a cache of Old World spices and nuts. Today moles continue to rely on chiles for color, body, and heat, and turkey remains enthroned as the bird that cooks prefer to sacrifice to impress a bishop or a hundred wedding guests.

AJÍ NEGRO AND COUSINS

Some of my favorite hot condiments belong to the family of heady, vinegary sauces based on yuca juice and very fiery peppers—a pre-Hispanic legacy that still flourishes among the indigenous peoples of the Orinoco and Amazonian regions. Still unknown to most US food-lovers, they have started attracting attention among avant-garde South American chefs.

Clans of the dwindling Witoto or Uitoto people in the Colombian Amazon still preserve the ancient rain forest technology of soaking, mashing, and squeezing bitter yuca to extract the juice before grinding the pulp to flour for

casabe. They denature the poisonous cyanide compounds of the juice by cooking it down for days, with hot peppers and perhaps fish bones, to make casarama or yomak, a dark sauce the consistency of condensed milk that is their main condiment. A more commercial Venezuelan cousin, bottled under different brand names, is making a crossover to high-end restaurants. Known as catara or katara, it has a sharp vinegary edge and packs a unique punch from being cooked with the tail segments of bachacos, a species of large leafcutter ants.

A road to the future for these traditional sauces is emerging in Peru, where the family has the general name of ají negro. The talented chef Pedro Miguel Schiaffino was so smitten by a version he tasted among the Bora people of western Amazonia that he not only now serves ají negro at his Lima restaurants Amaz and Malabar but commissions Bora women in the small community of Pucaurquillo to supply it. Dark and unctuous, it has the meaty umami depth of a demi-glace together with an addictive heat and tartness. Though primarily used now as a dip for casabe, it goes fantastically with many dishes. I hope to see chefs in North America and elsewhere follow Schiaffino's lead by providing a modern market for the ancient yuca-centered skills of threatened indigenous Amazonian-Orinocan peoples. Ají negro deserves to join harissa and Sriracha as one of the hot sauces that food-lovers anywhere can't live without.

Bora ají negro with casabe (yuca bread).

To make pepper powders, butterfly the dried peppers if they are large enough. They should be dry to the point of brittleness. If they are still pliable and soft to the touch, spread them on a baking sheet and place in a 200°F/95°C oven until completely dried, usually about 1 hour. Rotate the baking sheet and flip over the peppers every 30 minutes to dry evenly. Let cool completely. Break into bits by crumbling between your fingers or chopping with a heavy, sharp knife. The smaller the pepper bits, the easier they will be to grind. Grind to a powder in a spice mill or coffee grinder. I like a coarse texture, but grind twice if you prefer a very fine powder. If you have a large, powerful food processor, you can grind large amounts in one batch to the desired texture. Or use the food processor to get a coarse powder and then pulverize that into a finer powder in a coffee or spice mill.

Pepper Vinegars

I know that I'm in the presence of ancient culinary history when I sit down in an unpretentious Colombian or Venezuelan restaurant or walk into a country kitchen and see a bottle of vinegar sharpened with the bite of a few hundred tiny, scorching hot peppers. It could be a Coke or Pepsi bottle on the table with holes punched in the cap. But what the bottle holds is a link with the cuisine that was already in place when Columbus and his crew first broke *casabe* (the ubiquitous flatbread made from yuca flour) with their Taíno hosts on Hispaniola during that first expedition in 1492.

Thousands of years ago, these miniature, firey peppers reached the eastern Amazonian-Orinocan region from their place of origin in Bolivia. They entered the cuisine of civilizations in the lands that became northeastern Brazil, Venezuela, and Colombia as flavorings for the local vinegar fermented from yuca. Pepper vinegar, as an indispensable condiment for sprinkling over *casabe*, starchy vegetables, meat, and fish, accompanied people from the South American river basin societies when they moved to the Caribbean islands. Its use today persists throughout a broad region. I, a Cuban exile, feel an instant surge of recognition at first glimpse of the humble recycled bottle dispensing pepper vinegar anywhere in the Latin American tropics.

The truth is that all of us whose cuisines were touched by the ways of the island Taínos like acidic flavors in, or on, our food. We respond with familiar recognition to the ancient combination of acidity and stinging heat—though after the conquest we became the heirs of Spanish as well as indigenous food traditions. Vinegar from yuca has not disappeared as a commercial product. But depending on our different backgrounds, we may enjoy vinegar from apple cider or wine as well as today's most popular homemade version, pineapple vinegar, made from the peels trimmed off the fruit. But the principle hasn't changed since pre-Hispanic times: acid plus capsaicin heat.

HOW TO STERILIZE GLASS CANNING JARS

To store my pepper sauces and vinegars, I use glass canning jars and bottles. They can be easily sterilized to prevent bacterial contamination, and so they don't impart off-flavors to their contents. Plastic containers are convenient and plentiful but tend to add an unpleasant, chemical flavor. I often save glass vessels from store-bought condiments, wash them thoroughly, and sterilize them for storing sauces and vinegars. But I prefer glass jars with lid clamps and rubber gaskets for an airtight seal.

To sterilize jars or bottles and their lids, place them in a large stockpot and cover with water; push the vessels down so they fill with water. Bring the water to a boil over high heat and let boil for 10 minutes. Have another pot of water boiling on the stove and add to the stockpot if the vessels start to emerge from the boiling water. Remove the vessels from the water with tongs and place them upside down on a clean rack to drain until cool and dry.

This way of embracing capsicums sets apart the cuisines of northeastern South America and the Greater Antilles from those of other regions. In Central America and the Andean countries, people like pepper heat deeply infused into main-dish cooking sauces as well as some table sauces. People in the eastern river basins and the islands, on the other hand, do very little cooking with hot peppers. It comes naturally to us to grab a few handfuls of some tiny, stinging wild or loosely domesticated peppers, bruise them lightly to help release the heat, fit them into a jar or bottle, and cover them with vinegar. We reach for the steeped pepper vinegar to season anything from cooked starch tubers to grilled meats. When the vinegar level drops, we simply top up the bottle with some more. It takes many steepings for the peppers to lose their pungency.

Do not think that all containers for our beloved pepper vinegar are recycled soda bottles, even though this is emblematic of Latin American thrift and practicality. Nor does the steeped condiment always consist of just vinegar and peppers. Especially in Venezuela, well-to-do families pride themselves on the beauty of their *ajiceros*—elegant glass flasks or cruets filled with colorful, carefully arranged displays of peppers and other seasoning ingredients (often briefly cooked), such as sliced onions, carrots, garlic, and whole spices. Every region of the country has its own cherished variations. There is also a family of wonderful Venezuelan pepper-laced condiments where the basic liquid is milk or whey, not vinegar. I fell in love with this surprising combination after encountering it in the Orinoco and in the Andes and have been experimenting with different versions ever since.

I believe that the whole family of hot, vinegary condiments now adored by millions of US diners is a direct descendant of this general tradition. Even the smell of Tabasco sauce has a recognizable connection with the smell of South American frutescens peppers ripened in my garden. The Caribbean slave trade was the likely route of transmission for the family of pepper vinegar sauces, as well as the pepper wine that came to the North American colonies, and evidence of that remains in parts of the American South.

Fermented Hot Peppers

In Latin America we have our own style of fermentation based on such staple foods as yuca, corn, and pineapple. From a bacteriological—and culinary—point of view, they do not closely resemble the traditional preparations that evolved in cooler European and North American climates. Our classic approach to preserving peppers would be to put them in vinegar that is strong enough to stop fermentation rather than encourage it. Still, I enjoy the wonderful sauces made from fermented peppers in other cultures. I have followed the US fascination with Sriracha sauce, which now eclipses catsup as a table condiment, and I have tasted beautiful relishes of lightly fermented red peppers in Chinese and other Asian restaurants.

Fermenting vegetables by cutting up or mashing them and exposing them to dry salt is a very ancient method in many parts of the world. It works in two ways: The salt quickly draws out the original moisture from the cells of the vegetable by osmosis. It also creates an environment that is hostile to certain bacteria and favorable to others. The salt-avoiding ones that are deterred include many different kinds of pathogens. The salt-tolerant ones that colonize the food include several species of lactic acid bacteria that quickly get to work breaking down the available carbohydrates into lactic acid. The decreasing pH (or increasing acidity) of the drawn-out juices repels still more competing pathogens or agents of spoilage. Some kinds of lactic acid bacteria produce nothing but lactic acid, while others draw on the chemical complexities of the vegetable to contribute small amounts of other metabolic products, resulting in more subtle and varied flavors.

Different peoples around the world have developed a range of refinements to this basic dry-salting method, with strikingly varied results. And of course there are numerous other methods, often involving brine instead of dry salt, or extended fermentation in a cool cellar. For peppers, I am content with the simplest approach and a fermentation period of only one or two weeks at room temperature, which preserves much of the original freshness. I have also discovered a way of making it yield two products: the flavorful strained pulp and the coarser-textured remainder of the original chopped peppers, separated into two distinct but equally delicious condiments.

A cacao farmer's lunch in Barinas, Venezuela, is not complete without an ajicero.

Pepper Condiments

At the end of the season, when most of my plants have finished bearing and only handfuls of peppers remain on most of the stems, I hurry to extract the last of the fresh peppers' essence by putting them up in a simple vinegar solution in glass jars, which showcase their distinctive shapes and brilliant colors. I like to use different-size jars to accommodate the variable amounts that remain at this time of year. I vary the seasonings to go with whichever peppers I have on hand. Sometimes I like to play with a single cultivar or a group of related peppers with the same color, and other times I go for a colorful mélange. It is not necessary to refrigerate the finished vinegars. If you prefer to keep yours in the refrigerator, let them warm to room temperature on the kitchen counter before serving. (Personally, I don't like chilled table sauces, pepper vinegars, or condiments.) These *encurtidos*, or *curtidos* (as we call anything preserved in vinegar in Spanish), are showy table condiments, but they are also terrific kitchen resources. I use the spiced vinegar to add heat and acidity to stews, braises, soups, and beans. Combined with olive oil, a bit of fresh cilantro, and a dash of cumin and oregano, they become delicious salad dressings or marinades. And when fresh peppers are not in season, I only have to scoop out and lightly crush a couple of the pickled ones to add heat, flavor, and acidity to a table salsa.

Chile Salt

CHILE CON SAL

This seasoned salt packs a megaton of chile power and flavor. Use it as a finishing touch for anything that could use a boost of flavor and heat.

MAKES ABOUT 1⅓ CUPS CUPS/280 G

1½ oz/40 g (about 80) chiles de árbol, stemmed

1 garlic clove

1 cup/240 g kosher or sea salt

Heat a 12-inch/30.5 cm skillet or comal over medium heat and add the chiles and garlic. Toss with tongs until the chiles are charred in spots, 30 seconds to 1 minute. Make sure that your work space is well ventilated and avert your face when toasting the chiles; the powerful fumes will make you cough.

Transfer the chiles, garlic, and salt to a food processor and pulse into a well-blended coarse powder. Store in an airtight container at room temperature for up to 3 months.

Homemade Merkén with Guajillo

MERKÉN DE GUAJILLO

Merkén (see page 234) is a smoky ground hot pepper mixture from Chile's Patagonia region that calls for dried *cacho de cabra* pepper. I often make it with guajillo and use it whenever a recipe calls for chile powder and nuanced aroma.

MAKES ABOUT ⅓ CUP/40 G

1¼ oz/35 g (about 6) dried cacho de cabra peppers or guajillo chiles

2 tsp smoked Spanish paprika (preferably pimentón de La Vera)

2 tsp whole coriander seeds

2 tsp whole cumin seeds

1 bay leaf, crushed

Seed and butterfly the peppers according to the directions on page 238. Heat a cast-iron skillet or comal over medium heat. Add the peppers and toast for a few seconds.

Chop the peppers coarsely and then grind with the paprika, coriander seeds, cumin seeds, and bay leaf in a spice mill. Store in an airtight container for up to 3 months.

Basic Dried Pepper Paste

PASTA DE AJÍ SECO BÁSICA

In pepper-loving countries like Peru, seasoning pastes made with fresh or dried peppers are essential kitchen resources. The homemade pastes always surpass store-bought equivalents in quality and full, fresh flavor.

The idea is to process the peppers minimally to retain their flavor and color. In Peru and Bolivia, with a few regional exceptions, cooks don't toast the dried peppers before reconstituting them by soaking or boiling them until they are soft. (In Mexico and parts of Central America, however, the peppers are usually toasted before being reconstituted.) The peppers are then ground in a blender with a bit of the pepper-soaking liquid to make a smooth puree that has the consistency of tomato paste. This can become the foundation of a number of cooking sauces and adobos (marinades). If storing it for a few days, it is best to briefly sauté the paste in a little oil to reduce the water content, which will discourage spoilage. You can also double or triple the recipe to make larger amounts of the paste and freeze it in resealable freezer bags; I recommend dividing it into portions of ¼ cup/60 ml or ½ cup/120 ml for this purpose to make it easier to use when cooking. Use this recipe as a master formula for making a variety of pastes with a similar weight of other pepper varieties.

The paste can be made ahead and kept refrigerated until ready to use. I like to stir about 3 tablespoons of the paste into the egg batter for calamari (page 302) for heat, flavor, and color.

MAKES ABOUT ½ CUP/120 ML

1⅛ oz/32 g (about 6) dried panca peppers

Stem, seed, and reconstitute the peppers according to the directions on page 238. Drain the peppers, reserving ¼ cup/60 ml of the soaking or boiling liquid. (If using the liquid in the Simple Panca Pepper Cooking Sauce on page 267, reserve an additional 1 cup/240 ml liquid.)

Transfer the peppers and the ¼ cup/60 ml reserved liquid to a blender or small food processor and puree until smooth. Store in the refrigerator for up to 1 week, or freeze for up to 3 months.

Mirasol variation: For an equally flavorful sauce with a coppery tinge and more sweetness, substitute an equal amount of dried *mirasol* peppers for the *ají panca*.

Guatemalan Chile Cobán and Cacao Condiment

POLVO DE CHILE COBÁN Y CACAO GUATEMALTECO

The *chile Cobán*, also called by its Maya name *ululte*, is the quintessential pepper of the Q'eqchi' (also spelled Kekchi) Maya people who live in the highlands of Alta Verapaz in Guatemala. The chiles Cobán are very hot with a tart undertone and the subtle notes of menthol that I find in some chiltepines. They are gathered and ground to a paste and sold wrapped in corn husks, a preparation called *mucul ik*, or they are sun-dried or hung in baskets over a wood fire to gradually dry in the smoke.

My favorite Alta Verapaz recipe is a condiment made with smoked chiles *Cobán*, roasted cacao nibs, and salt, all ground into a coarse paste and sometimes shaped into balls to be dried and grated over the region's iconic turkey soup-stew, *kak-ik*. (*Ik* is the word for "chiles" in Q'eqchi' Maya.) Dried and smoked chile Cobán is often sold as chile piquín in Hispanic markets that cater to Central Americans. If you cannot find the smoked version, add the optional teaspoon of a quality hot or sweet smoked paprika, such as pimentón de la Vera, to give the mix a smoky edge.

Sprinkle it over cut fruit (see page 275) or salads or stir it into stews, braises, and soups as a seasoning.

MAKES 1⅓ CUPS/180 G

1 oz/30 g dried chiles Cobán or chiltepines

5 oz/140 g cacao nibs

1 to 2 tsp kosher or sea salt

1 tsp smoked hot or sweet Spanish paprika (preferably pimentón de la Vera; optional)

Prepare the dried chiles according to the directions on page 237. Heat a large cast-iron skillet or comal over medium-high heat. Add the chiles and toast briefly, tossing with tongs, for a few seconds; remove and set aside. Add the cacao nibs and toast until fragrant, about 1 minute. Transfer the cacao nibs to a bowl and let cool.

Combine all the ingredients in a bowl. Working in batches, transfer to an electric spice or coffee mill and grind to a powder. Alternatively, in a small food processor pulse to grind finely. Do not continue to process once the mixture is well ground or the cacao will start to melt and become sticky. Transfer the mixture to an airtight container and store in a cool place for up to 3 months.

Mole Coloradito Paste

PASTA DE MOLE COLORADITO

I thought long and hard about which mole recipes to include in a book about peppers. There are so many, and all so fascinating in their own right. In the end I decided to choose only this one—the beautiful *mole coloradito* (literally, "little red one").

It takes me back to the days when I was testing recipes for Zafra, my first restaurant. Already I knew that moles are incredibly diverse. They can be as bright as sunrise over Manhattan (*manchamanteles*) or as smoky and darkly sweet as midsummer midnight (the elusive mole negro). Some are like thin-bodied stews (*mole amarillo, chichilo*) and others are velvety with enrichments of chocolate or cacao. We settled for serving three moles at Zafra—and of these, *mole coloradito* is the one that has endured for fifteen years just as it was taught to me and to our staff by our first cooks, Hilda and Haydée, two Oaxacan women who will live forever in my heart.

From Hilda and Haydée, I learned that what is important about a mole is not sacrosanct ingredients that can't be changed but the role each one plays as part of the structured whole. In Oaxaca, *mole coloradito* is a thick but satiny brick-red sauce that is bright with the heat of guajillos and chilcostles and, at the same time, delicately fruity and mellow. The brick-red hue that makes the sauce true to its name comes chiefly from both of these thin-skinned dried peppers. When Hilda and Haydée started at Zafra, we had trouble finding chilcostles. Depending on the situation, we would use guajillos and the sharper *chiles puyas*, or add a few mellower, more complex anchos. If plantains were not perfectly ripe, Hilda and Haydée would find the desired qualities—the body, fruity sweetness, and light acidity essential for a *coloradito*—in apples. A properly made *coloradito* delivers a complex mixture: well-modulated pungency and acidity, deep fruitiness without cloying sweetness, spices that play against each other but surrender their individual personality to the symphony of the pot, chocolate as a backbone of flavor rather than a distraction, satisfying body contributed by bread and nuts that also mellow sharp edges of flavor, and chiles that provide color with medium heat. I also have Hilda and Haydée to thank for realizing that store-bought lard would overpower the sweetness and subtlety and for deciding to use a fruity Arbequina olive oil from northern Spain as the basic cooking fat for our moles.

The beauty of this mole is that you can plan ahead and pace your work instead of trying to cram everything in on one day. The dense, cooked-down paste can be kept in the refrigerator and deployed as needed, diluted to the right strength for final cooking. Often people will buy the paste from one of the great markets where mole pastes are displayed in big, colorful mounds. Dedicated cooks usually have at least a few different mole pastes in the refrigerator, ready to be used as needed. For me, it is like money in the bank—the portable foundation of a great dish whenever I have to cook away from the comfort of my own kitchen.

When you are ready to turn the mole paste into sauce, simply dissolve the paste in some broth in the proportion of 1 part mole paste to 2 parts broth. The sauce has many uses: dip fresh corn tortillas in it and fill them with beans and cheese or cooked meat for enchiladas. Or use it for rich meats, such as braised short ribs, roast pork, or panfried duck breasts, setting the meat on top of a pool of the mole. Or, in the full baroque glory of *mole coloradito*, bring braised meat or poultry to the table swimming in the rich and soupy sauce, which is in keeping with the original pre-Hispanic and colonial presentation.

continued

Mole Coloradito Paste, continued

MAKES 3 CUPS/840 G
CONCENTRATED PASTE,
9 CUPS/2.1 L DILUTED SAUCE
FOR COOKING THE MOLE

---

3 oz/85 g (about 14) guajillo chiles

1½ oz/40 g (about 6) chilcostles
or puya chiles

1¾ oz/50 g (about 3) ancho chiles

1 oz/30 g (about 1 slice) firm-
textured white bread from a French
or Italian baguette

¼ cup/40 g whole blanched
almonds

1 tsp allspice berries

1 tsp black peppercorns

1 tsp dried oregano

1 (3-inch/7.5 cm) Ceylon cinnamon
stick (canela), broken into 3 pieces

2 whole cloves

2 tsp sesame seeds

10 oz/280 g (2 medium) ripe
beefsteak tomatoes, cut in half
crosswise

8 oz/230 g (1 medium) white onion,
cut in half lengthwise

4 garlic cloves

½ cup/70 g seedless black raisins

6 to 7 oz/170 to 200 g (1 medium)
ripe plantain (yellow with black
spots and soft to the touch)

1 cup/240 ml extra-virgin olive oil
(preferably fruity green oil from
Arbequina olives), plus more for
storing

2 oz/55 g 60% cacao or higher
dark chocolate (preferably made
from Latin American cacao),
coarsely chopped

1 Tbsp sea salt

Seed, toast, and reconstitute the chiles according to the directions on page 238. Reserve 1 cup/240 ml of the cooking or soaking liquid. Working in batches as necessary, place the softened peppers in a blender and process into a thick paste, adding about ¼ cup/60 ml or more of the reserved liquid if necessary to help the action of the blades. Scrape out into a bowl and reserve. Rinse and dry the blender jar for later use.

In a skillet over medium-high heat, toast the bread until golden on both sides. Remove, crumble with your fingers into a small bowl, and set aside. Add the almonds to the skillet and toast until golden; set aside in another small bowl.

Lower the heat to medium and add the allspice, peppercorns, oregano, cinnamon, and cloves to the skillet. Toast briefly, about 30 seconds, then add to the bowl with the almonds. Put the sesame seeds in the skillet and toast just until golden, about 20 seconds; quickly scrape out into the same bowl. Grind the almonds and toasted spices in an electric spice or coffee mill. Pulse until the mixture is well ground, but do not overprocess to a paste. Return the mixture to the bowl.

Wipe the skillet clean with a damp clean kitchen towel and increase the heat to medium-high. Add the tomatoes and onion, cut-side up, and toast until slightly charred. Turn them cut-side down with tongs and toast for about 10 minutes, until somewhat charred on all sides. Remove from the skillet, peel away the charred bits, and chop coarsely. Place in the blender or food processor with the ground almond mixture and the garlic. Add the raisins and the toasted bread to the blender. You are now in the homestretch of making the basic paste.

With a sharp paring knife, slice off both ends of the plantain. Make a shallow cut through the skin and cut lengthwise along one of the pronounced ridges until you can remove and discard the peel. Cut on a diagonal into ½-inch/12 mm slices.

Heat the oil over medium-high heat in a heavy saucepan or Dutch oven at least 11 inches/28 cm wide and 4 inches/10 cm deep. Add the plantain rounds and fry on both sides until golden brown. Using tongs, transfer to the blender. Process into a thick but smooth paste, adding ¼ cup/60 ml or more of the reserved pepper-soaking liquid as needed to facilitate grinding.

Increase the heat to medium-high. Carefully stir the reserved chile puree into the skillet, averting your face because it will splatter furiously. Cook, stirring frequently, for about 20 minutes, until the oil begins to separate from the solids. Stir in the vegetable and fruit puree, and decrease the heat, simmer, stirring, for another 20 minutes, until the oil again separates from the solids and you can see the bottom of the pot while stirring.

Add the chopped chocolate and stir until it melts into the sauce. Add the salt and stir to dissolve.

Place a large mesh strainer over a large measuring cup or bowl. Force the mole paste through the mesh, pushing with a large wooden spoon or sturdy pestle, and then run a rubber spatula around the underside of the strainer to scrape off the paste that clings to the bottom of the strainer.

If not diluting the paste to make a mole sauce immediately, let it cool completely and then transfer it to a glass or stainless steel storage container. Pour a thin layer of oil over the paste to help preserve it. Cover tightly and refrigerate until ready to use, or for up to 6 months.

Cuban-Style Wild Hot Pepper Vinegar

MOJITO DE AJÍ GUAGUAO

In Yara, a small agricultural town in Cuba's easternmost region, the legacy of the indigenous Taínos lives on in the DNA of farmers who now call themselves Cuban, in the tuber crops that they grow, and in a native *C. frutescens* that is similar in flavor to Tabasco but much smaller and still called by its Taíno name, *ají guaguao*. This is the local hot pepper of choice for making a spiced vinegar condiment called *mojito*. Though the name conjures the famous mint-laced drink, it really has more to do with the quintessential Cuban *mojo*, a citrusy and garlicky sauce that is poured over boiled yuca just before serving.

In Yara, the *ají guaguao* is a semidomesticated plant that grows in backyards and on farms. It sprouts spontaneously in empty fields and along roadsides and the river's edge, transported by birds such as the sinsonte, Cuba's mockingbird. The plants begin to flower in March to April and produce fruit continuously until September or October. Local cooks, like my friend Amanda Viltrez, harvest the tiny peppers at different stages of ripeness and steep them in vinegar diluted with water, along with a few garlic cloves, and a bit of salt and sugar. The mixture is stored in a glass bottle and allowed to infuse for a couple of weeks. Once the vinegar is hot enough, the bottle moves to the dining table. Diners sprinkle the smoldering vinegar on their food, and cooks replenish the vinegar as it is consumed, topping the bottle with oil to protect the contents from oxidation. I make several versions of Amanda's recipes using a mixture of peppers similar to the *ají guaguao* in size, color, and pungency. My choices include the frutescens cultivars *malagueta*, Tabasco, and piri-piri, but also several annuums, such as a few chiltepín types (Sonora, Tarahumara, and Pima; and the Guatemalan *chile Cobán*). When my homegrown peppers are out of season, I buy tiny bird peppers in Asian markets so I can make the condiment year-round.

I like to blanch the peppers for the *mojito*, both to sterilize them and to fix the color. My Cuban friends skip this step.

3 to 4 oz/85 to 115 g very small hot peppers at varying stages of ripeness

4 garlic cloves, lightly crushed

1½ cups/360 ml distilled white vinegar

¼ cup/60 ml water

1 tsp salt

1 tsp sugar

1 tsp extra-virgin olive oil or vegetable oil (optional)

Sterilize a 16 fl oz/480 ml bottle according to the directions on page 243.

Rinse the peppers under running water in a colander and let drain. If you wish, blanch the peppers: Prepare a bowl of ice water. Put about 1 qt/960 ml water in a medium pot and bring to a boil over high heat. Add the peppers and blanch for 20 seconds. Scoop out with a slotted spoon and drop into the ice water. Scoop out, drain, and pat dry.

Remove the stems of the peppers and make a shallow cut across the stem ends to let the vinegar mixture penetrate. If using slightly larger and thicker-skinned bird peppers, you can place the peppers between two layers of paper towels and using a kitchen mallet or your fist, gently pound the peppers to bruise the flesh. (Bruising the peppers helps their flavor and heat seep into the vinegar.) Pack the peppers and garlic into the sterilized 16 fl oz/480 ml bottle, leaving ¾ inch/2 cm headspace to allow the peppers to expand as they absorb liquid and ferment slightly.

Pour the vinegar and water into a small saucepan and add the salt and sugar. Bring to a boil over high heat, stirring to dissolve the salt and sugar. Using a funnel, pour the vinegar mixture into the bottle and set aside to cool. Use chopsticks or the handle of a small wooden spoon to push down any peppers that float to the neck of the bottle. Top off with the oil and close the bottle tightly. For optimum flavor, store at room temperature and wait about 2 weeks before opening and using. The pepper vinegar can be refreshed with vinegar (and topped off with oil) for up to 6 months. If the peppers discolor or show signs of spoilage, discard and make a new batch.

Puerto Rican Hot Pepper–Spiced Pineapple Vinegar

PIQUE DE PIÑA

Puerto Ricans like to add heat to their food in the form of spiced table condiments like this *pique*, which is made by steeping tiny local peppers called *ají caballero* in a homemade vinegar made from pineapple peels or in regular distilled white vinegar with a touch of citrus juice added. In the Hispanic Caribbean, pineapple peel is also used to make a refreshing fermented drink called *chicha*. There are as many versions of this simple condiment as there are Puerto Rican cooks. In this recipe, which is from the Puerto Rican branch of my family, the peppers are quickly sautéed with sliced onions, garlic, peppercorns, and oregano before being combined with the vinegar and allowed to steep for a couple of weeks. It can also made with uncooked peppers, onion, and garlic. I prefer the latter because it yields a fresher tasting vinegar. As with the Cuban-Style Wild Hot Pepper Vinegar (page 254), a bottle of this vinegar sits on the table for all diners to add as much to their food as they like. I pack the peppers in a wide-mouthed 1 qt/960 ml jar because I like to scoop them out and crush them into soups.

MAKES 1 QT/960 ML

PINEAPPLE VINEGAR

3 lb/1.4 kg (1 medium) ripe pineapple

1 qt/960 ml distilled or spring water

2 Tbsp granulated sugar, demerara sugar, or light muscovado sugar

To make the pineapple vinegar: Rinse the pineapple under running water. Cut off the top and base of the fruit and discard. Remove the peel in thick strips with some flesh attached (reserve the remaining flesh for another use). Cut the strips into 3-inch/7.5 cm pieces and place in a 2 qt/2 L glass pitcher with the water. Cover loosely with plastic wrap and let ferment at room temperature for 3 days, or until the mixture begins to fizz and taste acidic. Stir in the sugar until dissolved and let ferment for another day or two. Strain, discarding the peel, and refrigerate until ready to use.

To make the spiced vinegar: Sterilize a 1 qt/960 ml jar and lid according to the directions on page 243.

Rinse the peppers in a colander and pat dry. Remove the stems and make a shallow cut across the stem ends or short lengthwise cuts through the bottom ends to let the vinegar mixture penetrate. You can also place the peppers between two layers of paper towels and using a kitchen mallet or your fist, gently pound the peppers to bruise the flesh. (Bruising the peppers helps their flavor and heat

SPICED PINEAPPLE VINEGAR

1 lb 5 oz/600 g malaguetas, Tabasco peppers, Puerto Rican ajíes caballeros, green bird peppers, or a mixture of several small, very hot peppers

2 Tbsp extra-virgin olive oil

4 oz/115 g (1 small or ½ medium) yellow onion, sliced into thin rounds

4 garlic cloves, thinly sliced lengthwise

1 tsp black peppercorns

2 sprigs fresh oregano, or 1 tsp dried oregano

2 tsp coarse sea salt

1½ cups/360 ml Pineapple Vinegar (previous recipe)

½ cup/120 ml distilled white vinegar

1 or 2 culantro leaves or 2 sprigs cilantro

seep into the vinegar.) You now have the option of sautéing the fresh ingredients or using them raw. For the latter choice, skip the next step and proceed with heating the pineapple vinegar.

To sauté the peppers, heat the oil over medium heat in a 12-inch/ 30.5 cm frying pan. Add the onion and garlic and sauté until soft, about 5 minutes. Add the peppercorns, oregano, and salt and sauté for 1 minute more. Add the peppers and sauté for 2 to 3 minutes. Remove from the heat and let cool.

Pour the pineapple vinegar into a saucepan and bring to a boil over medium heat. Let boil for 10 minutes, or until it has reduced to about 1½ cups/360 ml. Add the white vinegar and bring to a boil.

Meanwhile, use tongs to transfer the contents of the frying pan and the culantro to the sterilized jar, distributing the ingredients as evenly as possible to create the best appearance and flavor. When the pineapple mixture has finished reducing, remove it from the heat and pour over the pepper mixture. You may need to tamp down the peppers (I use cooking chopsticks) to get more liquid into the bottle or jar. Leave 2 to 3 inches/5 to 7.5 cm of headspace at the top of the container to allow for the mixture to expand during fermentation. Seal the jar and let rest at room temperature for 15 days. If you are planning to keep the peppers longer than that, open the bottle every few days to release the carbon dioxide that will have formed during fermentation. (I once left a bottle unopened for 6 months, and when I finally opened it, the spicy vinegar erupted like a geyser, drenching me from head to toe.)

Spicier Pineapple Vinegar: Any remaining reduced pineapple vinegar that doesn't fit into the jar can be stored separately and turned into a spicier vinegar by seasoning it with two yellow or red habanero peppers. Blanch the peppers and prepare them as instructed in this recipe. Place them in a small sterilized jar and add the vinegar. Cover tightly and let rest for 2 to 3 days. Taste the vinegar every few days and remove the habaneros when the vinegar is hot enough to suit you.

End-of-Harvest Superhot Mélange

ENCURTIDO MUY PICANTE DEL FIN DE LA COSECHA

I harvest a mixture of superhot and less incendiary peppers for this colorful pickle in late summer when they are very ripe, some even beginning to soften. At that stage, I like to blanch the peppers in boiling water to kill any pathogens and then quickly cool them in ice water. Omit this step if your peppers are in top condition, but blanch the carrot regardless.

Seeding the peppers through a slit cut in the side of each tones down their heat and helps them keep their shape. Latin-style brown sugar and sweet vegetables and fruits, such as carrots and mangoes, counterbalance the heat of the peppers and the acidity of the vinegar.

MAKES ABOUT 2 CUPS/480 ML

4 oz/115 g hot peppers, preferably a mixture of moderately hot and superhot in different colors, such as Trinidad Moruga scorpion, Trinidad Congo, dátil, Trinidad 7-pot, ají aribibiguanso quintisho, malagueta, and purple jalapeño

¾ oz/20 g (1 small) carrot, peeled and sliced into ¼-inch/6 mm rounds

4 oz/115 g (about ½) green or half-ripe mango, cut into 1-inch/ 2.5 cm pieces

1 garlic clove, thinly sliced crosswise

¼ tsp allspice berries

¼ tsp black peppercorns

1 bay leaf, coarsely crumbled

½ cup/120 ml distilled white vinegar

¼ cup/60 ml water (preferably distilled or spring water)

2 Tbsp plus 1 tsp light panela, demerara, or light muscovado sugar

2 tsp salt

2 tsp extra-virgin olive oil

Prepare a bowl of ice water. Sterilize a 1 pt/480 ml jar and lid, following the instructions on page 243.

Rinse the peppers in a colander under cold running water and pat dry. Bring 1 qt/960 ml water to a rolling boil in a small saucepan. Add the peppers and carrot and blanch for a few seconds. Using a slotted spoon, scoop the vegetables out of the pot and transfer them to the ice bath to stop the cooking. Drain and let dry on paper towels. Set the carrot aside.

Using kitchen gloves, remove the stems of the peppers and make a slit in the side of the larger peppers to let the vinegar mixture penetrate. Insert a small spoon in the slits and remove the seeds from those peppers. For the small peppers, such as the malagueta and quintisho, make a small cut across the stem ends to let the vinegar solution penetrate. Place the peppers, carrot, mango, garlic, allspice, peppercorns, and bay leaf in the sterilized jar. Toss to distribute the ingredients evenly.

Bring the vinegar, water, sugar, and salt to a rolling boil in a small saucepan, stirring to dissolve the sugar and salt. Pour the mixture into the jar. Set aside and let cool to room temperature. When completely cool, with top with the oil. Close the lid tightly and let stand at room temperature for about 5 days for the flavors to meld. Store at room temperature for up to 6 months.

Spicy Pickled Cucumbers

PEPINOS ENCURTIDOS PICANTES

This simple recipe is close to some versions of the fresh cucumber kimchi often served as one of the *banchan* that accompany many Korean meals. I love serving it as a bright, fresh-tasting relish for burgers and *bao*, but it goes beautifully with almost any main dish.

The dish owes its heat to the excellent Korean ground hot pepper, which is made primarily from the glossy, brilliant red peppers loosely called red finger hot peppers. Many of the attractively priced brands are not made from peppers grown in Korea. Some brands use peppers grown in China and India that are processed in Korean factories and some are 100 percent imported to Korea. In general, brands that list a specific Korean regional provenance are much higher-priced, but they also tend to be far fresher and fruitier, whereas those of Chinese or Indian origin often taste over-toasted. When I leave these pickles in the refrigerator longer than I should and the cucumbers have lost their crunchy bite, I strain the pickling sauce, discarding the cucumbers. I then boil the sauce in a saucepan for 10 minutes, let it cool, and use it for another batch of pickles. Sometimes I combine it with fresh garlic for a wet marinade for pork ribs. Delicious!

MAKES 12 SERVINGS

1½ lb/680 g (about 8 small) kirby cucumbers

1 Tbsp coarse sea salt

4 garlic cloves, finely chopped

1 cup/240 ml soy sauce

½ cup/100 g firmly packed grated light Columbian panela, Mexican piloncillo, or light muscovado sugar

⅔ cup/160 ml Japanese brown rice vinegar

1 tsp toasted sesame oil

1 Tbsp coarsely ground Korean hot pepper or milder ground ají panca

1 Tbsp toasted sesame seeds

Slice off the tips of the cucumbers and cut into rounds ¼ inch/6.5 cm thick or slightly thicker. Toss with the salt in a medium bowl and let rest for 10 minutes. Rinse under cold running water and drain for about 30 minutes in a colander set over a bowl. Combine the garlic, soy sauce, sugar, brown rice vinegar, sesame oil, and Korean hot pepper in a medium bowl and whisk until the sugar is dissolved. Add the drained cucumbers and toss gently to blend. Let rest at room temperature for about 30 minutes for the flavors to meld.

Spoon the pickles into a serving bowl and sprinkle with the toasted sesame seeds.

Store any leftovers in a tightly closed glass jar in the refrigerator for up to 2 days.

Miracha

MY SRIRACHA-STYLE FERMENTED PEPPERS AND PEPPER SAUCE

After a bumper crop of glossy red finger peppers, I decided to develop a fermented hot sauce. By configuring the ingredient proportions by degrees, I arrived at the ideal Asian-style sweet-sour hot sauce. It quickly became my husband's favorite table sauce—except that for him I had to customize it (using manzano peppers) to have more heat and less sweetness.

From this recipe I reap a light, pourable puree and a residue of coarsely processed pepper bits that don't go through the strainer. The reason for processing or chopping the peppers in the first place is to expose as much as the surface area as possible to the action of the salt and the lactic acid bacteria. Both the soupy puree and the crushed fermented pepper residue are multipurpose flavorings as table condiments or stirred into dishes. I particularly love the bite of the crushed pepper skins, which add texture, flavor, and color to everything.

The usual proportions are 2 teaspoons to 1 tablespoon of salt per 1 pound/455 grams of ripe, fleshy hot peppers. My favorite peppers to use are the moderately hot and very fruity red finger peppers sold at Korean markets. I also recommend Fresnos, ripe red jalapeños, or yellow Mexican manzanos. You can halve the recipe if you do not want to make so much, but do not halve the salt as it prevents the quick growth of salt-tolerant lactic acid bacteria. I use sea salt, but you can use any kind you prefer, except iodized salt or the exotic pink or red varieties.

This recipe is incredibly adaptable. You can dial up the pungency by using all or part scorching-hot peppers. You can reduce or increase the amounts of sugar and garlic to taste. You can add a little fresh ginger to the food processor with the peppers and garlic, or add some cumin, allspice, or another preferred spice. I like to use Japanese brown rice vinegar, but you may use plain rice vinegar, apple cider vinegar, or distilled white vinegar. It will be lovely in every iteration.

You can use the crushed pepper skins to flavor mashed potatoes and cheese spreads. And also as a spread for buttered country bread, put under the broiler for a few minutes, to make a spectacular tartine.

2 lb/910 g (about 36) fresh hot
peppers, such as Finger Red Hot
Peppers, Fresnos, red jalapeños,
or manzanos

6 garlic cloves, coarsely chopped

⅔ cup/110 g packed brown sugar
(preferably Latin American panela,
demerara, or light muscovado)

2 Tbsp coarse sea salt

1 cup/240 ml Japanese brown rice
vinegar or rice vinegar, apple cider
vinegar, or distilled white vinegar

Sterilize a 1 qt/960 ml jar with a clamping lid and rubber gasket, following the instructions on page 243.

Rinse the peppers in a colander and pat dry. Cut off the stem end of each pepper and cut the peppers crosswise into thick slices. Place half of the peppers in a food processor with half each of the garlic, sugar, and salt. Pulse until the peppers are coarsely chopped. Transfer the mash to the sterilized jar. Repeat with the remaining peppers, garlic, sugar, and salt, being sure to use all of the liquid that was expelled in processing. The jar should be about three-quarters full. Close the lid tightly and set aside to ferment at room temperature. The next day, open the lid and stir the mash with a sterilized spoon, then reseal. Repeat daily for 1 to 2 weeks. I find 1 week of fermenting time is usually enough.

Sterilize two 1 pt/480 ml jars with clamping lids and rubber gaskets, following the instructions on page 243.

Pour the fermented peppers into a bowl, add the vinegar and stir to mix thoroughly. Working in two batches, process the pepper mixture in a food processor to separate the pulp from the skins and seeds as completely as possible. Set a mesh strainer over a small saucepan and work the peppers through it with a wooden spoon, pressing hard to extract all the juice and pulp you can. Run a rubber or plastic spatula around the underside of the strainer to scrape any clinging pulp into the saucepan. Bring the puree to a full boil over medium-high heat, turn the heat to medium, and simmer for 10 minutes. Let cool to room temperature before transferring to one of the sterilized jars. Store in the refrigerator for up to 6 months.

Scrape the crushed pepper skins and seeds from the strainer into the other the sterilized jar, and store in the refrigerator for up to 6 months.

Peruvian Pickled Red Onions and Ají Amarillo

SALSA CRIOLLA PERUANA

This simple mixture of onions and peppers seasoned with a bit of lime juice and cilantro is the preeminent table condiment in Peru. Used as a relish in sandwiches and spooned freely over just about everything Peruvians eat, it is as ubiquitous in Peru as fresh chile salsas are in Mexico.

MAKES ABOUT 2 CUPS/340 G

8 oz/230 g (1 medium) red onion, cut in half lengthwise and into slivers

1 Tbsp kosher or sea salt, plus more

¼ cup/60 ml lime juice

2 Tbsp finely chopped cilantro

2 fresh or frozen ajíes amarillos (yellow Andean peppers), thawed if frozen and stemmed, seeded, and thinly julienned

Toss the onion with the salt in a small bowl; cover with cold water and let soak for a few minutes. Transfer to a colander and rinse under cold running water. Drain well and pat dry.

In a medium bowl, combine the onion with the lime juice, cilantro, and peppers, and toss well. Taste and add salt, as needed. Serve at once. This is best the day it is made because the onion will become soft overnight.

Chilean "Pig in Stone" Salsa

CHANCHO EN PIEDRA

The whimsical name of this terrific fresh salsa—"pig in stone"—does not seem to make sense. There is no pork in this recipe, just juicy tomatoes, onions, cilantro, and *ají cristal*, a mildly hot fresh pepper with translucent celadon-colored skin that plays an all-purpose role in Chilean cooking. But the *chancho* (pig) here might be a deformation of the Quechua verb *chanqay* (to crush). What makes this sauce different from a *pebre*, another traditional Chilean table sauce calling for the same ingredients, is that here everything is crushed in a stone mortar, not unlike the Mexican molcajete, to make a rough-textured sauce. In the central region of Chile, where *chancho en piedra* is very popular; it is served with *humitas* (small basil-scented fresh corn tamales), *tortillas al rescoldo* (homemade bread baked in cinders), and many traditional dishes. At home, I serve it as I would any fresh salsa: as a side for grilled fish, chicken, or pork; in tacos; on top of fresh corn tamales; and as a garnish for chicken or bean soups.

MAKES ABOUT 1½ CUPS/360 ML

1½ oz/40 g (about 2) ajíes cristal, green jalapeños, or unripe Santa Fe Grande peppers, seeded and coarsely chopped

3 garlic cloves, coarsely chopped

1 tsp sea salt

4 oz/115 g (1 small) red or yellow onion, coarsely chopped

10 oz/280 g (2 medium) ripe beefsteak tomatoes, coarsely chopped

1 Tbsp coarsely chopped cilantro leaves

2 Tbsp red wine vinegar

¼ cup/60 ml extra-virgin olive oil

Place the peppers, garlic, and salt in a rough stone mortar, preferably a molcajete, and crush into a paste with the pestle, using a circular motion. Add the onion and keep crushing to break down the ingredients. Add the tomatoes and continue crushing to make a coarse-textured sauce. Work in the cilantro, vinegar, and oil. Serve immediately.

Store any leftovers, tightly covered, in the refrigerator for up to 4 days.

Very Hot Rancho Chile Verde Salsa

SALSA DE CHILE VERDE DEL RANCHO

I learned how to make this fantastic and very hot tomatillo and chile salsa from a dear Oaxacan friend. It has been for sale at my store Ultramarinos since we opened in 2006, and it is a staple in my own kitchen. Just a tiny dollop gives a jolt of heat and fresh green acidity to any grilled meat or soup. The *miltomate* (tomatillo) plays the same role as the *tomate* in Mexican and Central American cooking. They come to markets and supermarkets covered with a waxy green or papery husk under which they look just like glossy and slightly sticky small green tomatoes. I adore the tomatillo's deep green-grass herbal acidity. It matches the similar vegetal notes of fresh serranos and jalapeños in many sauces. Here it also plays beautifully against the sharp heat of dried *chiles de árbol*.

MAKES ABOUT 2½ CUPS/600 ML

1 oz/30 g (about 58) chiles de árbol, stemmed

1 lb/455 g (about 16 small) tomatillos, husked, rinsed well, and patted dry

2 garlic cloves

1 tsp salt

Heat a cast-iron skillet or comal over medium heat. Add the chiles and toast, tossing with tongs until blackened in spots, about 30 seconds. Transfer the chiles to a blender. Add the tomatillos to the skillet and toast, turning occasionally, until charred in spots and softened, 18 to 20 minutes. Quarter the tomatillos and transfer them to the blender along with the garlic and salt and process into a textured sauce.

Transfer to a bowl and serve as a condiment. Store any leftovers, tightly covered, in the refrigerator for up to 4 days.

Clockwise from top: Rocoto and Tree Tomato Sauce (with red rocoto, page 270); Peruvian Ají Negro with Casabe (see page 240); Very Hot Rancho Chile Verde Salsa (this page); Romesco Sauce (page 268); Rocoto and Tree Tomato Sauce (with chile manzano, page 270); and Chilean "Pig in Stone" Salsa (page 263).

Serrano and Tomato Salsa

SALSA DE SERRANO Y TOMATE

In the molcajete (see page 238), ingredients are bruised and abraded with a circular motion, not pureed by pounding. The action releases their essential oils, leaving them with enough body and personality to make a textural difference. In this particular example, serrano chiles give a jolt of clean, sharp heat to the salsa that never overpowers the fresh acidity of the tomatoes. Smother grilled meats with it, spread it on hot tortillas, use it to spice up the filling of a taco, or stir it into scrambled eggs to make a soupy dish called salsa de huevos.

MAKES ABOUT 1¾ CUPS/420 ML

9 oz/255 g (about 3) very ripe plum tomatoes

4 green or red serrano chiles, or more to taste

3 large garlic cloves

½ tsp salt, plus more

2 Tbsp coarsely chopped cilantro leaves

⅓ cup/75 ml cold water

Heat a large cast-iron skillet or griddle or a comal over medium heat. Add the tomatoes and roast, turning with tongs until lightly charred and softened, about 10 minutes; transfer the tomatoes to a cutting board and quarter. Place the tomatoes in a mixing bowl. Add the serranos to the hot skillet and roast turning with tongs until blistered and charred, about 4 minutes.

Place the garlic and salt in a rough stone mortar, preferably a molcajete, and crush into a paste with the pestle. Add the serranos and crush coarsely. Repeat with the tomatoes. Add the cilantro and continue crushing the ingredients to blend them together into a coarse sauce. Loosen it up into a more fluid, pourable sauce by adding the cold water, 1 Tbsp at a time.

Alternatively process all the ingredients in a food processor with on-and-off pulses; do not keep processing and destroy the sauce's robust texture by turning it into a smooth, homogeneous sauce. Taste for salt and season as needed. Transfer to a bowl and serve as an all-purpose table salsa. Store any leftovers, tightly covered, in the refrigerator for up to 4 days.

Simple Panca Pepper Cooking Sauce

ADEREZO DE AJÍ PANCA SIMPLE

One of the secrets of Peru's regional cuisines is a simple but brilliant *aderezo* cooking sauce made with the paste of one of the country's two iconic dried peppers: *ají mirasol* or *ají panca*.

The sauce is a fantastic seasoning base for braises, stews, hearty soups, and rice dishes, and an adobo (spice rub) for pork, chicken, goat, or lamb. Just ¼ cup/ 60 ml of the sauce will flavor 2 lb/910 kg of chicken parts or meaty pork ribs. I begin by seasoning the chicken or pork with salt and pepper and perhaps a couple of crushed garlic cloves and browning it in some oil. Then I add the cooking sauce and about 2 cups/480 ml broth and braise the chicken or pork for about 30 minutes, until it is tender and the sauce has thickened. To flavor and color rice, sauté about 2 cups/440 g of rice in 1 Tbsp of oil and stir in 1 Tbsp of the sauce. Add about 2¼ cups/530 ml of equal parts chicken broth and water and cook as you would any rice. Not only will it taste delicious—just perfect to serve with any saucy dish—but it will also have a lovely and subtle brick-red hue.

MAKES ABOUT 1 CUP/240 ML

2 Tbsp extra-virgin olive oil or vegetable oil

4 garlic cloves, finely chopped

8 oz/230 g (1 medium) red onion, finely chopped

¼ tsp ground cumin

1 tsp wine vinegar

½ tsp sea salt, plus more

½ cup/120 ml Basic Dried Pepper Paste (page 248)

1 cup/240 ml reserved pepper-soaking liquid (see page 248)

Heat the oil in a 9-inch/23 cm skillet or saucepan over medium heat until it ripples. Add the garlic and sauté until golden, about 30 seconds. Add the onion and cook until golden, about 8 minutes. Add the cumin, vinegar, salt, and pepper paste. Cook, stirring occasionally, for about 5 minutes.

Stir in the pepper-soaking liquid and cook, stirring occasionally, until the sauce begins to separate from the oil, 5 to 7 minutes. Let cool to room temperature. Transfer to a blender and puree until smooth. Alternatively, do not puree if you prefer a coarser texture.

Store in a tightly sealed glass jar in the refrigerator until ready to use. It will keep for up to 3 weeks.

Romesco Sauce

SALSA ROMESCO

I have loved romesco since I first encountered it in Catalonia. My relationship with it has deepened and changed over the years because a key ingredient, ñora peppers, is now readily available in the United States and I have a keener sense of the sauce's diversity, which is rooted in medieval Spain and the Columbian exchange.

The port city of Tarragona, on the Catalan coast about 60 miles/95 kilometers west of Barcelona, is generally considered the birthplace of romesco. Some histories point to the city's Serrallo neighborhood. Though attributed to Tarragona's fishermen, it is clearly based on the family of medieval Spanish sauces thickened to a creamy consistency with nuts and bread. The Catalan linguist Joan Coromines suggested that the name came from the word *remescolar*, meaning "to mix" in one of the Mozarabic dialects of the Spanish Middle Ages. Beyond that, its origins are unclear. The one certain fact is that some of the usual ingredients, including tomatoes and the sweet, colorful dried *ñora* peppers, did not reach Spain until the early sixteenth century. Eventually Romesco became one of the most beloved Catalan sauces in an incredible range of different versions—thick or thin; cooked or uncooked; made with or without tomatoes, bell peppers, or various thickenings; and used as a table sauce, marinade, or (possibly the original form) as a cooking sauce incorporated into fish stews and braises.

Today some classic dishes are unthinkable without romesco. So is the late-winter *calçotada*, an outdoor festival celebrating the earliest *calçots*, a kind of spring onion grown like white asparagus with soil heaped up around the stalks to keep them white. People happily eat them grilled over charcoal and dipped in big bowls of romesco or a close variant of the sauce called *salbitxada*.

Among the changes that my own version has undergone are the addition of real *ñoras*, along with nuts and fried bread as thickeners, and I now sauté the sauce ingredients in olive oil for enhanced flavor before pureeing. This recipe reflects my growing awareness of romesco's ties with other old Spanish cooking sauces and Mexican moles.

The sauce's uses are too many to name. At Cucharamama, my South American restaurant in Hoboken, I use this sauce as a marinade for salmon roasted in our wood-fired oven. At home, I serve it with thick wedges of Spanish Potato Omelet with Roasted Peppers (page 291) or Grilled Japanese Spring Onions (page 276) in calçotada style. It also makes a great dip.

1⅛ oz/32 g (about 6) ñora peppers

⅝ oz/18 g (about 1) ancho chile

½ cup/120 ml extra-virgin olive oil

1⅛ oz/32 g (about 1½ slices) day-old country bread or French or Italian baguette

8 garlic cloves

12 oz/340 g (2 large) ripe beefsteak tomatoes, coarsely chopped

13 oz/370 g (2 medium) red bell peppers, roasted and seeded (see page 232), then cut into large strips

½ cup/60 g hazelnuts or ½ cup/80 g whole blanched almonds or a combination of both, lightly toasted

1 Tbsp sea salt, plus more

1 tsp wine vinegar (optional)

Seed, toast, and reconstitute the ñoras and ancho, according to the directions on page 238. Drain, reserving ¼ cup/60 ml of the soaking liquid.

Heat ¼ cup/60 ml of the oil over medium heat in a 12-inch/30.5 cm skillet. Add the bread and cook on both sides until golden. Remove from the pan and set aside. Add 4 of the garlic cloves and sauté for 20 seconds. Add the tomatoes and sauté until soft, about 8 minutes. Transfer the sautéed mixture, bread, and reconstituted peppers to a blender with the remaining ¼ cup/60 ml oil, remaining 4 garlic cloves, and the roasted bell peppers, nuts, salt, and vinegar. Process into a smooth creamy sauce. If desired, add the reserved liquid to thin slightly.

Store the sauce in a tightly closed glass jar in the refrigerator until ready to use. It will keep for up to 1 week.

Rocoto and Tree Tomato Sauce

SALSA DE ROCOTO Y BERENJENA AL ESTILO DE MOCHE

On a research trip to the northern Peruvian town of Moche in La Libertad Region, I had a fantastic lunch at a small restaurant called Mi Camote (meaning "my sweet potato"), a favorite spot for archaeologists excavating the ancient sites of the region. I was captivated by a dish of crunchy deep-fried toyo (baby shark) served with a hot orange sauce that we practically drank and asked for seconds because it was so good. I asked our server for the ingredients and she answered: "rocotos and berenjenas." I could recognize the heat and unmistakable flavor of the rocoto peppers, but I could not believe that there was any berenjena (eggplant) in the sauce. After some prodding the waitress took me back to the kitchen, where I learned that "berenjena" was the local name of the Andean tomate de árbol (tree tomato)

As soon as I got back home, I re-created the recipe for the menu of my restaurant Cucharamama. Remembering how delicious I had found the batter-fried morsels of shark dipped in the sauce, I decided to pair it with our similarly prepared Peruvian-style batter-fried calamari (page 302). The heat of the rocoto tempered the acidity and very subtle bitter edge of the tree tomato—a perfect complement to the sweetness of the squid.

MAKES ABOUT 2½ CUPS/600 ML

4½ oz/130 g (about 1) large red rocoto, fresh or frozen, or 3 or 4 yellow manzano peppers, stemmed and seeded

1⅔ cups/400 ml tree tomato puree (sold as *puré de tomate de árbol* in Latin markets)

3 garlic cloves

3 or 4 sprigs cilantro

¼ tsp ground cumin

1½ tsp salt

1 tsp sugar

Place the pepper, tree tomato puree, garlic, cilantro, cumin, salt, and sugar in a blender and process into a smooth puree.

Store the sauce in a tightly closed glass jar in the refrigerator until ready to use. It will keep for up to 2 weeks.

Ecuadorian Green Tree Tomato Sauce

LA SALSA VERDE DE TOMATE DE ARBOL DE SANTIAGO

This creamy sauce made with a combination of tree tomatoes, cilantro, and hot peppers is a staple at the table of Ecuadorian chocolate maker Santiago Peralta. It is perfect stirred into the simple broth of a chicken *maito* (see page 309) to round out all the flavors and lend tartness and heat.

Tree tomatoes (*Cyphomandra betacea*) are sold as tamarillos in specialty produce stores, or as *tomates de árbol* in Latin American markets (where you usually find them frozen). For the hot pepper, Santiago's choice is most likely an *ají ambateño*, which is also sold frozen in Latin American markets, or *ají amarillo*. You can also use serranos or jalapeños, or just 1 yellow Scotch bonnet pepper if you want more heat and perfume.

MAKES ABOUT 1½ CUPS/360 ML

10 oz/280 g (about 2) yellow tree tomatoes, fresh or frozen and thawed

4 oz/110 g (1 small) yellow onion, coarsely chopped

1.5 oz/40 g (1 or 2) hot peppers, such as ajíes ambateños, ajíes amarillos, serranos, jalapeños or 1 yellow Scotch bonnet, stemmed, seeded, and coarsely chopped

3 garlic cloves

1 cup/20 g coarsely chopped cilantro

½ cup/10 g coarsely chopped flat-leaf parsley

½ cup/120 ml extra-virgin olive oil

Juice of 2 limes
(about ⅓ cup/75 ml)

2 tsp salt, plus more

Make a shallow crosswise cut in the tip of each tree tomato. Put about 1 qt/960 ml of water in a small saucepan and bring to a boil. Add the tree tomatoes and blanch, for 2 to 3 minutes. Using tongs, lift the tree tomatoes out of the hot water and set aside to cool until you can handle them. Peel them, put them in a blender, and process into a creamy, smooth green puree. Add the onion, peppers, garlic, cilantro, parsley, olive oil, lime juice, and salt and process again into a smooth puree.

Store the sauce in a tightly closed glass jar in the refrigerator until ready to use. It will keep for up to 4 days.

Zafra's Chipotle and Vanilla Sauce

SALSA DE CHIPOTLE Y VAINILLA DE ZAFRA

In 1998, Gloria Casarin, the wife of Venezuelan vanilla grower Víctor Vallejo, intro-duced me to the women of an organization she directs: Alegría de Vivir, the Papantla chapter of INSEN, Mexico's National Institute for the Elderly. These women are on a mission to explore and expand the uses of vanilla in cooking while redressing the historical practice of exporting the best vanilla beans and using artificial vanilla extract for locally made desserts.

I had the privilege of cooking with the Alegría de Vivir members at their clubhouse and came away with a whole new understanding of an ingredient I thought I knew. Instead of only scraping the seeds from vanilla beans into sweet sauces and custards, they fearlessly ground handfuls of whole beans into a crumbly paste that they added to a range of savory, seriously spicy dishes made with other ingredients, such as tomatoes and, yes, lots of hot peppers (mostly jalapeños, chiltepins, and chipotles). It was a revelation. I was particularly drawn to a dish of shrimp and ripe plantains cooked in a delicious, very spicy sauce of chipotles perfumed and tempered at the last minute with vanilla. I remember the cook stirring the sauce and announcing, "Ya está chinita," alerting us that the sauce had reached the stage when the water had evaporated enough to let the oil separate and allow the solids to start frying again. That was the instant when generous amounts of ground vanilla beans were added, to release their aroma just before serving.

At first taste, it seemed as if the vanilla had been devoured by the powerful chile. Then its complex fragrance emerged, letting me detect other dimensions through the smoky chipotle heat. I had the sense that many other ingredients had been added, not just a spoonful of ground vanilla beans.

I now love various savory combinations of vanilla and hot peppers. At my restaurant Zafra, in Hoboken, New Jersey, this sauce is a vivid foil to our piquillos stuffed with refried beans (page 284). I often like to mellow it with a bit of chocolate and perhaps a dab of Latin American brown loaf sugar.

If making the sauce in advance, prepare it up to the point of adding the vanilla bean, and wait to grind and add the vanilla bean until you reheat the sauce before serving. In this way, the full vanilla fragrance will be emphasized.

A note about vanilla: Veracruz State in Mexico is inseparable from the jalapeño chile and its smoked incarnation, the chipotle. Sometimes it seems as if there is no escaping the insistent note of chipotles in every kind of table sauce, soup, or main dish. But the fertile green district of the Totonacapan and its capital, Papantla, in the northern part of the state, have historically been even better known for another New World treasure: vanilla.

Vanilla has been cultivated in Mexico since pre-Columbian times, but details of its early history are scant and clouded in myth. The delicate orchid *Vanilla planifolia* seems to have originated in or near the Totonacapan. Vanilla "beans," the long green fruits, were probably allowed to sun-dry on the plant until they turned dark brown and fragrant. The Totonacs called it *cacixanath* ("hidden flower") or simply *xanath* (also the name of the goddess identified with it). Eventually the imperialist highland Aztecs imported vanilla beans to Tenochtitlan as tribute, under the marvelously descriptive Nahuatl name of *tlilxochitl*, or "black flower."

Sometime around 1577, Franciscan friar Bernardino de Sahagún, author of the encyclopedic *General History of the Things of New Spain*, described vanilla as a flavoring for chocolate drinks. The pre-Columbian association of vanilla, chiles, and cacao lived on in complex chocolate drinks in colonial Mexico.

MAKES ABOUT 2 CUPS/480 ML

2 large, plump Mexican vanilla beans (see Resources)

2 lb/910 g (about 10) ripe plum or (8 small) beefsteak tomatoes, peeled, seeded, and quartered

3 canned chipotle chiles en adobo, with the sauce clinging on

¼ cup/60 ml extra-virgin olive oil

1 tsp salt

1 Tbsp grated Mexican piloncillo, Columbian panela, or light muscovado (optional)

1 oz/30 g 60% cacao dark chocolate (preferably made from Latin American cacao; optional)

Cut the vanilla beans into 1-inch/2.5 cm pieces with a sharp knife, put them in a small food processor or spice mill, and process until the texture resembles fine breadcrumbs. You should have about 1 Tbsp. Set aside.

Place the tomatoes and chiles in a blender or food processor and process to a fine puree.

Heat the oil in a 10-inch/25 cm skillet or medium saucepan over medium heat until it ripples. Stir in the puree and the salt. Sauté, stirring occasionally, for about 18 minutes, until the sauce thickens and the oil starts to separate from the solids. Stir in the ground vanilla, piloncillo, and chocolate and cook for about 2 minutes. Remove from the heat.

If not using immediately, store the sauce in a tightly closed glass jar in the refrigerator. It will keep for about 2 weeks.

Fresh Fruit with Guatemalan Chile Cobán and Cacao Condiment

FRUTAS FRESCAS CON POLVO DE CHILE COBÁN Y CACAO GUATEMALTECO

In summer, there is nothing more refreshing and uncomplicated than fresh fruit of varying degrees of ripeness sprinkled with ground hot peppers and salt or a more complex mixture of ground chiles and crunchy cacao nibs for texture and depth of flavor. While I look for perfectly ripe pineapple and melon for sweetness, I prefer mangoes just under the peak of ripeness for more acidity and flavor. Mexicans adore the Oro mango, which they eat green or half ripe, simply sprinkled with chile and salt. Among US cultivars developed in southern Florida, Keitt, which can be found in Latin and Asian markets, has a similar crunchiness and acidity and strikes the perfect balance with the hot peppers. If you have access to Indian mangoes, seek the Totapuri, which is extraordinarily delicious when green.

MAKES 8 TO 12 SERVINGS

2 lb/910 g (1 small) ripe pineapple, peeled and cut into 1-inch/2.5 cm wide sticks

14 oz to 1 lb/400 to 455 g (2 large) green or firm half-ripe mangoes, cut into 1-inch /2.5 cm wide sticks

2 lb 7 oz/1.1 kg (½ small) seedless watermelon, cut into 1-inch/2.5 cm sticks

2 Tbsp freshly squeezed lime juice, or to taste

Pinch of sugar

¼ cup/100 g Guatemalan Chile Cobán and Cacao Condiment (page 249) or Chile Salt (page 247)

8 to 12 lime wedges

Place the fruit in a large bowl and toss gently with the lime juice, sugar, and 2 tsp of the chile condiment or chile and salt.

Distribute the fruit sticks among shot glasses or other small glasses as if they were breadsticks. Sprinkle with more of the chile. Garnish with the lime wedges and serve immediately with the remaining chile in a small bowl for people to serve themselves.

Grilled Japanese Spring Onions with Romesco

CALÇOTS JAPONESES A LA PARRILLA CON SALSA ROMESCO

This recipe was born when I found the Japanese vegetable *negi* or *naga negi* at a Japanese market in my neighborhood and realized that it was a fine stand-in for the Catalan *calçots* served with romesco at the late-winter *calçotada*, the harvest festival for this prized regional specialty. Purists say that they are not identical. *Calcots* are members of the same species as regular yellow, white, or red onions. *Naga negi*, often sold under the misnomer "Japanese leeks," are a Far Eastern kind belonging to the species *Allium fistulosum*, that is popular in northern China, Korea, and Japan. Large *naga negi* are grown by the same technique as *calçots*, with earth mounded up around them as they grow to produce slender, elongated white stalks with a tender core that look like fat white asparagus and has a wonderful sweet onion flavor. They have the advantage of being longer than *calçots*, commonly 12 inches/30.5 cm or longer, and are even prettier, with a wandlike shape. They are great cooked in *calçotada* style—grilled over charcoal and eaten with romesco or any other hot pepper dipping sauce.

If you cannot get *naga negi*, substitute young white onions with partly formed bulbs and green stems attached often sold as spring onions. (Do not confuse them with scallions, which also sometimes go by the name spring onion.) Use the bulbs (roots trimmed) and about 1 inch/2.5 cm of the green stalks.

MAKES 12 SERVINGS AS AN
APPETIZER OR SIDE DISH

24 Japanese negi

¼ cup/60 ml extra-virgin olive oil

Coarse sea salt

Romesco Sauce (page 268) or another bright-flavored sauce

Prepare a grill over hardwood charcoal. Alternatively, the negi can be cooked on a gas grill or under the broiler.

Trim the roots and outer leaves of the negi along with most of the green stalks, leaving them 11 to 12 inches/28 to 30.5 cm long. Place them in a shallow container long enough to hold them, and then toss with the oil.

When the charcoal begins to get ashy, grill the negi in batches, turning with tongs, until charred and soft, about 5 minutes per batch. If using a gas grill, cook over medium heat with the grill covered. If cooking under the broiler, put the negi on a baking sheet and place about 2 inches/10 cm from the broiler. Once cooked, cut the negi in half crosswise and transfer to a serving platter. Sprinkle with salt to taste and serve with the romesco or other sauce.

Panfried Padrón Peppers

PIMIENTOS DE PADRÓN AL SARTÉN

Panfried Padrón peppers are addictive; a handful is never enough for anyone. Galicians like to fry the pimientos de Padrón in abundant olive oil, but I much prefer using just enough to give them flavor. Either way, sprinkle them with a sea salt that has soft, shard-like crystals such as Maldon or fleur de sel. The one pepper I've found that comes close to the Padrón's easy charm is the Japanese shishito, which is forgiving of warm climates and grows beautifully in my New Jersey garden. Serve with a fresh Galician Albariño.

MAKES 4 SERVINGS AS AN
APPETIZER OR SIDE DISH

1 lb 2 oz/510 g (80 to 100) pimientos de Padrón or shishito peppers, stemmed and seeded

Sea salt

¼ cup/60 ml extra-virgin olive oil, or more as needed

Place the peppers in a colander and rinse under cold running water. Dry thoroughly with paper towels.

Heat the oil in a 12-inch/30.5 cm heavy-bottomed or cast-iron skillet over high heat until sizzling. Add the peppers in batches, and cook, stirring rapidly, until they are blistered and softened but have not turned brown, 1 to 2 minutes, or 2 to 3 minutes for shishitos, which need a little more time.

Transfer the peppers to a serving plate, sprinkle with salt, and serve immediately.

Pan-Fried Padrón Peppers with Garlic and Serrano Ham variation: Though Padrón peppers are delicious cooked only with olive oil and salt, I also love to stir in garlic slivers and a bit of salty Serrano ham (about 1 oz/30 g) to provide a kick of extra flavor.

Tiger-Skin Peppers

HU PI QING JIAO

The name *hu pi* (tiger skin) comes from the mottled markings that the *qing jiao* (green peppers) get from the super heated wok. I serve them with plain rice, for a quick and delicious vegetarian lunch or as a side for any grilled meat.

The peppers used in Sichuan are a general cayenne type called "cow-horn" or "goat-horn" peppers. Use any sort of long, hot cayenne-type green pepper that you can find in Asian markets, milder peppers of the general New Mexico type or sweet and succulent Japanese Manganji peppers, which I like to use whole. Smaller thin-skinned peppers that blister easily, such as the Spanish Padrón and the Japanese shishito, are also good choices but should be used whole (with stems on). The total weight should be about the same in all cases.

I make this dish in a flat-bottomed carbon-steel wok, but a large cast-iron skillet will do. It is essential to use the mellow-flavored, slightly sweet Chinese black vinegar from Chinkiang (Zhenjiang), which is available in any Chinatown supermarket or grocery. Slightly reminiscent of balsamic vinegar, but more sour and pungent, it melds perfectly with the soy sauce to make a lovely pan sauce.

MAKES 4 SERVINGS

12 oz/340 g (about 12) long green peppers or an equal weight of manganji, padrón, or shishito peppers

2 Tbsp peanut or sunflower oil (or if preferred, extra-virgin olive oil)

5 garlic cloves, thinly sliced

¼ cup/60 ml soy sauce, plus more

2 to 3 Tbsp Chinkiang vinegar, plus more

Rinse the peppers under cold running water and pat dry. With a small sharp knife, slice off the stem ends and pointed tips of the long green hot peppers. Slit open lengthwise; remove the veins and seeds if you want to tame their heat. Cut the peppers in half crosswise. If working with manganji, Padrón, or shishito peppers, leave them whole.

Heat a well-seasoned 14-inch/35.5 cm wok or heavy skillet over medium-high heat. Add the oil and heat until fragrant and rippling, tilting the pan to oil the sides. Add the peppers and rapidly stir-fry, tossing and turning with a spatula (preferably a wok spatula) for about 5 minutes, or until dark, blistered patches appear on the peppers' skins. Add the garlic and stir-fry for another 20 seconds. Pour in the soy sauce and vinegar; continue to stir-fry while it comes to a boil. Taste for salt and acidity, and add more soy sauce or vinegar if desired. Using a slotted spoon or Chinese spider, transfer the peppers to a serving plate or shallow dish. Let the pan sauce return to a boil, then pour it over the peppers and serve at once. You can also refrigerate the peppers and serve them cold or at room temperature as a side dish like an escabeche.

Pepper "Steaks" with Pepper Leaf Chimichurri

CHURRASCO DE AJÍ Y CHIMICHURRI DE HOJAS DE AJÍ

When I first saw the showy Striped Holland Bells (also known as Enjoya Stripy Peppers, I fell in love with them instantly. Not only are they startlingly beautiful, with well-defined reddish pink and sunrise yellow streaks that penetrate all the way through the flesh, they also have thicker flesh and a mild sweetness. When cut into slabs and topped with chimichurri, they remind me of the well-marbled skirt steaks that most Latins call *churrasco* and Argentineans know as *entraña*. I like to serve this pair of spin-offs on the meat-centric Pampas cuisine as a satisfying vegetarian main course or side dish.

When the Spaniards invaded the Andean region, they found the natives using pepper leaves in stews and green pepper sauces. This chimichurri is ideal for the early summer, when pepper leaves are as tender as parsley.

MAKES 6 SERVINGS

PEPPER LEAF CHIMICHURRI

11 garlic cloves, finely chopped

4 oz/115 g (1 small) yellow onion

1 oz/30 g finely chopped tender pepper leaves

1 Tbsp finely chopped cilantro

1 Tbsp medium-hot ground red pepper (such as Korean, New Mexican red pepper flakes, panca peppers) or 2 tsp very hot cayenne

2 tsp ground cumin

2 tsp dried oregano

¼ tsp hot or sweet smoked Spanish paprika (preferably pimentón de la Vera)

¼ cup/60 ml red wine vinegar

1 cup/240 ml extra-virgin olive oil

2 lb 3 oz/1 kg (about 6) Striped Holland Bells (also sold as Enjoya Stripy Peppers)

Sea salt

¼ cup/60 ml extra-virgin olive oil

To make the chimichurri: Blend the garlic, onion, pepper leaves, cilantro, ground red pepper, cumin, oregano, paprika, vinegar, and olive oil in a bowl and let rest for about 30 minutes before using.

Roast and peel the peppers, following the instructions on page 232. Trim off about ½ inch/1.3 cm from both tops and bottoms of the peppers. Remove the placentas and seeds. Make a slit along one side of each pepper so that you can unfold the body into a strip. Trim any prominent veins. Spread the peppers flat on a baking sheet, skin-side down. Season with salt on both sides.

Heat the olive oil in a 12-inch/30.5 cm skillet over medium heat. Add the peppers in two batches and panfry for 2 to 3 minutes on each side, basting with the chimichurri, until golden and lightly charred in places. Serve with the remaining chimichurri on the side.

Chile Rajas with Epazote, Milk, and Cheese

RAJAS DE CHILE CON EPAZOTE, LECHE, Y QUESO

Here is one of my favorite recipes for *rajas* (roasted pepper strips), which is mostly poblanos or *chiles de agua* or other hot peppers (such as jalapeño) and sautéed onions, simmered in milk and epazote to make a rich, almost soupy blend enriched with chunks of fresh cheese that are allowed to soften and absorb the flavors of the milky broth but not to melt.

To understand this traditional dish, you need to visualize how people eat it at food stands in Zaachila and Tule, and in the Benito Juárez Mercado de Abastos in the city of Oaxaca: They spoon the mixture with some of its thin, wheylike broth onto bowls of black beans simply cooked with a piece of white onion, whole garlic cloves, epazote, and salt. Sometimes the beans are drained since the chile mixture has plenty of broth. The beans and *rajas* are eaten with tortillas as spoons. People also eat it with a serving spoon and pieces of *carne enchilada* (see Panfried Pork Steaks in Guajillo-Puya Adobo, page 326) rolled into hot tortillas.

What I love about this dish is that it can be made with several combinations of fresh peppers. Traditional versions call for poblanos and the hotter *chiles de agua* (when they are mostly green). You can also use a mixture of jalapeños and milder cubanelles or mild New Mexican chiles, and I have even made a Peruvian variation with *ají amarillo*, keeping the epazote, of course, since it is used in Peru, where it is called *paico*.

In the United States our tendency might be turn the sauce into a thicker creamy foil for the chiles, allowing the cheese to melt, reducing the milk, or adding cream to enrich it. None of that is necessary. Since you cook the dish over high heat, the milk will thicken a bit, but don't expect it to turn into cream. The acids in the peppers will coagulate the milk a bit, and you will see that the sauce becomes thin like whey. The milk solids, however, will cling to the soft peppers, onion, and epazote.

Make sure to cook the cheese just enough to soften it a little, and resist the temptation to cut it into smaller pieces. As for epazote, when Oxacans cook with it, they use lots of it. You can get fresh epazote in any Latin market catering to Mexicans.

1 lb 4 oz/475 g (about 5 large) poblanos or equal weight green chiles de aqua and 6 oz/170 g (about 10 large) jalapeños or a combination of jalapeños or Peruvian ajíes amarillos and NuMex Joe E. Parker or Big Jim, rinsed and patted dry

¼ cup/60 ml extra-virgin olive oil or vegetable oil

13 oz/370 g (about 1½) white onions, cut in half lengthwise and into long thick slices

12 sprigs fresh epazote, leaves only

1 tsp salt, plus more, depending on the saltiness of the cheese

1 qt/910 ml whole milk

1 lb/455 g queso blanco (preferably a soft Mexican-brand cheese like Jalisco), cut into 1-inch/2.5 cm cubes

Corn tortillas, warmed (optional)

Roast, peel, stem, and seed the peppers, according to the directions on pages 231 to 232. If using jalapeños, you may keep the seeds if they are not too hot. Cut the peppers into strips about ¼ inch/6 mm wide or a bit thicker; set aside.

Heat the oil in a medium pan over high heat until it sizzles. Add the onions and sauté, for about 2 minutes. Add the epazote, pepper strips, and salt and cook, stirring, for about 2 minutes. Pour in the milk, stir, and continue cooking over high heat, stirring occasionally, until the milk reduces and thickens a bit, about 8 minutes. Gently stir in the cheese and let soften for about 3 minutes. Serve in bowls with fresh tortillas alongside.

Refried Black Beans with Chile de Árbol

FRIJOLES NEGROS REFRITOS CON CHILE DE ÁRBOL

In Mexican cooking, refried beans are an important and multifaceted condiment. Cooks smother the thick paste on hot tortillas to create a flavorful base for other ingredients in tacos or bring the beans to the table with Mexican rice, as the vegetarian component of the meal's protein. I am partial to this Oaxacan recipe, which calls for licorice-scented avocado leaves and blazing hot *chiles de árbol*. These beans are also my filling of choice for stuffing piquillo peppers (see page 286). To make one of my favorite tacos, I spread a thick layer of refried beans on a freshly made corn tortilla and top it with bits of turkey or chicken pieces left over from Coloradito Mole (see page 317), and then I top that with the crunchy fried onions used to flavor the oil in this recipe and a dollop of a tart sauce, such as the Serrano and Tomato Salsa (page 266).

A note on Mexican avocado leaves: Avocados are classed into three main races—Mexican, Guatemalan, and West Indian. The avocados in today's markets are mostly crosses of the Mexican or West Indian types grafted onto Guatemalan stock. Unlike the leaves of the West Indian and Guatemalan avocados, which can be toxic, leaves of some Mexican cultivars have a delicate anise scent and are edible. They can be found dried in any Latin American market that caters to Mexican customers.

8 oz/230 g dried black beans

8 oz/230 g (1 medium) white onion, cut in half lengthwise

6 garlic cloves

3½ tsp salt, plus more

5 large dried Mexican avocado leaves

¼ oz/7 g (about 7) chiles de árbol, stemmed and seeded

½ cup/120 ml extra-virgin olive oil

4 to 5 oz/115 to 140 g (1 small) white onion, cut crosswise into ¼-inch/6 mm rounds, rings separated

Place the beans, halved onion, and garlic in a medium saucepan with 2 qt/2 L of water. Bring to a boil. Lower the heat, cover, and simmer. Season with 1 tsp of the salt just as the beans are beginning to soften. Cover and continue cooking until the beans are soft, about 1½ hours total cooking time. Strain the beans, reserving the cooking liquid. You will need about ⅔ cups/160 ml when you blend the beans and about ¼ cup/60 ml to store in the refrigerator to use to loosen the refried beans if storing for later use. (The beans thicken considerably when they cool.)

Pass the avocado leaves over a gas flame or add to a cast-iron skillet over high heat and char the edges to accentuate their licorice aroma. Crumble the leaves into a blender.

Heat a cast-iron skillet or comal over medium-high heat and add the chiles. Toast for about 15 seconds, tossing with tongs; chiles de árbol have very thin skins and can scorch easily. Transfer the chiles to the blender and add the beans, ⅔ cup/160 ml of the reserved cooking liquid, and the remaining 2½ tsp salt. Process into a smooth puree.

Heat the oil in a medium skillet over high heat and add the sliced onion. Sauté until the onion is golden brown and crunchy, with charred bits, and has released its flavor into the oil. Strain the oil through a sieve set over a bowl or measuring cup, pushing the onion down with a spoon to extract as much oil as possible. Reserve the crunchy onion for a topping; they are delicious in tacos. You should have about 2 tablespoons of oil. Pour the onion-flavored oil back into the skillet over medium heat. Pour in the bean puree and cook, stirring, until the puree burbles and erupts, 5 to 8 minutes.

If not using immediately, let cool completely. Store in a tightly covered glass container in the refrigerator until ready to use. The beans will keep for up to 4 days. To reheat, place the beans in a skillet over medium heat and loosen with some of the reserved cooking liquid. It is best to keep the beans as thick as possible if using them as a filling (as for the piquillo peppers, page 286), so they will not ooze out as the dish cooks (or when bitten into).

Zafra's Piquillo Peppers Stuffed with Refried Beans on Chipotle-Vanilla Sauce

LOS PIQUILLOS RELLENOS DE FRIJOLES REFRITOS EN SALSA DE CHIPOTLE Y VAINILLA DE ZAFRA

When I learned the sauce in this dish from a group of elderly women in Papantla, the vanilla-growing region of Veracruz State, I knew it was so special that I had to find other ways to showcase its goodness. It dawned on me that it would be a fantastic complement for a dish of piquillo peppers filled with refried beans. The recipe evolved into a gratin of sorts, with the bean-filled piquillos resting on a bed of the sauce. I added a thin layer of grated manchego to the bean filling for a savory barrier to help keep the beans from spilling out when broiled. The melted cheese also mingles with the sauce, adding another wonderful layer of flavor to an already complex mix. You could also serve these stuffed peppers on a bed of creamy polenta or with fresh corn tamales.

MAKES 4 SERVINGS AS AN APPETIZER OR A SIDE DISH

9½ oz/270 g (about 12) canned piquillo peppers, drained

1 cup/315 g Refried Black Beans with Chile de Árbol (page 284)

6 oz/170 g aged manchego cheese, grated

2 cups/480 ml Zafra's Chipotle and Vanilla Sauce (page 272)

To stuff the peppers, place one on the palm of one hand and hold it upright and open between your thumb and index finger. Fill with 1 Tbsp refried beans and top the filling with 1 Tbsp grated cheese. Gently transfer to a large plate. Repeat until all the peppers have been stuffed. Cover the plate with plastic wrap and refrigerate for 30 to 60 minutes for the beans to firm up.

Preheat the broiler. Pour about 1½ cups/360 ml of the sauce into a 12 by 9-inch/30.5 by 23 cm oval baking dish and spread evenly. Arrange the stuffed piquillos over the sauce. Pour the remaining ½ cup/120 ml sauce over the piquillos and sprinkle the rest of the cheese over the dish. Broil 5 inches/12 cm from the heat source until the sauce is bubbly and the cheese has melted, becoming golden brown and a bit charred in places. Serve hot. Store any leftovers, tightly covered, in the refrigerator for up to 2 days.

Alicante Fish "Paella" with Salmorrete

ARROZ A BANDA CON SALMORRETE

During a 1999 visit to my grandmother's family in Jauco, an isolated rural region of eastern Cuba near Baracoa, I discovered that my great-grandfather, Francisco Ferrer, was not born in Valencia as we had all believed, but in a small, ancient town called Benissa in the province of Alicante, halfway between the mountains and the Mediterranean. The discovery made me curious about the cuisine of a region of Spain better known as a tourist attraction for Germans and Britons than for its gastronomy. But as I soon discovered, Alicante has an ancient cuisine and a special way with rice. Even before I knew my connection to Alicante, I had become smitten with one of its most celebrated rice dishes, the *arroz a banda*. I much prefer it to more exuberant seafood paellas.

Arroz a banda is cooked in a paella pan but the resemblance ends there. The two signature elements are a concentrated fish broth and an unusual type of *sofrito* (cooking sauce) called *salmorrete*. (The name is probably a derivation of the Roman *moretum*, a thick sauce made with a mortar and pestle, and the root of the word *salmorejo*, a type of thick gazpacho also originally made with mortar and pestle.) The rice diffuses the essence of the local *morralla*, a collective name for small rockfish. The second is made with dark red dried ñora peppers that lend flavor and color to the rice. Some cooks also sauté bits of shrimp or squid with the rice to give it flavor and some textural interest (no wonder the seafood pieces are called *tropezones* (roadblocks). The rice comes to the table brick red in its paella pan and is eaten with dollops of rich aioli.

The term *a banda* means that the rice and the fish are eaten separately, side by side; the dish is said to be a fisherman's creation. I prefer to eat only the rice. The fish has already given up the ghost and surrendered its soul to the broth, while the rice has taken on the soul of the broth and the ñora peppers.

In Alicante, ñoras are consumed mostly dried, when the skin becomes a rich, leathery-looking reddish brown. Ñoras from the seaside town of Guardamar del Segura are justly renowned for a remarkable set-up where peppers grown farther inland are dried on the hot sand of nearby dunes under solar tunnels. Roasted or panfried before soaking in water to soften, ñoras are ubiquitous in the cooking sauces of the region, such as the ancient *salmorrete*, which is made from reconstituted ñoras sautéed in olive oil with garlic, onions, and tomatoes and ground to a paste with a mortar and pestle (though nowadays most people use blenders). This is what colors and flavors the *arroz a banda*.

continued

Alicante Fish "Paella" with Salmorrete, continued

SERVES 6

FISH BROTH

2 to 3 lb/910 g to 1.3 kg fish bones and heads, from white fish

2 qt/2 L water

8 oz/230 g (1 medium) yellow onion, peeled and cut in half lengthwise

8 garlic cloves, peeled

5 oz/140 g (1 medium) ripe beefsteak tomato, cut in half

½ bunch of parsley

1 bay leaf

1 Tbsp salt

SALMORRETE

1⅛ oz/32 g (about 6) dried ñoras

¼ cup/60ml extra-virgin olive oil

6 garlic cloves, finely chopped

4 oz/115 g (1 small) yellow onion, finely chopped

6 oz/170 g (about 2) plum tomatoes, seeded and chopped

1 tsp salt

AIOLI

1 whole egg

4 garlic cloves, coarsely chopped

½ tsp salt, plus more

1 cup/240 ml olive oil

1 tsp lime juice (optional)

RICE

2 Tbsp extra-virgin olive oil

8 oz/230 g squid, cleaned and cut into ½-inch/12 mm pieces

2 cups/440 g short-grain rice (preferably Bomba or Calasparra)

To make the fish broth: Place the fish in a large pot with the water, onion, garlic, tomato, parsley, bay leaf, and salt. Bring to a boil over medium heat. Decrease the heat and simmer gently for 30 to 40 minutes. Strain and measure out 5 cups/1.2 L of broth; keep it warm in a small pan. Freeze any remaining broth for another use.

To make the salmorrete: Seed the ñoras and place in a bowl. Cover with warm water; let soak until softened, about 20 minutes. Alternatively, bring to a boil with 1 qt/960 ml water for 20 minutes or until soft. Drain and reserve ¼ cup/60 ml of the cooking or soaking liquid.

Heat the oil over medium heat in a 12-inch/30.5 cm skillet. Add the ñoras and garlic and sauté for 20 seconds. Add the onion and sauté for 10 minutes, until golden. Add the tomatoes and sauté until soft, about 8 minutes. Transfer all ingredients to a blender with the reserved cooking liquid and salt and process into a smooth pureed sauce. You should have about 1 cup/240 ml sauce; reserve.

To make the aioli: Place the egg, garlic, and salt in a blender and process to combine. Add the olive oil in a stream while blending on high speed until the sauce is thick and emulsified. Add the lime juice and pulse to incorporate. Taste for salt. You should have about 1 cup/240 ml; reserve. The sauce will keep in the refrigerator for up to 1 week, tightly covered with plastic wrap. Bring to room temperature before serving.

To prepare the rice: Preheat the oven to 350°F/176°C. Add the reserved Salmorrete to the pan with the fish broth and bring to a low simmer over medium-low heat. Stir to blend well. Add the oil to a well-seasoned 14-inch/35.5 cm paella pan and place over medium heat. Add the squid and sauté, stirring, for 3 to 4 minutes. Add the rice and continue stirring to coat the grains with oil. Add the broth and continue stirring for 2 to 3 minutes until well distributed. Spread the rice evenly over the pan. When the liquid has reduced slightly and bubbles form on the surface, cover the pan with aluminum foil and transfer it to the bottom rack of the oven. Bake for 15 minutes. Unwrap and taste a forkful of rice. It should be al dente. Continue baking, uncovered, for 5 minutes more, until the top browns in some places. Serve spoonfuls of rice topped with dollops of aioli.

Spanish Potato Omelet with Roasted Peppers

TORTILLA DE PATATAS CON PIMIENTOS ASADOS

When I first went to live in Spain in the 1970s, I ate eggs almost every night for supper. I wasn't alone. Rain or shine, in every season, as night fell, the clatter of of forks beating eggs for *tortilla de patata* (potato omelet) would ring through my neighborhood. As soon as the clanging began to fade, I could hear the hiss of onions and potatoes being sautéed in olive oil, followed by waves of delicious aroma wafting through the air.

Spaniards eat *tortilla de patatas* at all hours of the day; hot from the pan for supper or lunch, at room temperature as a midmorning snack, or washed down with a glass of wine at a tapas bar. For long car trips and picnics, this is the food they are most likely to bring along—something portable and filling that they can eat without fuss. To this day I think of it as comfort food for all seasons.

There is nothing quaint or fluffy about a *tortilla de patatas*. Shaped like a round cake because it takes the form of the frying pan it is cooked in, the Spanish tortilla is a sturdy and substantial egg, onion, and potato dish—a type of frittata. In my student days at Valladolid, I would go to a small bar not far from the university for a slice of the largest tortilla I had ever seen. What I loved the most was its spiciness because it was flavored with guindillas, Spain's favorite hot pepper.

Making a great tortilla de patatas takes a bit of practice, as you need to flip the tortilla to cook it on both sides. It also requires a grassy olive oil and the freshest, most flavorful eggs you can find. I always look for free-range, organic eggs with bright golden-orange yolks. (You can always tell when an egg is fresh because the yolk is dome-shaped, never flat.) Don't be stingy with the oil when sautéing the onions and potatoes. Once the potatoes are tender and the onion has cooked down to the consistency of a confit, you drain off the oil and reserve it to flavor and cook the eggs. Some Spanish cooks I know claim that extra-virgin olive oil darkens the tortilla. They prefer to use sunflower oil, but I can't do without olive oil. Use a heavy-bottomed, well-cured or nonstick skillet and a gentle heat as high heat can result in a burnt crust and a runny interior.

My recipe is heavy on potatoes and roasted peppers, but you can reduce the amount for an eggier omelet. Bring it to the table on a platter with warm crusty bread, Romesco Sauce (page 268), and a crisp red wine from La Rioja or Ribero del Duero region for a rustic supper or lunch. To serve the omelet as tapas, cut into small squares and serve with romesco as a dipping sauce.

continued

MAKES 4 TO 6 SERVINGS
AS AN APPETIZER, AND
6 TO 8 AS A MAIN DISH

1 lb 4¾ oz/590 g (about 6 medium) hot green peppers for roasting, such as poblano or NuMex peppers

2 lb/910 g (5 large) russet potatoes, peeled and cut into ¼-inch/6 mm slices

1 lb/455 g (2 medium) yellow onions, cut into ½-inch/12 mm rings

1½ to 2 tsp salt

2 cups/480 ml light olive oil, or a mixture of 1 cup/240 ml corn or sunflower oil and 1 cup/240 ml extra-virgin olive oil

8 large eggs, lightly beaten

Roast the peppers, according to the directions on pages 232 to 233. Stem, seed, devein, and cut into 1-inch/2.5 cm squares.

Place the potatoes and onions in a medium bowl. Add the salt and toss well to coat. Warm the oil in a an 11-inch/28 cm nonstick or well-seasoned skillet over medium-high heat. When the oil is rippling but not smoking, add the potatoes and onions. Lower the heat to medium, cover, and cook, stirring occasionally, until the potatoes are fork-tender and the onions are soft and translucent, about 20 minutes. Add the roasted peppers and cook for about 5 minutes. Drain, reserving 2 Tbsp of the oil.

Transfer the vegetables to a large bowl. Pour in the eggs and stir gently with a rubber spatula to combine, being careful not to break up the potatoes. Return the reserved oil to the skillet over medium-high heat. Add the egg mixture and cook until the egg sets and separates completely from the sides of the pan, about 3 minutes. Using a spatula, lift the tortilla and check the bottom; it should be golden. To cook the other side, remove the skillet from the heat, cover with a plate that is slightly larger in diameter than the skillet, and, holding both the skillet and the plate firmly with oven mitts, flip the tortilla onto the plate. Return the skillet to the heat and very gently slide the tortilla back into the skillet. Cook until completely set and golden, about 5 minutes more.

Using the spatula, gently slide the tortilla onto a serving plate. Serve warm or at room temperature, ideally the day it is made, though it can be eaten cold from the refrigerator or brought to room temperature. Store, tightly covered, in the refrigerator for up to 2 days.

Puerto Rican Red Kidney Bean Stew

HABICHUELAS COLORADAS GUISADAS

Puerto Ricans use the lovely verb *guisar* to describe the cooking of beans, which means more than to simply *cocinar* (to cook) or *hervir* (to boil), but to braise or stew. It also conveys the building of flavors that are used to prepare beans and so many foods in Puerto Rico.

Making *habichuelas guisadas* involves a *recado* or *recao*, a chopped or pureed mixture that can include many seasoning elements, from tomatoes to garlic and onion, but always uses them in combination with the holy trinity of Puerto Rican flavors: cilantro; the similar-tasting broad-leaf culantro; and the tiny, heatless, and divinely perfumed chinense peppers they call *ají dulce*. The *recado* in turn goes into the sauce base that Latin American and Spanish cooks call the sofrito, a gently sautéed foundation built on a flavorful fat (such as olive oil or lard) with aromatics like garlic or onions—and in this case, flavorful salt pork and ham. The beans are first simmered by themselves with a few key flavorings before being combined with the sofrito and allowed to absorb its complex savor.

The dish should be a little soupy. Puerto Ricans serve it on its own in soup bowls or ladled over white rice. If serving without rice, I suggest accompanying it with wedges of the big Florida-type avocado—not as buttery as the popular Hass, but more like a refreshing vegetable—and one of the spicy vinegars on pages 254 or 256.

MAKES 6 TO 8 SERVINGS

BEANS

1 lb/455 g dried red kidney beans or pink beans, picked over and rinsed

2 cups/480 ml water

2 culantro leaves or 5 to 6 sprigs cilantro

4 sweet ajíes dulces, whole

1 cubanelle pepper, cut in half and seeded

5 oz/140 g (1 small) yellow onion, cut in half

To prepare the beans: Place the beans in a bowl, cover with water, and soak overnight. Place the beans and soaking water plus the 2 cups/480 ml of fresh water in a heavy-bottomed 6 qt/5.7 L pot with the culantro, ajíes dulces, cubanelle pepper, and onion. Bring to a boil over high heat. Lower the heat to medium, cover, and simmer until tender, about 1½ hours. While the beans cook, make the recado and sofrito.

RECADO

1 lb 2 oz/510 g (about 6) plum tomatoes, coarsely chopped

2 Tbsp tomato puree

6 oz/170 g (1 medium) green bell pepper, coarsely chopped

8 oz/230 g (1 medium) yellow onion, coarsely chopped

8 garlic cloves, coarsely chopped

18 ajíes dulces, seeded and cut in half

¼ cup/5 g cup coarsely chopped cilantro

2 culantro leaves

1 Tbsp apple cider vinegar

1 tsp dried oregano

SOFRITO

2 Tbsp Achiote-Infused Oil (see page 298)

3 oz/85 g salt pork, cut into ¼-inch/6 mm cubes

4 oz/115 g Smithfield-type ham (dry-cured country ham), finely diced

4 large garlic cloves, finely chopped

2 tsp salt, plus more

Freshly ground black pepper

To make the recado: Place the tomatoes, tomato puree, bell pepper, onion, garlic, ajíes dulces, cilantro, culantro, vinegar, and oregano in a blender or food processor and process into a coarse puree. Set aside.

To make the sofrito: Warm the oil in a medium skillet over medium heat until sizzling. Add the salt pork and sauté until golden brown, about 5 minutes. Add the ham and cook until golden, about 2 minutes. Add the garlic and cook, stirring, until golden, about 40 seconds. Stir in the recado and season with the salt and black pepper. Taste and add more salt or pepper if needed. Cook for 10 minutes, stirring occasionally.

When the beans are tender, stir in the sofrito and simmer for 20 minutes to let the flavors develop. Ladle into bowls and serve. Store any leftovers, covered, in the refrigerator for up to 5 days.

Tropical Shrimp Ceviche with Yuca

CEVICHE DE CAMARONES TROPICAL CON YUCA

The incomparable musky, citrusy flavor of chinense peppers, both sweet and hot, is what makes this shrimp ceviche special. (Note that "ceviche" is the most popular spelling of the word outside of Peru.) I first experimented with the Suave orange habaneros that I had gotten from the Chile Pepper Institute in New Mexico, which afforded me the luxury of using several deeply perfumed pods coupled with just one superhot habanero. Unfortunately, the Suave still is not widely available for retail sale, though seeds for planting are easy to find. But the effect can be duplicated by using a hot habanero or half of a very perfumed Scotch bonnet, such as the Trinidad 7-pot, with a handful of the tiny Caribbean sweet peppers that go by different names, including *ají cachucha* and *ají dulce* (preferably Venezuelan), which are deeply perfumed. When they ripen in my garden, I like to add a few tiny pods of the wonderfully perfumed Peruvian *charapita* or Brazilian *cumarí*, lightly crushed.

Achiote-infused olive oil gives this ceviche a terrific golden-orange color. Rather than serving the yuca alongside, as is done in Peru, I treat it like the Cuban *yuca con mojo*, which is doused in a citrusy *mojo* sauce. Garnish the ceviche with slices of ripe avocado and pair with ice-cold Cusqueña beer. You can prepare the sauce and the shrimp for the ceviche up to one day ahead of time.

continued

MAKES 6 SERVINGS
AS AN APPETIZER

ACHIOTE-INFUSED OIL

¼ cup/60 g achiote seeds

¼ cup/60 g extra-virgin olive oil

1 lb/455 g medium shrimp

1 qt/960 ml water

4 cilantro sprigs or
2 to 3 cilantro leaves

Peel of ½ orange

1 Tbsp allspice berries

½ tsp salt

8 oz/230 g (1 medium) red onion,
cut in half and thinly sliced

1 cup/240 ml freshly squeezed
orange juice

⅓ cup/80 ml freshly squeezed
lime juice

2 oz/55 g (6 to 8) NuMex Suave
orange or red habaneros or
(14 small) cachucha peppers
(ají dulce), stemmed, seeded,
and slivered or coarsely chopped

1 extra-hot habanero or any
Caribbean hot chinense, stemmed,
seeded, and slivered

1/16 oz/1.5 g (3 to 4 small) charapita
or cumarí peppers, lightly crushed

1 Tbsp finely chopped garlic

2 Tbsp finely chopped cilantro

1 lb/455 g fresh or frozen yuca or
sweet potatoes, (preferably a white-
fleshed type), peeled

1 Hass avocado, cut into 2-inch/
5 cm chunks or long slices

6 culantro leaves

To make the infused oil: Place the achiote seeds in a small skillet or saucepan with the olive oil. Warm over medium heat until the oil turns orange-red. Turn off the heat and let cool. Strain into a glass or metal container, cover tightly, and keep in a cool, dark place for up to 1 month.

Peel and devein the shrimp, leaving the tails intact. Place the shells in a medium pot with the water, cilantro sprigs, orange peel, allspice berries, and salt. Bring to a boil over high heat. Lower the heat and simmer for 10 minutes. Strain and return the liquid to the pot. Add the shrimp and cook for 3 minutes. Strain, reserving ¼ cup/60 ml of the cooking liquid. Place the cooking liquid in a medium bowl, cover, and keep at room temperature while you finish preparing the dish, or chill in the refrigerator along with the shrimp.

Place the onion in a medium bowl. Mix in the orange and lime juices and the reserved ¼ cup/60 ml cooking liquid. Add the peppers, garlic, and 2 Tbsp of the achiote oil. Add the cooked shrimp and season with salt. Add the chopped cilantro and mix well. Cover and refrigerate.

Place the yuca or sweet potatoes in a medium pot of salted water. Bring the water to a boil and cook until the tubers are tender and cooked through when pierced with a knife, about 20 minutes. Lift the cooked tubers out of the water and transfer to a bowl; cover to keep warm until ready to serve. Just before serving, remove the tough fibrous vein that runs though each yuca and cut the tubers into 1- to 2-inch/2.5 to 5 cm chunks.

Serve family style, mounding the the warm yuca on a large platter, topping with the ceviche, and garnishing with the avocado and culantro leaves.

Galician-Style Octopus with Paprika and Olive Oil

PULPO A FEIRA

The years I spent in the '70s studying medieval history in Valladolid, Spain, were the truly minimalist period of my life. I was on a shoestring budget that forced me to love the freshness and unencumbered flavors of the absurdly inexpensive fare at humble restaurants and tapas bars. The purity of much Spanish food was a revelation to me after the creolized, sometime baroque exuberance of most Caribbean cuisines. On research trips to many other parts of Spain, I discovered regional glories like pungent Extremaduran *pimentón de la Vera* (smoked paprika) and mildly hot Galician Padrón peppers. I also fell in love with Galician octopus, especially as served *a feira* (folk-festival style.) At any village, the *feira's* main attraction would be strong-armed women lifting out purplish *pulpo* (octopus) from huge, unlined copper pots and rapidly snipping off the tentacles with scissors before doling them out on small plates, drizzled with paprika, local olive oil, and a sprinkling of coarse salt.

Galician bars were also wonderful places to eat my fill of sweet, firm *pulpo a feira,* perfectly partnered with sharp, fizzy Ribeiro or Alvariño wine served in porcelain cups. I was captivated by the ingenious presentation of the octopus at some bars, with the knobby head tucked into a glass and the tentacles draped over the sides like flowering stems.

The following recipe was given to me by my assistant, Paloma Ramos, who comes from a family of Galician fishermen. Her father insisted that the best octopus was from the Rías Baixas, the fjord-like estuaries on the craggy Galician coast. Galicians usually cook very large octopus, which they beat to death to tenderize. In the United States, fish stores usually carry smaller (1½ to 3 lb/680 to 1.4 kg) precleaned octopus that are tender enough to not need this treatment.

I always follow the beautiful simplicity of Paloma's *pulpo a feira,* boiling the octopus without any fussy touches and serving the cut-up tentacles with the classic accompaniments of Spanish paprika, salt, and olive oil to be added as desired by each guest. The following amounts are more than enough to serve as one of several appetizers at a small dinner party. The recipe can easily be doubled or tripled for a larger gathering.

continued

MAKES 6 TO 8 SERVINGS
AS AN APPETIZER

1 (3 lb/1.4 kg) octopus, cleaned

¼ cup/30 g sweet smoked Spanish paprika (preferably pimentón de la Vera)

¼ cup/30 g hot smoked Spanish paprika (preferably pimentón de la Vera) or Homemade Merkén with Guajillo (page 247)

¼ cup/50 g coarse sea salt

½ cup/120 ml extra-virgin olive oil

Crusty bread, for serving

Bring a large stockpot of water to a boil over high heat. Holding the octopus by a tentacle, plunge it in and out of the boiling water three times to tenderize. Return the octopus to the pot. Cook at a rolling boil for 45 minutes, covered, checking for doneness after 30 minutes by piercing it with the tines of a fork. When it is fork-tender, either lift it out onto a platter at once or leave it in the cooking water until you are ready to serve it.

While the octopus cooks, set out the simple accompaniments in pretty vessels. Place the the sweet and hot paprikas in decorative saltshakers or small bowls, arrange the salt on a small plate, and pour the olive oil into a spouted beaker or a bowl with small wooden spoons for serving.

Some cooks like to remove the octopus's purplish skin. I never do. It is tasty and lends character to the octopus meat. Use a small sharp knife to cut all around the head and detach it. With kitchen shears or a knife, cut the tentacles into bite-size pieces. Place the octopus pieces on a serving platter or individual appetizer plates. Sprinkle the octopus with paprika and salt before drizzling it with olive oil. Serve with the crusty bread to mop up the flavored oil.

Crunchy Panca Calamari in the Style of Cucharamama

JALEA DE CALAMARES CUCHARAMAMA

When I was getting ready to open Cucharamama, I wanted to come up with a recipe for fried calamari that would come close to the crunchy texture and good flavor of the calamari in the Peruvian dish *jalea*, a tempura-like fried mix. My friend Pedro Miguel Schiaffino, one of Peru's most talented chefs, set us on the right track. He suggested dipping the raw squid in an egg mixture flavored with ground *panca* pepper before dusting it with flour and deep frying it. I fell in love with the idea and developed a recipe that never fails to produce deep-flavored calamari that is tender but coated in a light golden, crunchy crust that holds its texture.

MAKES 4 SERVINGS

1 lb/455 g cleaned squid, bodies and tentacles

SEASONED EGG COATING

3 large eggs

3 Tbsp panca pepper puree, homemade (see Basic Dried Pepper Paste, page 248), or store-bought (see Resources)

Juice from ½ lime (about 1 Tbsp)

¼ tsp sea salt

1 garlic clove, crushed to a paste

SEASONED FLOUR COATING

2 cups/250 g all-purpose flour

1 tsp kosher or sea salt

1 tsp freshly ground black pepper

3 cups/720 ml vegetable oil

Coarse sea salt

Ground Ají Panca (page 235)

Peruvian Pickled Red Onions and Ají Amarillo (page 262)

Rocoto and Tree Tomato Sauce (page 270)

2 Tbsp minced cilantro leaves

Cut the cleaned squid bodies into ½-inch/12 mm rings. Place the rings in a colander with the tentacles and let drain for a few minutes.

To prepare the egg coating: Place the eggs, panca pepper puree, lime juice, sea salt, and garlic in a bowl and whisk to mix.

To prepare the flour coating: Place the flour, kosher salt, and black pepper in a separate large bowl and stir to mix.

Heat the oil to 350°F/180°C in a medium heavy-bottomed pot. Line a baking sheet with paper towels.

Drop the calamari into the egg batter and toss to coat evenly. Lift out with a slotted spoon and drop in the seasoned flour. Toss gently with your fingertips to coat evenly, then transfer to a large strainer or colander; shake to get rid of excess flour. Lower the squid into the hot oil in batches and fry until golden, moving them around occasionally with tongs or a slotted spoon to cook evenly, about 2 minutes per batch. Lift out of the hot oil with a slotted spoon and place on the paper towels to drain.

Sprinkle with the coarse sea salt and dust lightly with ground panca pepper. Serve heaped on a plate topped with the pickled onions and cilantro. Pass the sauce for dipping.

Madame Carmelite's Red Snapper in a Spicy Creole Sauce in the Style of Guadeloupe

COURT-BOUILLON DE VIVANEAU

On a map, Guadeloupe—two large landmasses separated by a narrow saltwater channel—looks like a butterfly with wings outstretched, ready to take flight. Like Martinique, its neighbor, this Caribbean island is a French overseas department and a region of the European Union.

It is a twist of history that it was the French and not the Spanish who settled this island. By the time Columbus sighted Guadeloupe in 1493, its first inhabitants, the peaceful Arawak (Taíno) Indians, had been vanquished by the warlike Caribs. When Columbus's exploratory party found human remains leftover from a Carib ritual banquet, they left in a hurry. In 1635, after fierce battles with the Caribs, Norman nobleman Pierre Belain d'Esnambuc conquered the island in the name of France.

The centuries-old tie to France gives Guadeloupe a continental air of elegance and formality that surprises visitors looking for postcard Caribbean fun. By emphasizing the importance of a good education, speaking proper French, and Catholicism, the French government has helped create a native elite that looks to France for inspiration. Guadeloupe has an important creole cuisine, blending African, Native American, and other influences, but a strong French sensibility suffuses even the most traditional dishes.

I first went to Guadeloupe to do research on the Le Cuistot Mutuel, a culinary confraternity that brings together talented women chefs on the island. This is a powerful lot—an African matriarchy that controls the island's restaurant business. I stayed at the Village Caraibe, a small seaside hotel near Pointe-à-Pitre. The place is owned by Madame Jeanne Carmelite, a senior member of Le Cuistot Mutuel and the keeper of the clothes of St. Lawrence, the patron saint of the organization. Lawrence was grilled to death by the Romans, and the symbol of his martyrdom, a gridiron, adorns the aprons the women wear on his feast day, a serious yet joyful celebration known as the *Fête des Cuisinières* (the feast of the cooks).

My first meal at Madame Carmelite's hotel restaurant, La Nouvelle Table Créole, began auspiciously with blood sausages (*boudin noir*), malanga fritters (*accras de malanga*), and a delicious rum punch on the wide verandah overlooking the sea. As my main course, I ordered one of her specialties, a *court bouillon de poisson* made with red snapper.

continued

A power outage plunged us into darkness before I could take a good look at my food. Guided only by the fragrance wafting from my plate, I put a tiny morsel of fish in my mouth, fearful of bones. The fish was moist, perfectly seasoned, and deliciously fresh in a spicy but light tomato sauce with the tangy touch of lime that I adore in Caribbean seafood and the biting heat and musky aroma of Scotch bonnet pepper. I ate every bite in total darkness, concentrating only on flavor. By the time our waitress brought a candle to the table, only the bones remained on my plate.

The next morning, Madame Carmelite gave me a tour of the hotel grounds and then we walked to a rocky beach where fishermen had just moored their boat with the day's catch. We returned to her kitchen with an armload of fresh fish and bulbous hot peppers similar to the Scotch bonnet. My first lesson in French creole cooking began with *court bouillon de poisson*. I was able to see what I had missed the night before: the knowing hand of the cook, the layered seasoning, and a succulent fresh red snapper nestled in a vibrant red creole sauce spiced with the island's delicious but scorching hot pepper, all plated with meticulous French care and delicacy.

In classic French cooking, *court bouillon* (literally "short boil") refers to a savory broth used to poach fish or poultry. In the French islands, it is a generic term for seafood—from red snapper to octopus—seasoned in a lemony marinade and cooked in a savory sauce colored with achiote-infused oil and flavored with garlic, thyme, scallions, and tomatoes. What makes the court bouillon spicy is a type of Scotch bonnet pepper (*piment*), the island's favorite condiment. As a final touch, Madame Carmelite prepares a spicy garlicky table sauce, not unlike the Cuban *mojo* but with heat, that gives the fish a tangy kick and a touch of brightness. Like most island cooks, Madame Carmelite usually prepares the court bouillon with whole red snapper; I often use fillets or steaks for ease of serving. Serve this with rice and red kidney beans and a dry Sancerre or a Crios Rose de Malbec from Argentina.

FISH

Juice of 1 lime (about 2 Tbsp)

1 yellow Bonda Ma Jacques, Scotch bonnet, or habanero pepper, seeded and finely chopped

3 garlic cloves, mashed to a paste

1 tsp sea salt

3 lb/1.4 kg (about 4 small) red snapper fillets

TABLE SAUCE

Juice of 1 lime (about 2 Tbsp)

2 garlic cloves, mashed to a paste

¼ cup/5 g finely chopped parsley

1 yellow Bonda Ma Jacques, Scotch bonnet, or habanero pepper, seeded and finely chopped

2 to 3 Tbsp extra-virgin olive oil

½ tsp salt

COURT BOUILLON

¼ cup/60 ml Achiote-Infused Oil (see page 298)

4 oz/115 g (1 small) yellow onion finely chopped

6 scallions, including 3 inches/ 7.5 cm of the green tops, rinsed and finely chopped

10 oz/280 g (about 2 medium) ripe beefsteak tomatoes, peeled, seeded, and finely chopped

½ tsp minced fresh thyme, or ¼ tsp dry thyme

1 bay leaf

1 cup/240 ml well-flavored fish broth or chicken broth

½ cup/120 ml dry white wine

1½ tsp salt

½ tsp freshly ground black pepper

4 yellow Scotch bonnet peppers

To marinate the fish: In a small bowl, combine the lime juice, pepper, garlic, and salt. Rub the fish all over with this marinade and let rest, tightly covered with pastic wrap, in the refrigerator for at least 30 minutes and no more than 2 hours.

To make the sauce: In a small bowl, stir together the lime juice, garlic, parsley, pepper, olive oil, and salt. Set aside.

To make the court bouillon and finish the dish: Warm the oil over medium-high heat in a 12-inch/30.5 cm skillet, or a wider pan if cooking whole fish. Add the onion and scallions and sauté for 2 minutes. Add the tomatoes, thyme, and bay leaf and cook for 1 minute. Add the fish fillets and cook 1 minute on each side. Pour in the broth and wine, and season with the salt and black pepper. Cook for about 3 minutes, or until the fish is firm and flakes easily when pierced with a fork.

Spoon the cooked sauce onto a large platter and arrange the fish over it. Garnish with the whole Scotch bonnet peppers. Serve the table sauce in a bowl on the side.

Shrimp with Merkén

CAMARONES AL MERKÉN

Shrimp and lobster have a natural affinity for sauces spiked with hot peppers or pepper-based condiments. The capsaicin kick brings out their natural sweetness. This simple dish is a lively example. It draws on the smoky charm of *merkén*, a wonderful Chilean spice blend, to deepen the flavors of a tomato sauce lightly accented with citrus. I think it is delicious with my guajillo version of *merkén*, but artisanal versions of *merkén* available in the United States are also excellent. You can make an acceptable substitute using 2 tsp Spanish smoked paprika (preferably pimentón de la Vera) mixed with 1 tsp ground cumin and ¼ tsp ground coriander seed. The dish is especially good made with the hard-to-find rock shrimp (actually a tiny relative of lobster) but also great with any really fresh shrimp. Serve the shrimp over rice or toss with pasta, accompanied by a Riesling or Gewürztraminer from Chile's cool and humid Bio-Bio region.

MAKES 6 SERVINGS

1 lb/455 g medium shrimp or rock shrimp, shelled and deveined but with tails on

1 to 2 tsp sea salt

Freshly ground black pepper

2 Tbsp extra-virgin olive oil

4 garlic cloves, finely chopped

1½ lb/680 g (about 8) plum tomatoes, finely chopped

1 Tbsp Merkén (see page 247, or store-bought) or see headnote

1 cup/240 ml dry white wine or beer

1 Tbsp freshly squeezed orange juice

Finely chopped cilantro

Rinse the shrimp and pat dry. Toss in a bowl with the salt, season with black pepper and let sit for 5 minutes to 1 hour.

Warm the oil in a large skillet over medium heat until it ripples. Add the garlic and sauté until golden, about 40 seconds. Add the tomatoes and cook for 10 minutes. Stir in the merkén and cook for about 1 minute. Add the wine and orange juice and cook for 2 to 3 minutes. Add the shrimp and cook until curled and rosy, about 3 minutes more. Garnish with the cilantro and serve hot.

Amazonian Chicken Soup Cooked in Leaf Pouches with Hot Pepper Sauce

MAITO DE POLLO AMAZÓNICO

The peoples of western Amazonia, close to the original birthplace of peppers, most often use them as a condiment to accompany minimally seasoned dishes, rather than adding them during cooking. You see people eating very plainly flavored meals while periodically taking bites from a fiery chinese pepper, or putting a spoonful of a simple hot sauce on a dish. This recipe—a nearly unseasoned soup cooked in pouches fashioned from leaves, accompanied by an intensely flavorful hot sauce—is my homage to the pepper-eating ways of the Ecuadorian Amazon. It was inspired by visits to the small cacao-growing community of Santa Rita, close to Archidona in the rain forests of Napo Province.

The women of Santa Rita raise yuca, cacao, and several kinds of fruit on small plots of land while also foraging for ferns, mushrooms, and *palmito* (hearts of palm) in the surrounding forests. Their special preparations of food cooked in leaf wrappings are called *maito* in Kichwa (the local version of Quechua). The leaves come from the wild bijao plants (*Calathea* spp.) that grow along river banks. They are large (sometimes more than 3 ft/91 cm long) and sturdy, with a waxy surface that contributes a lovely flavor to anything cooked in them.

I watched cooks preparing *maitos* by placing the filling on two overlapping leaves, bringing the tips together, and tying the resulting pouch with strings of palm-leaf fibers before placing the *maitos* on makeshift wooden grills over a wood fire. I was amazed to see how strong and watertight the packages were. The outer bijao leaf scorches, but the inner one remains intact, imbuing the contents with a musky sweetness. Local fillings might include *garabato yuyo* (fiddlehead ferns), a cheesy-tasting white mushroom called *ala* that grows on fallen tree trunks, or shredded *palmito*. Some versions use small river fish or chicken. With a little added water, the filling becomes a wonderful broth with pure and concentrated flavor. I have eaten *maitos* together with a very hot, simple puree of chinese peppers, found growing in backyards and even along dirt roads, boiled with the white seeds of *Theobroma bicolor* (a cacao relative). On a visit to Santa Rita with my chocolate-maker friend Santiago Peralta, we successfully brought back some chicken-soup *maitos* from Archidona to Quito and ate them (miraculously still hot!) accompanied by boiled yuca and the rich green sauce that I call for in this recipe.

continued

Bijao leaves are not yet imported into the United States. But they are enough like banana leaves to allow US cooks to improvise. It is a more complicated undertaking than in Ecuador, because the frozen banana (or plantain) leaves have their pitfalls. They come to our markets in 1 lb/455 g packages, usually cut into about 8 folded pieces, each roughly 4½ to 6 ft/1.4 to 1.8 m long and about 12 inches/30 cm wide when unfolded. (The exact dimensions vary according to brand.) Unfortunately, frozen banana leaves are very vulnerable to tearing when thawed and handled. To make watertight pouches, it is necessary to allow for torn or split pieces by using extra pieces. Handle the leaves like fragile treasures. In this recipe, they impart a delicious herbal aroma to the simple but concentrated broth inside. When the chicken is done, the pouches are unfolded at the table to reveal the perfectly cooked chicken and rich broth cradled within. The sauce brightens the soup in color and flavor. Hot freshly boiled yuca is the ideal accompaniment.

MAKES 4 SERVINGS

3½ lb/1.6 kg (about 12 pieces) of chicken parts cut from a whole chicken, with the wings cut into two sections and tips on

1 Tbsp kosher or sea salt

4 (1 lb/455 g) packages of frozen banana leaves, thawed

5 cups/1.2 L water

Boiled yuca (see page 298)

Ecuadorian Green Tree Tomato Sauce (page 271)

Rinse the chicken parts, making sure to discard any fragments of bone clinging to the flesh. If you prefer, discard the skin, though this is not necessary. Pat dry and place in a bowl. Sprinkle with the salt, toss well to coat, and set aside.

Open the banana leaf packages and very carefully unfold the pieces. Rinse gently under cold running water until soft and flexible, trying not to tear them. Set aside any with obvious splits. Pat the intact pieces dry with paper towels. One at a time, place them on a cutting board. With a small sharp knife, cut the leaves into long 18-inch/46 cm sections. To make four *maitos*, you will need at least 16 sections, but it doesn't hurt to allow for a few more. Carefully inspect them again and set apart any that are split. Tear off 8 thin strips (10 to 12 inches/25 to 30.5 cm long by about 1 inch/2.5 cm wide) from the split pieces to use later as strings for tying the pouches.

continued

To release the natural oils in the leaves, singe them by running each side over a gas flame or an electric burner set on high for a few seconds. (This allows their flavor and fragrance to better permeate the chicken during cooking.) The leaf will immediately become supple and its outer side shinier. Again examine all the pieces to be sure that you have 16 intact ones. If some are ripped, you may need to compensate by using several extra pieces.

Preheat the oven to 400°F/200°C. Choose a medium stainless steel bowl or a large soup bowl as a mold. Begin by lining it with two pieces of banana leaf crossed at right angles, the ends draped over the sides. Rotate the bowl a quarter turn and place two more pieces over the first two, also crossed at right angles. With your hands, gently but firmly press the leaves together against the sides of the mold to create a secure nest for the chicken and liquid. If you have had to use some split pieces, carefully press several more over the four original pieces.

Place 3 pieces of the chicken in the bottom of the bowl. Very carefully dribble in 1¼ cups/300 ml of the water from one side (do not pour it over the chicken). Gather the ends together and twist gently to create a pouch. Tie with a couple of strings made from the banana leaves. Carefully lift the leaf pouch onto a baking dish that is just large enough to hold all four pouches snugly. Continue with the remaining leaf sections, chicken pieces, and water. Slide the baking dish into the oven and bake for 1 hour and 10 minutes. The outer leaves might scorch, but the ones inside will remain fresh.

When done, place each maito in a large soup bowl and bring to the table. With a sharp knife or kitchen scissors, cut the plantain strings and open up the leaf wrappings. Add a few pieces of yuca and a spoonful of the sauce to each bowl and serve.

Big Tamal Pie Filled with Chicken in Chile Ancho Adobo

TAMALÓN

A big *tamal* (or tamalón) wrapped in banana leaves and baked in the oven is practical because it saves cooks the trouble of wrapping dozens of individual tamales. It is also a thing of beauty—a spectacular way to showcase the elegance of an ancestral food cooked in the embrace of banana leaves and unveiled at the table. As you open the package, the musky aroma of the charred banana leaves mingles with the sweet scent of corn and the earthy aroma of the adobo, awakening the appetite. I like to use a handsome terra-cotta-colored earthenware baking dish, like a *cazuela*, which you will find at kitchenware and gourmet shops that sell Spanish ingredients and cookware.

MAKES 8 SERVINGS

1 (1 lb/455 g) package of frozen banana leaves, thawed

ADOBO

3½ oz/100 g (about 6) ancho chiles

1 head garlic, separated into cloves and peeled

Juice of 2 oranges (about ¾ cup/180 ml)

1 Tbsp apple cider vinegar

1 tsp ground cumin

½ tsp dried oregano

2 Tbsp Achiote-Infused Oil (page 298)

1 tsp sea salt

CHICKEN

1 (3½ lb/1.6 kg) chicken

Kosher salt

Freshly ground black pepper

2 qt/1.9 L water

8 oz/230 g (1 medium) white onion, cut in half

1 bunch cilantro

Unfold the banana leaves and rinse under cold running water until soft and flexible, handling gently and being careful not to rip them. Pat dry with paper towels or a kitchen towel. Working on a cutting board, use a small sharp knife to cut the leaves into eight 12 by 6-inch/30.5 by 15 cm rectangles. If not using immediately, keep the leaves between sheets of damp paper towels or store in the refrigerator wrapped in a damp kitchen towel.

To make the adobo: Seed, toast, and reconstitute the anchos according to the directions on page 238. Drain, reserving ¼ cup/60 ml of the soaking liquid. Add the softened chiles and reserved soaking liquid to a blender, along with the garlic, orange juice, vinegar, cumin, oregano, achiote oil, and salt and process into a smooth puree. Set aside.

To prepare the chicken: Season the chicken inside and outside with salt and black pepper. Place in a pot with the water, onion, and cilantro. Bring to a boil over high heat. Lower the heat to medium and simmer for 20 minutes, until just barely tender. Remove the chicken from the broth. Strain the broth and reserve ½ cup/120 ml; refrigerate the remaining broth and save for another use.

continued

TAMAL DOUGH (MASA)

8 cups/1.5 g (about 16 ears) fresh corn kernels

2 Tbsp Achiote-Infused Oil (page 298)

8 garlic cloves, finely minced

8 oz/230 g (1 medium) yellow onion, finely chopped

12 oz/340 g (about 4) plum tomatoes or canned plum tomatoes, coarsely chopped

1 tsp ground cumin

1 Tbsp crushed or ground hot red pepper (see page 235)

2 Tbsp coarse salt, plus more

½ cup/120 ml chicken broth

½ cup/120 ml whole milk

¼ cup/55 g salted butter, softened

1 cup/140 g fine yellow cornmeal, or more as needed

Serrano and Tomato Salsa (page 266), Chilean "Pig in Stone" Salsa (page 263), or Rocoto and Tree Tomato Sauce (page 270)

Peruvian Pickled Red Onions and Ají Amarillo (page 262)

Strip the meat from the bones, removing the skin if you like, and cut the meat into 2-inch/5 cm pieces; place in a bowl, pour the adobo over the chicken, and set aside to marinate for 1 to 12 hours, refrigerating it if marinating for more than 1 hour.

To make the dough: Put the corn in a blender or food processor and process into a smooth puree. In a heavy pot, warm the achiote oil over medium heat. Add the garlic and sauté until lightly gold, about 20 seconds. Add the onion and sauté for about 5 minutes, until translucent and golden. Add the tomatoes, cumin, ground hot pepper, and salt and sauté for 5 minutes more, stirring occasionally. Add the corn puree, broth, milk, and butter and stir to combine. Stream in the cornmeal while stirring continuously and cook for 5 to 6 minutes, until thick and creamy.

Preheat the oven to 350°F/180°C. Line a round 10 by 2½-inch/25 by 6 cm) cazuela or other baking dish with the banana leaves layered in a crosshatch pattern. Spoon in half of the corn dough and cover with the chicken. Add the rest of the dough over the filling and smooth with a spatula. This second layer needs to be just thick enough to cover the filling. Fold the leaves over the top to close. To prevent the leaves from burning, cover with aluminum foil.

Bake the tamal for 1 hour, then remove the aluminum foil and bake for 15 minutes more to brown the top and form a delicious crust. If you bake the tamal in a cazuela, do not bother transferring it to a serving plate. Or, transfer it to a large round serving platter or rustic wooden cutting board using two large spatulas. Unwrap the tamal at the table. Slice the tamal into generous wedges or scoop out as you would a spoonbread. Serve with a spoonful of salsa and spoonsful of the pickled onions.

Turkey in Mole Coloradito

MOLE COLORADITO DE GUAJOLOTE

More than any other category of Latin foods, the marvelous moles of Mexico are edible history, revealing the mixing of complementary techniques and ingredients from two venerable but very different culinary traditions during the early colonial period. The mole is the Latin hybrid sauce par excellence—the aromas and body might point to the Mediterranean, but the color and pungency are New World, with chiles, and chocolate, playing a starring role.

When cooking mole for a large event, cooks usually work with members of their family in an assembly line to process every ingredient efficiently. In rural communities, the making of a mole is a ritual that begins with a journey to local markets, lighting the fire, readying the comal to toast the chiles, and the backbreaking work of kneeling behind a metate to reduce toasted chiles, seeds, and cacao to the smooth and aromatic paste. That paste is then transformed into mole sauce in a cavernous earthenware pot and cooked poultry is added and allowed to simmer gently to absorb the wonderful flavors of the mole.

For centuries, the preferred vehicle for the great moles was turkey (see page 239). It can also be made with chicken drumsticks and thighs or whole legs, which will absorb the sauce more quickly (but you will miss the pre-Hispanic richness of turkey).

I usually make my mole paste ahead and finish the dish a couple of hours before I plan to serve it to let all the flavors meld. Mole tastes even better the next day. Leftover turkey or chicken in mole is delicious in tacos—smear a bit of refried black beans (page 284) on hot tortillas and top with leftover mole. Or use leftovers for filling tamales and enchiladas.

continued

Turkey in Mole Coloradito, continued

3¼ to 4 lb/1.5 to 1.8 kg turkey wings, legs, and drumsticks or the equivalent weight of chicken legs or drumsticks and thighs (skinless or not, as preferred)

12 garlic cloves

5 tsp sea salt

3 tsp dried oregano

11 oz/310 g (1 extra-large) white onion, cut in half lengthwise

5 or 6 sprigs cilantro or parsley

4 qt/3.8 L water

3 cups/840 g Mole Coloradito Paste (page 250)

2 tsp sesame seeds, toasted

Corn tortillas, warmed, for serving

Cooked white rice or Mexican rice, for serving

Rinse the turkey or chicken and pat dry. Transfer it to a large bowl. With a mortar and pestle, crush 6 of the garlic cloves, the salt, and 1 tsp of the oregano into a paste. (In my restaurants, where Cubans and Mexicans work together and both have the tradition of marinating every meat they cook, even a complex dish like a mole gets a rub of crushed garlic, salt, and spices.) Smear the paste all over the turkey or chicken pieces. Cover with plastic wrap and let rest for 1 to 12 hours, refrigerating it if allowing it to rest for more than 1 hour.

Place the poultry pieces, with the flavoring paste that clings to them, in a large pot with the onion, remaining garlic, remaining 3 tsp of salt, 2 remaining tsp of oregano, cilantro, and water. Bring to a boil over medium-high heat. Lower the heat and simmer, uncovered, until the poultry is barely tender, about 45 minutes for turkey and 25 to 30 minutes for chicken; check for doneness and continue cooking a little longer if necessary. Lift the poultry pieces from the pot, place in a large bowl, and keep warm while you finish the dish.

Strain the broth through a mesh strainer into a large bowl, pressing lightly with the back of a spoon to extract as much liquid as possible. You should have about 3 qt/2.8 L broth; discard the solids. Transfer the broth to a saucepan and simmer until reduced to about 6 cups/1.4 L.

For turkey, remove the turkey meat from the bones and cut into 3-inch/ 7.5 cm serving pieces; for chicken, keep the pieces whole. Return the meat to the bowl, cover with plastic wrap, and finish the sauce.

Put the mole paste in a large Dutch oven or other heavy, lidded saucepan about 11 inches/28 cm wide by 4 inches/10 cm deep. Add about 6 cups/1.4 L of the reserved broth. Bring to a gentle boil over medium heat. Lower the heat and simmer for about 5 minutes. You should have about 9 cups/2.1 L of diluted mole sauce. Add the turkey or chicken pieces and simmer, stirring occasionally, for 10 minutes.

Transfer the contents of the pot to a large serving bowl and sprinkle with the sesame seeds. Serve with the corn tortillas and rice. Store any leftovers, covered, in the refrigerator for up to 3 days.

Slab Bacon in Hibiscus Hot Pepper Adobo with Chocolate

TOCINO EN ADOBO DE JAMAICA Y CHILES CON CHOCOLATE

The marinade for this succulent slow-roasted slab bacon dish is a garlicky adobo of dried Mexican chiles and aromatic spices combined with a scarlet hibiscus flower syrup. A rich mahogany glaze made by mixing some of the sauce with chocolate is added about 30 minutes before the end of cooking, providing the backbone of flavor along with a sultry shine. This dish can be served as an appetizer, cut into 2-inch/5 cm squares and set on a cushion of pureed root vegetables (I suggest Caribbean sweet potato or *arracacha*) or creamy polenta. Alternatively, you can present it in its full glory as the centerpiece of a festive meal, carved at the table and accompanied by a starchy puree or fresh corn tamales. I also love to serve it Chinese-style, folded into small steamed *baos* and garnished with Korean-style Spicy Pickled Cucumbers (page 259).

You may need to order the meat in advance from a butcher because such large slabs of bacon are seldom sold in supermarket meat departments. A Latin or Italian pork butcher is your best bet. A large slab of pork belly will give a different flavor but an equally delicious result. The pork needs to marinate for about 6 hours so plan to start the day before.

continued

MAKES 12 SERVINGS AS AN
APPETIZER OR 6 AS A MAIN

5 lb/2.3 kg slab bacon or skin-on pork belly, boneless

1 Tbsp sea salt

HIBISCUS SYRUP

2 oz/55 g (about 1 cup) dried hibiscus blossoms

½ cup/100 g granulated sugar

½ cup/100 g grated brown loaf sugar (preferably Mexican piloncillo or Colombian panela) or muscovado sugar, plus more

2 cups/480 ml water

ADOBO

5¼ oz/150 g (about 9) ancho chiles

1⅛ oz/32 g (about 9) dried guajillo peppers

⅝ oz/18 g (about 3) dried puya, chilcostle, or taviche chiles

1 Tbsp extra-virgin olive oil

12 large garlic cloves, coarsely chopped

2 tsp ground cumin

1 tsp dried oregano

½ tsp aniseed

¼ tsp ground allspice

¼ cup/60 ml aged dark rum

1 Tbsp sea salt, plus more

½ cup/120 ml water

Rinse the pork and pat dry. Use a heavy sharp knife to score a grid pattern on the skin side without cutting through the skin. The size of the grid can be adjusted according to the way you want to serve the meat. Rub with the salt. If using the pork belly, let rest about 20 minutes.

To make the syrup: Place the hibiscus blossoms, both sugars, and the water in a small pot. Bring to a boil over medium heat and simmer for 15 minutes. Strain through a mesh strainer, pressing to extract as much liquid as possilbe. Return the liquid to the pot and cook over medium heat for 10 minutes, until reduced to about 1¼ cups/300 ml.

To make the adobo: Rinse and dry the peppers according to the directions on page 236. Warm a skillet or comal over medium heat. Add the dried peppers in several batches (first the anchos, followed by the guajillos, and then the smaller peppers), and toast lightly, 3 to 4 seconds on each side. As they are done, transfer them to a medium bowl. To soften, either cover them with 8 cups/2 L warm water and soak for 20 to 30 minutes, or simmer over medium heat for 15 minutes and then drain. Working in batches if necessary, process to a smooth paste in a blender or food processor with the hibiscus syrup, olive oil, garlic, cumin, oregano, aniseed, allspice, rum, and salt. If desired, work the puree through a mesh strainer to eliminate any fibrous bits (I don't always bother with this step). You should have about 3 cups/720 ml.

Place the meat in a baking or roasting pan that is 2 inches/5 cm deep and large enough to hold the meat snugly but easily. Pour 2 cups/480 ml of the adobo over the meat, reserving the rest for the glaze. Rub it thoroughly into the surface. Cover with plastic wrap and let marinate for at least 6 hours or overnight, refrigerated. When ready to roast, preheat the oven to 350°F/180°C. Remove the plastic wrap and add about ¼ cup/60 ml of the water to the pan. Cover tightly with aluminum foil and roast on the middle oven rack until golden brown and fork-tender, 1½ to 2 hours. About 1 hour into cooking, uncover the meat, add the remaining ¼ cup/60 ml of water to keep the sauce from getting too thick, and cover again.

GLAZE

2 to 3 oz/55 to 85 g 60% cacao or higher dark chocolate (preferably made from premium Latin American cacao)

1 Tbsp grated brown loaf sugar (preferably Columbia panela) or muscovado (optional)

Salt (optional)

To make glaze: Combine the reserved 1 cup/240 ml of adobo and the chocolate in a small pot over medium-low heat and cook, stirring constantly, until the chocolate has melted. Taste and add the sugar and season with salt, if needed. (You might need the sugar if using a 70% cacao).

Blanket the meat with the glaze and roast uncovered for another 30 minutes, until it has a moist, glistening look.

Using two large, broad spatulas to keep the meat from falling apart, carefully lift it onto a large cutting board. Pour the pan juices into a small pot and keep warm over low heat, then bring the warm sauce to the table in a sauceboat. Slice the meat and serve. Store any leftovers, tightly wrapped, in the refrigerator for up to 2 weeks.

Panfried Pork Steaks in Guajillo-Puya Adobo

CARNE ENCHILADA

Pork shoulder is a great cut for thin steaks because, unlike steaks from the loin, it remains succulent and juicy after cooking. Thinly sliced and brightly seasoned with a pungent paste of dried guajillo and puya chiles, it is an ideal filling for soft tacos smeared with refried beans (page 284) or cooked whole beans, Very Hot Rancho Chile Verde Salsa (page 264), and Chile Rajas (page 282). The pork needs to marinate for 1 to 2 days, so start this recipe a couple of days ahead.

MAKES ENOUGH FOR
24 SMALL TACOS

2 lb/910 g boneless pork shoulder, rinsed and patted dry

Coarse sea salt

Freshly ground black pepper

ADOBO

3 oz/85g (about 14) guajillo chiles, wiped clean, stemmed, and opened flat (see pages 233 and 236)

⅛ oz/3 g (about 3) dried puya chiles or chiles de árbol, wiped clean, stemmed, and opened flat (see pages 233 and 236)

1 tsp ground cumin

1 tsp dried oregano

⅛ tsp ground cloves

8 garlic cloves

3 Tbsp extra-virgin olive oil

2 Tbsp apple cider vinegar

1 tsp sea salt

Extra-virgin olive oil

Sea salt

Cut the meat into steaks ⅛ to ¼ inch/4 to 6 mm thick. Place in a bowl and season generously with coarse salt and black pepper, rubbing it all over the meat.

To make the adobo and marinate the meat: Seed, toast, and reconstitute the chiles, according to the instructions on page 238. Strain, reserving ¼ cup/60 ml of the soaking liquid. Place the chiles and reserved liquid in a blender with the garlic, cumin, oregano, cloves, olive oil, vinegar, and salt and process into a smooth puree.

Set a mesh strainer over a bowl and work the puree through it with a wooden spoon, pressing hard to extract as much sauce and pulp as you can. Run a rubber spatula along the underside of the strainer to scrape any clinging sauce into the bowl.

Pour about 1 cup/240 ml of the sauce over the meat, coating it well on both sides. Let marinate in the refrigerator, covered tightly with plastic wrap, for 1 to 2 days. Store the remaining adobo in a tightly covered jar in the refrigerator.

Warm 1 to 2 Tbsp of olive oil in a 12-inch/30.5 cm cast-iron skillet over medium-high heat. Add the pork in batches and pan fry, then season with sea salt. Remove the pork from the marinade, letting the excess drain away. Cook for 5 minutes on each side, basting with some of the reserved adobo and the olive oil and seasoning with sea salt. Slice the meat, and serve.

Poblanos Stuffed with Beef Hash in a Savory Tomato Sauce

CHILES RELLENOS

Chiles rellenos belong to a wonderful family of stuffed vegetables popularized by Islamic cooks in southern Spain. This ancient Levantine tradition was brought by the Spaniards to the Americas and vigorously took root in colonial Mexico, where the technique flourished, spawning many clever interpretations often starring the beautiful poblano pepper.

These peppers are ideal for stuffing. Most have a lovely heart shape, thin skin that is easy to peel, and very few seeds conveniently clustered around a knobby placenta. In addition, they are usually large enough to hold a generous amount of filling. Preparing them for stuffing involves roasting, a basic technique that you will find used for many types of peppers, both fresh and dried, not only to peel them, but also to intensify their flavor and mellow their heat.

The choice of stuffing varies all over Mexico. Many cooks love to fill the peppers with a savory pork hash. Others prefer beef or chicken, a combination of potatoes and chorizo, or simply cheese. The most famous of the whole family is *chiles en nogada*, attributed to (among several candidates) a group of nuns from Puebla. It has a savory pork stuffing with sweet fruits, such as apples, and is served blanketed in a creamy walnut sauce and garnished with ruby pomegranate seeds.

In this recipe, the spongy fried batter encloses the pepper like an omelet soufflé, absorbing the delicious tomato sauce and giving a succulent richness to the pepper. Whatever your choice of stuffing, it is important to remember that traditional recipes, true to their Spanish and Islamic antecedents, tend to feature elements that are both sweet (dried fruits and raisins) and nutty (almonds or walnuts). My version was inspired by the Cuban picadillo, a beef hash with sweet-and-sour counterpoints. Serve these chiles rellenos with Mexican rice, white rice, or any type of rice and bean dish.

continued

MAKES 6 TO 8 SERVINGS

2 lb/910 g (about 8) large poblano peppers, with stems attached

STUFFING

¼ cup/60 ml extra-virgin olive oil

6 garlic cloves, finely chopped

8 oz/230 g (1 medium) yellow or white onion, finely chopped

6 oz/170 g (1 medium) green bell pepper, finely chopped

12 oz/340 g (about 4) ripe plum tomatoes, peeled and finely chopped

1 tsp ground cumin

1 tsp dried oregano

¼ tsp ground cinnamon

1½ tsp coarse sea salt

1 lb/455 g coarsely ground beef

½ cup/85 g cup slivered almonds

½ cup/70 g cup dark raisins

½ cup/120 ml chicken or beef broth

Roast the peppers, according to the instructions on page 232. Seed by making a lengthwise slit along the sides of the peppers, from about 1 inch/2.5 cm above the tip to about 1 inch/2.5 cm below the stem end. (This will keep the filling from spilling out of the pepper when frying.) Scrape out the seeds that cling to the knobby placenta with a small paring knife or a spoon. Set the peppers aside on a plate or baking sheet until ready to stuff.

To make the stuffing: Warm the oil in a 10-inch/25 cm skillet or sauté pan over medium heat. When the oil ripples, add the garlic and sauté until fragrant, about 20 seconds. Add the onion and sauté until golden, about 5 minutes. Stir in the green bell pepper and cook, stirring occasionally, for about 3 minutes more. Add the tomatoes, cumin, oregano, cinnamon, and salt and cook for about 10 minutes, or until the oil begins to separate from the solids. Stir in the meat and break up any lumps with a wooden spoon. Add the almonds and raisins and cook, stirring occasionally for about 10 minutes. Stir in the broth and continue cooking, stirring, for about 3 minutes. The mixture should be moist but not overly juicy. Transfer to a bowl and set aside.

To make the sauce: Warm a cast-iron skillet or comal over medium heat. Place the onion, cut-side down, and the tomatoes on the heated surface and toast for about 10 minutes, until charred on all sides. Peel away the charred bits and chop the vegetables coarsely. Place in a blender or food processor and process into a coarse puree.

Warm the oil in a 10-inch/25 cm skillet or sauté pan over medium heat. When rippling, add the garlic and sauté for about 20 seconds. Carefully stir in the tomato puree, averting your face because the sauce will spatter fiercely. Cook, stirring occasionally, for about 15 minutes, or until the oil begins to separate from the solids. Stir in the cumin, oregano, salt, and cilantro. Remove from the heat and keep warm. The sauce can be made a day ahead and stored, covered, in the refrigerator.

TOMATO SAUCE

8 oz/230 g (1 medium) yellow onion, cut in half lengthwise

2 lb/910 g (about 10) ripe plum tomatoes

¼ cup/60 ml extra-virgin olive oil

4 garlic cloves, finely minced

1 tsp ground cumin

1 tsp dried oregano

2 tsp coarse salt

1 Tbsp finely chopped cilantro (optional)

COATING

1 cup/125 g all-purpose flour

¼ to ½ tsp salt

4 large eggs (at room temperature), separated

1 qt/910 ml vegetable oil

Fill each pepper with about ½ cup/85 g beef hash and press the cut edges together. Set aside. The peppers can also be stuffed a day ahead and stored, well wrapped, in the refrigerator.

To make the coating: Place the flour on large plate or in a shallow bowl and mix with the salt. Separately beat the egg whites to soft peaks by hand or with an electric mixer at medium speed. Lower the beating speed and add the yolks one at a time, beating thoroughly to incorporate. Use a rubber spatula to transfer the mixture to a wide, shallow bowl.

Line a baking sheet with paper towels. Put the oil in a 10-inch/25 cm deep skillet or Dutch oven and heat to 350°F/180°C over medium heat. (If the stuffed peppers and sauce have been made ahead, reheat the tomato sauce gently as you proceed with coating and frying the peppers.) Coat each stuffed pepper lightly with the flour, making sure that the flour does not get into the stuffing. Holding a pepper by the stem, dip it into the egg batter and coat it thickly on all sides. Lower it gently into the hot oil and do not turn until the bottom side is firm and golden brown. Using a metal spatula, turn and continue cooking until the batter looks evenly cooked and golden brown on all sides. Transfer to the paper towels to drain. Repeat until all the peppers have been fried.

Pour the hot tomato sauce into a baking dish that can hold all the stuffed peppers in one layer. (I love using a round copper paella pan.) Arrange the peppers over the sauce and bring to the table. If you must make the whole dish a few hours ahead, heat in a 350°F/180°C oven until the sauce is bubbly.

Resources

GENERAL INFORMATION AND ADDITIONAL SOURCES

Peppers of the Americas

peppersoftheamericas.com

This is my online supplement to this book, with links to additional sources for supplies, tools for the pepper kitchen, updates on current research, and travel highlights.

SEEDLINGS

The Chile Woman

thechilewoman.com

Hoosier Susan Wasland (aka the Chile Woman) has been in the pepper-growing business for 25 years, growing her plants organically with a method that she describes as Hoosierorganic. I especially love the Latin American selection, which shows her penchant for flavorful as opposed to overly hot peppers. I have had excellent late-season results with her panca and ají amarillo peppers (as good as any that you can buy in the Andean region). She is meticulous in her packing, so plants arrive strong, healthy, and ready for battle.

Cross Country Nurseries

chileplants.com

Owner Janie Lamson was my first pepper-gardening inspiration. Her vigorous seedlings consistently arrive in perfect shape and are carefully labeled, with clear instructions on how to best start the plants in the ground or transplant them into bigger pots. She also sells fresh peppers beginning in September each year (check for availability).

First Coast Technical College AgriScience

fctc.edu/news/peppers-for-sale

To order *dátil* plants for shipment during the growing season, contact the dedicated gardeners of this agricultural college.

SEEDS

The Chile Pepper Institute

chile.nmsu.edu

This celebrated center, devoted to chile breeding and improvement as well as genetic research, has an online shop that offers books and seeds of Suave Habanero and other NuMex varieties developed at the institute.

Native Seeds/SEARCH

nativeseeds.org

The Tucson-based Native Seeds/SEARCH is a heritage seed bank founded by plant researcher and environmentalist Gary Paul Nabhan. If you are interested in starting chiltepines from reliable seed, this is an excellent source. The enticing, informative catalog also offers seeds of various Mexican and Southwestern chiles as well as a fascinating range of other desert food plants.

Pepper Joe's, Inc.

pepperjoe.com

Pepper Joe's is a reliable source that focuses on exotic peppers and super-hot varieties such as Bhut Jolokia and Carolina Reaper.

Refining Fire Chiles

superhotchiles.com

This is the site of Jim Duffy, a grower who achieved cult status among fans of superhot peppers by introducing horticulturist Paul Bosland of the Chile Pepper Institute to seeds of the fabled Trinidad Moruga Scorpion, a 2012 Guinness World Record–breaker. Specializing in superhots, Jim sells both quality seeds and seedlings.

Seed Savers Exchange

seedsavers.org

Seed Savers is a purveyor of heritage seeds with a mission to preserve biodiversity though a process of participatory preservation. They are an excellent source for the hard-to-find heirloom Bull Nose Pepper seeds.

FRESH PEPPERS

Happy Quail Farms

happyquailfarms.com

Farmer David Winsberg is passionate about peppers and sells his crops at several San Francisco Bay Area farmers' markets and online. This is my favorite long-time source for high-quality various-colored bell peppers, Padrón peppers, chile manzano, red rocotos, and the best fresh ají amarillo I have found in the US (check late in the season). A pioneer in Padrón pepper cultivation, he grows them in large quantities for retail stores and restaurants, though you can order just a couple of pounds (or a kilo) for home use.

DRIED PEPPERS/PEPPER POWDER

Despaña

despanabrandfoods.com

Spanish pimientos choriceros, ñora peppers, jarred guindillas in vinegar, Spanish paprika, paella pans, and more are available at Despana's Soho-neighborhood retail shop and online.

La Tienda

tienda.com

La Tienda sells a range of Spanish peppers, jarred guindillas and pimientos del piquillo, dried ñora peppers, and quality Spanish paprika. They are also a good source for traditional paella pans and accessories and short-grain rice for arroz a banda and paellas.

Zocalito Latin Bistro

zocalito.com

Zocalito is a source for high-quality rare Oaxacan chiles—chilhuacle, smoked pasilla de Oaxaca, chilcostle, taviche, and more—personally sourced by chef/owner Michael Beary.

Bibliography

Acosta, Joseph de. *Historia natural y moral de las Indias*. Mexico City: Fondo de Cultura Económica, 1985. [First published in 1590.]

Albrecht, Elena et al. "Genetic diversity in *Capsicum baccatum* is significantly influenced by its ecogeographical distribution." BMC Genetics 13 no. 1 (2012): 1–15.

Alegría, Francisco Abad. *Pimientos, Guindillas y Pimentón: Una Sinfonía en Rojo*. Gijón, Sp.: Ediciones Trea, 2008.

Andrews, Jean. *The Pepper Trail: History and Recipes from Around the World*. Denton, TX: University of North Texas Press, 1999.

_____. *Peppers: The Domesticated Capsicums*. Austin, TX: University of Texas Press, 1984.

Ayala, Vargas, and Helmer Dagoberto. *Le ik: Los chiles en Guatamala*. Guatemala City: Universidad de San Carlos de Guatemala Facultad de Agronomia, n.d.

Berdan, Frances F., and Patricia Rieff Anawalt. *The Essential Codex Mendoza*. Berkeley, CA: University of California Press, 1997.

Bird, Junius B. "The Preceramic Excavations at the Huaca Prieta, Chicama Valley, Peru." *Anthropological Papers of the American Museum of Natural History*, 62 pt. 1 (1985): 1–294.

Borges, Karla Morais et al. "Caracterização morfoagronômica e físico-química de pimentas em Roraima." *Agro@mbiente On-line* 9 no. 3 (2015): 292–299.
doi: http://dx.doi.org/10.18227/1982-8470ragro.v9i3.2766

Bosland, Paul. W, and Danise Coon. "Novel Formation of Ectopic (Nonplacental) Capsaicinoid Secreting Vesicles on Fruit Walls Explains the Morphological Mechanism for Super-hot Chile Peppers." *Journal of the American Society for Horticultural Science* 140, no. 3 (2015): 253–256.

Bosland, Paul W. et al. "'Trinidad Moruga Scorpion' Pepper is the World's Hottest Measured Chile Pepper at More Than Two Million Scoville Heat Units." *HortTechnology* 22, no. 4 (2012): 534–538.

Bosland, P.W., and E.J. Votava. *Peppers: Vegetable and Spice Capsicums*. Wallingford, UK: CABI Publishing, 2000.

Bryant, Vaughn M., and Glenna W. Dean. "Archaeological coprolite science: The legacy of Eric O. Callen (1912–1970)." *Palaeogeography, Palaeoclimatology, Palaeoecology* 237 (2006): 51–66.

Cárdenas, Juan de. *Problemas y Secretos maravillosos de las Indias*. Madrid: Alianza Editorial, 1988. [First published in 1591.]

Casas, Bartolomé de las. *Apologetica Historia Sumaria*. [First published in 1566.] Digital edition published by Fundacion el Libro Total: La Biblioteca Digital de America,

www.ellibrototal.com/ltotal/?t=1&d=4072_4167_1_1_4072 [This work originally was intended to form part of Las Casas's *Historia de las Indias*.]

_____. *Brevísima relación de la destrucción de las Indias*. Madrid: Ediciones Cátedra, 1984. [Completed in 1542.]

_____. *Historia de las Indias*. 3 vols. Mexico City: Biblioteca Americana, 1965. [Completed ca. 1561.]

Chanca, Diego Alvarez. "Letter of Dr. Chanca on the Second Voyage of Columbus." *American Journeys Collection*, Document no. AJ-065. Wisconsin Historical Society Digital Library and Archives, 2003. www.americanjourneys.org.

Chiou, Katherine, and Christine A. Hastorf. *Capsicum* spp. at the Preceramic Sites of Huaca Prieta and Paredones, Chicama Valley, Peru. *UC Berkeley McCown Archaeobotany Laboratory Reports*, 74. University of California, Berkeley: Archaeological Research Facility, 2012.

_____. "Documenting Cultural Selection Pressure Changes on Chile Pepper (*Capsicum baccatum L.*) Seed Size Through Time in Coastal Peru." *Economic Botany* 68 no. 2 (2014): 190–202.

_____. Pachacamac, Peru, Archaeological *Capsicum* Seed Analysis. *UC Berkeley McCown Archaeobotany Laboratory Reports*, 82. University of California, Berkeley: Archaeological Research Facility, 2015.

_____. "A Systematic Approach to Species-Level Identification of Chile Pepper (*Capsicum* spp.) Seeds: Establishing the Groundwork for Tracking the Domestication and Movement of Chile Peppers through the Americas and Beyond." *Economic Botany* 68 no. 3 (2014): 316–336.

Choden, Kunzang. *Chilli and Cheese: Food and Society in Bhutan*. Bangkok: White Lotus Press, 2008.

Christenson, Allen J., trans. and ed. *Popol Vuh: The Sacred Book of the Maya*. Norman, OK: University of Oklahoma Press, 2003.

Cobo, Father Bernabé. *History of the Inca Empire: an account of the Indians' customs and their origin, together with a treatise on Inca legends, history, and social institutions*, trans. and ed. Roland Hamilton. Austin, TX: University of Texas Press, 1979. [Completed in 1653.]

Coe, Sophie D. *America's First Cuisines*. Austin, TX: University of Texas Press, 1994.

Colmenero de Ledesma, Antonio. *Curioso tratado de la naturaleza y calidad del chocolate*. Madrid: Francisco Martinez, 1631.

Colquitt, Harriet Ross. *The Savannah Cook Book*. Charleston, SC: Colonial Publisher, 1960. [First published in 1933.]

Cortés, Hernán. *Letters from Mexico*, trans. and ed. Anthony Pagden. New Haven, CT: Yale University Press, 1986.

De Oviedo, Gonzalo Fernández. *Sumario de la natural Historia de las Indias*. Madrid: Historia 16, 1986. [First published in 1526.]

DeWitt, Dave, and Janie Lamson. *The Field Guide to Peppers*. Portland, OR: Timber Press, 2015.

DeWitt, Dave, and Paul W. Bosland. *The Complete Chile Pepper Book: A Gardener's Guide to Choosing, Growing, Preserving, and Cooking*. Portland, OR: Timber Press, 2009.

_____. *Peppers of the World: An Identification Guide*. Berkeley, CA: Ten Speed Press, 1996.

Díaz del Castillo, Bernal. *Historia verdadera de la conquista de la Nueva España. Texto comparado*. 3 vols. Cuidad Real: Universidad de Castilla-La Mancha, 2001. [First published in 1568.]

Durán, Fray Diego. *The History of the Indies of New Spain*, trans. Doris Heydon. Norman, OK: University of Oklahoma Press, 1994. [First published ca. 1581.]

El Punto de Ají: Investigaciones en Capsicum Nativos, Numeros 1 y 2. Programa de Hortalizas. Lima: Universidad Nacional Agraria La Molina (UNALM), 2012.

Eshbaugh, W. Hardy. "Peppers: History and Exploitation of a Serendipitous New Crop Discovery." In: J. Janick and J.E. Simon (eds.), New Crops (pp. 132–139). New York: John Wiley & Sons, Ltd, 1993.

Friese, Kurt Michael, Kraig Kraft, and Gary Nabhan. *Chasing Chiles: Hot Spots along the Pepper Trail*. White River Junction, VT: Chelsea Green Publishing, 2011.

González-Jara, Pablo et al. "Impact of Human Management on the Genetic Variation of Wild Pepper, *Capsicum annuum* var. *glabriusculum*." PLoS ONE 6(12): e28715.

Guaman Poma de Ayala, Felipe. *El Primer Nueva Corónica y Buen Gobierno*. 3 vols. Mexico City: Siglo XXI Editores, 1980. [Completed ca. 1615–1616.]

Hernández, Francisco. *Cuatro Libros de la Naturaleza y Virtudes Medicinales de las Plantas y Animales de la Nueva España*. Morelia, Mexico: 1888. [First published ca. 1615.]

Ibiza, Vicente P. et al. "Taxonomy and genetic diversity of domesticated Capsicum species in the Andean region." *Genetic Resources and Crop Evolution* 59 (2012): 1077–1088.

Jäger, Matthias et al. *Las cadenas de valor de los ajíes nativos de Bolivia, compilación de los estudios realizados dentro del marco del proyecto "Rescate y Promocion de Ajies Nativos en su Centro de Origen."* Rome: Bioversity International, 2013.

Kim, Seungill et al. "Genome sequence of the hot pepper provides insights into the evolution of pungency in *Capsicum* species." *Nature Genetics* 46 (2014): 270–278.

Kraft, Kraig H. et al. "Multiple Lines of Evidence for the Origin of Domesticated Chili Pepper, *Capsicum annuum*, in Mexico." *PNAS* 111, no. 17 (2014): 6165–6170.

Labat, Jean-Baptiste. *Nouveau Voyage Aux Isles de L'Amerique*, 3 vols. Paris: Delespine, 1742.

Landa, Friar Diego de. *Yucatan: Before and After the Conquest*. trans. William Gates. New York: Dover Publications, 1978. [Translation of *Relacion de las cosas de Yucatán*, completed ca. 1566.]

Long, Edward. *A History of Jamaica*, vol. III. London: T. Lowndes, 1774.

Long-Solis, Janet. *Capsicum y Cultura: La Historia del Chilli*. Mexico City: Fondo de Cultura Economica, 1986.

López de Gómara, Francisco. *Historia General de las Indias*. 2 vols. Barcelona: Editorial Iberia, 1966. [First published in 1552.]

Monardes, Nicolás. *Herbolaria de Indias*. Mexico City: Instituto Mexicano del Seguro Social, 1990. [First published as *Primera y segunda y tercera partes de la Historia medicinal de las cosas que se traen de nuestras Indias Occidentales*, Seville: 1574.]

Morison, Samuel Eliot. *Admiral of the Ocean Sea: A Life of Christopher Columbus*. Boston: Northeastern University Press, 1970. [First published in 1942.]

_____, trans. and ed. *Journals and Other Documents on the Life and Voyages of Christopher Columbus*. New York: The Heritage Press, 1963.

Moses, Marissa, and Pathmanathan Umaharan. "Genetic Structure and Phylogenetic Relationships of *Capsicum chinense.*" *Journal of the American Society for Horticultural Science* 137, no. 4 (2012): 250–262.

Pastor, Humberto Rodriguez, ed. *El Ají Peruano en sus Regiones y Pueblos*. Lima: Universidad de San Martín de Porres, 2014.

Perry, Linda, and Kent V. Flannery. "Precolumbian use of chili peppers in the Valley of Oaxaca, Mexico." *PNAS* 104, no. 29 (2007): 11905–11909.

Perry, Linda et al. "Starch Fossils and the Domestication and Dispersal of Chili Peppers (*Capsicum* spp. L.) in the Americas." *Science*, 315 (2007): 986–988.

Pfefferkorn, Ignaz. *Sonora: A Description of the Province*, trans. Theodore E. Treutlein. Tucson, AZ: The University of Arizona Press, 1989.

Pichardo, Esteban. *Diccionario Provincial casi Razonado de Vozes y Frases Cubanas*. Havana: Editorial de Ciencias Sociales, 1985. [First published in 1836.]

Pickersgill, Barbara. "Domestication of Plants in the Americas: Insights from Mendelian and Molecular Genetics." *Annals of Botany* 100 (2007): 925–940.

Piperno, Dolores R., and Deborah M. Pearsall. *The Origins of Agriculture in the Lowland Neotropics*. San Diego, CA: Academic Press, 1998.

Powis, Terry G. et al. "Prehispanic Use of Chili Peppers in Chiapas, Mexico." *PLoS ONE* (2013)

_____. *Gran Cocina Latina: The Food of Latin America*. New York: W. W. Norton & Company, 2012.

Presilla, Maricel. *The New Taste of Chocolate: A Cultural and Natural History of Cacao with Recipes*, rev. ed. Berkeley, CA: Ten Speed Press, 2009.

_____. "A World of Peppers: Chiles bring a lot more to the table than just heat." *Saveur* 122 (2009): 27–34.

Reeves, Caroline. "How the Chili Pepper Got to China." *World History Bulletin*. Spring 2008, vol. XXIV, no. 1: 18–19.

Rojas, Rosario et al. *Ajíes Nativos Peruanos: Caracterización Agro-Morfológica, Químico-Nutricional & Sensorial*. Lima: Universidad Peruana Cayetano Heredia, 2016.

Sahagún, Fray Bernardino de. *Historia general de la cosas de Nueva España*. Mexico City: Editorial Porrúa, 1992. [Completed ca. 1577.]

Smith, Bruce D. "Reassessing Coxcatlan Cave and the early history of domesticated plants in Mesoamerica." *PNAS* 102 no. 27 (2005): 9438–9445.

Stuart, David. "Maya Decipherment: Ideas on Ancient Maya Writing and Iconography." *Decipherment*, decipherment.files.wordpress.com.

Tewksbury, Joshua J. and Gary P. Nabhan. "Seed dispersal: Directed deterrence by capsaisin in chillies." *Nature* 412 (2001): 403–404.

Tewksbury, Joshua J. et al. "Evolutionary ecology of pungency in wild chilies." *PNAS* 105 no. 33 (2008): 11808–11811.

Vega, Garcilaso de la. *Comentarios Reales*. Augusto Cortina, ed. Buenos Aires: Editora Espasa-Calpe Argentina, 1970. [First published in 1609.]

_____. *Los Incas: Comentarios Reales de los Incas*. Arequipa, Peru: Ediciones El Lector S.R.L., 2012.

Wafer, Lionel. *A New Voyage and Description of the Isthmus of America*. Cleveland, OH: The Burrows Brothers Company, 1903. [First published in 1699.]

Weaver, William Woys. *Heirloom Vegetable Gardening: A Master Gardener's Guide to Planting, Seed Saving, and Cultural History*. New York: Henry Holt & Co., 1997.

Zurita Muñoz, Ricardo. *Los Chiles Nativos de México*, 3rd ed. Mexico City: DGE|Equilibrista, 2015.

Acknowledgments

I, like my father, Ismael Espinosa, a painter who opened my eyes to the beauty of food plants as well as the curious cook who taught me to relish the bite of hot peppers, am often an impulsive, baroque gardener who depends more on luck and excess than prescribed method. But I am also the granddaughter of Santiago Parladé, a disciplined horticulturist, who was born on a farm and taught me to nurture plants with care, respect, and patience. I planted my first fruit tree, a Surinam cherry, following his detailed directions when I was about seven, and to this day I remember my astonishment in seeing it grow, prosper, and bear delicious fruit. This is the same feeling of disbelief and accomplishment that fills me when I walk into my backyard and see the scrawny pepper plant I grew from seed in the early spring laden with pods ready to be cooked. My husband, Alejandro Presilla, never seems to get bored of eating our home-grown peppers, from the sweetest to the hottest in every form and in everything I cook. His delight is my inspiration.

The visual story of my home-grown peppers was told beautifully by the two Cuban-born artists who collaborated with me on this book: Photographer Romulo Yanes and botanical illustrator Julio J. Figueroa. Romulo followed my garden through several growing seasons and captured many of my peppers at the peak of their glory, arranging them like jewels for every artful still life. He even did them justice when the weather gods conspired against them in the aftermath of Superstorm Sandy, when he helped me save specimens that had been bruised and battered by a freak snowstorm; we kept them in the book to remind us that nature's imperfections are also beautiful. Working with Julio, a thirty-year veteran of the Cuban National Botanical Garden in Havana, made me closely examine my plants' patterns of growth, textures of leaves, color nuances, delicate flower details, and even the shapes of their seeds.

As a farmer's daughter, my editor Lorena Jones understood the challenges of publishing a book on a seasonal crop and decided to turn it into a more serious and complex undertaking than merely a cook's visual gallery. I will be forever grateful for her thorough editing and for inviting me to be a part of the entire creative process. My warm gratitude and appreciation goes to designer Kara Plikaitis for molding so many disparate visual elements and text into a seamless work of beauty. My thanks also to publisher Aaron Wehner and the team at Ten Speed for supporting this multifaceted project.

My gratitude extends to James Oseland, journalist and former editor of *Saveur,* for laying the groundwork for *Peppers of the Americas* in our collaborative article, "A World of Peppers," back in 2009. This book has benefited enormously from the steady, intelligent contribution of my longtime friend and fellow medievalist Anne Mendelson, who revised the text with her characteristically critical eye and offered invaluable guidance and encouragement during every step of the project. My deep thanks to Kathy Martin, my food editor at the *Miami Herald*, for encouraging me to explore peppers in my columns and for her sound advice and unforgettable writing lessons. My gratitude to historian and my friend Marc Aronson for reading the manuscript and offering valuable suggestions. My thanks to my agent Madeleine Morel for taking care of many important threads.

As *Peppers of the Americas* draws heavily on archaeology and botany, I sought the advice of noted experts: Horticulturist Dr. Paul Bosland took the time to show me the extraordinary work he and his team carry out on behalf of the US pepper industry in Las Cruces, New Mexico, at the Chile Pepper Institute, a one-of-a kind pepper research center that is a tribute to the legacy of legendary Mexican-born horticulturist Fabián García. I am grateful to professor Pathmaratha Umaharam, a cacao and pepper expert working at the University of the West Indies, for alerting me to the special genetic ancestry of the Trinidadian superhot peppers. It was a pleasure to visit the pepper research division of the Universidad Nacional Agraria La Molina in Lima with chief horticulturist and professor of agroecology Roberto Hugo Ugás to understand the state of pepper research in Peru. My thanks to Dr. Rosario Rojas, of the Universidad Peruana Cayetano Heredia, for sharing her research on the chemical, nutritional, and sensorial analysis of native Peruvian peppers. My gratitude to sociologist Mirtha Salinas for sharing research and insight on small-scale pepper farming in Peru. I'll always be thankful to the dynamic and generous Carmen Rosa Sánchez, from the Peruvian Ministerio de Agricultura y Riego, for keeping me abreast of pepper projects and statistics there. I was introduced to the wonders of El Brujo by archaeologist George Gummerman IV of Northern Arizona State University, who invited me to visit his laboratory in 2003 when he was leading the Moche Foodways Archaeological Project. I was guided to the El Brujo site by Peruvian archaeologist César Gálvez, who gave me a masterful introduction to the ancient foods of the region, including peppers. My thanks to admired archaeologist Michael D. Coe for useful leads and to food science authority Harold McGee for inspiring me to always keep asking more questions. My gratitude to Peruvian chef Pedro Miguel Schiaffino for sharing his knowledge of Amazonian foodways and countless kindnesses.

In decades of travel in Latin America, I have benefited from the wisdom of countless home cooks, chefs, farmers, scientists, and historians. Special thanks to Raquel Torres, Patricia Quintana, Gloria Casarín, Victor Vallejo, Alma Vallejo, and Jaime González in Mexico; to Domingo Tzep, Walter Maldonado Osorio, and Pepe Miguez and his wife, Leticia, in Guatemala; to Veronica Peralta, Susana Polo, Patricia León Guerrero, and chefs Carlos Gallardo and Edgar León in Ecuador; food writer and ají lover Miro Popic and his wife, Yolanda, and their daughter, Veronica Popic, in Venezuela; to Peruvian restaurateur Arturo Rubio and his wife, Natalia Grasses, and their daughter, Natalia Rubio; chef Marilú Madueño of the Huaca Pucllana, journalist Diego Salazar, Stella Coello of USAID, and Marisela Pedroza of Technoserve; fearless explorer Josefa Nolte (who works with indigenous communities in the Peruvian Amazon), Ana María Rojas Lombardi, her late mother Judith Lombardi de Rojas, and my dear late friend chef Felipe Rojas-Lombardi, who taught me much about cooking with Peruvian peppers; Oscar and María Eugenia Baeza, Ana Baeza, and Sofia Chanilao in Chile; and Jurici Martins da Silva in Salvador, Bahia. Colombian-born horticulturist Dr. Noris Ledesma, who works at the Fairchild Tropical Botanical Garden and has years of experience in Amazonian crops, shared many useful gardening techniques. Special thanks to my international chocolate and cacao community for generous support: Santiago Peralta, Carla Barboto, Martin Christy, Monica Meschini, Lisi Montoya, Giovanna Maggiolo, Samir Giha, Eduardo Lanfranco, Eduardo Espinosa Tamariz, Oliver Eggers, Susumu Koyama, Kanako Satsutani, Clay Gordon, Brady Brelinski, and Nat Bletter. And also George Gensler, who helped me track sources, tag pepper plants, and organize my sizable collection of scholarly papers and books with great efficiency.

I learned much about cooking with peppers from the cooks of my restaurants, Zafra and Cucharamama, and I owe thanks to my business partner, Clara Chaumont, for her embrace of my pepper-centric menus. Artist Mary Lou Schempf created lovely backdrops for some peppers. My longtime cooking assistants Paloma Ramos and Amanda Viltres have kept a hawkish eye on my peppers, caring for their health and safety. With the assistance of my paternal cousin, Liss Espinosa, who helped me codify my collection, we came together as a team, creating an effective gardening routine and a true pepper kitchen that has given all of us much pleasure every year. If I were to choose the season when my garden and kitchen feels most alive, I would have to say it is pepper season, from beginning to end.

Index

End-of-Harvest Superhot
Mélange, 258
Enjoya Stripy Pepper. *See* Striped
Holland Bell
Enza Zaden, 108, 109
Escabeche, ají. See Amarillo, ají

F

Ferdinand, King, 44, 66
Fermented hot peppers, 244
Ferrer, Francisco, 289
Fertilizing, 224
Finger hot pepper, 75, 147
   Miracha, 260–61
Fish
   Alicante Fish "Paella" with
      Salmorrete, 289–90
   Madame Carmelite's Red Snapper
      in a Spicy Creole Sauce in the
      Style of Guadeloupe, 305–7
Fish pepper, 148
Flannery, Kent V., 52
Fresh Fruit with Guatemalan Chile
   Cobán and Cacao Condiment,
   275
Fresh peppers
   broiling, 233
   buying, 230–31
   preparing, 231–32
   roasting, 232–33
   storing, 231
   tasting, 228
   See also individual peppers
Fresno, 149
   Miracha, 260–61
*Frijoles negros refritos con chile de
   árbol,* 284–85
Fruit
   Fresh Fruit with Guatemalan
      Chile Cobán and Cacao
      Condiment, 275
   See also individual fruits
*Frutas frescas con polvo de chile Cobán
   y cacao guatemalteco,* 275
Fuchs, Leonhart, 72, 150

G

Galapagos Islands, 5, 116
Galician-Style Octopus with Paprika
   and Olive Oil, 299–301
García, Fabián, 158, 159, 160
García, Frank, 152, 154
Gómara, Francisco López de, 53, 66
Gonzalez, Eriberto, 185
Gran Chaco, 115
Grenada hot seasoning pepper, 149

Grenada pimiento seasoning
   pepper, 151
Grilled Japanese Spring Onions with
   Romesco, 276
Growing tips, 219–26
Guacanagari, 41
Guadeloupe, 305
Guaguao, ají, 94–95, 198, 254
Guajillo, 132, 206, 209
   ground, 235
   Homemade Merkén with
      Guajillo, 247
   Mole Coloradito Paste, 250–53
   Panfried Pork Steaks in
      Guajillo-Puya Adobo, 326
   Slab Bacon in Hibiscus Hot
      Pepper Adobo with Chocolate,
      321–23
Guaman Poma de Ayala, Felipe, 62
Guampinha de veado, pimenta, 171
Guardamar del Segura, Spain, 217
Guatemalan Chile Cobán and Cacao
   Condiment, 249
Guernica pepper, 70
Guindilla, 72, 150–51
Guitarrero Cave, 61

H

Habanero, 26–27, 29, 58, 152–55, 164
   Madame Carmelite's Red Snapper
      in a Spicy Creole Sauce in the
      Style of Guadeloupe, 305–7
   Tropical Shrimp Ceviche with
      Yuca, 296–98
Habichuelas coloradas guisadas,
   294–95
Ham
   Panfried Padrón Peppers with
      Garlic and Serrano Ham, 277
   Puerto Rican Red Kidney Bean
      Stew, 294–95
Happy Quail Farms, 32, 105, 109, 122,
   168, 173
Harissa, 73
Harper, Roy, 159, 160
Harvesting, 224
Hastorf, Christine A., 10
Hatch, New Mexico, 158
Hazelnuts
   Romesco Sauce, 268–69
Heat levels, 17–22, 30, 35–36
Hernández, Francisco, 56–57, 94, 203,
   204, 208
Hibiscus Hot Pepper Adobo with
   Chocolate, Slab Bacon in,
   321–23
Hijueputa (hijo de puta), 155

Holland red finger hot pepper. *See*
   Finger hot pepper
Homemade Merkén with
   Guajillo, 247
Homocapsaicin, 19, 20
Homodihydrocapsaicin, 19, 20
Hot Chocolate Jamaican, 156
Huaca Prieta, 3, 6, 7–8, 10, 61
Huacle, 124–27, 209–11
Hungarian Hot Wax. *See* Yellow
   Hot Wax
Hu pi qing jiao, 279

I

Inca Red Drop, 156
Incas, 58–59, 61–63
Isabella, Queen, 44, 66

J

Jalapeño, 128, 130, 204, 205
   Chilean "Pig in Stone" Salsa, 263
   Chile Rajas with Epazote, Milk,
      and Cheese, 282–83
   Ecuadorian Green Tree Tomato
      Sauce, 271
   End-of-Harvest Superhot
      Mélange, 258
   Miracha, 260–61
Jalea de calamares Cucharamama, 302
Jamaican Hot Red, 156
Jauco, Cuba, 289
Jefferson, Thomas, 104
Jerónimos, 67, 71

K

Kennedy, Diana, 27
Kitchiner, William, 117
Kraft, Kraig H., 138

L

Lambayeque, Peru, 177
Landrace, definition of, 20
Las Casas, Bartolomé de, 44–45,
   48, 55
Lawson, Edward W., 144
Lemon Drop, 157
Limo, ají, 96–97
Limón, ají, 97
Linnaeus, 24
Locoto. See Rocoto
Lodosa, Spain, 176
Long, Edward, 50

M

Macho, 130
   Madame Carmelite's Red
      Snapper in a Spicy Creole

Published in the United States by Ten Speed Press, an imprint of the
Crown Publishing Group, a division of Penguin Random House LLC,
a Penguin Random House Company, New York.

www.crownpublishing.com

www.tenspeed.com

Ten Speed Press is the registered trademark of
Penguin Random House LLC.

Lorena Jones Books and the Lorena Jones Books colophon are
trademarks of Penguin Random House LLC.

Library of Congress Cataloging-in-Publication Data
on file with publisher

Hardcover ISBN: 978-0-399-57892-2

ebook ISBN: 978-0-399-57893-9

Design by Kara Plikitas

Printed in China

10 9 8 7 6 5 4 3 2 1

First Edition